The VERY QUICK JOB SEARCH

Get a Better Job in Half the Time!

Third Edition

Michael Farr

Works

America's Career Publisher

The Very Quick Job Search, **Third Edition**
Get a Better Job in Half the Time!

© 2004 by JIST Publishing, Inc.

Published by JIST Works, an imprint of JIST Publishing, Inc.
8902 Otis Avenue
Indianapolis, IN 46216-1033

Phone: 1-800-648-JIST   Fax: 1-800-JIST-FAX
E-mail: info@jist.com   Web site: www.jist.com

Note to Instructors

This book is widely used in courses and workshops on career planning and job seeking. Instructional support materials include a complete curriculum titled The Very Quick Job Search Instructor's Curriculum, *a student workbook titled* The Very Quick Job Search Activity Book, *transparencies, and a 10-video series titled* The Video Guide to JIST's Self-Directed Job Search. *Call 1-800-648-JIST or visit www.jist.com for details.*

Visit our Web site at **www.jist.com** for information on JIST, free job search information, book excerpts, and ordering information on our many products. For free information on 14,000 job titles, visit www.careeroink.com. Quantity discounts are available for JIST books. Please call our sales department at 1-800-648-JIST for a free catalog and more information.

Acquisitions Editor: Randy Haubner
Development Editor: Nancy Stevenson
Editor: Susan Pines
Cover Designer: Trudy Coler
Interior Designer: Aleata Howard
Interior Layout: Carolyn Newland
Proofreaders: David Faust, Jill Mazurczyk, Jeanne Clark, Lori Cates Hand
Indexer: Henthorne House

Printed in Canada

09 08 07 06 05 04 03   9 8 7 6 5 4 3 2 1

Library of Congress Cataloging-in-Publication Data

Farr, Michael.
  The very quick job search : get a better job in half the time! /
Michael Farr.— 3rd ed.
        p. cm.
Includes bibliographical references and index.
  ISBN 1-59357-007-4
  1. Job hunting—United States. I. Title.
  HF5382.75.U6F37 2004
  650.14—dc22
                                                        2003021423

We have been careful to provide accurate information throughout this book, but it is possible that errors and omissions have been introduced. Please consider this in making any career plans or other important decisions. Trust your own judgment above all else and in all things.

Trademarks: All brand names and product names used in this book are trade names, service marks, trademarks, or registered trademarks of their respective owners.

ISBN 1-59357-007-4

Relax. You Don't Need to Read This Entire Book!

Just a Few Chapters Will Tell You Enough to Make a Big Difference in Your Job Search

While this is a big book, reviewing just a few chapters can make a huge difference in your job search. Even reading just Chapter 4 (Dramatically Improve Your Interviewing Skills) in the morning can considerably improve your interviewing skills for that afternoon. To get your job search off to a quick start, Section 1 includes the information I think is most important for you to know. The topics I cover there are most likely to result in your getting a better job in less time.

But there is much more to this book than the content of Section 1. Section 2 provides chapters on important labor market trends, career planning, exploring alternative job options, resumes, advanced interviewing and job search skills, and other topics that could help you get the best job for you. Some chapters in Section 2 may be more important to you than others, so review the table of contents to identify topics of particular interest.

The focus of this book is quite simple: To help you get a better job and to reduce the time it takes to get it.

While this book includes a lot of information, I have arranged it so you can read essential chapters in Section 1 today and be looking for a job tomorrow. Depending on your situation, you could begin your job search quickly and then review the more-detailed material as you need to in Section 2. If your need for a job is less urgent, it would be wise to learn more from the content in Section 2 before you begin your job search.

Whatever your situation, it may interest you to know that most of the information in this book is arranged around seven major themes. These seven concepts are VERY important if you want to get a better job in less time. Here they are:

The Seven Steps to Getting the Job You Want

1. **Know your skills.** If you don't know what you are good at, how can you expect anyone else to figure it out? One survey of employers found that about 80 percent of those they interview did not do a good job of presenting the skills they had to do the job. The 20 percent that did present their skills well were those most likely to be hired.

2. **Have a clear job objective.** If you don't know where you want to go, it will be most difficult to get there. Take the time to clarify what you want to do with your career and your life, and your job search will be far more effective.

3. **Know where and how to look for job openings.** Because about 3 out of 4 job openings are never advertised on the Internet or elsewhere, you should learn and use job search methods that help you find these unadvertised jobs. Some job search methods work better than others and, because few people have had any formal training in looking for a job, most people think this information is very helpful.

4. **Spend at least 25 hours a week looking.** Most job seekers spend far less than this and, as a result, are unemployed longer than they need to be. Organize your job search as if it was a full-time job, and you will be likely to get a job in much less time than the average.

5. **Get two interviews a day.** This sounds impossible to do but it can be done once you redefine what counts as an interview, as I will explain in this book.

6. **Improve your interviewing skills.** Even minor improvements in your interviewing skills can make a huge difference in whether you get an offer over someone else. You can quickly learn enough to make a difference in this most critical area of your job search. For example, if you want the job, tell the employer you do and why he or she should hire you.

7. **Follow up on all contacts.** Just sending thank-you notes and e-mail to the people who help you in your job search can make a difference in whether you get job leads. And following up with a potential employer is one of the things that does make a difference in getting a job offer over others.

While this book covers a lot of topics, they all have something to do with just these seven themes—the things that will make the most difference to you in getting a better job in less time. I hope you enjoy the book and that it helps bring you happiness and prosperity, or both.

Dedication

My mother lived to be 93 years young and had a talent for being happy in almost all she did. As a little girl, she learned poetry in school and would often repeat from memory the poems of her youth. She liked Ralph Waldo Emerson. Here is some of his work that fits the philosophy of this book:

How do you measure success?
To laugh often and much.
To win the respect of intelligent people and the affection of children.
To earn the appreciation of honest critics and endure the betrayal of false friends.
To appreciate beauty.
To find the best in others.
To leave the world a little better, whether by a healthy child, a redeemed social condition, or
a job well done.
To know even one other life has breathed because you lived.
This is to have succeeded.

Ralph Waldo Emerson, 1803–1883

And here is another piece of wisdom, from a successful woman:

The harder you work, the luckier you get.

Anna Veronica (McLaughlin) Farr, 1908–2002

Acknowledgments

I can't begin to thank the many job seekers who helped me figure out which job search approaches worked better than others, but I appreciate their efforts. I thank the many researchers, data collectors, and analysts at the U.S. Department of Labor and other sources for their important work on labor market, career, and job-seeking research.

There are also people I can thank by name for their substantial help with this book.

Very special thanks to writing contributor
Karine B. Blackett, MS

Kari helped a great deal in updating many details, as well as in writing Chapter 18. Thank you to other writing contributors, Eric Oestmann, Ph.D., and Frank Cawley. Thanks also for research assistance to Paul Hubbeling.

Nancy Stevenson, the developmental editor for this book, provided many updates and improvements in the text. Randy Haubner, acquisitions editor, and Sue Pines, associate publisher at JIST, led the project and handled many details that got the book done quickly and well. Other JIST staff, including Trudy Coler, Aleata Howard, Carolyn Newland, Jill Mazurczyk, Jeanne Clark, and Lori Cates Hand, did great work on design, layout, proofreading, and so many other things. Everyone involved was supportive, demanding, friendly, and professional all at the same time. Their collective efforts make this book, we all hope, simple to use and helpful. To a great team: You did well, thanks.

Finally, a special thanks to our many customers who have used this book. In particular, thank you to the instructors and students at National American University and Corinthian College for feedback on the second edition and the valuable ideas that I incorporated into the third edition to make it an even more valuable tool.

Table of Contents

Introduction: Why This Book Could Be Worth Thousands of Dollars to You — *The Economics of Career Planning and Job Search*

Here is a quote from a study titled "Workplace Basics," completed jointly by the U.S. Department of Labor and the American Society for Training and Development:

> *Research shows that roughly half of the differences in earnings [between people] can be attributed to learning in school or on the job. Accidents of geography, career choices, and the selection of an employer account for the other half.*

Another way to summarize the study's conclusion is to say that good career planning and job seeking skills can make a huge difference in how much you earn. Education and training remain very important, of course, but even a good education or advanced technical skills are not enough if you don't know where or how to find the right jobs. And then, of course, there is the issue of finding a job you really enjoy.

Why a New Approach Is Needed

Back in the good old days, larger employers ruled the land and the job search was simple. To get a job, you sent out resumes to what was then called the "Personnel Department," or went there to fill out an application. You responded to want ads and you went down to the employment service office for free referrals. And you went after government jobs because there were many of those available. Sure, there were also private employment agencies, but the larger companies usually paid their fees. No problem.

Things were simpler then. College graduates were in demand (there were fewer of them then), and factory jobs were plentiful. You got a job with a big employer, and you kept it until you retired.

Of course, that rosy picture was not quite perfect for everyone during those times in the sixties and early seventies—there were problems. However, traditional job search methods did work better back then.

The labor market has changed. An enormous number of new workers have come into the labor market, more than 36 million since 1980 and another 17 million are projected through 2010. Almost all of the new jobs that absorbed these new workers have been in the service (non-manufacturing) sector of the economy.

The fact is that about 70 percent of all people now work for small employers (under 250 employees), and the majority of new job growth has been with very small employers (those with fewer than 50 employees). People also change jobs and careers far more often than they did in the past, and few employees expect to stay with their current employer until retirement. For example, a longitudinal study by the Department of Labor found that workers changed jobs an average of 9.6 times from age 18 to 36.

The Cost of Unemployment Is Very High

With all these changes, it is likely that most people will experience unemployment one or more times during their working lives. And the cost of this can be enormous: about $11,000 in lost wages per bout of unemployment and well over $100,000 during the average person's working life.

For all the reasons mentioned here, the old ways of looking for a job no longer make sense. Small employers, for example, usually don't have human resource departments and are far more likely to depend on referrals from current employees than on traditional sources such as want ads. More importantly, because small employers are better able to make decisions, they are more likely to create a new position for someone they want to hire—even if there is no formal opening. The Web hasn't changed this situation, because most jobs will never be posted there or, in fact, advertised in any way.

Getting a job today requires more knowledge of how the labor market works than in the past. While traditional job search methods still work for some, they have become increasingly less effective for most. This is one of the reasons that I say that career planning and job search skills are more important than ever. Not only will you need to gain these new skills, but, with more frequent job and career changes, you will need to use your job search skills more often.

Career planning and job seeking skills are essential survival skills in our new economy. How well you plan your career and conduct your job search can make a tremendous difference in how much you earn, how rapidly you advance in your career, and how much you enjoy your work—and your life.

What This Book Is Designed to Accomplish

This book is about getting a good job in less time. Many books claim to do this, but this one is different. In addition to showing you how to write a good resume and find job openings, it will help you do the following:

1. **Define what you want in a job**: I've included information to help you define and find "THE" job rather than just "a" job. This is important because what you do for a living is a big part of how you feel about yourself and your life.

2. **Find your next job in less time**: Some job search methods work better than others, and I have spent many years looking for techniques that reduce the time it takes to get a good job. The techniques presented in this book have been used by many thousands of people and programs and have been proven to cut job search time in half.

3. **Negotiate for a higher salary**: Using the right approach when negotiating salary can result in a significantly higher starting salary. It's easy enough to do, and I will show you how.

4. **Develop a skills language**: Many people tell me that learning to identify their skills—and deciding how best to use them—is an important life experience for them. Of course, it will also help you in the interview process and throughout your job search.

5. **Learn how to network effectively**: Networking is one of the keys to finding hidden jobs. You will learn how to network "warm" and "cold" contacts, and find out precisely what to say to get results.

6. **Use current technology to expand your search**: The Internet and computers, when used effectively, can open new avenues for your search.

In writing this book, I have tried to keep things interesting, to emphasize the most important information, and keep the book to a manageable size. I hope you like it. More importantly, I hope it helps you find a satisfying job and a more meaningful life in less time than you could have otherwise done. That is why this book has been titled *The Very Quick Job Search*.

How Well Do the Job Search Methods Presented in This Book Work?

There are hundreds of job search books and Web sites offering job search advice, but hardly any offer proof that their methods work better than others. Most writers of career materials are good people who learned what they know as teachers, counselors, or human resource experts. I have a different background.

During the recession of the early 1980s, the national unemployment rate went over 10 percent. That is as high as it has gotten in over 40 years, but in some areas it was much higher. I had been operating successful job search programs since the early 1970s, and in the early 1980s I won a contract to run a demonstration job search program. The U.S. Department of Labor tracks the unemployment rates for the 200 largest cities in the U.S., and the rate in the location of our project, with lots of auto plant closings, went over 24 percent. That was the highest unemployment rate of any city in the entire United States at that time.

I was told by the government agency that hired us that there were no job openings in this area—none. Our project was to work with people who were unemployed but who were to receive no other services than attending our job search program. We did no screening other than a two-hour orientation session, where we explained the program and asked participants to attend only if they could commit themselves to a full-time job search and attend our program for six hours daily for four weeks or until they found a job. They were not compensated for attending.

We kept careful records on participants. Their average length of unemployment before they started our job search program was 4.5 months. Average age was 31.6 years, with 48 percent women and 50 percent minorities.

Program Results

Sixty-six percent of all participants found jobs within 2.3 weeks of program initiation. Of those who attended the first two weeks of the program without absence, 96 percent found jobs within 2.03 weeks.

These results are incredible but true. There was no magic to it; the jobs were there all along, although no conventional approach found them. Our job seekers got them because they went to potential employers before the jobs were advertised and convinced an employer that they could do the job. The people waiting for a job to get advertised stayed unemployed.

The Internet, e-mail, and other technologies have added new approaches to the job search and have been incorporated throughout this book, but many of the same principles apply now as did then. Programs across the U.S. and Canada have obtained similar results in difficult settings using the techniques presented in this book, adapted to their local situations.

> The techniques in this book work, and thousands of those who have used them will agree. As I was writing this, I got a call from someone who had interviewed me a year earlier on a radio station in Wichita. He told me that, after the radio show, his wife had obtained a job as a result. She loved gardening but had no formal training in it, so he simply called a large gardening center and spoke with the owner about her. There was no job opening then, but she followed up, got an interview, and began working there soon after.

While the job search is not always this easy, the basic techniques I present in this book do work well for many people. And now you have access to the same techniques. They are described in detail in this book and, taken together, represent a body of experience and common sense that has been developed and tested over many years. They can work if you make them work. Nothing more and nothing less. Making them work will, of course, be up to you.

I hope that you enjoy this book. When you are done with it, after you have found your own job, pass it along to someone else or buy another copy for him or her. That and your offering another person a little bit of caring and support will let you become part of a grassroots movement to help us help each other find satisfaction in our careers and our lives.

SECTION 1
The Seven Things That Make the Most Difference in the Job Search

CHAPTER 1

What It Takes to Get a Good Job in Less Time—

And Why Traditional Job Search Methods Don't Work Very Well

≡≡≡Quick Overview

In this chapter, I review the following:

- ✔ Traditional job search techniques
- ✔ Why nontraditional methods are more effective
- ✔ Two things that can cut your job search time in half
- ✔ Why some people take longer to find jobs
- ✔ The hidden job market is where most of the jobs are
- ✔ How people really find jobs
- ✔ Why many employers don't like to advertise
- ✔ Why resumes don't get jobs, interviews do
- ✔ How to search for civil service jobs
- ✔ How to make better use of human resource departments, application forms, newspaper help wanted ads, employment Web sites, employer's online classified advertisements, and resumes
- ✔ How to take advantage of government employment services, private employment agencies, school programs, and other resources
- ✔ How to manage the stress of being unemployed or under-employed

"If you use better job search methods, you can get a better job in much less time!"

It's true. I have spent many years looking into which job search methods work better than others. It is clear that some techniques can reduce the time it takes to find a job. This fact has been demonstrated many times in well-run job search programs, as well as in research that I and many others have conducted.

You can cut your job search time in half or more—and this book will teach you the basic principles of how to do it.

If you are currently looking for a job, the job search "how to" aspects of this book will probably appeal to you the most. But another element of this book may be far more important to you over time: I have included a variety of tools and advice to help you understand yourself and what you want. This self-knowledge is an essential element in helping you define just what sort of job you want.

If you don't know what you want you are not likely to find it. I help you refine your goals and give you the tools you need to reach them.

If you know what your ideal job would be, you are more likely to find one that comes close to it. This may be far more important to you in the long run than just finding any job quickly.

Why Some People Take Longer to Find Jobs and How You Can Avoid This

Looking for a job is a learned skill. If you are lucky, you may find one quickly. But finding even entry-level jobs can take a long time to find if you don't know how to look.

According to the U.S. Department of Labor, the average adult spends three to five months finding a new job. It can take even longer when unemployment rates are high, if you earn more than average, or have skills that are not in demand in your area.

But some people find jobs faster than others with similar credentials, even in times of high unemployment. Why do they get quicker results? While the answers can be complex, there are only two primary reasons why some people get jobs faster than others.

Doing Just Two Things Can Cut Your Job Search Time in Half

The average job seeker spends fewer than 15 hours a week looking for a job and gets fewer than two interviews.

What It Takes to Get a Good Job in Less Time

1. Job seekers who spend more time actually looking for work find jobs faster than those spending less time.

2. Job seekers who get more interviews find jobs faster because the more interviews you get, the more likely you are to get a job offer.

   The bottom line is that people who spend more time on their job search and who get more interviews will usually get jobs faster.

There Are Two Major Problems with Traditional Job Search Methods

Part of the problem with the traditional approach to the job search is that it leads to many dead ends and rapid discouragement.

Traditional techniques encourage you to be passive in your job search. They don't work well for most people, and often result in you being out of work or under-employed longer than necessary.

Another major problem with the traditional job search is that job seekers define an interview too narrowly. By doing this, they overlook many opportunities and make obtaining an interview harder than it needs to be.

Two Problems with Traditional Approaches

1. Traditional techniques encourage you to be passive in your job search.

2. Traditional techniques encourage you to define an interview too narrowly.

This book, particularly the next chapter, tackles both of these problems. Of the variety of job search methods, some clearly work better than others. The most effective ones help you remain active in your job search and do not encourage you to wait until someone calls you. Using more effective techniques can dramatically increase the number of interviews you get. But more effective methods will only work, of course, if you use them.

Most Job Openings Will Never Be Advertised

Most jobs are not advertised, and people who use traditional job search methods never find out about these jobs. A variety of research studies find that most job openings are not visible to job seekers using traditional job search methods.

For example, job openings posted on the Internet and in newspaper want ads are considered public knowledge—anyone can find out about them. But these advertised openings add up to only about 25 percent of all job openings. The other 75 percent or so are hidden from you if you use traditional job search methods. Your job search should be a search for these hidden jobs.

Should "Luck" Be How You Find a Job?

For most people, "luck" is the most important element in their job search. Many people eventually get a job offer through a job lead that they found almost by accident. But you can do things to increase your chances of finding job openings and, therefore, create your own good luck.

In spite of all the books telling us how to read want ads, find openings on the Internet, or send out resumes, and in spite of the national "system" of private and public employment agencies, most people get their jobs by informal methods, such as hearing about a job opening from someone they know or going directly to an employer. Even though these are clearly the most effective methods, few people are organized in their use of these approaches. The result is lost time, and time spent unemployed really equals money lost. Because very few people have any formal job search training, many waste much of their time using ineffective methods that needlessly lengthen their unemployment and drain their confidence.

Traditional Ways of Finding Job Leads

Very few people have any real training on how to find jobs. Few have even read a book or attended a workshop on job seeking, and very few have attended a seminar or class on job seeking. As a result, they go about using well-known job search methods that may or may not work well.

To learn more about the job search, let's begin by examining the job search techniques that are traditionally used by most people. By "traditional" I mean the way people have always done things. That doesn't mean it's the best way, it's just the way that everyone knows. Traditional job search methods are not always the most effective ones, but some people do find jobs using them so you need to know what they are to use—and not use—them most effectively.

Frequently Used Traditional Job Search Methods

✓ Reading help wanted ads in the newspaper and online

✓ Going to human resource departments and filling out applications

✓ Posting your resume on the Internet

✓ Sending out unsolicited resumes

✓ Getting leads from a private or government-funded employment agency

✓ Applying for civil service/government jobs

As you will soon discover, these traditional job search approaches all have their limitations. It is important for you to understand these limitations so that you do not rely on these methods too heavily.

Because so many people use traditional job search methods, let's take a closer look at each of them. For each one, I present their disadvantages as well as tips to increase their effectiveness.

Traditional Job Search Method 1: Internet Job Postings and Print Help Wanted Ads

Almost everyone who is looking for a job reads the newspaper's want ads and almost all Web users use the well known job posting sites to look for openings. Smart job seekers also find openings posted in specialized journals; association newsletters; and school, professional, or association-sponsored Web sites. That means that these sources must be a good place to look for jobs, right? Not really.

One of the very reasons advertised jobs are *NOT* great sources for good job leads is that so many people do use them. With thousands of people looking at each advertised job, the odds are not in your favor. (See the sidebar titled "With Advertised Jobs, the Odds Are Not in Your Favor" for more on this.)

As if that is not bad enough, there is another major problem with limiting your job search to jobs that are advertised: Most job openings are never advertised at all. To understand why, see the Quick Case Study later in this chapter "Why Many Employers Don't Like to Advertise."

Various studies have found that about only 15 percent of all job openings are advertised, which leaves abut 85 percent that are not. The Internet has not really changed this much. The major job posting sites do show thousands of job openings but research finds that most are old and no longer open.

The fact is that employers prefer to fill their openings through more reliable methods. Some good jobs are advertised online, in the newspapers, and other publications, but those jobs tend to be there for one of the following reasons:

✓ Many of advertised jobs are relatively low paying or have high turnover, requiring constant rehires to fill vacant positions.

✓ Other advertised jobs are highly specialized or very much in demand, with few qualified applicants available.

In other words, employers advertise these jobs because they can't fill the openings by more reliable methods.

WITH ADVERTISED JOBS, THE ODDS ARE NOT IN YOUR FAVOR

Let's do a little arithmetic to illustrate my point. I'll use the newspaper want ads as an example but the same principles apply for online ads.

The research indicates that about 10 percent of the workforce read the newspaper want ads at any given time.

 It's easy to accept that 10 percent figure since the unemployment rate is often half or more of that percentage. Then add to that the people who are looking for better jobs, wanting full-time instead of part-time, soon-to-graduate students, and those entering or re-entering the labor market.

For example, in a city of 200,000 people, about 65 percent or 130,000 people are in the workforce. This means that about 13,000 will be reading the want ads in that area at any given time. If the local paper had 500 want ads, that would be an average of 260 people per advertised job!

It can get even worse for the most desirable jobs. For a want ad that said something to the effect of "good pay and benefits, no previous experience required," there would be even more interested people. Let's say that twice as many people as usual are interested in this ad. That would result in 520 people reading and perhaps responding to that particular advertised job. If you were one of them, you would be about one-fifth of 1 percent of those interested—offering you a slim chance indeed of getting an interview for that job, let alone a job offer. And the odds get even worse in larger metropolitan areas.

The situation is even worse for jobs advertised on the Internet, because anyone, anywhere, can see those job listings and apply for them. The numeric odds against you for jobs posted on larger Web sites are astoundingly against you.

The poor odds of getting an interview or offer for an advertised job is one reason that those who depend too much on them get so discouraged—it always seems that someone else is more qualified.

WHY MANY EMPLOYERS DON'T LIKE TO ADVERTISE

Quick Case Study

A business associate had advertised online and in the newspaper for a receptionist and told me that 80 applicants responded within a few days. The large number of inquiries disrupted the phones and required considerable time to handle. Some e-mails had resume or other attachments that could not be opened (several because they contained viruses), and a number of people "followed up" by e-mailing additional attachments and asking for more information. Most applicants were not appropriate, and all but five were screened out based on their resumes. They interviewed five and got down to the final two, plus another applicant who came in after hearing about the opening from the receptionist who was leaving. After all that work, they hired the job seeker who had never read the ad and was referred and recommended by a trusted employee.

This is not an unusual situation; some research indicates that about half of all jobs that are advertised are filled by people who did not read about the job and who found out about the opening in other ways.

Employers find that advertising causes unnecessary work

Employers don't advertise job openings for a variety of reasons. Let's consider a couple of the most important ones. Doing so will help you understand why employers often prefer to hire people using other methods.

When employers advertise their jobs, they often receive many responses and, in turn, have to screen all sorts of strangers. Most employers are not trained interviewers, don't enjoy it, and don't have the time for it. They have to interview job seekers who do their best to create a good impression. Their job is to eliminate most of them by finding their weaknesses. It's not fun for either side.

Phone calls have to be handled, e-mails answered, applications and resumes collected and reviewed, interviews scheduled, and follow-up activities conducted. It takes a great deal of time. Employers know that screening strangers is a risky business because few are willing to present their weaknesses or limitations in an honest way.

Some organizations get hundreds of applicants for each job opening. To the employer, they are all strangers that may or may not be telling the complete truth. Employers would really rather not have to interview strangers unless they have to.

Often, employers don't need to advertise

Most jobs are filled before advertising is needed. The employer may already know someone who seems to be right for the job. Or someone hears about the job and gets an interview before it is advertised. Often, employers hire someone who has been recommended to them by a friend, employee, or associate. Employers are much more comfortable hiring a person based on a personal reference rather than someone they don't know at all. Personal referrals matter, it's that simple.

There is also some evidence that employees who are hired as a result of a personal referral make better employees than those hired through want ads. I think this is the result of a current employee only being willing to refer someone who they think is a very good match and not recommending those who are not.

Tips to increase your chances of getting interviews for advertised openings

The fact is that some people do get jobs from following up on advertised openings, and some advertised jobs are good ones. So go ahead and look for advertised openings on a regular basis. Just remember that you should spend most of your job search time using other methods. Here are some tips to increase your chances of success when looking for advertised openings.

- ✓ While many ads ask you to send your resume or fill out an application, you don't have to follow those rules. It is often to your advantage to make a direct contact first. Attempt to get directly with the person who will supervise the advertised position. Do this by sending an e-mail or calling and asking for the name of the person in charge of the area that interests you. When you reach that person, ask for an interview, even if you meet with resistance, then set up a specific time to meet.

- ✓ To make advertising more attractive to employers, larger newspapers list their printed ads online. Many newspapers have cooperative arrangements that allow you to see jobs advertised in many areas listed on one Web site. Check your local paper to see if it refers you to a Web site for its listing and see what it offers. If you want to see want ads for another city, go to one of these sites and search for the ads in that region—and you don't have to buy the newspaper for that area.

- ✓ Web sites listing newspaper ads will often allow you to view expired ads. Some of these jobs may not have been filled and could still be open. They also help you find employers in the area who hire people with skills similar to yours. Even if that employer doesn't have an opening now, ask for an interview so you can be considered for future openings. You can, of course, also see expired ads by reviewing past editions of the printed newspaper at home or in your local library.

✓ Many Web sites post job openings, and the larger ones allow you to take advantage of all sorts of helpful features. For example, you can post your resume for employers to review; sort job openings by region, job title, and other criteria; get information on resume writing; get an e-mail with new job listings that meet your criteria when they appear; and much more. Sure, go ahead and use one or more of these sites on a regular basis. Just understand that many others will be doing the same thing, and your chances of success are quite slim. Use them as one source of job leads, but spend most of your time using more effective methods.

✓ Use more specialized print and Web resources. Join one or more professional associations in your field so you can access their Web sites, journal, and news. Look for any sources listing job opportunities and interact on their Web site with other members, letting them know that you are looking.

✓ Jobs that interest you may not be listed in an obvious way. An accounting job, for example, could be listed under "Accounting," "Bookkeeper," "Controller," "Chief Financial Officer," or several other key words. On Web sites, browse multiple job titles and categories to find appropriate openings. In print ads, read each and every newspaper ad at least weekly, and then mark any job that appears interesting and respond to each one, even if you don't have all the qualifications listed.

✓ Employers sometimes list things they do not absolutely require to limit the responses. If you are well qualified to do a job but don't have the degree or number of years experience listed, apply anyway. Emphasize your other credentials and abilities and go after an interview.

✓ Follow up in appropriate ways. Most job seekers do not follow up at all, or do so in inappropriate ways. For example, if you first e-mailed your resume, follow up with a mailed letter that includes your printed resume and asks for an interview. Or call or even drop in and ask to see the person in charge. Try a combination of things if the position really does interest you because doing so will separate you from the others who do not follow up—and greatly increase your chance of getting an interview.

✓ If an ad does not include an address, e-mail address, or phone number, you can often look the company up. Use Internet sites such as www.whitepages.com or www.yellowpages.com to look up employers by address, phone number, person, or organization name. Larger libraries may also have a printed "criss-cross" directory with which you can do the same thing. Or enter the organization name in your Web browser to see if the company has a Web site.

✓ Find out more about the prospective employer. If the company has a Web site, use it to find out as much as you can about it. You can often get the e-mail addresses of staff members from these sites, or at least an e-mail address of the Web site administrator or some other general address. Then send an e-mail to the person most likely to supervise you and ask for an interview—or ask him or her to send you the name of the person to contact. You can do the same thing via phone.

What I am suggesting here is that you be creative. Don't simply accept that you "should" only be passive and wait for the employer to contact you. Instead, try to make a direct and personal contact with someone specific, and then ask that person for an interview, even if there isn't a job opening right now. The worst thing that can happen is that you get blocked or rejected for an interview. This is the likely outcome for anyone seeking an advertised job anyway, but your efforts are far more likely to get you an interview than waiting passively for a response.

Traditional Job Search Method 2: Contacting Human Resource Departments and Filling Out Application Forms

Quick Alert

The human resource department (which is sometimes called "Personnel") is often not a job seeker's best friend, and neither is an application form.

Consider what the function of the typical human resource department (HR) really is. A person who works there might tell you that his or her job is to help the organization find qualified people to fill jobs by screening applicants. The question is, from the job seeker's point of view, who is getting screened out? Usually it's most of the job applicants (including you) because HR's function is to eliminate most applicants.

If you don't believe this, ask people who have worked in a human resource department. They will tell you that for each person who is hired, 20 or more are not. Sometimes hundreds are screened out for each person hired. What makes this situation even worse is that HR staff doesn't actually hire anyone other than those who will work in the human resource department. They screen out most job seekers and then, if the position is still open, and if you weren't screened out, you get to meet the person who could eventually hire you.

If you make it to the interview stage—and the chances are slim that you will—you will be just one of several others being interviewed. This further reduces your chances of getting a job offer to maybe 5 percent or less.

While those odds seem terrible, they are even worse when you consider that many employers end up hiring someone who wasn't even referred by the human resource department. Jobs are often filled before people in HR even know they are open.

I have hired many people while working within larger organizations, and I know this hiring scenario to be common. I often would recruit informally for weeks before the position I was trying to fill worked its way through the formal channels and became posted in the human resource department. By then, I often had one or more good candidates who had the inside track on that job. The last thing I wanted was to get many people referred to me from HR. They would all be strangers, they would all try to manipulate me into thinking they were great, and they would take up too much of my time.

HUMAN RESOURCE DEPARTMENTS MAY NOT EVEN BE FRIENDLY

HR departments in large organizations can be busy places with strict procedures that can make them feel a bit unfriendly to would-be employees. Have you ever noticed how job seekers are treated in most human resource departments? The furniture is usually inexpensive, and uncomfortable. The walls are decorated with signs saying everything but "sit down and be quiet." Even if the signs don't say that, the HR receptionist might. Job seekers in busy HR departments may be told things such as "Take one of those pencils and complete this application, and then wait until someone can give you an interview." It does not make you feel very important, does it?

One more thing: Only larger organizations have departments of human resources. Smaller organizations are not likely to have them at all, nor will many branch offices of larger organizations. Yet most job openings are in smaller organizations. A job seeker who assumes that getting a job requires finding the human resource department will miss most of the job opportunities that are out there.

Filling out applications

Much of what I said about human resource departments applies to applications as well. Application forms are specifically designed to collect information that can be used to screen most people out. The same is true for online applications and those that are completed on a computer at the employer's location. Furthermore, many smaller organizations don't even use them.

It is almost always better to ask to see the person in charge than to ask to complete an application. Fill out an application if you are asked to, but don't expect it to get you an interview.

Completing an application is also a passive way to try to get interviews, which is one of the reasons it does not typically work well. The exception is for young people, where completing applications is a bit more effective. This is because many of the jobs young people seek are entry level jobs that do not pay well, require night and weekend hours, require little training, and have high turnover rates. Many employers have difficulty filling these positions and are more willing to hire someone based on an application and a brief interview.

 I give you more details on completing applications in Chapter 15.

Traditional Job Search Method 3: Posting Your Resume Online or Mailing Unsolicited Resumes

The resume has been around for ages. So have the "experts" who will advise you to send yours out by the hundreds or to post them on any and all Internet sites. This approach does have its appeal because it seems easy, and almost every job search and resume book recommends it. The problem is that this approach does not work very well.

Like an application, a resume is the near-perfect tool for an employer to use to screen you out. As a result, you should expect a very low response rate, in the neighborhood of 2 to 5 percent, if you mail out unsolicited resumes and even worse if you post a resume online.

The effectiveness of sending out unsolicited resumes or posting them online varies by industry and job. It might be that you have skills in short supply, such as a registered nurse; in that case, sending out unsolicited resumes or posting your resume on a Web site is more likely to get you interviews. But, overall, it is clear that this is not an effective approach for most people.

While a high percentage of Internet users post their resumes on one or more Web sites, only a small percentage get a job offer from this approach. I do encourage you to post your resume on the Internet, but suggest you don't count on this one approach too heavily. I'll teach you some of the effective ways to use the Web and how to create a successful online resume in Chapter 12.

Farr's Rule: Resumes don't get jobs; interviews and networking do.

Many resume books will tell you that the way to get an interview is to create a superior resume that will somehow jump out of a pile of resumes or stand out from the thousands of online resumes and get an employer's attention. If you only follow their advice, they say, they will show you how to create a better, best, or perfect resume.

While this advice seems to make sense, it assumes that the job search consists of submitting your resume to someone who will compare it to many other resumes. But this approach to the job search limits your options and is not the only or even the most effective approach. For example, it is almost always better to contact an employer directly (a proactive approach) rather than to send a resume and hope for the best (a passive approach). The more effective approach is to make a direct and personal contact with the employer, set up an interview, and then send or bring your resume to the interviewer.

I do think that print and online resumes have an important place in the job search. Most people can write a superior resume in a matter of hours—once they have clarified what they want to do and have to offer in support of that objective. Writing a good resume is worth doing; it is how and when you use your resume that makes the biggest difference.

Quick Reference

I cover resumes in more detail in Section 2 and cover networking and other job search methods throughout this book.

Traditional Job Search Method 4: Employment Agencies

There are two very different types of employment agencies. The first type is operated by the government and charges no fees. The other type is run as a business. Since these are very different, I will cover each type separately.

The government-run employment service

Required by federal law, each state (and province, in Canada) has local offices that provide assistance to job seekers in locating job openings. These offices also administer unemployment compensation programs and are often referred to as the "unemployment office" as a result. These agencies have different names in different areas and can be located in the government "blue pages" of your phone book.

While these agencies have their limitations, I suggest you register with them early in your job search. There are several reasons for doing this, including:

✓ Obtaining any unemployment compensation that may be due you.

✓ Finding out about any special services they may offer.

✓ Seeing if they have any appropriate job listings to refer you to.

Because they are publicly funded, one of the big advantages of the public employment service is that they *never* charge a fee for their services. But they also have limitations that you need to understand. The most important limitation is that they know of only about 5 percent of the existing job openings in their area—which means that you will have to use other methods to find the other 95 percent of the openings. This is one reason why only about one in twenty of all job seekers get their jobs through this source. Another limitation is that many of the jobs it lists are relatively low paying and hard to fill.

Go to "America's Job Bank" at www.ajb.org to search all the jobs listed by the public employment service throughout the country. Run by the U.S. Department of Labor, it lists about a million job openings and allows you to sort them by region, type of job, and other criteria.

Tips for Using a Government Employment Service

While the overall results of using the government employment service is quite modest, I still suggest you use their services throughout your job search. Here are some points to consider in getting the most out of what they have available.

- ✓ If you qualify for unemployment compensation benefits, it is essential that you apply for them as soon as possible after you leave a job.
- ✓ Some offices, in some areas, are much more active than others, listing as many as 30 percent of the available openings in that area. Some states and provinces provide job search workshops and other helpful services, too.
- ✓ Many offices have staff and services for specific groups of people such as veterans, professionals, temporary workers, and others. Ask what services are available and use those that apply to you.
- ✓ Try to see the same staff person on a regular basis so that he or she gets to know you over time. It is important to create a good impression, so dress as if you are going to an interview and treat the staff with respect. If you impress them, they might remember you when they see a good job opening listed and refer you to it.
- ✓ Use the Internet (at www.ajb.org) to search for jobs listed with the public employment service by region and job type.

Private employment agencies

At one time I warned job seekers not to use private employment services, because you can do pretty much the same things yourself and save a lot of money. There were also a lot of dishonest operations that took advantage of unsuspecting people—and there are still some. But I'm a bit more positive about using private employment agencies now for a variety of reasons.

Private employment agencies are businesses and they charge a fee for their services. There is nothing wrong with this, and many people use them with good results. Over the years, the research has improved on the results job seekers obtain by using private employment agencies. They are more effective, for example, with young people and with those with specific occupational skills that are in demand, such as accounting, technology, or medical skills.

Most private agencies charge employers fees rather than charging job seekers directly, which has reduced the pressure tactics used on job seekers to accept a job so the agency can get its fee.

These changes have softened my position on using fee-based employment agencies, but you still need to use them cautiously, knowing what to expect and not expect in the way of services and fees.

Consider Using Private Employment Agencies, But Use Caution

 About 5 percent of all job seekers get their jobs through a private employment agency, about the same percent using the public employment service. This means that for each 20 people who use these agencies, only one or two get jobs, so you do need to use other approaches as well.

Employment agencies charge fees, often substantial ones, to either you or the employer. Typical fees range from 10 to 15 percent of your annual salary. For each $10,000 you earn a year, your fee will be between $1,000 and $1,500. Figure it out for your annual salary. That is a lot of money—entirely too much, I think, for most people to consider if you are paying it. Request only employer-paid referrals and make sure you will not pay a fee if you find your own job.

You should watch for want ads placed by these agencies; there are lots of them in most newspapers. The advertised job may not exist, and they may try to refer you to another one that pays less.

NEVER sign an agreement without taking it home and studying it. Never. Make sure an agreement allows you to actively look for and accept a position on your own, and agree to pay only for job leads they refer to you. If you are pressured to sign an agreement, walk away.

The people who work in private employment agencies are salespeople who are paid a commission on the fees they earn. Most are not career counselors, so don't expect much help if you have a problem (been fired, changing careers, new graduate, and so on).

The Seven Things That Make the Most Difference in the Job Search

In spite of some problems, most private employment agencies are ethical and can be very useful in finding job leads that might be difficult to find using other methods. If you are working and have limited time to look on your own, or have skills that are in demand, agencies can be of great help.

Consider agencies specializing in temporary jobs

Both public and private employment agencies will list temporary jobs, and some private agencies specialize in these opportunities. There are good reasons to consider these jobs, particularly if you need income right away or could benefit from getting some work experience in different settings. Many employers hire "temps" for short or even longer projects, and then make permanent job offers to those who best meet their needs. Temp jobs are a good alternative to unemployment and will often allow you to learn new skills that will help you get a better long-term job. Some agencies provide skills training, health insurance, and other benefits for those temps who meet their criteria. Temporary agencies often specialize in areas such as accounting, executive, general labor, office support, medical, and other areas, so find one that best fits your needs and see what it can do for you.

Traditional Job Search Method 5: Civil Service Jobs

About one in ten workers is employed by a government agency or in a government-funded job of some kind. With about three million employees, the federal government is the largest employer in the country. There are additional millions of workers employed by state, province, county, city, township, and local government sources. Almost any job you can imagine can be found somewhere within the public sector: teachers, police officers, laborers, engineers, scientists, technicians, office workers, managers, short-order cooks, librarians, technicians, aircraft mechanics, environmental workers, and many others.

Most civil service jobs require you to fill out many forms, take tests, or meet other criteria in order to be considered. These procedures are intended to make the hiring process fair to all who apply. However, you should know that applying and actually being considered are two different things.

The procedures for being considered for government positions often take a long time before a decision can be made; so if you are in a hurry to find a job, this source is probably not for you. It takes months to be considered for some positions, and there is often intense competition for the more desirable jobs. In spite of all this, it could be worthwhile to find out what jobs you may qualify for and how to apply for them.

Quick Tip

For federal jobs, the best place to get information is on the Internet. Here are some helpful sites:

✓ The official U.S. government site for federal job information: www.usajobs.gov

✓ U.S. Office of Personnel Management: www.opm.gov

✓ Federal Jobs Digest: www.jobsfed.com

✓ Federal Jobs Central: www.fedjobs.com

✓ The Resume Place (advice on writing a federal resume): www.resume-place.com

Procedures for applying to state, city, and local government agencies vary by area. Start by contacting the entities that interest you and asking them how to find out about openings and their application procedures. Most phone books have a special government section, often printed on blue pages, that list general information numbers to call, as well as specific agencies. States, Canadian provinces, and many other government entities have Web sites that provide employment information; use your Web browser to search for these sites by name. Larger governmental systems typically have a centralized office that screens applicants and lists available openings.

Looking for government jobs can require a lot of work and time, so be prepared for this if you are interested.

Traditional Job Search Methods Encourage You to Be Passive

A major problem with the traditional job search methods covered in this chapter is that they encourage you to be passive. Traditional methods, used in the traditional way, all require you to depend on *someone else* to do something to let you know about an opening.

They assume that you can't do anything until *someone else* decides to create a position, announces the opening in some public way such as by an ad in the paper or online, reads your resume or application, does not screen you out, and finally allows you to interview for a job opening.

You send in a resume and hope someone else will call or e-mail you back. You depend on an employer to place a help wanted ad or post their opening online—and hope you don't get screened out. You fill out an application—and hope you get an interview. I believe that all traditional methods are designed to help the employer screen people out. They all create barriers to a job seeker getting in and talking to the person who is most likely to actually hire you. And, most importantly of all, traditional job search methods all assume that a prospective employer and a job seeker can't see each other unless there is a job opening.

Traditional job search methods do work for some people, and I've given you some tips in this chapter to improve the effectiveness of these approaches. While you are likely to use these traditional methods in your search for a job, it is important to recognize the limitations of such passive methods.

Traditional Job Search Methods Lead to Hopelessness

Many of the traditional job search methods would make sense in a labor market dominated by a relatively few large employers—but not by the many smaller employers that employ about 70 percent of today's workers.

By narrowly defining who can talk to whom, traditional job search methods have the effect of encouraging people to believe that there are fewer jobs out there for which they are qualified.

Private or governmental employment agencies know about only a small percentage of openings, so those who use them exclusively will never know of most of the jobs never listed there. Newspapers only list about 15 percent of all openings, and Internet listings include many jobs that have already been filled or are not the best job openings. All of these methods allow large numbers of people to see the relatively few openings.

After people use traditional job search methods and nothing happens, they tend to believe that there is nothing more they can do. Eventually, they tend to sit at home becoming increasingly discouraged.

The longer people are unemployed or under-employed, the fewer hours they tend to spend looking for a job. So even those who have good work habits, years of reliable work experience, and many skills begin to believe that there are no jobs out there for them and that *they* are undesirable and unemployable.

While any one of the traditional methods can and does work for some people, they represent, in total, only about 25 percent of the methods people use that actually get them jobs. Therefore, each technique should be used only as one of a combination of methods. Taken individually, with virtually every traditional job search method, the odds are stacked against you.

I suggest that you can do much better.

In the rest of this book, you will learn about more effective and—nontraditional—job search methods. Other techniques explained in this book will be far more effective for most people than traditional methods.

The techniques I encourage you to use are proactive ones. I teach you to look at the job search in a new and different way from the traditional approach. I encourage you to be self-reliant, self-directed, and active rather than passive. As you learn about more effective job search approaches, you can use them in addition to the more traditional approaches to boost your effectiveness considerably.

Your objective is to find better job opportunities, get more and better interviews, and do well in those interviews. If you do, you are likely to get a better job, in less time, than the average job seeker who uses less effective methods.

How to Manage Being Unemployed or Under-employed while Looking for the Job You Want

 Quick Reference

If you are currently unemployed, you are not alone. There are about ten million unemployed workers in the United States at any one time. Although this seems grim, there is good news as well: U.S. employers are hiring approximately 125,000 workers each day—more than 800,000 a week.

Chapter 17 provides detailed advice about coping with job loss. However, if you are currently unemployed, you might want to review these few tips right now to help you get through this difficult time and focus on your job search.

✔ **Apply for benefits without delay.** Don't be embarrassed to apply for unemployment benefits as soon as possible, even if you're not sure you are eligible. Unemployment compensation is an insurance program that is intended to help you make a transition between jobs, and you helped pay for it by contributing during your previous employment. Depending on how long you have worked, you can collect benefits for up to 26 weeks and sometimes even longer. Contact your state Labor Department or Employment Security Agency for further information. Their addresses and telephone numbers are listed in your phone book.

✔ **Set goals.** Like a grocery list, write down your daily "to do" list, including small, achievable tasks. Divide the tasks on your list and make a list for every day so you will have some "successes" daily.

✔ **Prioritize.** Remember first things first. You cannot handle everything at once. Don't even try. I suggest doing the most important things first, even if they are not enjoyable.

✔ **Establish a workable schedule.** When you set a schedule for yourself, make sure it is one which can be achieved. As you perform your tasks, you will feel a sense of control and accomplishment. Use your daily to do list and check off the items, large and small, as you do them.

(continued)

(continued)

✔ **Make a budget.** Use free consumer credit counseling services. Look for ways to increase your income and cut expenses. Find a way to reward yourself that does not harm you or your family financially or emotionally, but gives you a sense of freedom.

✔ **Reduce stress.** Learn relaxation techniques or other stress-reduction techniques. This can be as simple as sitting in a chair, closing your eyes, taking a deep breath and breathing out slowly while imagining all the tension going out with your breath. There are a number of other methods, including listening to relaxation tapes, which may help you cope with stress more effectively. Many of these tapes are available at your public library.

✔ **Avoid isolating.** Keep in touch with your friends, even former coworkers, if you can do that comfortably. Unemployed people often feel a sense of isolation and loneliness. See your friends, talk with them, and socialize with them. You are the same person you were before unemployment. The same goes for the activities that you may have enjoyed in the past. Evaluate them. Which can you afford to continue? If you find that your old hobbies or activities can't be part of your new budget, perhaps you can substitute new activities that are less costly.

✔ **Picture success.** Practice visualizing positive results or outcomes and view them in your mind before the event. Play out the scene in your imagination and picture yourself successful in whatever you're about to attempt. What you focus on expands, so focus on the results you want. Worry is negative goal setting, so keep worry at bay.

✔ **Surround yourself with positive people.** Socialize with family and friends who are supportive. You want to be around people who will "pick you up," not "knock you down." You know who your fans are. Try to find time to be around them. It can really make a difference.

✔ **Become accountable for yourself.** Try not to complain or blame others. Save your energy for activities that result in positive experiences. You are in charge of you. Often a couple of good decisions can wipe out a string of "bad luck," so focus on making good choices.

✔ **Learn to accept what you cannot change.** However, it is largely not what happens to you, but how you react to the situation that will determine your success. Your reactions and your behavior are in your control and will influence the outcome of events.

> ✔ **Keep the job search under your own command.** This will give you a sense of control and prevent you from giving up and waiting for something to happen. Enlist everyone's aid in your job search, but make sure you do most of the work. People like to help and having a positive attitude will attract those who can and want to assist you.
>
> ✔ **Face your fears, and try to pinpoint them.** "Naming the enemy" is the best strategy for relieving the vague feeling of anxiety. By facing what you actually fear, you can see how realistic your fears are. And remember FEAR stands for False Evidence Appearing Real. Now is the time to dig in and do something positive, not become immobilized by fear.
>
> ✔ **Think creatively, stay flexible, take risks, and don't be afraid of failure.** Don't take rejection personally. Think of it as information that will help you later in your search. Take criticism as a way to learn more about yourself. Keep plugging away at the job search despite those inevitable setbacks. See all set backs as temporary. Success is often failure turned inside out, so press on. Most important, forget magic—you will learn in this book how to create your own good luck. With perseverance and diligence you will get the job you seek.

≡ *Quick Summary*

✓ You can cut your job search time in half (or more) and get a better job.

✓ Some job search methods work better than others.

✓ There are proactive steps you can take to reduce the stress of finding a job.

✓ If you are currently looking for a job, the job search "how to" aspects of this book will probably appeal to you most.

✓ Self-knowledge (regarding your skills and interests) is an essential element in helping you define just what sort of job you want. If you know what your ideal job would be, you are more likely to find one that comes close to it.

✓ Job seekers who get more interviews find jobs faster because the more interviews you get, the more likely you are to get a job offer.

✓ One of the things that traditional job search methods have in common is that they encourage you to be passive. The result is discouragement and being out of work or under-employed longer than is necessary.

✓ Traditional job search approaches have job seekers define an interview too narrowly and make obtaining an interview harder than it needs to be.

✓ The most effective job search methods help you remain active in your job search and can dramatically increase the number of interviews you can get and valuable contacts you can make.

✓ Most jobs are not advertised. Only about 25 percent are publicly advertised in some way.

✓ Employer Web sites and online classified advertisements are increasingly being used by employers to develop applicants. Being able to connect with computer-dependent employers is a skill you will want to learn and use.

✓ Private employment agencies and search firms have a place in the job search. You can learn how to use these professional networkers to your advantage.

✓ Studies show that only two job-seeking methods—direct contact with employers and getting leads from people you know (networking) are used to find about three out of every four jobs.

✓ In this chapter, I reviewed job search techniques that are traditionally used by most people. For each one, I present their disadvantages as well as some nontraditional tips on increasing their effectiveness.

✓ The techniques I encourage you to use throughout this book are active ones. I teach you to look at the job search in a new and different way from the traditional approach. I encourage you to be self-reliant, self-directed, and proactive rather than passive. I teach you how to use technology to your advantage in this process and how to make valuable contacts wherever you go.

CHAPTER 2

The Two Best Job Search Methods—

Why They Work and How to Use Them

═══Quick Overview

In this chapter, I review the following:

✔ Why the nontraditional methods I outline work best

✔ What frictional unemployment is

✔ The four stages of a job opening

✔ Networking in detail

✔ How to make warm and cold contacts

✔ Redefining the job interview

✔ How to use the *Yellow Pages* or Internet directories and other traditional tools to find job leads

✔ A preview of other job search methods presented in greater detail in later chapters

✔ Some "little things" that you can do to make a big difference in your job search

I mentioned in the previous chapter that some job search methods work better than others. It turns out that two methods—networking and direct contacts with employers—work better than any of the traditional techniques.

In this chapter, I review these methods and give you a good idea of how to use them during your job search. I also present a few key ideas about where to look and why the techniques I suggest work better than others.

I've already shown you the data on how people find jobs, and as you've learned, the most effective technique is getting leads from people you know. I've also pointed out that most jobs are with smaller organizations.

Well, you might say, all this is very enlightening, but just going around talking to people doesn't seem like a substantial job search method. It's true, there is more to it than that, and I will give you the details in this chapter. But in order to understand just how to be most effective in your job search, I first want you to understand a bit about *why* networking and direct employer contacts work best.

Some Reasons Why Networking and Direct Contacts Methods Work Best

Many of the traditional job search methods made sense 25 years ago or more. Back then, a large percentage of our workforce was employed in large organizations. Today many people continue to use outmoded job search methods, despite the fact that the labor market has changed.

Small Organizations—Where Most of the Jobs Are

Whatever job search methods you use, it is essential that you begin with a sense of where those jobs are, and most jobs are now with smaller organizations.

My most recent review of the data indicates that about 70 percent of all non-governmental workers now work for small employers. These are employers with 250 or fewer workers. Look at the following chart to see the importance of small organizations in your job search.

Most of the new jobs in our economy now come from small organizations, and this has been true for many years now. Some studies indicate that virtually all of the net job growth in recent years has come from very small employers—those with 20 or fewer employees.

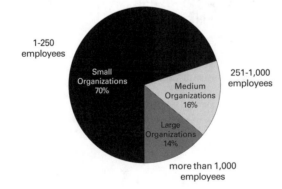

Smaller employers tend not to have a human resource department, so asking to fill out an application or to send in a resume to the HR person doesn't make much sense. Furthermore, because there are many more small employers than large ones, they are often harder to find or even to know about. Even larger corporations have decentralized, passing along hiring decisions to smaller local branches that are too small to have their own human resource department. While local offices of large organizations do have to follow corporate hiring procedures, they often act more like small ones in the way that they hire people—and the traditional job search approaches are even less effective.

It is clear that more people are working for small employers than large ones today, and this trend is likely to continue. You should also note that the opportunities for learning and advancement are often better in smaller organizations than in larger ones.

Many of the job search methods presented in this chapter and throughout this book are very effective with smaller organizations. The same methods also work well with larger, more formal organizations. The traditional job search methods reviewed in the previous chapter were designed for a very different time and economy, when large employers dominated the labor market. They just aren't as effective or sensible today.

Frictional Unemployment—Where the Job Search Action Is

Friction, according to the dictionary, is "a resistance to motion when two surfaces touch." According to the U.S. Department of Labor, a similar phenomenon occurs in the job market. Called "frictional unemployment," it is a situation where job openings exist and qualified job seekers are looking for them, but the employer and job seeker don't connect with each other right away.

An example of frictional unemployment is when a job opening occurs because of someone leaving, but the position remains unfilled for a time before a qualified candidate is selected and actually begins working. The U.S. Department of Labor estimates that over 40 percent of all unemployment is due to this friction. The other sources of unemployment indicated in the following chart include "cyclical" unemployment, which is the product of a sluggish economy, and "structural" unemployment, which stems from the restructuring of our economy in fundamental ways such as restructuring due to new technologies.

Some researchers believe that 40 percent of unemployment attributed to friction is a conservative estimate. They argue that frictional unemployment is a major source of unemployment because the longer it takes to fill or find a job, the higher the unemployment rate.

Quick Fact

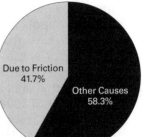

If you could reduce the average length of time it takes to find a job by just one day, it would reduce the number of unemployed by more than 300,000 people. If you could reduce it by just 10 percent, it would have the same economic impact as creating 2.5 million jobs.

This may all seem somewhat theoretical until you realize that the major cause of frictional unemployment is that most job seekers do not know how to find the jobs that exist at any given time. What this means is that there are jobs open right now and qualified people to fill them, but the employer and job seeker have not yet met. For you, this means it is very likely that an employer would hire you today for a job opening he has now, if only the two of you could find each other.

The impact of frictional unemployment is even more important now than in the past. This is due to people changing jobs more frequently, resulting in a higher percentage of people experiencing at least some unemployment each year. When the overall unemployment rate is higher, that's an indicator that even more people will experience some unemployment that year.

The good news for you is that once you learn the proper job search techniques, you can dramatically reduce the time it takes to find a job. In other words, you are more likely to find those jobs that are open but unfilled as a result of "friction." This reduction in job search time is something that programs using my job search methods have demonstrated many times—people can cut their job search time in half if they use the right techniques.

Once you understand that good jobs are out there for you that are not advertised—and that you qualify for these jobs—the next step is learning how to find them.

The Four Stages of a Job Opening

There is a practical application to the idea of frictional unemployment. It comes in an examination of how a job opening comes to be. Jobs, you see, don't just open up one day with no notice. Someone typically knows a job might open up before it actually does. Often, these jobs get filled by someone before the employer needs to advertise. The result is that the job is never advertised at all, because it is filled before there is a need to. But how do you find these openings if they're not advertised? Here is the answer:

Find employers before they advertise the job you want.

To do this, you need to understand how most jobs become available.

I have found it useful to think of a job opening as a process that occurs over time. Before a job is filled, a series of events typically occur. Thinking in these terms, I have identified four major stages that most job openings go through before they are filled. Each of the four stages represents a distinct phase in the history of a job opening. To help you understand this, let's go through each stage of a job opening in more detail. Each stage is defined and illustrated in the graphic that follows.

THE FOUR STAGES OF A JOB OPENING

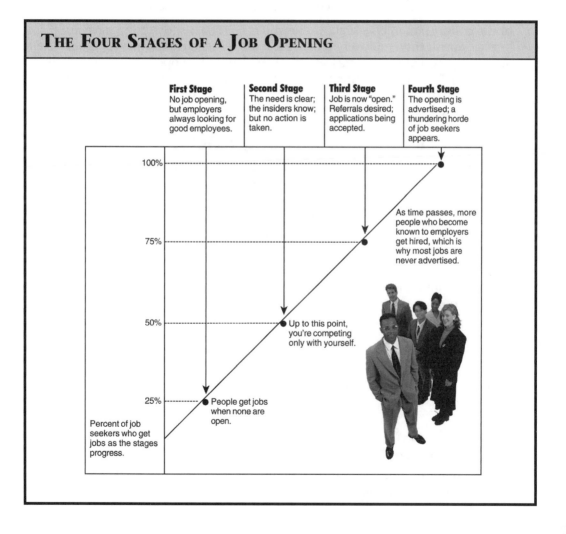

First Stage
No job opening, but employers always looking for good employees.

Second Stage
The need is clear; the insiders know; but no action is taken.

Third Stage
Job is now "open." Referrals desired; applications being accepted.

Fourth Stage
The opening is advertised; a thundering horde of job seekers appears.

100%

As time passes, more people who become known to employers get hired, which is why most jobs are never advertised.

75%

50%

Up to this point, you're competing only with yourself.

25%

People get jobs when none are open.

Percent of job seekers who get jobs as the stages progress.

More Details on the Four Stages of a Job Opening

It's important to understand that most jobs are filled before employers need to advertise them. To find these opportunities, you have to get in to an employer before the job is made fully public. Here are some more details on the four stages of a job opening to help you understand better how this works.

Stage 1: There is no job open now

Before a job is actually created or available, it obviously does not exist. If you asked an employer if they had a job opening at this stage, they would say "No." Perhaps no openings are planned or all positions are occupied.

In the conventional job search, there would be no basis for you to have an interview with this employer. In fact, most job seekers will completely ignore the opportunities that exist in this situation. Yet, should an opening become available at any time in the future, those who are already known to the employer will be considered before all others. About 25 percent of all jobs are filled by people the employer knows of before the job is even open.

Stage 2: No formal opening exists, but one or more insiders know of a possibility

As time goes on, someone in an organization can usually anticipate a possible future position becoming available before one actually opens up. It could be the result of a new marketing campaign or product, an increase in business, an observation that someone is not doing well on the job, someone is thinking about relocating, or a variety of other things. It's not always the boss who knows first, either.

In previous jobs, I have often known that a coworker was looking for another job even though the boss did not. Or I wondered why that person didn't get fired. Typically, if you were to ask an employer if there were any job openings at this stage, you would be told "No" once again. In fact, there is no job opening—yet. And, for this reason, most job seekers keep on looking, not realizing that a job opportunity is right before them. Unfortunately for them, about 50 percent of all jobs are filled by people who are known to the employer by this stage of an opening.

Stage 3: A formal opening now exists, but it has not been advertised

At some point in time, the boss will finally say that, yes, they have a job opening and that they are looking for someone to fill it. However, with few exceptions, days or even weeks go by before that job will be advertised in some public way. If you were to ask if there was a job opening at this stage, you might still get a "No," depending on whom you ask.

In larger organizations, even the human resources department doesn't get formal notice of an opening for days or even weeks after the opening is known to people who work in the affected department. In large organizations, people who work there often don't know of openings in other departments. In smaller organizations, of course, most staff would know of any formal openings.

In any case, once a job opening finally reaches this stage, it is the first time a person using a conventional approach to the job search might get a "Yes" response. And about 75 percent of all jobs are filled by someone who finds out about the job before it leaves this stage.

Stage 4: The job opening is finally advertised

As more time goes by and a job opening does not get filled, it might be advertised in the newspaper or posted online, a sign may be hung in the window, career services are notified, or some other action is taken to make the opening known to the general public. This is the stage where virtually every job seeker can know about the opening, and if the job is reasonably desirable, a thundering horde of job seekers will now come after it.

What the Four Stages Mean to You

The "four stages of a job opening" concept shows that you can be considered for a job opening long before a formal opening exists—and long before it is advertised. In fact, that is why most jobs are never advertised. Someone like you gets there before it needs to be advertised. Employers don't like to hire strangers. They prefer to hire people they already know or who are referred to them by someone they know. Many are willing to talk to a job seeker even before they have a job opening—if you approach them in the right way. Once you know each other, of course, you are no longer strangers.

About 25 percent of the people who get hired become known to the employer before a job opening exists. Another 25 percent or so of those who get hired find out about the opening during the second stage of a job opening. Jobs that are filled during the first and second stages of a job opening are simply not available to someone using traditional job search methods. Half of all jobs are filled by the time traditional search methods come into play.

Only about half of all positions make it to the third stage of a job opening. During this stage the job is at least available to a job seeker using traditional methods. If that job seeker just happens to ask the right person at the right time and if there is a job opening, he or she will, for the first time, get a "Yes" response. During this third stage another 25 percent land their jobs. With 75 percent of the jobs getting filled during the first three stages, that leaves the remaining 25 percent that get advertised, and in other ways, made available to the public.

The most important job search rule of all

The four stages of a job opening make it clear that most jobs are filled before they are advertised. This pattern illustrates the most important job search rule of all:

Don't wait until the job is open before asking for an interview!

The best time to search for a job is before anyone else knows about it. Most jobs are filled by someone the employer meets before a job is formally "open." So the key is to meet people who can hire you before a job is available. This is why these jobs are sometimes referred to as the hidden job market, or the networked job market. Instead of saying "Do you have any jobs open?" say "I realize you may not have any openings now, but I would still like to talk to you about the possibility of future openings." With this simple approach many employers will say "Yes" instead of "No." Not all, but many.

More bad news for traditional job search methods and good news for you

In addition to missing out on half of the available job openings, there are other disadvantages to those using traditional job search methods. The first negative is that the positions that remain unfilled by the third and fourth stages of a job opening tend to be less desirable or harder to fill. The best jobs are often filled by then. This is even truer for the jobs that are left unfilled long enough to get advertised. There are exceptions, of course, but the better jobs tend to be filled long before they are advertised.

Jobs that make it to the third and fourth stage of a job opening face another distinct negative—more people know about and compete for these jobs. This is particularly true for advertised jobs because there are often many applicants for these jobs.

During the third and fourth stages, an employer has the task of screening out all but one of those who are interested. Virtually all of the applicants are now strangers who will try to manipulate the employer by "marketing" or "selling" themselves, which means emphasizing their strong points and hiding their weaknesses. Employers know this, so they try to find out something "wrong" with each applicant in order to eliminate them from consideration. It is the nature of the game and it is not pretty.

So the job search takes on a decidedly competitive and distasteful flavor for those seeking jobs in the third, and more so, in the fourth stage of a job opening. I am not saying you should not consider jobs that are advertised—you should—it's just that you need to find ways of finding potential openings before others do. If you do insist on looking for jobs in the fourth stage of a job opening, you need to know that you will probably be unemployed longer than you need to be.

You can get an "interview" even before a job opening formally exists

You may not have noticed, but what I have done in the previous narrative is to redefine what counts as an "interview." In the conventional job search, an interview is something you can obtain only when an employer has a clearly defined job opening for which you qualify. But this definition eliminates opportunities available during the first two stages of a job opening. Here is my new definition of an interview which I ask you to consider:

A New Definition of an Interview

An interview is any face-to-face contact with a person who hires or supervises people with your skills—even if there is no job opening now.

This definition is a very important one to remember because it allows you to "interview" with all sorts of people you would otherwise overlook in a job search. For example, it allows you to talk to a potential employer during the first or second stages of a job opening—before a job is formally open at all.

Instead of waiting for a job to be advertised, this new interview definition allows you to go out and find potential employers who may not have job openings now, but who might in the future. Understanding and using this new definition of an interview will give you a distinct advantage in finding job possibilities while others use traditional job search methods—and remain unemployed longer than they need to.

The rest of this book assumes this new and broader definition of an interview. This mind-set opens a world of possibility. More importantly, it can help you get a job in much less time than would be possible otherwise.

The Two Most Effective Job Search Methods—Warm and Cold Contacts

I find concepts easier to understand if I keep things simple. One simple idea that I have applied to the job search is that of warm and cold contacts. Let me explain: Salespeople who call on potential customers via phone or by dropping in without an appointment call this technique making "cold contacts." While I do not think that the sales analogy is completely appropriate when applied to the job search, I like the "cold contacts" term. It quickly communicates a style of contact that can be adapted for the search for potential job openings.

So, in the job search context, cold contacts are job leads obtained from contacting people you don't know—employers in particular. Using this term also allows me to create the term "warm contacts" to describe leads for job openings that come from people you already know. These warm contacts include friends, relatives, and acquaintances.

Start by Making Warm Contacts: The Most Effective Job Search Method

If you remember the data on how people find jobs presented in the previous chapter, you may recollect that warm contacts—job leads obtained from friends and relatives—account for about one-third of all job leads. The reality is probably higher than that. More recent studies that asked job seekers for lead sources other than friends or relatives found other groups such as "business associates" and "acquaintances" provided leads as well.

Quick Fact ▶ All personal referrals together probably account for about 40 percent of the ways that people find jobs. That makes using personal contacts the most important job search technique of all.

Leads developed from direct contacts with employers are also very important. About 30 percent of all job seekers find their jobs using this method. Together, these two techniques—leads from people you know and direct contacts with employers—account for about 75 percent of all job leads. With a little practice, getting leads from your warm contacts may be the only job search techniques you need.

GETTING WARM AND COLD CONTACTS IS A FORM OF NETWORKING

Many people use the term "networking" to refer to the technique of getting job leads from people you know or meet during your job search. Networking is essentially the same thing as the warm and cold contact approach I present here, although I think my approach is a bit easier to understand and put to use. I will provide more specific networking methods in this and later chapters.

Use These Three Steps to Identify Hundreds of Warm Contacts

The people who know you are the same ones who are most likely to help you—if only they knew what to do. Yet few job seekers seem willing to ask for meaningful help from the people they know in developing job leads. If job seekers ask their friends, relatives, and acquaintances for help at all it is of the vague, "Tell me if you hear of anything," variety.

While this crude approach does work often enough, people you know—your warm contacts—can and will be much more helpful if you learn to ask them to help you in more specific ways.

Knowing that leads provided by warm contacts are the most effective source of jobs for most people, it makes sense to systematically develop these contacts. Yet few job seekers go about developing their warm contacts in an organized way. With just a few simple techniques, you might be amazed at how many people you know—or can come to know.

Step 1: List contact groups of the people you know

To give you an idea of how this works, let's start by defining just who you know (that is, your "warm" contacts). You know far more people than you may at first realize, and many of them will help you uncover job leads that cannot be found in any other way. To demonstrate this, begin by listing the *types or categories* of people you know.

Look over the list of contact groups that follows. Notice that some of the listings are of groups of people with whom you might share something in common, even though you would not know all those within the group.

A Sample List of Warm Contact Groups

Friends

Relatives

Clients

Former employers

Former coworkers

School friends

Alumni lists

Members of my political party—in and out of elected positions

Members of my church

Members of social, fraternal, or other clubs

Present or former teachers

People at my children's sport games/events

Neighbors

People in my athletic club

People I play sports with

Members of a professional organization I belong to (or could join)

People who sell me things or provide me with professional services (insurance, hair salon, mechanic, shop clerks, etc.)

People I play cards with

Warm Contact Groups Worksheet

Directions: Now create your own list of "groups" of people you know. Use any of the groups from the previous sample as well as your own groups and list them in the spaces below. I have already included the friends and relatives groups since almost everyone has some—and because they are an important source of job leads. Be as specific as possible in the categories you add. Remember you want the groups, not the specific names of people at this point.

Groups	#	Groups	#
Friends			
Relatives			

Step 2: Create warm contact lists

While most people agree that "you have to know someone to get a job," most job seekers often tell me they "don't know anyone." One of those assumptions is true; namely, that people very often *do* get jobs through someone they know. But job seekers are mistaken if they think they don't know people. To show you what I mean, let's take a few of the groups you listed in the preceding exercise and see how many people they represent.

You know far more people than you might realize

Right now, if I asked you to take the first group on your list (which is "friends," which I put there) and write a list that includes everyone you are friendly with or who is even somewhat friendly to you, how many people would you guess that would be? Ten? Twenty-five? Two-hundred? Don't feel insecure here: some very good people just can't call a lot of people "friends." The truth is we all would be very fortunate to have just a *few* good friends during our lives. Instead, I'm suggesting that you think of people who are "friendly" to you, not close friends. Jot that number on your Warm Contact Groups Worksheet, next to the "friends" entry. Next, estimate how many people are in each of the other groups and note your estimate next to each entry.

When you are finished, don't be surprised if the number of people you know is larger than you anticipated. It's not at all unusual for someone to get hundreds of potential contact people this way. Some groups, such as people who belong to your religious group or who went to the same school, can be enormous. They don't all know about job openings, of course, but they are a place to start. Remember, each contact on your list is a source of potential job leads.

Some contact groups are ideal for making out-of-town contacts. For example, while you may not personally know everyone who graduated from your school, an alumni list can help you locate past graduates who live all over the country. If you have a specific location you want to move to, you can contact alumni who live in that area and ask them to help you to locate job leads there; many will be willing to help you.

I'll provide more details on looking for a job out of town later in this book and easy methods of going online to find these alumni and other lists.

Now create lists of specific contacts—the actual people in the groups

I know from experience that leaving you with the idea that you know lots of people is not enough. To make this an effective job search technique, you will need to contact those people. To accomplish this, it is essential that you make— you guessed it—more lists. (I know you are resisting creating these lists now. But these lists can be VERY important to you in your search for a job, so please, do go ahead and complete them.)

For each of the contact groups you listed previously, use a sheet of paper to make a separate list. Begin with friends and write as many friends' names on that list as you can think of. Then do the same thing for relatives. When you have completed these two lists, you should have a significant number of names of people who know you. You can save the other lists to do later in your job search. You may only need the first two.

Step 3: Use your warm contacts to develop an expanding network of contacts

Armed with your lists of friends and relatives, you have the beginning of a larger list of people who, in turn, can refer you to others. Of course, some of the people on your lists will be more helpful than others. Keep in mind though that these people are the ones who will be most likely to want to help you. Many job seekers do not follow through with their warm contacts and do not get the job leads from these important contacts that they could. The information that follows will help you greatly improve the results of using your warm contacts.

Networking basics

Networking sounds sophisticated and complicated, but it's really a simple idea. You use one person you know as a source to introduce you to one or more people you don't know. The best approach is to get at least two names of new people to contact from each one of your warm contacts, like this:

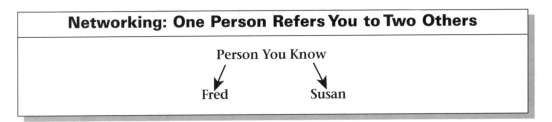

Networking: One Person Refers You to Two Others

Person You Know

Fred   Susan

The first person you contact is clearly a warm contact, because you know him or her directly. The people your warm contact then refers you to will also give you a warm reception, because you have a personal connection with them. In a sense, they are also warm contacts once you get to know them.

Quick Fact

There is a substantial amount of research (popularized by the movie *Six Degrees of Separation*) that finds that we can usually contact anyone on the planet through the personal contacts in a chain of just six or fewer people. So, if you want to work for a specific organization, you can use the networking methods I suggest here to locate people who already work there, or who know people who do, quickly.

KEEP YOUR CONVERSATIONS FRIENDLY AND INFORMAL

Depending on the situation, it is often best to work into your request for help casually. For example, don't just say "Hey, I am looking for a job, do you know of anything?" or "I want to talk to you about a job." A better approach depends on the situation but would normally begin with some informal conversation. For example, say you are sitting at your kid's game, near a woman you've seen there before. First you just chat about the game and are friendly. You might then ask her what sort of work she does, listen, be interested, and ask questions. She will probably ask you what you do, and you can tell her you are looking for a job, if currently unemployed, or tell her about whatever work you do now, if employed, but admit that you are considering other options. Keep chatting until you get the names of two or three people she knows who might be able to help you. Then stay in touch with this person, by at least sending her a thank-you note and letting her know how things went when you contacted the people she referred you to.

Treat friends and others you know in similarly thoughtful ways.

After meeting with Fred and Susan (or chatting with them on the phone), they will often be willing to give you names of others to contact. As you repeat this referral process with each person, this is what happens:

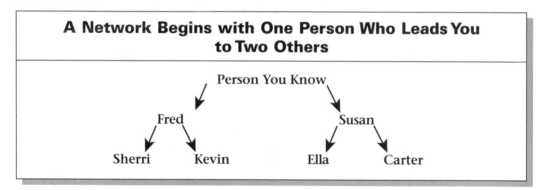

A Network Begins with One Person Who Leads You to Two Others

Networking arithmetic

The number of people you could contact through networking is amazing. In the example I just presented, if you kept getting two referrals from each person, you would have 1,024 people in your network after only the tenth level of contact. And that is starting with only one person!

THE SIX RULES FOR DEVELOPING A SUCCESSFUL NETWORK OF CONTACTS

Networking is a simple idea and it does work. It helps you meet potential employers you would not find using any other method. These employers may be a friend or a friend of a friend. And they will be willing to see you because of your common acquaintance.

Of course, not all of your contacts will be helpful to your job search, but there are some things you can do to increase this possibility. Here are my basic rules of successful networking:

Rule 1: Get Started—Set Up a Meeting

An essential criterion for a person to be in your network is that he or she is willing to talk to you. Because almost everyone will be willing to talk to you, select those who seem most likely to know lots of other people. Friends, relatives, and other warm contacts are an ideal place to start, because they are usually very willing to help you if they can.

To set up a meeting, simply call your contact and say something like:

> "Hi there, Uncle Albert, I'm looking for a job and wonder if you could help me out. When would be a good time for me to come over?"

While some short explanatory conversation is in order in your initial phone call, your objective is to get an appointment.

In a later chapter you will learn about a job search tool called a JIST Card and use this as a basis for making phone calls. These techniques will assist you in making more effective phone contacts; but more on this later.

Rule 2: Present Yourself Well

It is most important that all the contacts in your network end up thinking well of you. To increase the chances that they will, it helps to be friendly, well organized, polite, and interested in what they have to say. Even Uncle Albert doesn't have to see you, so be on your best behavior and behave as if you are going to an interview with a stranger, even if you know the person well.

Rule 3: Learn Something

Be open to learn from your contacts, even if they don't know very much about the type of job you are seeking. Do try, however, to keep things centered on your goal. Your goal, of course, is to get more job leads.

In situations where the contact does know about the type of job you want, there is often much that he or she can tell you about what is going on in the field and other details that would be helpful for you to know.

Rule 4: Get Two Referrals

Getting referrals is essential to developing a network, so don't give up until you have at least two names of other people who might help in your job search. You can get referrals from virtually anyone, but only if you keep asking for them. I have developed three questions that will typically get you one or more referrals, but often only after you ask the second or third question.

The Three Essential Questions to Get Referrals

1. Do you know of anyone who might have an opening for a person with my skills? If no, then,

2. Do you know of anyone else who *might* know of someone who would?

3. Do you know someone who knows lots of people?

It is essential that you ask all three questions!

 It is unusual to get a "No" if you ask all three questions. But I know from many years of experience that you will resist asking the second and, particularly, the third questions. Most people are willing to ask the first question but stop there.

Even untrained job seekers ask the first question, although typically using less direct language than I suggest here. Even so, untrained job seekers get about 40 percent of all their job leads in this way—more than from any other method. But my point here is that asking the second and third questions can dramatically increase the effectiveness of your warm contacts.

So get used to asking each of the three questions until you get what you want: either a lead for a possible job opening or the names of two people who might be of assistance to you in your search.

As you ask each of the three questions, be prepared for an occasional "yes" response to your first question. Whenever this happens, get the details about the person to contact regarding the job opening, including the correct spelling of the name and how to contact them. Then call or e-mail the contact yourself and ask for a time to come in and talk as soon as possible.

(continued)

(continued)

Rule 5: Follow Up on Referrals

There will be occasions when you do get the name of a person who has a job opening. When this happens, obviously you should follow up on this right away. In most cases, you are better off to make the contact yourself, rather than waiting for your warm contact to contact them for you. This approach allows you to make sure that there is no delay in making the contact and assures that you maintain control of the contact process.

The networking process is far more likely to provide you with contacts that are not likely to have a job opening for you at this time. In these situations, you can call them and say something like this:

Hello, my name is Jean Porter, a friend of Fred Janney. He suggested I call and ask you for help. I am looking for a position as a retail sales manager and he thought you might be willing to see me and give me a few ideas...

The conversation pretty much takes care of itself from there on, but do keep your phone conversation short. Remember that you want an interview in person, not over the phone. You can use e-mail in similar ways, just adapt the approach a bit to put your inquiries in writing.

Once you make the first few contacts with people you know, you will quickly begin to be referred to people you don't know. The nature of the process encourages each person to refer you to someone who knows even more about the kind of job you want than they do.

As you get referred along, you will begin to meet some very knowledgeable people who will tell you things you need to know. The more of them you see, the more you learn, and the better prepared you are for future contacts and for interviews. With each level of referrals, you are also more likely to meet people who have the ability to hire you or who know someone who can.

Quick Tip As you make contact with referrals who do employ people with your skills, it is important that you NOT interview them via e-mail or phone.

If the contact is local, make brief phone contact to set up a face-to-face meeting—e-mail is OK for this too, if this makes sense. If the potential employer is in a distant location, it is logical to adapt the approach of sending a paper resume and JIST Card and making additional e-mail or phone contacts to follow up. If the lead is important enough to travel for an interview, focus on setting up a number of interviews in the same area while you are there.

You are now in the hidden job market. Most of the people you meet through networking in this way do not have jobs open or are unlikely to hire someone like you. But they do know other people and are often willing to refer you to them—or tell someone else about you who, in turn, does have an opening.

This is networking and it really does work. After just a few levels of contacts, you will begin to talk to people who do supervise or need people with skills similar to yours. They may or may not have a job opening now, but you are now in a position to be considered for future openings. You will then be known to them in the early stages of a future job opening. While others are waiting for jobs to be advertised in the want ads, you are getting there before they are—and have a chance to get a job before it is ever advertised.

Questions You Can Ask in a Referral Interview

If you are shy and conversation does not come easily to you, here are a few questions you can ask in your referral interviews that should keep things moving:

- ✓ How did you get into this line of work?
- ✓ What are the things you like best (or least) about your work?
- ✓ Do you have any ideas how a person with my background and skills might find a job in this field?
- ✓ What trends do you see in this career field? How could I take advantage of them?
- ✓ What projects have you been working on that excite you?
- ✓ From your point of view, what problems are most important to overcome in this career area?

Rule 6: Send Thank-You Notes

Sending someone a thank-you note or e-mail is a simple act of appreciation. While sending a thank-you note is good manners, very few people do it today. Good manners alone justify sending thank-you notes to people who help you in your job search. They may have spent an hour or so interviewing you, given you the name of someone else to contact, or helped you in some other way. I believe that the job search can and should be conducted on a person-to-person level. Thank-you notes help reinforce this one-on-one relationship.

(continued)

(continued)

Sending thank-you notes also has a practical benefit because the person who receives a note is far more likely to remember you. The contact will perceive you as thoughtful and well-organized. I have been told by hundreds of employers that they rarely or never get a thank-you note from the people they interview. They describe the people who do send them as being "thoughtful," "well-organized," "thorough," and use other positive terms.

While thank-you notes will not get you a job for which you are not qualified, they will often help people remember you in a positive way. Thank-you notes can also help these referrals become effective members of your network of people willing to help you. If they do know of a job opening, or meet someone who does, you will be remembered when others will not.

 A thank-you note is an important and often overlooked tool in the job search. I cover them in more detail in a later chapter and I encourage you to use them regularly. These notes are a small detail that can make a big difference in the immediate and future success of your job search.

 Sending e-mail thank-you notes is fine for many situations but sending an actual paper thank-you card and note through the mail is even better. Consider sending paper notes to those who have helped you in substantial ways or when you want to make a positive impression on a potential employer.

Cold Contacts: Making Direct Contacts with Prospective Employers

Many people need only use their warm contacts to develop a network that results in a job offer. As I have pointed out, warm contacts are the number one source of job leads, accounting for about 40 percent of successful job searches. With the techniques I presented earlier in this chapter, you can use your warm contacts even more effectively than the norm.

Even though networking with your warm contacts may be the only job search method you really need, it is wise to use a *variety* of job search methods. This section presents basic techniques that you can use to develop direct contacts with prospective employers. This is an important topic, because the research indicates that contacts made in this way account for about a third of successful job searches. That makes this method one of the two most effective job search methods.

Although getting jobs by directly contacting an employer is clearly an important source of leads, there are things you can do to dramatically improve your results when doing so. While making cold contacts is intimidating for many people, doing so can make a dramatic difference, if you know how.

There are two basic methods for making cold contacts. The first is using the phone to set up interviews with people who work in organizations that are likely to use or need someone with skills similar to yours. The second involves your personally dropping in to a potential employer's location and asking for an interview. Let me cover each of these methods in turn.

Remember the New Definition of an Interview

When making cold contacts with employers, it is important for you to remember just what your objective is. Very simply put, your objective is to get an interview. But you also need to keep reminding yourself that you are not just looking for an interview in the traditional sense. Instead, you are looking for interview opportunities in a broader context and with a nontraditional definition.

Just to help you remember this definition of what it is you are looking for, let me again present the definition I provided earlier in this chapter:

A New Definition of an Interview

Quick Definition

An interview is any face-to-face contact with a person who hires or supervises people with your skills—even if there is no current job opening.

Keep this in mind at all times as you consider how to make cold contacts. It is a key concept, and if you use it fully, it will help you find many opportunities that others overlook.

Using the Yellow Pages or Online Lists as a Source of Job Leads

If you think about it, the *Yellow Pages* telephone directory is the ideal source for finding prospective employers. Virtually every business, not-for-profit, and governmental organization is listed in this one place. Big organizations as well as the smallest of organizations are listed. And the *Yellow Pages* book is free and readily available.

If you are looking for a job in a distant location, the online versions of the *Yellow Pages* for that location are an important source of job leads. Most Web portal sites such as Yahoo.com or AOL.com point to online *Yellow Page* sources such as www.yellowpages.com that allow you to look up potential employers by region anywhere in the country—or world.

For the advice that follows, understand that *"Yellow Pages"* can refer to either the printed or online directory, depending on your needs.

THE FABULOUS FOUR-STEP *YELLOW PAGES* COLD CONTACT PROCESS

The *Yellow Pages* are a gold mine of job leads if you know how to use them. Once again, it pays to be systematic in how you go about your job search. Using the *Yellow Pages* can be intimidating unless you approach it in an organized way. After considerable trial and error I have developed an approach to using the *Yellow Pages* that I suggest you use, too. If you do, the *Yellow Pages* can become one of your best friends. Here are some tips to get the best results.

Yellow Pages Step 1. Identify Index Headings

Begin by looking at the index that is usually in front of the *Yellow Pages* book or the area that is used to organize the Web directory you are using. It lists the categories within which various businesses and other organizations are arranged. Both print and online versions of the *Yellow Pages* use hundreds of similar groupings, from "Abrasives" and "Accident & Health Insurance" through "Zoning Consultants." Each category, of course, refers to a listing of specific organizations under that heading. While most printed *Yellow Pages* include phone numbers and street addresses, online *Yellow Page* directories will often include an e-mail address, when one is available.

I think it best to do the following activities with the printed *Yellow Pages*, because doing so will help you learn the system better. Later, you can use the same approach with online directories.

Go through each and every heading in the print version of the *Yellow Pages* index, and for each, ask yourself this question:

Could this organization use a person with my skills?

The only possible answers are "Yes" or "No." Doing this will result in your saying "Yes" to some strange options, things you would never seriously consider, but humor me, and just answer yes or no for each listing.

Yellow Pages Step 2. Define Which Headings Are of Most Interest

If your answer is "Yes" to a particular *Yellow Pages* category, then mark it with one of the following numbers:

Mark each "Yes" index entry with a 1, 2, or 3

1 = This type of organization sounds very interesting as a possible place to work.

2 = This type of organization sounds somewhat interesting.

3 = This type of organization does not appeal to me at all (or is possible, but weird).

Sample
Yellow
Pages
Listing

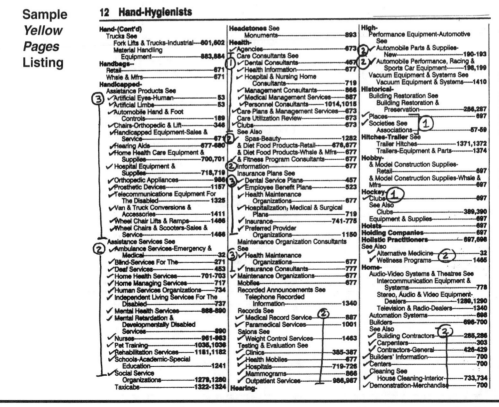

(continued)

(continued)

Yellow Pages Step 3. Identify Specific Prospects

Each and every *Yellow Page* index entry refers you to a section in the *Yellow Pages* which, in turn, lists specific organizations and businesses to contact. Each and every one of these individual listings is a potential target for you. Let's look at a way to identify which organizations you should contact.

The obvious place to begin would be the ones you rated with a "1"—those that sounded particularly interesting to you. But these entries may not be the best place to begin. If you are just beginning your job search, it is often a good idea to improve your job search and interviewing skills with organizations where you have less to lose. So consider contacting organizations you listed as a "3" first.

Even if you mess up these contacts, you can't hurt yourself badly because you did not rate them as highly desirable potential employers. If you are looking for a specialized job where few positions—and even fewer organizations—exist, it is especially wise to start with your "3s" until your techniques improve. As you do this, though, you just may get a job offer. It happens often enough, even from the least likely of sources. And you just might want to consider such an offer, too.

As you get more comfortable and effective with making cold contacts, you can begin to contact your more desirable potential employers. These contacts can be very important to you, so handle them carefully.

By now, you should have expected me to suggest you create yet another list. And why not? In identifying specific places to contact, I have found it most effective to write down the name of each targeted organization in a simple list along with the phone number and/or e-mail address for each. Use a separate form for each general type of organization that you identify in the index.

Yellow Pages Contact List

Desired Position: accountant

Employer Name	Phone Number	E-mail
Jon Murphy, Bartlett Insurance	555-9936	jmm5@bi.com
Kareem Anderson, Acme Corporation	555-3201	kander66@ac.com

For many jobs, there are hundreds—and in larger cities, perhaps thousands—of places you can identify using just this technique. The odds are excellent that one of them will hire you. And you only need one.

Yellow Pages Step 4. Make the Initial Contact

In most cases, you should just pick up the phone and call. If you are calling a smaller organization, ask for the manager or person in charge. In a larger organization, ask for the person in charge of the functional area you are interested in, like accounting, information technology, or whatever.

If the organization has a Web site, it may contain a list of staff names, positions, and contact information. If you can't get the name of the person you want from the Web or through an initial call, try e-mailing the "info" address or webmaster for the site. Ask for the name and e-mail address or phone number of the person in charge of the area you want. I've been surprised how often I get information I want in this way that I could not easily get using the phone.

In making cold phone contacts, remember that you are not looking for a job opening—you want to meet with the person who has the authority to hire or supervise someone with your skills, even if there is no job opening now. This is a very important point, because doing otherwise will result in many more negative outcomes than would otherwise be the case.

Never ask for the human resources or personnel department when making these kinds of contacts!

Keep in mind that you want to get to the person who directly hires or supervises someone with your skills. Unless you want to work in a human resources department, you should not be asking for that department.

Most people who make cold calls based on the *Yellow Pages* techniques I present here get one or more interviews from each hour of using the telephone. There are few other techniques that can get you this kind of result.

Making Cold Telephone Calls Is Not Easy, but It Does Work

I know that making a phone call to an unknown, prospective employer is not easy for most people. Ask yourself what is the worst thing that can happen to you? At worst, the employer might be annoyed that you called. They might even get angry and hang up on you. However, my experience—and that of many job seekers who have used this technique—is that most employers don't mind you calling at all. You see, employers are interested in talking to good people, even if they don't have an opening when you call. Employers are people, too—and they know from experience that they just might need someone soon.

You can combine e-mailing and phone calling in appropriate ways. Because e-mailing someone is less threatening than cold calling, most people prefer to send an initial e-mail, and then follow up with a phone call. This approach can be effective if done professionally, although it is less direct than making initial phone contacts.

The chapter "Use the Phone and E-mail to Get Lots of Interviews," later in this book, provides considerable detail on how to create and use a telephone script that you can adapt for use in making contacts with people you know or in making cold contacts. While there is a bit more to learn about making cold phone contacts work well, the basic techniques are quite easy and they do work.

Another Effective Cold Contact Technique: Dropping in Without an Appointment

If you keep your eyes open, there are sources of job leads everywhere you go. For example, if you are interested in photography, drop in at a camera store. If you are looking for a position in accounting, drop in on any interesting business or other organization and ask for the person in charge. On your way to a job interview at 2:00 p.m., look for places along the way that might need someone with your skills. On your way home, when you don't have anything important to do anyway, stop in at these places and see if you can get an interview.

Managers in many small organizations will often see you if you just drop in and ask to see them. Even managers in large organizations may see you if you ask to see the person in charge of the area most likely to use someone with your skills. While doing this may frighten you, it does work and you might be surprised at how many people are willing to talk to you if you approach the situation correctly.

It is important that you are dressed appropriately for an interview if you are making cold contacts in person. First impressions do count. An opportunity can present itself in unexpected ways, so you should pay more than normal attention to your dress and grooming throughout your job search. Doing so will allow you to create positive impressions with even casual contacts and to pursue cold contact and interview opportunities on short notice.

Be willing to try several times

You will find often enough that the person you want to see is busy or not available. You do need to be sensitive to this and shouldn't push for an interview if you sense that this is a bad time for the person.

If the person you want to see is busy, offer to get back with him or her at a better time. Make sure that you have the correct name and title, then set a specific time that would work out best for that person by getting a specific day (next Tuesday, for example) and time (between 9 and 10 a.m. or when?) for you to call or come back. In most cases, you will be better off to call at that time and set up an appointment for a later time, because this will save you transportation time. An exception to this would be if you sense that this would be an above-average opportunity for you based on what you observed in your initial contact.

Use e-mail for an initial cold contact if a better option does not exist

Everyone gets lots of junk e-mail. Employers are busy, so sending an e-mail to someone you don't know is likely to result in your message being deleted or ignored. That is why e-mail is more effective when sent to someone who does know you in some way, or has a common connection with you.

For example, you can send an e-mail to members of your alumni group or professional organization, even if you don't know them personally. If you are referred to someone who does not know you, include in an e-mail subject line that states that "Kathy McCarty" (or whomever it is that they already know) suggested you contact them. Quickly explain your connection to them, and then ask for their help in the form of setting up an interview, referring you to someone else, providing information, or whatever action you think appropriate.

Sending unsolicited e-mail to someone you don't know is not nearly as effective as e-mailing someone you do know. One problem is that you will often not know the name of a specific person to send the e-mail to. You might visit a Web site for an organization and find the person most likely to hire or supervise someone with your skills. More often, however, you will have to send an e-mail to the main Web address and hope it gets forwarded to the appropriate person. While doing this does allow you to avoid the stress of actually making a real phone call to someone you don't know, sending an e-mail "to whom it may concern" is not likely to get you much attention, is it?

There are situations where sending unsolicited e-mail to prospective employers can make sense, depending on the context. For example, maybe you have access to an e-mail address for a specific person and have had difficulty getting through to him or her by phone. Because the e-mail can be addressed to an individual, go ahead and give it a try. In all cases, though, make your initial contact personal and avoid a depersonalized "form" or "broadcast" e-mail approach because these are most likely to be deleted before they are read. This is, come to think of it, the very same fate of unsolicited resumes that are snail-mailed.

If you do make initial contact via e-mail, follow up with a phone call so that you can personalize your interaction a bit more. Use your good judgment and make your online contacts as direct and personal as you can.

Should you attach a resume or JIST Card to your initial e-mail? It depends on the situation.

If you know the person, sure, go ahead and attach one or both. If you don't know them or have been referred, your initial contact should be friendly and not aggressive. Remember that you are asking them to help you in some way. In these situations, I think it best to include the text of your JIST Card in the e-mail itself, not as a separate attachment. It is far more likely to be read this way, because they can be certain that it is not a virus, as some attachments from unknown people can be. If you attach a separate resume file, give it a clear name like "Dallas Green's resume" so it is less likely to be seen as a potential virus attachment.

Follow up!

Next Tuesday, at 9:00 a.m., the odds are very good that this particular employer is not even thinking about or expecting you to call them. Of course, because you WILL call at the time you had promised, you are bound to make a positive impression. In your phone call, go after setting up a specific time to come in. If no job is open now, ask to come in and "discuss the possibility of future openings."

Persistence pays off, so get over your fear of rejection in making cold contacts in person or by phone. Keep asking for an interview, even if there is no job opening just yet. Doing so will help you identify opportunities long before they would be known to job seekers using more passive and traditional methods.

Little Things Make a Difference

I often observe that if you take care of the little things the big things will take care of themselves. In closing off this chapter, I want to review a variety of little things that matter in the job search. In some cases, other sections of the book will cover these things in more detail but, in case you don't take the time to read those sections in detail, I wanted you to know about them.

Know What You Want to Do

Too many people look for a job without having a clear sense of what they really want to do. This lack of a job objective puts an employer in the position of having to figure this out for you and this is not the way you want this done. Worse yet, not having a clear objective greatly increases your chances of getting a job that you hate.

  Chapters 10 and 11 help you define what you want to do and put it into the form of a job objective. It is essential that you take the time to do this because it is so very important to helping you find a job you love.

Emphasize Your Skills and Accomplishments

When I ask them, few people can quickly tell me why an employer should hire them over someone else. Yet the key question you will have to answer in an interview (though it is rarely asked this clearly) is "Why should I hire you?" Answering this question requires you to have a thorough understanding of the skills you have that can be used in the job you want. And this requires most of us to do some homework.

Several of the chapters in this book give you lots of information to use in the interview process, and I strongly suggest that you review those chapters carefully.

Send Thank-You Notes

Thank-you notes in mailed or e-mailed form make a difference, and while mentioned in this chapter, are more thoroughly covered later in this book. You should routinely send them right after each significant contact you make in your job search: after an interview, after setting up an interview, after getting the name of someone to contact from a friend, and in many other situations.

To help you understand why I emphasize thank-you notes, consider their effect. For example, if you had made a cold contact but had only arranged to make a call back again next Tuesday at 9:00 a.m., it is highly likely that the employer will quickly forget about this discussion. But, on the same day you spoke with that person, you send him or her a thank-you note saying that you appreciate their willingness to talk to you and that you look forward to calling next Tuesday morning. My experience is that most employers are impressed with this attention to detail, and that impression will help you to be considered for a job offer just a little bit more than other candidates.

As a few days pass, the potential employer is likely to put you out of his or her mind again, but not as much. When you call next Tuesday as you promised, he or she is likely to be just a bit more receptive to setting up a time to see you. After you set up an appointment, *send another* thank-you note or e-mail, thanking that person for seeing you and enclosing a JIST Card (more on this later) or resume. If you do this, you will have again created a positive impression and increased your chances of getting a good reception.

Little things count, in the job search as well as in life. I've always appreciated people who send thank-you notes—and so will most potential employers.

Spend More Time Looking

The Chapter 7 will help you organize your job search as if it were a job in itself. Plan on looking full-time for your next job. This approach, along with some non-traditional techniques I present in this book, can reduce your job search time substantially.

Chapter 2

Set a Goal of Two Interviews per Day

Using traditional job search methods looking for mostly advertised openings, getting two interviews a day just isn't possible for most people. That's why I suggest a nontraditional definition of an interview because this new definition allows you to get more interviews, including interviews where no job opening formally exists—yet. Lots of people using the techniques I present in this book do get two interviews a day. And, they get better jobs in less time as a result.

Stay in Touch

Stay in touch with the meaningful contacts you make during your networking. Ask them if it is OK to call them every few weeks during your job search, then do so if it is OK (and it almost always is). If you sent them a thank-you note or e-mail after your first contact, they will probably remember you fondly. When you call, let them know what happened from your follow up with any referrals they gave you.

People in your expanding network will hear of job openings that they did not know of when you last had contact. In a very real sense, they will know of jobs in the first, second, or third stages of the job opening—long before these jobs are advertised, and before others have a chance to apply. Because people in your network already know you, staying in touch with them is often a far more effective source of good job leads than making new contacts.

Organize Your Contacts

In case you haven't noticed, using the techniques I have covered in this chapter can solve one of the major problems job seekers normally have—not having enough job leads or interviews. While that problem can be solved if you use the job search methods I suggest, a new one is often created—having too many job leads to keep track of in your head.

The only way to solve this new "problem" is to organize your contacts on paper. Computer time management or contact management programs and electronic schedulers and PDAs (personal digital assistants) can do this task very well but simple non-computer systems will work just fine too. For example, you can use a follow-up system based on 3-by-5-inch index cards that have the advantage of being inexpensive, easy to find, and portable.

Quick Reference

I review basic job search time and contact management systems in Chapter 7.

More Good Job Search Methods

There are a lot of clever job seekers out there, so almost anything you can imagine has been tried by someone and has probably worked. Let's look at some of the more important of these other techniques. Most are covered in more detail later in the book.

✓ **JIST Cards:**

JIST Cards are covered later in this book, but I want to show you an example here because they are so effective. JIST Cards are an excellent tool for enclosing in a thank-you note, giving to people in your network, attaching to your resume or application, including in or attaching to an e-mail, and for many other uses. Look in Chapter 6 on JIST Cards for additional examples of and tips on using these most effective job search tools. They work!

John Kijek   **Phone Message:** (219) 637-6643
       Email: jkijek@squigley.com

Position Desired: Management position in a small- to medium-size organization.

Skills: B.A. in business plus over five years experience in increasingly responsible management positions. Have supervised as many as 12 staff and increased productivity by 27 percent over two years. Was promoted twice in the past three years and have excellent references. Started customer follow-up program that increased sales by 22 percent within 12 months. Get along well with others and am a good team worker. Computer and Internet literate.

Willing to travel and can work any hours

Hardworking, self-motivated, willing to accept responsibility

---

✓ **School or Other Placement Office:**

About five percent of all people get their jobs either from school placement programs or from referrals from teachers. That may not sound like much, but it can be a very important source of leads if you have access to this resource. There are some very good job search programs operated by schools, government agencies, and other organizations—and most are free. Some people even choose to attend a specific school because of their record for helping graduates find good jobs. If you have access to any such program, find out what is available and use it. Often, these services can be of excellent quality.

✓ **Take an Entry-Level Job:**

For example, if you want to manage a restaurant but you are short on experience, get a job as a waiter or waitress. Take the jobs that are easy to get, and then volunteer to help out at other, more responsible tasks. Ask to move up to increasingly responsible jobs until you get what you want.

✓ **Ask for the Job:**

Once you decide you are interested in a particular job, telling an employer that you want it is a way to communicate your enthusiasm for it. Be prepared to say exactly why you want that job and why you think you can handle it well. An employer is likely to be impressed with your enthusiasm for this particular job and will assume you to be more energetic and committed to it. Say you want the job and you are more likely to get it. It's amazing how many people don't do this. Just say "I'm really interested in this position. When can I start?!" It makes a difference, when it is true.

✓ **Define a Problem You Can Solve:**

If you look for them, opportunities for you to solve an employer's problem will often become obvious to you in your job search. Let's say you know something about marketing. During an interview, you conclude that you could substantially increase the sales of that organization.

Go home and develop a simple written plan, including projected income and expenses, and set up a later interview to present your ideas. You could do this at any place you really wanted to work.

✓ **The Armed Services:**

Don't overlook them as an important source of training and employment. They are a major employer of young people and have a lot to offer, including funds for attending college.

✓ **Volunteer to Work for Free:**

In some situations, consider offering an employer a day or more of your time to demonstrate that you can do the job. If you really do want the job, this is a technique that can get an employer to take you seriously over other candidates who might appear to have better credentials.

✓ **Self-Employment:**

More than ten percent of all workers are self-employed or run small businesses. Though often overlooked as a source of jobs, you could create your own job. It's not easy, but some jobs—such as painting or consulting—cost very little to start. People with substantial management or professional experience often offer consulting services while continuing their job search. Some people successfully turn their unemployment into opportunities to start a business they have always dreamed of.

If you are considering self-employment, do be cautious. While some people succeed in starting up a profitable business, many more do not. The best way to approach this may be to define what sort of activity you want to be self-employed in and begin doing that part-time while employed elsewhere. Many hobbies and part-time jobs help you develop the necessary skills that later help you avoid business failure.

If you are now unemployed—or soon will be—consider self-employment as a way to earn temporary income. Paint houses, do tax returns, design Web sites, or do whatever else you know how to do to earn cash. The extra income will help get you through to your next "real" job.

If you know you want to be self-employed or start a particular type of business, it may also be wise to seek a job in your area of interest. Depending on the job, you can then gain the skills and contacts you need to succeed in that work on your own.

SELF-EMPLOYMENT RESOURCES

There are many good books and Internet resources for those interested in starting a small business. Check out the U.S. Small Business Administration's Web site at www.sba.gov for basic information on starting your own business and links to other sites. JIST publishes several books on this topic, including *Self-Employment: From Dream to Reality.*

✓ **Consider a Temporary or Contract Job:**

If you have a difficult time finding the right long-term job, need some work experience, or have to pay the rent now, consider taking a "temp" or contract job while you look for longer-term opportunities. Assignments can last from a day or two to many months. Some employment agencies specialize in these sorts of jobs. You will see their ads in the Sunday want ads, or look in the *Yellow Pages* under Employment Agencies for contact information.

Some agencies specialize in labor or general office help, others in accounting, information technology, health care, or other specialized areas. A few agencies provide testing and training in such areas as word processing, spreadsheets, and other basic skills needed by employers. You will do best as a temp if you have skills that are in demand and are flexible in what you are willing to do.

Some people like the freedom of temp jobs so much that they work temp jobs only, sometimes getting health insurance and other benefits from the temp agency as part of the deal. Most people, however, should consider them for other reasons. One distinct advantage is that the job assignments can give you good experience in a variety of work settings. Another is that many employers use these services to screen for good employees instead of using conventional hiring procedures.

It is not unusual, if you do a good job, to get a job offer from the company where you worked as a temp. However, before you accept such a job offer,

Chapter 2

find out if you or they are required to pay the agency a fee as a condition of you being hired.

✓ **Head Hunters:**

True head hunters are not interested in most unemployed job seekers. They are hired by employers to look for specific kinds of highly compensated people who are in short supply. Unless you are employed now in a responsible job, making good money, and on your way up, head hunters are not likely to be interested in you.

✓ **Other Sources of Information:**

There are thousands of sites on the Internet that provide information that will be useful to you throughout the job search. There are too many sites to list here, but refer to the appendix at the back of this book for other resources.

Consider using the library, still a wonderful resource for job seekers. One of the library's best resources is the research librarian, who can help you find answers to the most difficult questions you might have. A good library will have a variety of newspapers, professional journals, business directories, career information, job search books, and other resources. Almost all libraries also have free Internet access—and a librarian to help you find the best Web sites to meet your needs. Many will let you use their computers to write resumes and cover letters, which can be useful if you don't have access to your own computer.

Libraries are also quiet, free, and open days, evenings, and weekends. Consider using them as an "office" between interviews or when you want to do quiet research, work on your resume, or other tasks.

INTERNET USE MAY HARM, NOT HELP, YOUR SEARCH FOR A JOB

A research project by Christine Fountain from the University of Washington looked at U.S. Census and Department of Labor data on the employment status of 50,000 households. One finding was that those who used the Internet in their job search were 4 percent less likely to find a job within three months than non-users. How could this be so? Fountain suggests the reason is that the Internet has become less helpful as more people use it. Earlier research found the Internet helped slightly in finding a job, but this advantage disappeared as employers began getting too many applicants.

Fountain speculates that "as employers continue to get huge stacks of applicants, personal recommendations become more important as a way to distinguish among potential employees." She suggests that Internet users not depend on posting their resumes online, but use the Internet to build and interact with communities of users such as acquaintances, people you went to school with, and professional contacts who can be a good source of information. In other words, use the Internet to network and not just to post your resume and wait for a response. Be active, not passive.

Quick Summary

✓ Whatever job search methods you use, it is essential that you understand that most jobs are now with smaller organizations. More than 70 percent of all nongovernmental workers now work for employers with 250 or fewer employees.

✓ *Frictional unemployment* is a situation where job openings exist and qualified job seekers are looking for them, but where the employer and job seeker don't connect with each other right away. The U.S. Department of Labor estimates that over 40 percent of all unemployment is due to this friction. This is VERY important, because it means that jobs are often out there, but people don't find them right away. So, those with better job seeking skills often will find better jobs in less time than less savvy job seekers.

✓ There are many opportunities to find out about job openings long before others know about them. The Four Stages of a Job Opening makes this very clear:

Stage 1: There is no job open now.

Stage 2: No formal opening exists, but insiders know of a possibility.

Stage 3: A formal opening exists, but it has not been advertised.

Stage 4: The job opening is finally advertised.

✓ Learn to find employers before they advertise the job you want. Unfortunately for most job seekers, but fortunately for you, about 75% of all jobs never get advertised. This means that you can use job search methods to find and get the many jobs others will never know of.

✓ Don't wait until a job is open to ask for an interview.

✓ The New Definition of an Interview: An interview is any face-to-face contact with a person who hires or supervises people with your skills—even if there is no job opening now.

✓ The two most effective job search methods: Warm contacts and cold contacts.

✓ All personal referrals together probably account for about 40 percent of how people find jobs. That makes using personal contacts the most important job search technique of all.

✓ Cold contacts are job leads obtained from contacting people you don't know, employers in particular. Using this term also suggests the use of the term "warm contacts" to describe leads for job openings that come from people you do already know. These warm contacts include friends, relatives, and acquaintances.

✓ Armed with your lists of friends, relatives, and acquaintances, you have the beginning of a list of people who, in turn, can refer you to others. This process is what is called "networking."

✓ The three steps to use to identify hundreds of warm contacts are:

Step 1: List contact groups of people you know

Step 2: Create warm contact lists

Step 3: Use your warm contacts to develop an expanding network of contacts

✓ The six rules for developing a successful network of contacts are:

Rule 1: Get started—Set up a meeting

Rule 2: Present yourself well

Rule 3: Learn something

Rule 4: Get two referrals

Rule 5: Follow up on referrals

Rule 6: Send thank-you notes

✓ The *Yellow Pages* in book form or on the Internet is an important source of job leads.

Other techniques discussed in this chapter provide important job search methods that are discussed in further detail in later chapters of the book.

Identify Your Key Skills—

An Essential Step for a Successful Job Search

====**Quick Overview**

In this chapter, I review the following:

✔ What skills are

✔ How to develop a skills language

✔ The Skills Triad: Job-related skills, adaptive skills/personality traits, and transferable skills

✔ The skills that employers want

✔ Three basic employer expectations

✔ How to use knowledge of your skills to help you find a satisfying job

✔ How to create the key word component for your resume

✔ How to quantify your skills

While this is a book about getting a job, I believe that this chapter is one of the most important in the book. It will help you identify the skills you have and begin to develop a "skills language" that is tremendously important throughout your job search and, more importantly, your life.

Knowing what you are good at is an essential part of doing well in a job interview. It is also important in other ways. For example, unless you use the skills that you enjoy using and are good at, it is unlikely that you will be fully satisfied in your job.

Most people are not good at recognizing and listing the skills they have. I can tell you this based on many years of working with groups of job seekers. When asked, few people can quickly tell me what they are good at, and fewer still can quickly present the specific skills that are needed to succeed in the job they want.

Many employers also note that most job seekers don't present their skills effectively. According to one survey of employers, more than 90 percent of the people they interview cannot adequately define the skills they have that support their ability to do the job. They may have the necessary skills, but they can't communicate about them.

In an exhaustive study titled "Job Search: A Review of the Literature," Steve Mangum cites a variety of research studies and concludes that "No single factor carries more negative connotations in the interview than an inability to communicate." It is "Problem #1" in the job search and interview process.

This chapter is designed to help you fix that problem.

Skills: They May Not Be What You Think They Are

Webster's dictionary defines a skill as an ability to do something well, especially as the result of long, practical experience. However, like the definition of "love," there is much more to understanding the word "skill" than reading a dictionary can tell you. Because knowledge of your own skills is such an important issue, it is worth more space than this chapter can provide. But because one chapter is all there is, let's get started.

A Skill Is Something You Can Do

True enough. There are many skills that any of us could demonstrate to someone else. These demonstrative skills relate to performance of various kinds, such as riding a bike or baking a cake. In turn, most of these types of activities can be broken down into "smaller" skills that must be used together to perform the more complex tasks. For example, baking a cake seems simple enough to do, but only if you have some of the component skills such as using measuring cups and other devices, reading a cookbook (and following directions), shopping for ingredients, using timing devices, using an oven properly, organizing the work area, and other related skills.

In turn, each of the above skills can be further broken down. For example, in order to use an oven with a dial, you would need to be able to read the numbers or words on the dial and be able to turn that dial to the correct setting, which requires fine motor coordination. You get the point: If you carefully analyze even simple tasks, more skills are required than you realize at first.

A Skill Can Be Something You Own, as Part of Your Personality

For example, some people just seem to be "organized." Others seem to "get along well with others" or have "leadership abilities." Yet others might be "creative thinkers" or "good writers." Such skills are more abstract than riding a bike or baking a cake, and it may be difficult to define how you acquired them. Nevertheless, they are legitimate and important job and life skills.

How Many Skills Do You Have?

Many people don't realize that everyone has hundreds of skills, not just a few. When I ask someone in a job search workshop what skills they have, too often they say, "I can't think of any."

> **Quick Case Study**
>
> I was leading a workshop for a group of about 30 people, and we were doing a series of exercises to help each person in the group identify his or her skills. Most of those in the group had been unemployed for a long time, and they lived in a small town with an unemployment rate of about 15 percent.
>
> I asked one man in the group to tell me what he was good at. He couldn't think of one thing! I asked him some questions and found out that he had worked as a cabinet maker on the same job for over 15 years. He never missed a day of work and had been late once, over 10 years ago. He took pride in his work and had one of the lowest reject rates in his department of over 20 people. No skills?
>
> Young people often underestimate their skills in the same way. So do women who have been "just" a homemaker and have "no work experience." This is also true for some people who have had very responsible and well-paying professional positions. In my workshops over the years, countless job seekers have told me they have "no skills" when in fact, they have hundreds. And so do you.

The Three Types of Skills

Simple skills such as closing your fingers to grip a pen (which is not simple at all if you consider the miracle of complex neuromuscular interactions that sophisticated robots can only approximate) are building blocks for more complex skills, such as writing a sentence, and even more complex skills, such as writing a book.

Even though you have hundreds of skills, some will be more important to an employer than others. Some will be far more important to you in deciding what sort of job you want. In order to simplify the task of identifying your skills, I have found it useful to think of skills in the three major categories that make up the Skills Triad.

Chapter 3

The Skills Triad

As I have already suggested, analyzing the skills required for even a simple task can become quite complicated. A useful way to organize skills for obtaining the job you seek is to divide them into three basic types. Each of these is explained briefly below. Much of the rest of this chapter will help you identify your own key skills in each of these areas.

THE SKILLS TRIAD

Transferable Skills

Job-Related Skills

Adaptive Skills

Adaptive Skills/Personality Traits

You probably take for granted the many skills you use every day to survive and function. I call these skills adaptive or self-management skills because they allow you to adapt or adjust to a variety of situations. Some of them could be considered part of your basic personality. Such skills, which are highly valued by employers, include getting to work on time, honesty, enthusiasm, and getting along with others.

Transferable Skills

These are general skills that can be useful in a variety of jobs. For example, writing clearly, good language skills, or the ability to organize and prioritize tasks would be desirable skills in many jobs. These are called transferable skills because they can be transferred from one job—or even one career—to another.

Job-Related Skills

These are the skills people typically think of first when asked, "Do you have any skills?" They are related to a particular job or type of job. An auto mechanic, for example, needs to know how to tune engines and repair brakes. Other jobs also have job-specific skills required for that job in addition to the adaptive and transferable skills needed to succeed in almost any job.

This system of dividing skills into three categories is not perfect. Some things, such as being trustworthy, dependable, or well-organized, are really not skills as much as they are personality traits that can be acquired. There is also some over-lap between the three skills categories. For example, a skill such as being organized might be considered either adaptive or transferable. For our purposes, however, the Skills Triad is a very useful system for identifying skills that are important in the job search.

Quick Tip

It's ironic that schools teach traditional educational subjects: math, history, science, language, keyboarding, etc. However, studies have concluded that there is a difference in what is taught versus what employers look for in an employee.

Employers want dependability, honesty, a good attitude, critical thinking skills, self-motivation, high self-esteem, personal accountability, and other skills that can't be taught. So although it is important that you have the minimum degree or certificate required, most employers will train you if you have "what they want."

Now it is time to identify the skills you do have that are desirable to employers.

Identify Your Skills

Because it is so important to be aware of your skills, I include a series of checklists and other activities in this chapter to help you identify your key skills. It's impor-tant that you recognize these skills so that you can select jobs that you will do well in. They are also important to recognize and emphasize in a job interview.

Developing a skills language can also be very helpful to you in writing resumes and conducting your job search.

Adaptive Skills—Skills That Allow You to Adapt to New Situations

On the following lines, list three things about yourself that you think make you a good worker. Take your time. Think about what an employer might like about you or the way you work.

1. _____

2. _____

3. _____

The skills you just wrote down may be among the most important things that an employer will want to know about you. Most (but not all) people write adaptive skills when asked this question.

Whatever you wrote, these skills are often very important to mention in the interview. In fact, presenting these skills well will often allow a less experienced job seeker to get the job over someone with better credentials. Most employers are willing to train a person for skills he or she lacks, but who has the qualities that the employer is looking for in a candidate. In fact, some employers prefer job seekers with better adaptive skills than job-related skills because they are more malleable and not set in their ways.

Identify Your Adaptive Skills and Personality Traits

I have created a list of adaptive skills that tend to be important to employers. The ones listed as "The Minimum" are those that most employers consider essential for job survival and many will not hire someone who has problems in these areas.

Look over the list and put a check mark next to each adaptive skill that you possess. Put a second check mark next to those skills that are particularly important for you to use or include in your next job.

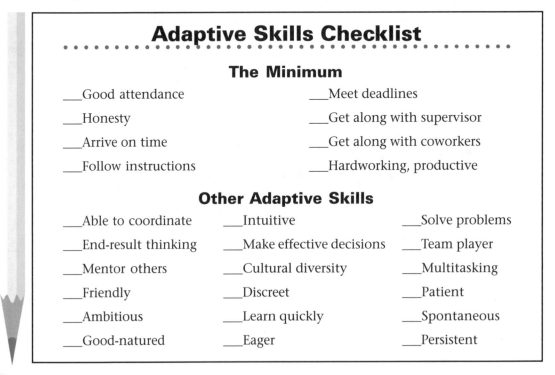

Adaptive Skills Checklist

The Minimum

___Good attendance   ___Meet deadlines

___Honesty   ___Get along with supervisor

___Arrive on time   ___Get along with coworkers

___Follow instructions   ___Hardworking, productive

Other Adaptive Skills

___Able to coordinate   ___Intuitive   ___Solve problems

___End-result thinking   ___Make effective decisions   ___Team player

___Mentor others   ___Cultural diversity   ___Multitasking

___Friendly   ___Discreet   ___Patient

___Ambitious   ___Learn quickly   ___Spontaneous

___Good-natured   ___Eager   ___Persistent

___Assertive   ___Loyal   ___Steady

___Helpful   ___Efficient   ___Physically strong

___Capable   ___Mature   ___Tactful

___Humble   ___Energetic   ___Practice new skills

___Cheerful   ___Methodical   ___Take pride in work

___Imaginative   ___Enthusiastic   ___Competent

___Modest   ___Reliable   ___Independent

___Expressive   ___Tenacious   ___Complete assignments

___Motivated   ___Resourceful   ___Industrious

___Flexible   ___Thrifty   ___Natural

___Responsible   ___Conscientious ___Formal

___Trustworthy   ___Informal   ___Open-minded

___Self-confident ___Creative   ___Optimistic

___Versatile   ___Intelligent   ___Sincere

___Sense of humor ___Dependable   ___Original

___Well-organized

Other Similar Adaptive Skills You Have

Add any adaptive skills to the list above that were not listed but that you think
are important to include.

_____

_____

_____

_____

_____

_____

Chapter 3

Your Top Adaptive Skills

Carefully review the checklist you just completed and select the three adaptive skills you feel are most important for you to tell an employer about or that you most want to use in your next job. These three skills are EXTREMELY important to include in your resume and to present to an employer in an interview.

1. _____

2. _____

3. _____

Identify Your Transferable Skills — Skills That Transfer to Many Jobs

Over the years, I have assembled a list of transferable skills that are important in a wide variety of jobs. In the checklist that follows, the skills listed as "Key Transferable Skills" are those that I consider to be most important to many employers. The key skills are also those that are often required in jobs with more responsibility and higher pay, so it pays to emphasize these skills if you have them.

The remaining transferable skills are grouped into categories that may be helpful to you. Go ahead and check each skill you are strong in, and then double-check the skills you want to use in your next job. When you are finished, you should have checked 10 to 20 skills at least once.

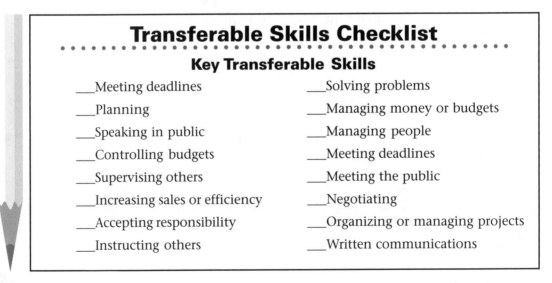

Transferable Skills Checklist
Key Transferable Skills

___Meeting deadlines

___Planning

___Speaking in public

___Controlling budgets

___Supervising others

___Increasing sales or efficiency

___Accepting responsibility

___Instructing others

___Solving problems

___Managing money or budgets

___Managing people

___Meeting deadlines

___Meeting the public

___Negotiating

___Organizing or managing projects

___Written communications

Other Transferable Skills

___Drive or operate vehicles   ___Operate tools and machinery

___Assemble or make things   ___Repair things

___Build, observe, inspect things   ___Good with my hands

___Construct or repair buildings   ___Use complex equipment

Dealing with Data

___Analyze data or facts   ___Negotiate

___Investigate   ___Compare, inspect, or record facts

___Audit records   ___Count, observe, compile

___Keep financial records   ___Research

___Budget   ___Detail-oriented

___Locate answers or information   ___Synthesize

___Calculate, compute   ___Evaluate

___Manage money   ___Take inventory

___Classify data   ___Use technology to analyze data

Working with People

___Administer   ___Pleasant   ___Diplomatic

___Patient   ___Counsel people   ___Supervise

___Care for   ___Sensitive   ___Help others

___Persuade   ___Demonstrate   ___Tactful

___Confront others   ___Sociable   ___Insightful

___Teach   ___Tough   ___Understand

___Interview others   ___Listen   ___Outgoing

___Tolerant   ___Trust   ___Kind

___Negotiate

(continued)

Chapter 3

(continued)

Using Words, Ideas

___Articulate

___Correspond with others

___Design

___Inventive

___Speak in public

___Communicate verbally

___Remember information

___Edit

___Write clearly

___Logical

___Research

___Ingenious

___Create new ideas

Leadership

___Arrange social functions

___Motivate people

___Competitive

___Negotiate agreements

___Decisive

___Plan

___Delegate

___Run meetings

___Direct others

___Self-controlled

___Explain things to others

___Self-motivated

___Get results

___Solve problems

___Mediate problems

___Take risks

Creative, Artistic

___Artistic

___Music appreciation

___Dance, body movement

___Perform, act

___Drawing, art

___Play instruments

___Expressive

___Present artistic ideas

Other Similar Transferable Skills You Have

Add any transferable skills to the list above that were not listed but that you think are important to include.

_____

_____

_____

_____

_____

Your Top Transferable Skills

Write in the margins any other transferable skills you have that were not listed. Then select the five top transferable skills you want to use in your next job and list them below.

1. _____

2. _____

3. _____

4. _____

5. _____

The Skills Employers Want

Because I am particularly interested in personal and career development issues, it is nice to know that employers value those who have done their homework in these areas. The reason they do is that people who have done career planning have a better idea of what they want to do long-term. These job seekers also understand the training and skills needed to get there. Because they are clearer in what they want to do, they are more likely to be in the right jobs for the right reasons—and they are also more likely to be motivated and prepared to do them well.

Finding Out What Employers Want— The Results of a Survey of Employers

As a way to illustrate that employers value adaptive and transferable skills very highly, I have included the results of a survey of employers here. This information comes from a study of employers conducted jointly by the U.S. Department of Labor and the American Association of Counseling and Development.

The study, titled *Workplace Basics—The Skills Employers Want,* was conducted to discover what employers want in the people they hire. It turns out that most of the skills they want are either adaptive or transferable. Of course, specific job-related skills will remain important, but basic skills form an essential foundation for success on the job.

Here are the top skills employers identified in the Workplace Basics survey:

The Top Skills Employers Want

1. Learning to learn
2. Basic academic skills in reading, writing, and computation
3. Good communication skills including listening and speaking
4. Creative thinking and problem solving
5. Self-esteem, motivation, and goal setting
6. Personal and career development skills
7. Interpersonal/negotiation skills and teamwork
8. Organizational effectiveness and leadership

Note that all of these skills are either adaptive or transferable skills. What is most interesting is that most of these skills are not formally taught in school. Try to find a course on "creative problem solving" or "personal goal setting," for example. Yet these "soft" skills are those that employers value most. Of course, job specific skills are also important—an accountant will still need to know accounting skills, but the adaptive and transferable skills are the ones that allow you to succeed in any job.

Again, this study shows the importance of being aware of your skills and using them well in career planning. If you have any weaknesses in one or more of the skills that were listed, consider improvements. And, always remember to turn your weaknesses into strengths. For example, if you don't have a specific skill that's required for a job let the employer know that you don't; but add that you are eager to learn and you are a quick study. This will show the employer that you are not afraid of learning new skills and that you are confident in your abilities. Furthermore, if you are already strong in one or more of the top skills employers want, look for opportunities to develop and use them in your work—or to present them clearly in your next interview.

You can never assume that you are exempt from new training because your duties involve routine tasks. Competitive pressures compel employers to shift employees between jobs and responsibilities, which places a premium on your ability to absorb, process, and apply new information quickly and effectively.

From the organization's perspective, having an employee who knows how to learn and who is flexible is more cost-effective because it reduces the time and resources spent on training. Your adaptability also means you'll have reason to stay longer, and every employer values the money he or she can save by hiring a long-term employee.

Meeting Employer Expectations

I've been playing around with the "employer's expectations" concept for many years, when I was looking for a way to help people in my job search workshops improve their performance in an interview. After looking at the research on how employers make decisions, I concluded that there are a few simple concepts that could help one job seeker be seen more positively by an employer than another. While there is considerable research to support what I suggest on this topic it is also good common sense advice.

Back in the 1970s Sidney Fine, a labor market expert who was the principal researcher for the U.S. Department of Labor's job classification system, estimated that one-half of all jobs could be learned by the average adult in two weeks or less. To do so, they would use their adaptive and transferable skills to compensate for their lack of specific job knowledge and job-related skills.

While many jobs have become more complex since then, it is still true that you could use your current skills and abilities to quickly learn to handle many, many jobs that you had not done previously. The point is that many employers are willing to overlook a lack of job content skills or "credentials" and hire people who present themselves more effectively in an interview. If an employer has two job seekers with similar credentials, the one who makes a better impression will get the job. Even if one has better credentials, the one who *presents* his or her ability to learn and do the job best will often get the job over the more qualified candidate.

Identifying Your Job-Related Skills

Many jobs require skills that are specific to that occupation. An airline pilot will obviously need to know how to fly an airplane, and, thankfully, having good adaptive and transferable skills would not be enough to be considered for that job.

Job-related skills may have been gained in a variety of ways including education, training, work, hobbies, or other life experiences.

I've included a variety of information and activities in Chapter 9 to help you identify your job-related skills. These skills can be found through education, work, and other life experiences. You should find Chapter 9 particularly thorough in helping you identify key job-related skills to emphasize in your job search and interviews.

Knowing Your Skills Is the Basis for Your Job Search

Knowing what you are good at is an essential part of your job search. It will help you to answer interview questions, write a resume, and complete applications. More importantly, knowing the skills you *like* to use can help you make a better decision about what sort of job you really want. Your jobs, careers, and personal situations will change, but your adaptive and transferable skills will remain with you throughout your life. They are important for an employer to know about, but even more important for you to recognize.

THREE BASIC EMPLOYER EXPECTATIONS

An important principle throughout this book is that the opinion of an employer does matter. In the interview, where an employer's opinion matters most, there are three basic employers' expectations for you to meet, and each is covered below.

Employer Expectation 1. Appearance: Do You Look Like the Type of Person Who Will Do Well in the Job?

There is a variety of research that indicates that employers react to how a job seeker looks, and one survey indicates that 40 percent of all interviewees create a negative first impression based on their appearance. Once you create a negative impression it is most difficult to overcome, yet an appearance-related problem is often relatively easy to correct.

Employers react within a few seconds to people they first meet—just as all people do. If their initial reaction to you is negative, you probably will not be hired. I suggest that "appearance" in this context is more than just dress and grooming, although these things are clearly of great importance in an interview. Employers will also react to a variety of things including whether you are on time to the interview, your verbal skills, body language, ability to handle "small talk," and other adaptive skills.

In an interview, if the employer feels you will not fit in or will not get along well with coworkers, you will not be hired—even if you have the experience to handle

---

the job. Job seekers who can effectively present their ability to adapt to a new work situation often get jobs over people with more experience. I have seen this happen countless times. It is the better prepared job seeker who gets the job, not necessarily the better qualified one.

To further illustrate how important adaptive skills are to employers, note that most people who are fired or lose their jobs do so because of an inability to adapt and get along rather than an inability to do the job itself.

Robert Half & Associates conducted a survey of personnel directors from the 1,000 largest U.S. corporations. Only 4 percent listed "not doing job" as the most disturbing employee behavior. Responses related to actual job performance totaled only 32 percent. The remaining responses related to poor adaptive skills. The most frequently noted problems were lying and dishonesty (14%), absenteeism and tardiness (12%), arrogance and overconfidence (10%), and lack of dedication (6%).

Employer Expectation 2. Dependability: Can You Be Counted On to Get the Job Done?

Even if you have superior job-related skills, you won't get an offer unless the employer feels that you are a reliable employee who does not miss work, can be relied upon to get things done, and will hang around long enough to pay off their training investment.

Many interview questions are designed to probe this very issue. An employer will not hire a person who may move out of town soon, take another job (overqualified), has a history of leaving jobs, may have an attendance problem (alcoholism, sick kids), has no family or friends living in town (will move soon), is late often, or for any other reason that suggests he or she can't be depended upon. Some of the issues may not seem fair for an employer to wonder about—and some are probably illegal to ask about—but they are a legitimate concern to an employer. These would be your concerns as well, if you were hiring someone.

An employer is clearly not concerned with job-related skills here, but in your adaptive skills and motivations for wanting to work. Once an employer is satisfied that you have acceptable adaptive skills, your transferable skills are often next in importance. Your ability to learn the new job quickly, for example, together with other desirable personal traits or skills, will be more important than if you simply have the necessary experience with that type of work.

Most employers have learned that, despite whatever you already know, you will have to be retrained in their system. If a job seeker impresses the employer as disorganized, rigid, unmotivated, or lacking in other important transferable or

(continued)

(continued)

adaptive skills, someone else with less experience is likely to get the job. Your skill in organizing things could be more important to the employer in the long run than someone else's knowledge of a specific procedure.

Employer Expectation 3. Credentials: Do You Have the Job-Related Skills, Experience, and Training?

Your education, training, and prior work experiences are weighted heavily by employers in determining whether you are capable of doing a particular job. I have listed this expectation third since it becomes important only if you don't get screened out based on the first and second criteria.

People without the minimal job-related skills required for a job typically will not get an interview. However, many employers will waive their requirements for education, training, and previous experience for the right candidate. That's why I have listed job-related skills third among the three employer expectations.

This is not to say that job-related skills are unimportant, especially in certain professional or technical jobs. They are. For example, no matter how nice you are or how good you are with your hands (another transferable skill) you can't get a job as an airline pilot unless you know how to fly an airplane and have the appropriate credentials. This is a fact that I am very comfortable with since I travel on airplanes a great deal of the time. But if you do meet the minimal criteria for a job and get an interview, you will be considered, unless you create a negative impression based on expectations #1 and #2.

Translating Your Knowledge of Your Skills to Your Resume

Once you have an awareness of your skill set, you need to be sure you communicate about those skills with potential employers. One of the best ways to do that is by including information about your skills in your resume.

 Section 2 of this book includes much more detailed information on building a successful resume.

Formulate Key Words from Your Skills to Add to Your Resume

Armed with knowledge about the skills you have, both adaptive and transferable, you should find the **Key Words** to identify them. These key words should be used in your resume. You should put on the hat of the "hiring person" and think of what matters to that person. What words describe the skill set for the position you are seeking?

For example, if you were seeking a sales rep position, you would look at your skills and the skills that the employer wants and use key words that relate to those skills in your resume.

In this case you would use words such as **cold calling**, **new business development**, **account management**, **meeting quotas and maintaining margin**.

These concepts are discussed further in Section 3 on resume writing.

The Importance of Quantifying Your Skills for Your Resume

Keep in mind most people will say that they are a "good communicator," "team player," or "have manager skills." What you should do is to separate yourself from the ordinary in your resume and hit them with specifics, (i.e., quantify your skills). Take the above example of applying for a sales rep position. You should say things such as:

Helped "x number" of people in events planning produce for "such and such event."

Coordinated "such and such" conference of 300 people.

Top Producer—met quota in last six months.

Developed 10 new accounts over the last year.

You get the idea; the point is that this kind of specific experience is what a hiring manager would look for in filling this position.

Quick Summary

✓ Most job seekers don't present their skills effectively. According to one survey of employers, more than 90 percent of the people they interview cannot adequately define the skills they have to support their ability to do the job. They may have the necessary skills, but they can't communicate them.

✓ One researcher concludes that "No single factor carries more negative connotations in the interview than an inability to communicate." It is problem number one in the job search and interview process.

✓ Most people underestimate their skills. A skill can be something you do, or something you own as part of your personality.

✓ Three types of skills, making up the skills triad, are adaptive skills/personality skills, transferable skills, and job-related skills.

Chapter 3

✓ The top skills employers want: 1) Dependability, 2) Honesty, 3) Competence, 4) Good attitude.

✓ Other important skills that business owners say they want in a new employee include 1) Learning to learn, 2) Basic academic skills in reading, writing, and computation, 3) Good communication skills including listening and speaking, 4) Creative thinking and problem solving, 5) Self-esteem, motivation, and goal setting, 6) Personal and career development skills, 7) Interpersonal/negotiation skills and teamwork, 8) Organizational effectiveness and leadership.

✓ Three basic employer expectations are 1) Appearance: Do you look like the type of person who will do well in the job? 2) Dependability: Can you be counted on to get the job done? 3) Credentials: Do you have the job-related skills, experience, and training?

✓ Meeting employer expectations in an interview can get you the job over those with better credentials.

✓ Most people who are fired or lose their jobs do so because of an inability to adapt and get along rather than an inability to do the job itself.

✓ Utilize key words and quantify your skills to give you the leading edge in your resume.

CHAPTER 4

Dramatically Improve Your Interviewing Skills

≡≡≡Quick Overview

In this chapter, I review the following:

- ✔ Tips on traditional and nontraditional interviews
- ✔ Eight things to do to have a successful interview
- ✔ The three types of interviews
- ✔ The seven phases of an interview
- ✔ The three-step process for answering problem interview questions
- ✔ How to use "control statements" effectively in an interview
- ✔ How to use nonverbal indicators strategically
- ✔ The best questions to ask in the interview
- ✔ How to close all interviews to your advantage

The interview is the most important 60 minutes in the job search. There is a great deal at stake, yet the research indicates that most people are not well prepared for the interview process. This can be good news for you, because I believe it is fairly simple to substantially improve your interviewing skills, thereby giving you an advantage over other job seekers who do not know what you will soon learn.

I have observed many employers that are willing to hire people who present themselves well in an interview over others with superior "credentials." This chapter is based on substantial research into how employers actually decide on hiring one person over another. While the interview itself is an incredibly complex interaction, I have found that there are certain simple things you can do that make a big difference in getting a job offer. This chapter will present some of the things I have learned over the years, and I hope you find them helpful.

The Most Important 60 Minutes in Your Job Search

Most interviews last about 60 minutes. One hour. It is the most important 60 minutes in your job search, and you should do everything in your power to see that it goes well. Even though you are likely to have many interviews, each one is important and each one could be the one that gets you the job offer.

There is a lot of research indicating that interviews are not a particularly good way to select employees. Most employers would agree. While it is not always the best method, the fact is that how you do in an interview is very important to whether or not you will be considered for a job. Doing well in an interview is, more or less, a requirement for getting a job.

Eight Things You Must Do to Have a Successful Interview

While we know that the interview is important to both you and the employer, few job seekers have a clear sense of what they need to accomplish during those critical minutes. Before I teach you interview techniques, I ask you to consider just what it is you want to accomplish in an interview. Here are the things I believe are most important:

Eight Things to Do to Have a Successful Interview

1. Make a positive impression.
2. Communicate your skills.
3. Use control statements to your advantage.
4. Answer problem questions.
5. Ask key questions.
6. Help the employer know why they should hire you.
7. Close the interview properly.
8. Follow up after the interview.

These are interview essentials, and if you do them well, you can dramatically increase your chances of getting a job offer. This chapter will show you, step-by-step, how to do well in a job interview. By dividing the interview into sections and mastering one section at a time, those crucial 60 minutes won't seem so intimidating.

Don't Be Intimidated by the Interview Process

An interview is intimidating and stressful to most people. We aren't often evaluated as intensely as we are in an interview and the stakes are high. I believe one of the reasons so many people withdraw from an active job search is because of their fear of rejection, which is unavoidable in most traditional interviews. If you don't get a job offer, does it mean that you are a bad person? Of course not. Even so, it is hard not to avoid the stress of hoping to be selected and the disappointment of not getting the job. There are some things you can do to reduce the stress of interviews.

Reject rejection

The word "interview" is derived from the French entrevu, which means to see each other. In a job interview, that is precisely what should be going on. More often, however, there is the one-sided feeling that the all-powerful employer is giving the job seeker a thorough looking over.

The job seeker conducting a conventional job search is likely to get rejected, which does not feel good. You need to get over these feelings and understand that rejection is a necessary part of eventual success in the job search. The more rejections you get (and the faster you get them), the closer you are to being accepted. One way to look at this is to understand that success is often the result of many previous failures. It is the persistence beyond the failures that will often lead to success.

You Have to Get Rejected Before You Can Get Accepted

One way to look at the interview is as a series of rejections, like this: No No No No No No No No No No No No No No No No No No No No No No No No No No No No No No No No No No No No No No No No No No No No No No No No No No No No No No No No No No No No No No No No No No No No No No No No No No No No No No No No No No No No No No No No No No No Yes

---

Chapter 4

Finally, you meet someone who makes you a job offer. If you accept, that's a "yes." Along the way, however, the rejection doesn't have to be one-sided. An interview should be, after all, a two-way communication. Employers are not the only ones who can say no. You are looking for a good fit and you get to make that call as well.

Understand "intuition" and use it to your advantage

Many employers claim they get a "feel" for a person during an interview. I have often heard interviewers say they did or did not hire someone based on a "gut reaction." This can be a very unnerving thought until you understand that what they feel is often based on something you do that can be changed. Is your dress or grooming a problem? When you are nervous, do you have unconscious behaviors that an employer might interpret as negatives? The odds are high that you can improve your performance in the interview if you know what it is that you do that may turn some people off.

 Most gut reactions are really responses to nonverbal cues.

Many of your most powerful signals can be nonverbal. As evidence of this, think about how a lie detector works. Your body gives off electrochemical signals that can be measured. Even if you try, you can't keep this from happening—and the machine can read your "real" reaction. Your voice, facial expressions, posture, and other subtle signals communicate to an interviewer, too. Are you sending the "signals" you wanted to send?

My point here is that employers will react to little things you do in an interview. It is not just what you say, it is how you say it as well as a variety of behaviors you may not even be fully be aware of. All of us make assumptions about people based on how they dress and look, for example.

Of course you are nervous, you just don't want to look that way. To that end, there is some well-known body language you should avoid. Don't cross your arms or legs, which can make you seem defensive. If you avoid eye contact an interviewer may think you lack self-confidence. Avoid talking too much, which may be an indicator that you are not a good listener.

In addition to avoiding negatives, it is in your best interest to "look" confident, friendly, and interested in the interview. Sit up straight and lean a bit forward in your chair to show that you are listening, make eye contact with the interviewer, and nod and smile occasionally.

If you are trying to hide a negative, an evasive response is likely to leave the interviewer wondering what you are hiding. Or if you overstate your abilities, you are likely to unconsciously communicate that you are hiding something, which many interviewers will notice. Practicing how to answer difficult questions in an honest and positive way will help. If you have positive answers, you are much more likely to "look" confident than if you are not comfortable with your responses.

Often, you may be completely unaware of how your nonverbal signals are creating a negative impression. Perhaps your grooming is inappropriate or out-of-date; maybe you play with your hair or slouch in your chair; or you may have a hard time expressing yourself without moving your hands too much. Employers notice these things and may interpret them in ways that hurt your chances of getting a job offer.

Quick Case Study

Some time ago, I worked with a college graduate who had been chronically unemployed or underemployed for over 10 years. His credentials were great—a prestigious school, good grades, a desirable degree in business. Yet, I immediately knew why he had such a hard time getting a decent job—his handshake was limp, he slouched terribly, his hair looked oily, and he looked like he slept under a bridge. While many of his problems were personality-related, his job search was bound to be unsuccessful simply based on his appearance. Any employer would react negatively to him. When he corrected his appearance-related issues and specifically sought a "back office" job out of the public eye, he quickly found a decent job.

Quick Tip

The good news is that you can change many of your undesirable mannerisms. Ask an objective person or friend to role-play interviews with you and provide constructive feedback on your verbal and nonverbal communications. By becoming aware of negative signals, and by practicing to eliminate or change them, you can make an employer's "intuition" work for you.

I suggest you videotape and then view these mock interviews, looking for things you can improve. Although you may be uncomfortable in front of the camera, the practice will pay off in the real interview.

Reasons for interviewers to be nervous

Interviewers are people, too. If you tend to think of an interviewer as the enemy, you should reconsider. It is helpful to remind yourself that most bosses started out as job seekers and will very likely take on that role again. You should also realize that most interviewers have reasons of their own to be nervous. For example:

✓ **Most employers have no training in interviewing.** Just as most job seekers don't know how to find jobs, interviewers often don't know how to interview. How would they have learned? It is not at all unusual for a well-trained job seeker to be a better interviewer than the interviewer. (Really!) I often hear job seekers say, "They didn't even ask me any hard questions! I had to tell them what I was good at because they never asked."

Chapter 4

✓ **If they hire you, and you don't work out, they lose.** If they make a mistake, their boss will know. Since it is very costly to train new staff, their decision is literally worth thousands of dollars. In small organizations or departments, if one person does not work out, everyone else feels the extra workload. The person who hired you could lose credibility (and maybe even his or her job).

✓ **Everyone likes to be liked.** I've known employers who hate to interview because they don't like to turn people down. They are not comfortable in screening people out. You don't have to feel sorry for them, but it is something to think about.

So, you see, interviewers are not to be feared at all. Employers are just like us because they are us. Their roles are just a little different at the moment.

The Three Types of Interviews— A Very Important Concept

Too many people think of a job interview too narrowly. One of the big tasks in a successful job search is to get more interviews. But if you define an interview in a narrow and traditional way, you will miss out on meeting many perspective employers who in many cases are willing to talk to you even before a job opening exists.

For this reason, how you define an interview is a critical part of a successful job search. To open yourself up to a more creative and effective job search, consider that there are many types of interviews. I've defined just three major types of interviews. Understanding the distinctions among them can help to find jobs that others may overlook.

The Three Types of Interviews

1. The traditional job search interview

2. The JIST job search interview

3. Information interviews and other miscellaneous types of interviews

---

Much of this book is based on the assumption that an interview can include something more than the "traditional" interview. All three types of interviews share some characteristics, but there are significant differences too. If you know how to conduct yourself in each type of interview, you will have a distinct advantage over most job seekers.

Let's take a closer look at the first two interview types.

The First Interview Type: The Traditional Job Interview

The following is what job seekers usually think of when the word "interview" is used.

A Traditional Interview Is...

...a meeting with a person who has a job opening for which you might qualify, who is actively looking for someone to fill it, and who has the authority to hire you.

A traditional interview situation is clearly a real interview, but it presents some limitations for you to overcome. For one thing, most jobs get filled before a traditional interview is needed. This means that your search for these traditional interviews will overlook job openings that are not advertised. For the jobs that are advertised, many employers hire someone they came to know before the job was advertised—or who found out about it through a personal referral. An important lesson to learn is that if you wait until the opening is advertised, the job is likely to be filled by the time you apply for it.

This is not to say that traditional job interviews are not important. They are. But it would be irresponsible not to tell you that more than half of all jobs are filled in a different way. If you believe in your heart that an interview can happen only if you get a "Yes" to your question, "Do you have any job openings for me?" you will miss some of the very best opportunities.

Manipulation and counter-manipulation are the basis for the traditional interview

In the traditional interview, your task is to present yourself well. The task of the interviewer is to find out what's wrong with you so you can be eliminated from consideration. This is not the friendliest of social situations. If the interviewer has any training on how to interview, you will face techniques intentionally designed to reveal your flaws.

Chapter 4

In a book considered by many to be required reading for interviewers, The *Evaluation Interview*, Richard Fear wrote,

> *"Since most applicants approach the interview with the objective of putting their best foot forward, the interviewer must be motivated from the very beginning to search for unfavorable information."*

In a traditional interview, any good interviewer will encourage you to be yourself and let your guard down. In an article by John and Merna Galassien entitled "Preparing Individuals for Job Interviews: Suggestions from More Than 60 Years of Research," they conclude that the primary role of interviewers is to weed out the "undesirables." The interviewer's goal, in the traditional interview, is to manipulate you to reveal negative information, if at all possible.

A job seeker's reaction to all this manipulation is natural enough: You try to hide your faults and emphasize your strengths. Your objective, in these traditional interviews, is to keep from being screened out and to get a second interview. If you leave the interview without a scheduled second interview, go after a second interview in your follow-up efforts. (I'll tell you more about following up later in this chapter.)

THE MAJOR TYPES OF TRADITIONAL INTERVIEWS

While most traditional interviews are relatively unstructured, employers might use one or more of a variety of approaches to screen applicants applying for a job in the conventional way. These approaches are designed to manipulate the interaction so that you are more likely to reveal negative information and be screened out.

So that you will not be taken by surprise, here is a quick review of the more common methods used in traditional interviews.

The Preliminary Screening Interview

This is by far the most common preliminary interview, where you meet with a person whose role is to screen applicants and arrange follow-up interviews with the person who has the authority to hire. Other times, you may meet directly with the hiring authority whose primary focus is to eliminate as many applicants as possible, leaving only one or two. These one-on-one interviews are the focus of the techniques presented later in this chapter.

The Group or Panel Interview

While still not as common as the one-on-one interview, group interviews are gaining popularity. It's possible you could be asked to interview with two or more people involved in the selection process. I've even known of situations where a group of interviewers met with a group of applicants—all at the same time. Many of the techniques used in this book will work well in these settings, too.

The Stress Interview

Some interviewers intentionally try to get you upset. They want to see how you handle stress, whether you can accept criticism, or how you react to a tense situation. They hope to see how you are likely to act in a high-pressure job.

For example, this type of interviewer might try to upset you by not accepting something you say as true. "I find it difficult to believe," this person might say, "that you were responsible for as large a program as you claim here on your resume. Why don't you just tell me what you really did?"

Another approach is to quickly fire questions at you, but not give you time to completely answer, or to interrupt you mid-sentence with other questions. Not nice.

Now you've been warned. I hope you don't run into this sort of interviewer, but if you do, be yourself and have a few laughs. The odds are the interview could turn out fine if you don't take the bait and throw things around the room. If you do get a job offer following such an interview, you might want to ask yourself whether you would want to work for such a person or organization. (It might be fun not to accept the job and then tell them what you think of their interviewing technique.)

The Structured Interview

Employment laws related to hiring practices have increased the use of a structured interview, particularly in larger organizations. This type of interview provides a list of questions the interviewer is to ask of all applicants and a form to fill out to record the responses and observations. Your experience and skills may be compared to specific job tasks or criteria. Even if highly structured, there is usually the opportunity for you to present what you feel is essential information.

The Reality Interview

Many large organizations now use a method known most commonly as "reality interviewing." These companies believe that the more traditional way of rating candidates' answers to questions only encourages the interviewers to pick new employees who are just like themselves.

(continued)

(continued)

According to Arthur H. Bell, author of *Extraviewing*, there are three simple steps to the reality interview:

1. **Ask applicants to describe their realities: What they did do or are doing, rather than their impressions, attitudes, or ideals.**

   The idea here is to sidestep canned answers. Instead of being asked, "What do you believe is the best way to handle conflict?" the question will be phrased, "Tell me about a time you experienced conflict with another worker. How did you handle it?"

2. **Probe the applicant's past and present realities in direct relation to his or her future responsibilities with the company.**

   Simply stated, the past is dead and buried as far as the interviewer is concerned. In the reality interview, interviewers want to know which parts of your past will be useful for the specific job you now want with their organizations. In this situation, do not expect any questions that require you to judge or give value to anything—that is the interviewer's task. As Bell reports one interviewer's explanation, "I want an applicant to tell me about what he ate, not how he liked it." Questions here will be posed as, "What were the events that led to the incident?" "Who was involved?" "What exactly did you do and say?" "What was the outcome?"

3. **Pose situational questions in addition to past experience questions.**

   Again, the situational questions are specific, which prevents you from answering vaguely. For example: "As a seafood buyer, you are responsible for the availability of halibut to supermarkets in our chain. You manage to lock in a large purchase of halibut at an attractive price from suppliers. Based on this purchase, management decides to feature halibut prominently at rock-bottom prices in its double-page newspaper ads. The ads work too well: Within hours of ad publication, customers have cleaned out the supermarkets of their halibut stock. Managers from most of the stores are calling you for more halibut. What would you do?"

   Notice this does not invite an "I-think-buying-should-always-be-done-within-budget" answer! Nor is it a good idea to blurt out, "I'd just buy more halibut as fast as I could and get it out to the stores," Bell said. Your answer must keep the company's interests firmly in mind, as well as saving your own rear end.

Although the reality interview demands more, it can stack the cards in your favor. The *Wall Street Journal* reported that S.C. Johnson & Co. interviewed a woman for a sales position using this situational method. Her background was in theater—not exactly an area that excited interviewers. Furthermore, she was up against several experienced salesmen and the interviewers had never hired a woman for such a position. However, the reality interview gave her a chance to score higher than the other applicants and get the job offer. She eventually broke the sales record in the company.

There is also some research that employees hired using this approach are less likely to be terminated later on and more likely to be promoted than those hired using other interview methods.

The Disorganized Interview

Let's face it; you will come across many inexperienced people who will not do a good job interviewing you. They may talk about themselves too much or neglect to ask you any meaningful questions. Many people are competent managers but poor interviewers and few have had any formal interview training. The best way to help such lost souls learn about the true you is by providing some answers to questions they may not ask.

The Second Interview Type: The JIST Job Search Interview—An Essential Concept for Getting More Interviews

Traditional interviews, conducted in the traditional way, are designed to screen you out and put the control in the hands of the employer. This and other chapters in this book will help you handle traditional interviews more effectively, but it is important for you to understand that traditional interviews are only one type of interview.

Over the years, I have come to define an interview in a way that is quite different from how most people define an interview. Instead of the narrow definition of a traditional interview—where your job search consists of looking for job openings—I suggest that an interview can also be one where no job exists at all. Here is my simple definition of an interview:

A JIST Job Search Interview Is...

...any face-to-face contact with someone who hires or supervises people with your skills—whether or not that person has a job opening now.

The implications of this new definition of an interview are enormous: It allows you to talk to people who might hire you in the future, but may not have an opening now. For example, if you seek an interview for a job that is now open (a traditional job opening) you would ask, "Do you have any job openings?" Very often, the answer would be "No." If, on the other hand, you said, "I would like to speak with the person in charge of (this or that)," you would probably get to talk to them. That would be an interview in the way I define it, even if there is no job opening yet.

Almost everyone thinks of the job search in the traditional way: of getting in to talk to employers about jobs that are now open. But I believe that this traditional approach results in those people being out of work longer than they need to be.

While I encourage you to look for traditional interviews during your job search, I believe that these interviews represent only a small percentage of the opportunities for jobs. Opening up your job search to include an emphasis on interviews with potential employers that don't have a job opening now, allows you to access the 75 percent or so of all jobs that are never advertised. Understanding and using this new definition of an interview fundamentally changes how you approach your search for a new job and it has profound implications on your ability to get more "interviews," both traditional and nontraditional.

Three Things You Need to Know or Do for a JIST Job Search Interview

Because there are far more employers who don't have a formal job opening for you at any one time, it should be obvious that this new definition of an interview allows you to talk to more employers because it doesn't restrict your search to specific openings. But not every conversation with an employer is an interview. To get the most from this type of interview, here is what you need to know or do:

1. You must know what sort of job you want, and

2. You must be able to communicate clearly why someone should hire you for that job, and

3. The interviewer must know something about the sort of job you are looking for or, at the very least, know other people who may know.

Using the JIST Job Search Interview approach provides a tremendous advantage to you. Now you can interview with employers before they have a job opening and often completely avoid competition from other job seekers. And, because the employer won't be trying to eliminate you from the pool of applicants (as is done in the traditional interview), the interview can be much more relaxed.

Keep the new definition of an interview in mind as you continue reading this book. It is an important definition that can make a very big difference in how effective you are in finding job openings.

The Seven Phases of an Interview

In a traditional interview, the objective is to get a job offer. It is that simple. But in situations where there may not be a job opening just yet, the objective may be to make a good impression and get referrals to other people.

A certain amount of judgment is required for you to know how to act in various sorts of interviews. If there is a job opening and you want it, you would behave differently than in an interview where no opening existed. But just what *do* you do during the interview?

Fortunately, there has been much research on the interview process. That research indicates that some things are clearly very important to an employer in deciding on one person over another. For example, it should be obvious that your dress and grooming can create a positive or negative first impression. But just *how should* you dress and groom for an interview? What else do employers find important—and what can you do about it? The answers to these and other questions fill this book. I think you will find the following review of the interview process will give you enough information to anticipate most situations.

Overview of the Seven Phases of an Interview

A job interview is a complex interaction, but dividing one into distinct sections makes it easier to understand. After extensive consideration, I've divided a typical interview into seven distinct sections (actually, it could have been some other number, but seven seemed just right). Here they are:

Chapter 4

FARR'S SEVEN PHASES OF AN INTERVIEW

Phase 1. Before You Go In.

Before you even meet the interviewer, you will create an impression. If it's bad, nothing good can come of it.

Phase 2: Opening Moves.

An interview isn't a game, exactly, but how you begin it will often affect whether you win or lose.

Phase 3: The Interview Itself.

This is the longest and most complex part of an interview. It's here that you are asked problem questions and have the opportunity to present your skills. The impression you make here is highly dependent on your self-awareness of what you have to offer and your ability to communicate it.

Phase 4: Closing the Interview.

There is more to ending an interview than simply saying good-bye. This phase can allow you to wrap up the interview in a positive way and close the interview to your advantage. You can effectively arrange for the next phase.

Phase 5: Following Up.

In my opinion, an interview is not over until you send a thank-you note and schedule additional follow up. People who follow up get jobs over those who do not. It's that simple.

Phase 6: Negotiating for Salary and Other Benefits.

Discussing money in an initial interview can quickly get you screened out. Knowing what to do, and how, can be worth many, many dollars.

Phase 7: Making a Final Decision.

Once you get a job offer, you have to decide to accept it, reject it, or negotiate for something "better." The stakes are high here and you may have to live with a bad decision for some time. I'll provide you with a simple decision-making process and other tips to help you evaluate such an important life decision on its own merits.

A Review of the Seven Phases of an Interview, Including Tips on Handling Each One

Once the interview process has been cut into more manageable chunks, each one becomes easier to master. The section that follows provides information on each phase along with tips on improving your performance. Pay attention: Even small improvements in your interviewing skills can make the difference between getting an offer and getting screened out.

Phase 1: Before You Go In—You Make an Impression Before You Even Get There, So Make Sure It Is a Good One

While often overlooked, what happens before the interview is very, very impor-tant. Before you actually meet prospective employers, you often have indirect contact with those who know them. You might even contact the interviewer directly, through e-mail, a phone call, or correspondence. Each of these contacts creates an impression. Let's take a look at the issues here and see what you can do to prepare yourself.

Create a positive impression in preliminary contacts

There are three ways an interviewer may form an impression of you before meeting you face-to-face:

1. The interviewer already knows you

There are many situations where an interviewer may know you from previous contacts or from someone else's description of you. When this is so, your best approach is to acknowledge that relationship, but to treat the interview in all other respects as a business meeting. Even if you are the best of friends, remember that a decision to hire you involves hard cash. It will not be done lightly.

2. Through previous e-mail or phone contacts

E-mail and the phone are important job search tools. How you handle these con-tacts will create an impression, even though the contacts are brief. For example, both contact via the phone and e-mail will give an impression of your language skills and ability to present yourself in a competent way; e-mail will also quickly communicate your level of written communication skills. So, if you set up an interview with the employer, you have already created an impression, most likely positive enough or you wouldn't have gotten as far as setting up an interview.

Chapter 4

Administrative Assistants, receptionists, and other staff you have contact with, may also mention their observations to the interviewer, and so be professional and courteous in all encounters with staff.

You should call the day before to verify the time of your interview. Say something like: "Hi, I want to confirm that our interview for two o'clock tomorrow is still on." Get any directions you need. This is just another way of demonstrating your attention to detail and helps to communicate the importance you are placing on this interview.

3. Through your resume and other job search correspondence

Prior to most interviews, you will provide the employer with some sort of information or paperwork that will create an impression. Sending a note, letter, or e-mail beforehand often creates the impression that you are well organized. Copies of applications, resumes, and JIST Cards sent or e-mailed in advance help the interviewer know more about you. If they are well prepared (as they must be), they will help to create a positive impression. For these reasons, everything you present to an employer must be as professional as possible.

 The JIST Card presented on this page is a type of mini-resume that presents key information about you on a 3-by-5-inch card. It is covered in more detail in Chapter 6, but here is an example, just so that you know what it is:

Jonathan Michael   **Phone messages:** (614) 788-2434
                                              e-mail: jonathanm@mindquest.com

Objective: Management Position

Skills: Over 7 years of management experience plus a B.S. degree in Business. Managed budgets as large as $10 million. Experienced in cost control and reduction, cutting over 20% of overhead while business increased over 30%. Good organizer and problem solver. Excellent communication and computer skills.

Prefer responsible position in a medium to large business

Cope well with deadline pressure, seek challenge, flexible

Research the organization, interviewer, and job

Knowing something about the organization and the interviewer will pay off. Doing this may not be practical in situations where you call or drop in unexpectedly, as when making a cold contact, but it does make sense in other situations.

For example, let's say you have targeted a particular organization as one of the few that seem able to provide you with the kind of position you want. Because of that interview's importance to you, it would be wise to be well prepared for it. Briefly, here are the major ways of researching for an interview.

The Internet. Find out if the organization has a Web site and, if so, learn as much as you can by visiting it. Then do a keyword search using any good search engine, entering the organization's and interviewer's names. This may or may not get you much useful information, particularly for a small business, but it is worth a try.

The library is another place to research. Ask the librarian for sources of information on the organization that interests you. There are often national, state, and local directories listing businesses and other organizations that provide some information. Newspapers might contain articles and news releases regarding the organization, and back issues are often available at the library. Major newspapers are indexed and articles are cross-referenced to help you find what you are looking for. Libraries also often have access to online information sources that may not be available to you for free.

The organization itself is a good source of information. Call the receptionist or interviewer and ask them to suggest materials you might read. Annual reports, brochures, or catalogs are sometimes available, but anything you get will help. It won't hurt for your interviewer to know how thorough you are, either.

Ask others who might know about the organization or the interviewer. This is often the best source of information. An hour or so of contacting people you know who might know something about the employer can give you information you could not obtain otherwise. Use the networking technique by contacting someone who seems likely to know what you want or knows someone who would. Find out what you can, and then ask for the name of someone else who would know more.

Contact past employees. If you can find out who the person was who had the position you are applying for, you may see if he or she will tell you about the job. This can work to your advantage. Do not reveal anything to this person that you do not want shared with the boss or organization, however. If you know of others who work there or have worked there, contact them as well.

Here are some things you might want to find out about before you go to a job interview:

The organization: Size, number of employees; major products or services; competitors and the competitive environment, major changes in policies or status; reputation, values, and major weaknesses or opportunities.

Chapter 4

The interviewer: Level and area of responsibility; special work-related projects, interests, or accomplishments; personal information (family, hobbies, etc.); and management style.

The position: If an opening exists or if similar jobs now exist; what happened to others in similar positions; salary range and benefits; duties and responsibilities; and what the last person did wrong (to avoid it) or right (to emphasize it).

The more you can find out before you begin, the better you are likely to do in the interview. Employers appreciate people who do their homework. You will be better prepared for any questions that may come up, and you will be able to more readily direct the interview to focus on presenting your skills well.

An appendix at the end of this book provides many more sources you can use to obtain more information on employers and other job-related topics.

Getting to and waiting for the interview

There are several details to consider before the interview itself and each one makes a difference.

Get there on time. Try to schedule several interviews within the same area of town and time frame to avoid wasted time in excessive travel. Ask for directions from the receptionist or office manager and be sure you know how to get there and how long it will take. Allow plenty of time for traffic or other problems and plan on arriving for the interview 5 to 10 minutes early.

Check your appearance. Arrive early enough to slip into a restroom and correct any grooming problems your travel may have caused, such as wind-blown hair. You would be surprised how many people go into the interview with pen marks on their face or smudged lipstick on their teeth. Use a breath mint or gum just to be on the safe side. Do not spray on perfume, cologne, or hair spray right before the interview because many people are sensitive to chemicals or scents.

Be nice to the receptionist, office manager, or administrative assistant. Many organizations have a receptionist or office manager, and this person is important to you. Assume that everything you say or do will get back to the interviewer, because it typically will. A friendly chat with the receptionist can also be a productive way to find out more about the organization. For example, if it seems appropriate, ask the person what it is like to work there, what he or she does in the job, or even what sort of a person the boss is. They are often happy to share these things with you in a helpful way. A thank-you note to the receptionist following your interview will surely create a positive impression. Treat all support personnel with respect and they will help you by saying nice things about you to the boss; mistreat them and you will probably not get a job there.

I once worked in a busy office with a waiting room that was often crowded. When I was interviewing people, the receptionist and other staff often interacted with applicants as they waited for me. If the person being interviewed acted strangely or did not treat all staff with respect, they would give me a thumbs-down sign in a way that the applicant could not see. Those interviews were very short.

I figured that if that applicant did not treat one of my staff well before the interview, he or she would only show the same lack of interpersonal skills on the job. The moral: Every person you interact with is a real person and their opinions of you do count.

Use appropriate waiting room behavior. It is important to relax and to look relaxed as you wait for the interview to begin. Occupy yourself with something businesslike. For example, this could be a good time to review your notes on questions you might like to ask in the interview, key skills you want to present, or other interview details. Bring a work-related magazine to read or pick one up in the reception area. They may also have publications from the organization itself that you may not have seen yet. You could also update your daily schedule.

During the entire interviewing process, I advise you not to smoke because a non-smoker is often seen as a more desirable worker. You may have other mannerisms that create negative impressions, too. Don't slouch in your seat. Don't create a mess by spreading out your coat and papers across the next seat. Don't take this time to crack your knuckles or neck. Etcetera.

Be prepared if the interviewer is late. Hope that it happens. If you arrive promptly but have to wait past the appointed time, that puts the interviewer in a "Gee, I'm sorry, I owe you one" frame of mind. If the interviewer is 15 minutes late, approach the office manager or administrative assistant and say something like: "I have an appointment to keep yet today. Do you think it will be much longer before (insert interviewer's name) will be free?"

Be nice, but don't act like you can sit around all day either. If you have to wait more than 25 minutes beyond the scheduled time, ask to reschedule at a better time. Say it is no problem for you and you understand things do come up. Besides, you say, you want to be sure Mr. or Ms. So-and-So doesn't feel rushed when he or she sees you. Set up the new time, accept any apology with a smile, and be on your way. When you do come back for your interview, the odds are that the interviewer will apologize—and treat you very well indeed.

Chapter 4

Phase 2: Opening Moves—First Impressions Do Count!

You've gotten to the right office, you're on time, and the interviewer now walks into the room. What is the first thing that will happen? While this may seem obvious, the first thing that will happen is that he or she will see and react to you. You have a very short time period during which the interviewer forms a first impression. The impression the interviewer has formed during the first few minutes will often result in you being eliminated from consideration or allowed to move on in the application process.

Appearance counts

In a thorough review of the research on interviewing entitled *Job Search, A Review of the Literature,* Steven Magnum found that "Appearance, communication skills, and attitudes dominate the research. Attire and physical attractiveness visibly influence the hiring process."

Appearance counts and I cannot stress enough the importance of your appearance in the job search. It is a major factor in the interview process and in getting a job offer—or getting eliminated from consideration.

The importance of appearance is highlighted by the results of a study which evaluated the effect of nonverbal communication style on employers. Two actors, one male and one female, were videotaped while role-playing an interview. Two videos were made of each, using precisely the same responses to the same questions. In one video, the actors made good eye contact while speaking, spoke clearly, and presented good posture. In the other, they did not. They dressed the same for each series of videos, and I emphasize, used the same words in responding to the same questions.

These videos were then randomly shown to 52 professional interviewers who were asked to score the interviews in various categories. No interviewer saw the same actor in both roles. What do you suppose happened? Naturally, the "good" interview was chosen over the "bad" one.

What was astonishing was that, of all the interviewers, not one would have invited back the person who had poor nonverbal skills. The same people using the same responses but who had good nonverbal communication skills would have been invited back by 88 percent of the interviewers. The results of this study show that your appearance and various personality traits (adaptive skills) are observed by—and are very important to—interviewers.

Let's look at some of the other appearance-related issues employers use to make hiring decisions.

Be particular about your dress and appearance

How you dress and groom can create a big negative or positive impression, especially during the first few seconds of an interview. With so many options in styles, colors, and other factors, determining the "correct" approach can get quite complex. Entire books have been written on the subject and there are many differences of opinion on just what is right for various occasions. To avoid the complexity, I present this simple rule for you to follow:

☑ Mike Farr's Interview Dress and Grooming Rule

Dress and groom like the interviewer is likely to be dressed, but just a bit better.

For example, a job seeker interviewing for a job as an accountant would be likely to dress differently from someone interviewing for a position as an auto mechanic. If you are not sure how to dress for a particular interview, go a bit on the conservative and professional side. Even if the culture of the organization is business casual, you can revert to that when you have the job.

Pay attention to details. Do your shoes look presentable? Are your clothes clean and pressed? Is your hair neat? Are you absolutely clean? Have you looked closely at yourself in the mirror?

This is your one chance to make a first impression, and it counts. It is best to get someone else's opinion on the impression you make. A better clothing store can help you select a coordinated job search outfit. Plan to invest some money in at least one set of good quality interviewing clothes. Notice, when you are all dressed up, how good you feel. That can affect your whole performance in the interview.

A firm handshake and good eye contact

Shaking hands is a common custom and, while it seems a small detail, do learn to execute this formality properly. If the employer offers his or her hand, give a firm-but-not-too-firm handshake as you smile.

As ridiculous as it sounds, a little practice helps. Avoid staring, but do look at the interviewer when either of you is speaking. It will help you concentrate on what is being said and indicate to the employer that you are listening closely and have good social skills.

Other nonverbal behaviors make an impression

The very best way to see yourself as others see you is to role-play an interview while it is videotaped. Ask a friend to be the interviewer and ask that person to be tough. Looking at and listening to the video playback is sometimes shocking to

Chapter 4

people. If video equipment is not available to you, all is not lost. Pay close attention to your own posture, mannerisms, and other body language. Ask yourself how employers might evaluate you if they saw that behavior. Look at other people and copy the posture and behavior of ones you think would look good in an interview situation. Here are some additional tips on improving your interview behavior.

Act interested. When you are sitting, lean slightly forward in your chair and keep your head up, looking directly at the interviewer. This helps you look interested and alert.

Eliminate annoying behaviors. Try to eliminate any distracting movements or mannerisms. A woman in one of my workshops saw herself in a videotape constantly playing with her hair. It was only then that she realized she did it at all, and how distracting it was. Listen to yourself and you may notice that you say "aaahhh" or "ummmmm" frequently, or say "you know what I mean?" over and over, or use other repetitive words or phrases. You may hardly be aware of doing this, but do watch for it. Seek out and eliminate similar behavior from the interview.

Pay attention to your voice. If you are naturally soft-spoken, work on increasing your volume slightly. Listen to news announcers and other professional speakers who are good models for volume, speed, and voice tone. I, for example, have a fairly deep voice. I have learned to change my intonation while doing presentations, so everyone doesn't go to sleep. Your voice and delivery will improve as you gain experience and conduct more interviews.

Tips to help you quickly establish a positive relationship

Open the interview with an approach intended to establish a relaxed, social tone. Here are some ideas of what to say in the first few minutes.

Use the interviewer's formal name as often as possible. Do this particularly in the early part of the interview and again when you are ending it. Use "Mr. Jones," "Ms. Smith," or "Dr. Johnson," unless the interviewer suggests otherwise.

Play the chit-chat game for awhile. The interviewer will often comment on the weather, ask if you had trouble getting there, or make some other common opening. Be friendly and make a few appropriate comments. Do not push your way into the business of your visit too early because these informal openings are standard measures of your socialization skills. Smile. It's nonverbal and people will respond more favorably to you if you smile at them.

Comment on something personal in the interviewer's office. "I love your office! Did you decorate it yourself?" or "I noticed the sailboat. Do you sail?" or

"Your office manager is great! How long has he been here?" The idea here is to express interest in something that interests the employer and encourage her or him to speak about it. It is a compliment if your enthusiasm shows. This tactic can also provide you the opportunity to share something you have in common, so try to pick a topic you know something about.

Ask some opening questions. As soon as you have both completed the necessary pleasant chit-chat, be prepared to use your control statement or question to get the interview off in the direction you wish it to go. This can happen within a minute of your first greeting, but is more likely to take up to five minutes. You could use some of the transitional questions that follow in a traditional interview setting, while other questions assume that you are interviewing before a job is actually open.

Use a Control Statement

A control statement is the statement you make that will be the roadmap for where the conversation (interview) is going. While you might think that you are at the mercy of the interviewer, you do have some ability to set the direction of the interview from the chit-chat to the focus you desire.

For example, you might say something direct like "I'd like to tell you about what I've done, what I enjoy doing, and why I think it would be a good match with your organization." Your control statement can come at the beginning if things seem fuzzy after the chit-chat or anytime in the interview when you feel it is slipping away.

Questions to Ask Early in an Interview

"How did you get started in this type of career?" (or business or whatever)

"I'd like to know more about what your organization does. Would you mind telling me?"

"I have a background in _____ and am interested in how I might be considered for a position in an organization such as yours."

"I have three years experience plus two years of training in the field of _____. I am actively looking for a job and know that you probably do not have openings now but would be interested in future openings. Perhaps if I told you a few things about myself, you could give me some idea of whether you would be interested in me."

Phase 3: The Interview Itself—A Few Simple Techniques Can Dramatically Improve Your Performance

If you have created a reasonably positive image of yourself so far, an interviewer will now be interested in the specifics of why they should consider hiring you. This back-and-forth conversation usually lasts from 15 to 45 minutes and many consider it to be the most important—and most difficult—task in the entire job search.

Fortunately, by reading this book, you will have several advantages over the average job seeker:

1. You will know what sort of job you want.

2. You will know what skills are required to do well in that job.

3. You have those very skills.

The only thing that remains to be done is to communicate these three things. This is best done by directly and completely answering the questions an employer asks you.

Be prepared for problem interview questions

Quick Fact ➠ According to employers in Northwestern University's Endicott Survey, about 80 percent of all job seekers cannot provide a good answer to one or more problem interview questions.

All employers will try to uncover problems or limitations you might bring to their job. Everyone has a problem of some sort and the employer will try to find yours. Expect it. Let's say, for example, that you have been out of work for three months. That could be seen as a problem, unless you can provide a good reason for it.

Meet an employer's expectations or you are unlikely to get the job

Your task in the interview is to understand what an employer is looking for. After reviewing the research on what employers react to in an interview, I've selected three things that are of particular importance. If any of these "employer expectations" are not met, it is unlikely that you will get a job offer. Following are the three major employer expectations.

The Three Major Employer Expectations

1. Appearance—Do you look like the type of person who will succeed on the job and readily fit into the organization's culture?

2. Dependability—Can you be depended on to be reliable and to do a good job for a reasonable length of time?

3. Credentials—Do you have the necessary training, experience, skills, and credentials that indicate that you are able to do the job well?

Because few employers will ask you questions about your appearance, most problem questions have to do with either the second or third expectations.

View every interview question as an opportunity to support your ability to do the job. Your interview will be short, so you must make the most of it. Each question provides a chance to present the skills you have that are needed by the employer. Remember that the interviewer is a person, just like you. You must be honest and be able to support, with proof, anything you say about yourself. If you have carefully selected your job objective and know your skills, you will find it easy to present reasons why the employer should hire you.

Aside from your control statement or question, you should also be prepared to ask some other questions early on. Some interviewers are happy to discuss details of the position you seek. If possible, find out as much as you can about the position early in the interview. Ask about the type of person they are looking for to fill this position, what sort of people have done well in similar jobs before, or what sorts of responsibilities the job requires. Once you know more about what the interviewer is looking for, you can "fit" your later responses to what you now know the company wants.

Let's say you've found out that the position requires someone who is good at meeting people and who is organized. Assuming you have those skills, you could later emphasize how good you are at meeting people and provide a few good examples. The examples you offer could also provide evidence of how organized you are.

The Three-Step Process for answering most interview questions

There are thousands of questions that could be asked of you in an interview and there is no way you can memorize a "correct" response for each one. Interviews just aren't like that, because they are often conversational and informal. The unexpected often happens. For these reasons, it is far more important to develop an *approach* to answering an interview question rather than memorizing a "correct" or canned response for each.

I have developed a technique that you can use to fashion an effective answer to most interview questions. To make it easy, I have given the technique a name: The Three-Step Process for Answering Interview Questions.

THREE-STEP PROCESS FOR ANSWERING INTERVIEW QUESTIONS

Step #1: Understand What Is Really Being Asked.

Most questions relate to Employer Expectation #2—regarding your adaptive skills and personality. This includes such questions as: Can we depend on you?; Are you easy to get along with?; Are you a good worker? The question may also relate to Employer Expectation #3, namely, do you have the experience and training to do the job if we hire you?

Step #2: Answer the Question Briefly, in a Non-Damaging Way.

A good response to a question should acknowledge the facts of your situation, and present them as an advantage, not a disadvantage.

Step #3: Answer the Real Question by Presenting Your Related Skills.

An effective response to any interview question should answer the actual question being asked in such a way that also presents your ability to do the job well.

An example of an answer using the Three-Step Process

To show you how the Three-Step Process can be used, let's use it to answer a specific question:

Problem Question: "We were looking for someone with more experience in this field than you seem to have. Why should we consider you over others with better credentials?"

Here's how one person might construct an answer to this question, using the Three-Step Process.

Step 1: Understand What Is Really Being Asked

The question above is often asked in a less direct way, but it is a frequent concern of employers. To answer it, you must remember that employers often hire people who present themselves well in an interview over those with better credentials. Your best shot is to emphasize whatever personal strengths you have that could offer an advantage to an employer. The person wants to know whether you have anything going for you that can help you compete with a more experienced worker.

Well, do you? Are you a hard worker? Do you learn fast? Have you had intensive training or hands-on experience? Do you have skills from other activities that can transfer to this job? Knowing in advance what skills you have to offer is essential to answering this question.

Step 2: Answer the Question Briefly, in a Non-Damaging Way

Here is an example of how one person might answer the question without damage:

"I'm sure there are people who have more years of experience or better credentials. I do, however, have four years of combined training and hands-on experience using the latest methods and techniques. Because my training is recent, I am open to new ideas and have gotten used to working hard and learning quickly."

Step 3: Answer the Real Question by Presenting Your Related Skills

While the above response answers the question in an appropriate and brief way, you might continue with additional details that emphasize key skills needed for the job:

"As you know, I held down a full-time job and family responsibilities while going to school. During those two years, I had an excellent attendance record both at work and school, missing only one day in two years. I also received two merit increases in salary and my grades were in the top 25 percent of my class. In order to do all this, I had to learn to organize my time and set priorities. I worked hard to prepare myself in this new career area and am willing to keep working to establish myself. The position you have available is what I am prepared to do. I am willing to work harder than the next person because I have the desire to keep learning and to do an outstanding job. With my education complete, I can now turn my full attention to this job."

This response presents the skills necessary to do well in any job. This job seeker sounds dependable, which meets Employer Expectation #2 (Dependability). And she gave examples of situations where she had used the required skills in other settings, thus meeting Employer Expectation #3 (Credentials). It is a good response.

The next chapter shows you how to use the Three-Step Process to provide thorough answers to 10 interview questions that, in one form or another, are asked in most interviews. If you can answer those questions well, you should be prepared to answer almost any question. Chapter 16 provides answers to a wide variety of more specific interview questions you may be asked. That chapter also includes a list of nearly 100 additional questions that are frequently asked in an interview.

Because you are probably curious, here is my list of the 10 most frequently asked problem questions.

The Top 10 Problem Interview Questions

1. Why don't you tell me about yourself?

2. Why should I hire you?

3. What are your major strengths?

4. What are your major weaknesses?

5. What sort of pay do you expect to receive?

6. How does your previous experience relate to the jobs we have here?

7. What are your plans for the future?

8. What will your former employers (or teachers, if you are a recent student) say about you?

9. Why are you looking for this sort of position and why here?

10. Why don't you tell me about your personal situation?

Questions you might ask the interviewer

Even if you don't ask any questions during an interview, many employers will ask you if you have any. How you respond will affect their evaluation of you. So be prepared to ask insightful questions about the organization.

Good topics to touch on include:

✓ The competitive environment in which the organization operates

✓ Executive management styles

✓ What obstacles the organization anticipates in meeting its goals

✓ How the organization's goals have changed over the past three to five years

Generally, it is most unwise to ask about pay or benefits or other similar areas. The reason is that doing so tends to make you seem more interested in what the organization can do for you, rather than in what you can do for them. It is also not a good idea to simply have no questions at all. Doing so makes you appear passive or disinterested, rather than curious and interested.

Phase 4: Closing the Interview—The Last Few Minutes Are Very Important

There are a few things to remember as the interview is coming to an end. Let's review them briefly.

Don't let the interview last too long. Most interviews last 30 to 60 minutes. Unless the employer asks otherwise, plan on staying no longer than an hour. Watch for hints from interviewers, such as looking at a watch or rustling papers, which indicate that they are ready to end the interview. Exceptions to the one-hour rule should be made only at the interviewer's request.

Summarize the key points of the interview. Use your judgment here and keep it short! Review the major issues that came up in the interview with the employer. This is an optional step and can be skipped if time is short.

If a problem came up, repeat your resolution of it. Whatever you think that particular interviewer may see as a reason not to hire you, bring it up again and present your reasons why you don't see it as a problem. If you are not sure what the interviewer is thinking, be direct and ask, "Is there anything about me that concerns you or might keep you from hiring me?" Whatever comes up, do as well as you can in responding to it.

Review your strengths for this job. This is another chance for you to present the skills you possess that relate to this particular job. Emphasize your key strengths only, and keep it brief.

If you want the job, ask for it. If you do want the job, it is important that you say so, and why. Employers are more willing to hire someone they know is excited about their job, so let them know if this is the case. Ask when you can start. This may not always be appropriate, but if it is, do it. The "Call-Back Close" that follows is an assertive approach that does work.

The Call-Back Close

This approach requires some courage, but it does work. Practice it a few times and use it in your early interviews to help you get more comfortable with using it.

1. **Thank the interviewer by name.** While shaking their hand, say: "Thank you (Mr. or Mrs. or Ms. _____) for your time today."

2. **Express interest.** Depending on the situation, express your interest in the job, organization, service, or product:

   "I'm very interested in the ideas we went over today." or,

   "I'm very interested in your organization. It seems to be an exciting place to work." Or, if a job opening exists and you want it, definitely say,

   "I am definitely interested in this position."

3. **Mention your busy schedule.** Say "I'm busy for the next few days, but..."

4. **Arrange a reason and a time to call back.** Your objective is to leave a reason for you to get back in touch and to arrange for a specific day and time to do so. For example, say, "I'm sure I'll have questions. When would be the best time for me to get back with you?"

   Notice that I said "When" rather than "Is it OK to...." because asking when does not easily allow a "no" response. Get a specific day ("Monday") and a best time to call ("between 9 and 10 a.m.").

5. Say "thank you" and "good-bye."

Phase 5: Follow Up after Each Interview

The interview has ended, you made it home, and now it's all over, right? Wrong. Effective follow-up actions can make a big difference in getting a job offer over more qualified applicants.

As I say throughout this book, following up can make the difference between being unemployed or under-employed and getting the job you want fast. Here is what you should do when you get home.

Make notes on the interview. While it is fresh in your mind, jot down key points. A week later, you may not remember something essential.

Schedule your follow up. If you agreed to call back next Monday between 9:00 a.m. and 10:00 a.m., you are likely to forget unless you put it on your schedule.

Send your thank-you note. Send the note the very same day if possible. Send an e-mail thank you that day, and follow this with a snail mail thank-you note.

Call when you said you would! When you call when you said you would, you create the impression of being organized and wanting the job. If you do have a specific question, ask it at this time. If a job opening exists and you do want it, say that you want it and why. If no job opening exists, say you enjoyed the visit and would like to stay in touch during your job search. If they referred you to others, let them know how these contacts went. Ask them what they suggest your next step should be. This would also be a good time to ask, if you had not done so before, for the names of anyone else with whom you might speak about a position for a person with your skills and experience. Then, of course, follow up with any new referrals.

Schedule more follow up. Then schedule the next time you want to follow up with this person. And, of course, send them another thank-you note or e-mail.

Phase 6: Negotiating for Salary and Other Benefits

Once a job offer is made, negotiations can be as simple as saying "When can I start?" However, there is far more you should know about negotiating a job offer, and I will provide additional details on this in Chapter 5. If you handle this well, you can earn thousands of dollars a minute. Meanwhile, here are a few essential tips to remember:

1. The time to negotiate is after you've been offered the job.

Do not discuss your preferred salary or any other negotiable subject in an interview until after a job offer has clearly been made. Many, many job seekers have been eliminated from consideration over this very issue.

2. Don't say "no" too quickly.

NEVER, EVER turn down a job offer in an interview! Even if you are certain that you won't accept the job because, say, it pays too little, always tell the employer that you'd like to consider the offer overnight. You can always say no tomorrow. If your decision to refuse the job as offered remains firm, you can always suggest (tomorrow) that you appreciate the offer but ask that they consider you for other opportunities, give you higher wages, or whatever. This is no time to be playing games, but many people have turned down one job only to be offered a better one later simply because the employer had time to think it over.

3. Don't say "yes" too quickly either.

As with saying "no" too quickly, take time to think about accepting a job too. If you do want the job, do not jeopardize obtaining it with unreasonable demands. Ask for 24 hours to consider your decision and, when calling back, consider negotiating for something reasonable. A bit more money, perhaps—or the promise of a salary review after 90 days. Make it clear that you do want the job in any case and don't be difficult. If you want the job, say so—and don't quibble over things that are not that important to you.

MONEY ISN'T EVERYTHING: SOME OTHER THINGS YOU MIGHT NEGOTIATE

Let's assume that you get a job offer that is close to, but not quite in the pay range you wanted. Before you turn it down, think about what other things you might ask for that would make the job acceptable. Then ask for them. For example:

Title: Some job titles look better on a resume and sound better in an interview. Just by changing the wording, you can position yourself for more responsibility ("office manager" vs. "secretary," for example).

Hours: I once accepted a job that paid a bit less than I wanted, but it let me take one afternoon off per week. I still worked over 40 hours but those afternoons off sure felt good.

Salary Review: Ask to have your salary reviewed for an increase after three to six months. Negotiate a specific increase to be given at that time, if your performance is good.

Advancement: Discuss the next level of responsibility toward which you might work. Find out how you might get there and how long it might take.

Education and Training: Some organizations pay for course work, seminars, or other training. This can be a tremendous benefit, if you can get it.

Vacations: Smaller organizations are more flexible on this. Ask for more and you just might get it.

Fringe Benefits: "Fringes" are often standard for everyone in the same organization, but sometimes there is flexibility. For example, negotiation for special insurance benefits (by showing that you are more valuable than some other employees), could be worth real money to you.

Working Conditions: Perhaps you like to do some work from home, come in at 8:15 a.m. instead of 8:00, prefer to have your own office (with a window), or some other special request. The time to negotiate these things is before you start working there.

Phase 7: Making a Final Decision

It is rare to find the perfect job. There are usually compromises to be made. Too often, a job is accepted without thorough knowledge of just what it would be like to actually work there. At the time, it seems to be a good idea. Unfortunately, what seemed good at first doesn't always turn out that way later. The major problem is that many people never make a careful decision at all. They don't take the time to weigh the pros and the cons of their decision. One job leads to another and careers develop almost by accident. There is an alternative.

In a book entitled, *Decision Making,* Irving Janis and Leon Mann present research and theory on the process and consequences of making important decisions. They found that various groups who used this process were more likely to stick to their decision and have fewer regrets afterwards then those who did not. To make any important decision, they suggest that you consider the alternatives in a systematic way.

You can easily adapt their decision-making process for use in making career decisions. Let's say that you are considering a job offer, but it requires you to move, something you would rather not do. They suggest that you create a simple form with four boxes, like the sample one I provide here. Simply writing in the pros and cons for yourself and for others (if this is an issue for you) will help you make a good decision. It's that simple.

THE CAREER CHOICE BALANCE SHEET	
Positives	**Negatives**
For me:	
For others:	

Information Interviews and Other Miscellaneous Types of Interviews

It is impossible to cover all the creative interview approaches that have been used by people over the years. Some of these approaches are well known or can be very helpful for some job seekers to use in certain situations. These are the interview types I cover here.

Information Interviews

This type of interview has become widely-used, and often abused, since Richard Bolles popularized it in his book *What Color Is Your Parachute?* It is supposed to be used by job seekers who have not yet decided what they want to do—or where.

An Information Interview Is...

...used by someone who isn't yet sure of what they want to do, to obtain career information or advice from a knowledgeable person who shares a common interest or who works in a career area of possible interest to the interviewee. It is not supposed to be used by someone who is actively seeking a job.

To correctly use the technique, you must first define your ideal job in terms of skills required, size and type of organization, salary level, interests, what sort of coworkers you prefer, and other preferences. The next step is to gather information on just where a job of this sort might exist and what it might be called.

If you are interested in defining your ideal job, if you do your homework before using this method, and if you are truly honest and sincere about seeking information but not a job, then the information interview technique is both effective and fun.

Unfortunately, this technique is often misused. People who really want to get a job use the technique as a trick to get in to see someone. ("I'm not looking for a job but I am conducting a survey...") Well, that is dishonest and most employers resent the misrepresentation. Many employers are now wary about anyone, even the sincere ones, asking to see them for any reason. Many who support the use of information interviews lament this and point out that some career counselors and others who should know better have encouraged this dishonesty. Proponents do point out, however, that the technique is still useful, particularly outside larger cities and with smaller organizations.

"Profit" Interviews

Years before "information interviewing," Bernard Haldane developed a similar technique for those seeking managerial and professional positions. He explained his approach in a book that I consider to be a classic, titled *How to Make a Habit of Success.* Haldane explained that first you have to identify an employer that is of particular interest. That organization meets most of the criteria set by the job seeker *and* the job seeker clearly sees how that organization could benefit from employing him or her.

Once that happens, the job seeker carefully puts together a written proposal to be presented to the person (or persons) within that organization who makes decisions. The plan would address what you propose to do; how it would be done; how much money (or other benefits) the project or activity will generate; how much it will cost (including your salary and benefits); and why you are the one person uniquely qualified to successfully fill the position.

The keyword in all this is "profit," because if you propose other benefits, but not more profit, your case is surely weakened. If all goes well, you have a job created for you where none existed before. It *does* happen! In fact, Haldane and Associates, the career counseling firm founded by Bernard Haldane, provides data indicating that more than half of the people they work with have jobs created just for them by using this technique.

VIDEO AND TELECONFERENCING INTERVIEWS

While relatively novel at present, employers can use Internet and other technologies to interview applicants at remote locations, a trend that will accelerate as technologies improve. This approach is not as interactive as a physical interview but is much less costly for an employer or job seeker, because no travel is required. In many ways, these interviews can be the same as face-to-face interviews and are used to screen applicants who make the initial cut.

═══ *Quick Summary*

✓ Eight things you must do to have a successful interview:

1. Make a positive impression.
2. Communicate your skills.
3. Use control statements to your advantage.
4. Answer problem questions.
5. Ask key questions.

6. Help the employer know why they should hire you.

7. Close the interview properly.

8. Follow up after the interview.

✓ The three types of interviews are: 1) Traditional, 2) JIST Job Search Information, and 3) Information and other miscellaneous types of interviews.

✓ Major types of traditional interviews include: The Preliminary Screening Interview, The Group or Panel Interview, The Stress Interview, The Structured Interview, The Reality Interview, The Disorganized Interview.

✓ One type of information interview is called the Profit interview.

✓ A JIST Job Search interview is "Any face-to-face contact with someone who hires or supervises people with your skills—whether or not they have a job opening now."

The Seven Phases of an Interview:

✓ Phase 1: Before You Go In—You Make a Positive Impression Before You Even Get There, so Make Sure It Is a Good One.

✓ Phase 2: Opening Moves—First Impressions Do Count!

✓ Phase 3: The Interview Itself—A Few Simple Techniques Can Dramatically Improve Your Performance

✓ Phase 4: Closing the Interview—The Last Few Minutes Are Important

✓ Phase 5: Following up—Effective Follow-Up Actions Can Make a Big Difference in Getting a Job Offer over More Qualified Applicants

✓ Phase 6: Negotiating for Salary and Other Benefits—If You Handle This Well, You Can Earn Thousands of Dollars a Minute

✓ Phase 7: Making a Final Decision

The Three-Step Process to Answering Interview Questions:

✓ Step 1: Understand what is really being asked

✓ Step 2: Answer the question briefly, in a nondamaging way

✓ Step 3: Answer the real question by presenting your related skills

CHAPTER 5

Answers to 10 Key Interview Questions

≡Quick Overview

In this chapter, I review the following:

✔ The 10 most frequently asked interview questions

✔ Comments and analysis of each question

✔ Sample answers to each question

✔ The "Prove It" Technique

✔ How to handle obvious and not-so-obvious problems

✔ How to leave them with "Why wouldn't you hire me?"

Doing well in an interview is so important that I put this chapter in the first section of this book. The reason is that improving your performance in the interview even a little bit can result in your getting a job offer over someone else. I provide more information on answering problem questions in Chapter 16 and encourage you to review that chapter carefully. Most job seekers do reasonably well in basic interview skills but stumble in answering one or more problem questions. This is true even for experienced people who have lots of good credentials. Many employers I've spoken with say that they would have hired someone if he or she had just done a little better in the interview. So spend a little time to learn how to answer the questions covered in this chapter—it can make an enormous difference to you in getting a job over other qualified applicants.

Let me also suggest to you that reading this chapter can be worth thousands of dollars to you, because one of the questions is "What sort of pay do you expect to receive?" Knowing how to answer this one question will quickly pay for this book—and, over the years, leave enough left over for you to buy a new car.

The 10 Most Frequently Asked Interview Questions

Knowing and practicing answers to a relatively small but important cluster of difficult questions will prepare you to answer many other related interview questions. Employers tend to ask some questions more than others. Several of the questions I present here are seldom asked directly but provide the basis for other common questions. For example, a conversational question about any aspect of your family relationships may really be an attempt to discover whether or not you will be a reliable worker.

From the thousands of questions that could be asked, I have constructed 10 questions that represent the types of issues that concern most employers. The following list of questions is partly based on questions employers actually ask, and partly on my sense of which questions provide the best patterns for teaching you the principles of constructing good overall responses.

The Top 10 Problem Interview Questions

1. Why don't you tell me about yourself?

2. Why should I hire you?

3. What are your major strengths?

4. What are your major weaknesses?

5. What sort of pay do you expect to receive?

6. How does your previous experience relate to the jobs we have here?

7. What are your plans for the future?

---

8. What will your former employers (or references) say about you?

9. Why are you looking for this sort of position and why here?

10. Why don't you tell me about your personal situation?

In the previous chapter, I reviewed the Three-Step Process for answering interview questions. Because each applicant is different—and each interview is different—there isn't only one correct way to answer an interview question. Instead, this chapter teaches you to provide short and positive responses to most interview questions.

In order to do well in interviews, you will need to use a general approach to answering interview questions because memorizing responses is simply not a reasonable option. Because this Three-Step Process is such an important concept, I present it again below to help you in this chapter.

The Three-Step Process to Answering Interview Questions

Step 1: Understand What Is Really Being Asked. This usually relates to Employer Expectation 2, regarding your adaptive skills and personality: Can we depend on you? Are you easy to get along with? And, are you a good worker?

Step 2: Answer the Question Briefly, in a Non-Damaging Way. Acknowledge the facts, but present them as an advantage, not a disadvantage.

Step 3: Answer the Real Question by Presenting Your Related Skills. Once you understand the employer's real concern, you can get around to answering the often hidden question by presenting your skills and experiences related to the job.

The "Prove It" Technique

The Three-Step Process is important for understanding that the interview question being asked is often an attempt to discover underlying information. The 4-step technique that follows will help you provide that information in an effective way.

1. **Present a Concrete Example:** People relate to and remember stories. Saying you have a skill is not nearly as powerful as describing a situation where you used that skill. The example should include enough details to make sense of the who, what, where, when, and why.

2. **Quantify:** Whenever possible, numbers should be used to provide a basis for what was done. For example, give the number of customers served, the percent you exceeded quotas, dollar amounts you were responsible for, or the number of new accounts you generated.

3. **Emphasize Results:** It is important to provide some data regarding the positive results you obtained. For example, sales increased by 3 percent over the previous year or profits went up 50 percent. Use numbers to quantify your results.

4. **Link It Up:** While the connection between your example and doing the job well may seem obvious to you, make sure it is clear to the employer. A simple statement is often enough to accomplish this.

If you do a thorough job in completing the activities in this book, it should be fairly easy to provide proof supporting the skills you discuss in an interview. The Three Steps and Prove It techniques are the basic interview strategies to use. I will refer to these techniques in sections that follow and it is most important that you remember the basic steps.

Answers to the Top 10 Problem Interview Questions

In this section, I use the Three-Step Process and Prove It techniques to create sample answers to the 10 problem questions listed earlier in this chapter. For each question, I provide an analysis of what the question is really asking, followed by a strategy for answering it. I also provide one or more sample responses. In each case I use the Three-Step Process, including the Prove It approach for constructing a response.

While your answers will differ from the sample answers provided, you will learn how to use the basic techniques and apply them to your own interview situation.

Problem Interview Question #1: "Why Don't You Tell Me About Yourself?"

Analysis of the question:

This is an open-ended question. You could start anywhere, but telling your life's history in two hours or less is not what is really being asked. Instead, such a question is a test of your ability to select what is important and communicate it clearly and quickly. Obviously, the questioner expects you to relate your background to the position being considered.

A strategy to use in answering the question:

There are several basic approaches that could be used. One would be to go ahead and provide a brief response to the question as it is asked, and the other is to request a clarification of the question before answering it. In both cases, you would answer the question and then quickly turn your response to focus on your skills, experience, and training that prepared you for the sort of job you now want. In other words, you want to relate what you say about yourself to the job at hand. Talk about your experiences as they relate to the position.

Sample answer #1:

If you answered the question as it was asked you might say something like this:

> *"I grew up in the Southwest and have one brother and one sister. My parents both worked and I was active in sports growing up. I always did well in school and by the time I graduated from high school I had taken a year's worth of business courses. I knew then that I wanted to work in a business setting and had several part-time office jobs while still in high school. After high school I worked in a variety of business settings and learned a great deal about how various businesses run. For example, I was given complete responsibility for the daily operations of a wholesale distribution company that grossed over two million dollars a year. That was only three years after I graduated from high school. There I learned to supervise other people and solve problems under pressure. I also became more interested in the financial end of running a business and decided, after three years and three promotions, to seek a position where I could have more involvement in key strategies and long-term management decisions."*

Comments on this answer

Notice how this job seeker provided a few bits of positive personal history and then quickly turned the interviewer's attention to skills and experiences that directly relate to the job this applicant is now seeking.

You could ask interviewers to help you focus on the information they really want to know with a response such as this:

Sample answer #2:

> *"There's so much to tell! Would you like me to emphasize my personal history, the special training and education I have that prepared me for this sort of position, or the skills and job-related experiences I have to support my objective?"*

Chapter 5

Comments on this answer:

If you do this well, most employers will tell you what sorts of things they are most interested in, and you can then concentrate on giving them what they want.

Honesty is always the best policy, but that old adage doesn't rule out marketing yourself in the best light during an interview. Virtually all career counselors encourage job seekers to be positive about themselves and don't consider this as unethical in any way. But they also caution you to stay away from taking credit for something you don't deserve, claiming to have experience you don't have, or bragging about your performance. This is also not the place to talk about an unhappy childhood or make negative comments about past employers. Instead, focus on the positive by saying that your childhood helped you become self-motivated, resilient, and a hard worker. It is just fine to talk up your achievements, awards, and promotions without fear of misrepresenting yourself.

Problem Interview Question #2: "Why Should I Hire You?"

Analysis of the question:

This is a direct and fair question. Though it is rarely asked this clearly, it is the question behind any other question that is asked. It has no hidden meaning.

A strategy to use in answering the question:

A direct question deserves a direct response. Why SHOULD they hire you? The best response to this question provides advantages to them, not to you. A good response will give proof that you can help them make more money by improving efficiency, reducing costs, increasing sales, or solving problems (by coming to work on time, improving customer services, organizing one or more operations, offering knowledge of a particular software or computer system, or a variety of other things).

Sample answer:

Here is an example of a response from a person with considerable prior experience:

> *"You should hire me because I don't need to be trained and have a proven track record. I have over 15 years of education and experience related to this position. Over 6 of those years have been in management positions similar to the one available here. In my last position, I was promoted three times in the 6 years I was there. I most recently had responsibility for supervising a staff of 15 and a warehousing operation that processed over 30 million dollars worth of materials a year. In the last 2 years, I managed a 40 percent*

increase in volume processed with only a 6 percent increase in expenses. I am hard working and have earned a reputation as a dependable and creative problem solver. The opportunities here excite me. My substantial experience will help me to know how to approach the similar situations here. I am also willing to ask questions and accept advice from others. This will be an important factor in taking advantage of what has already been accomplished here."

Comments on this answer:

This job seeker's response emphasized the Prove It technique and included a variety of specific numbers to support her accomplishments. While she presented her skills and experience in a direct and confident way, she avoided a know-it-all attitude by being open to others' suggestions. She also made it clear that she wanted this particular job and why she should be considered for it.

Because having good reasons for why someone should hire you over others is so important to your job search success, I have included the brief activity that follows. Completing it will be a challenge unless you first complete some of the activities elsewhere in this book. If you find it difficult to clearly identify why someone should hire you, come back to this activity after you have completed or reviewed Chapters 3, 9, and 10.

The Reasons Why Someone Should Hire You

In the spaces below, list the major advantages you offer an employer in hiring you over someone else. Emphasize your strengths. These could be personality traits, transferable skills, special training, prior experience, or anything else you think is important. These are the things to emphasize in your interview.

1. _____

   _____

   _____

2. _____

   _____

   _____

3. _____

   _____

   _____

Chapter 5

Problem Interview Question #3: "What Are Your Major Strengths?"

Analysis of the question:

Like the previous question, this one is quite direct and has little hidden meaning.

A strategy to use in answering the question:

This question allows you to focus on the credentials you have that are most important to doing well in the position you are seeking. Your response should emphasize your key adaptive or self-management skills. The decision to hire you is largely based on these skills; you can deal with the details of your specific job-related skills later. Remember that here, as elsewhere, your response must be brief and direct.

A good source for the basic information needed to answer this question is the JIST Card you complete in Chapter 6. If this is carefully written, it will include the key skills to emphasize in responding to this question.

Sample answer:

Here is a response from a person who has little prior work experience related to the job he now seeks:

> *"One of my major strengths is my ability to work hard toward a goal. Once I make a decision to accomplish something, it gets done, and done well. For example, I graduated from high school four years ago. Many of my friends started working and others went on to school. At the time I didn't know what I wanted to do, so furthering my education at that point did not make sense. The jobs I could get at the time didn't excite me either so I looked into joining the Navy. I took the test and discovered a few things about myself that surprised me. For one thing, I was much better at understanding complex problems than my grades in high school would suggest. I signed up for a three-year hitch that included intensive training in electronics. I worked hard and graduated in the top 20 percent of my class. I was then assigned to monitor, diagnose, and repair an advanced electronics system that was worth about 20 million dollars. I was promoted several times to the position of Petty Officer and received an honorable discharge after my tour of duty. I now know what I want to do and am prepared to spend extra time learning whatever is needed to do well here."*

Comments on this answer:

Once you begin speaking about one of your strengths, the rest of your response often falls into place naturally, as the sample response above illustrates.

Remember to provide some proof of your skills, as this response did when citing results of Navy entrance testing and repeated advancement in a highly responsible position. These specifics about your skills can make a difference.

Problem Interview Question #4: "What Are Your Major Weaknesses?"

Analysis of the question:

This is a trick question that some interviewers will ask and that you must be prepared to answer. If you answer the question as it is asked, you could easily damage your chances of getting the job. By trying to throw you off guard, the employer can see how you might react in similar tough situations on the job. I have often asked this question to groups of job seekers and usually get one of two types of responses. The first goes like this:

"I really don't have any major weaknesses."

That response is obviously untrue and evasive. The other type of response I usually get is an honest one like this:

"Well, I am really disorganized. I suppose I should do better at that, but my life has just been too hectic, what with the bankruptcy and embezzlement charges and all."

While this type of response might get an "A" for honesty, it gets an "F" for interview technique.

A strategy to use in answering the question:

What's needed here is an honest, undamaging response followed by a brief, positive presentation to counter the negative. The best approach is to present a weakness in a way that does not harm—and could help—your ability to do a good job. Here are some examples.

Sample answer #1:

"Well, I have been accused by coworkers of being too involved in my work. I usually come in a little early to organize my day and stay late to get a project done on time."

Sample answer #2:

"I need to learn to be more patient. I often do things myself just because I know I can do them faster and better than someone else. This trait has not let me be as good at delegating tasks as I want to be. But I am working on it.

Chapter 5

I'm now spending more time showing others how to do the things I want done and that has helped. They often do better than I expect because I am clear about explaining what I want and how I want it done."

Comments on these answers:

These responses could both be expanded with some Prove It content but they successfully use the three basic steps in answering a problem question, as outlined earlier in this chapter. In both cases, the answers responded to the question as it was asked, but did so in a way that presented the weakness as a positive.

Problem Interview Question #5: "What Sort of Pay Do You Expect to Receive?"

Analysis of the question and tips for a good answer:

If you are unprepared for this question, it is highly probable that any response will damage your ability to get a job offer. The employer wants you to name a number that can be compared to a figure the company has in mind. For example, suppose that the employer is looking to pay someone $36,000 a year. If you say you were hoping for $40,000, you will probably be eliminated from consideration. The employer will be afraid that, if you took the job, you may not stay. If you say you would take $29,000, one of two things could happen:

1. You could get hired at $29,000 a year, making that response the most expensive two seconds in your entire life.

2. The employer may keep looking for someone else, since you must only be worth $29,000 and the employer is looking for someone, well, worth more.

This question is designed to help the employer either eliminate you from consideration or save money at your expense. You could get lucky and name the salary the employer had in mind, but the stakes are too high for me to recommend that approach. Which brings me to the most important salary negotiation rule:

Farr's Salary Negotiation Rule 1

Never talk money until after they decide they want you.

Discussions of pay in an initial interview are often used by employers to screen people out.

Because it is unlikely you will get a firm job offer in a first interview, your objective should be to create a positive impression and not be rejected. If the topic of pay does come up, avoid getting nailed down. Here are some things you could say:

"Are you making me a job offer?" (A bit corny, yes, but you just might be surprised at the result.)

"What salary range do you pay for positions with similar requirements?"

"I'm very interested in the position and my salary would be negotiable."

"Tell me what you have in mind for the salary range."

"I prefer to hear more about the position before I can come up with a solid number."

"Employers are anxious to know how your joining the organization will impact their bottom line, and they'll try to get to the subject as soon as possible," says Doug Matthews, managing principal of Right Management Consultants, Cincinnati office—an executive outplacement firm. Salary issues are the main reasons candidates are knocked out of the running during screening interviews and informational meetings, according to outplacement industry surveys. In fact, responding appropriately to salary questions can get you past screening interviewers, who rarely have authority to negotiate salaries and get you in front of decision-makers with whom the real negotiations take place.

So put off discussion of pay until you are sure it's the real thing and not just part of a screening process. Then, when the timing is right, maneuver the interviewer into naming the starting point. **Remember the most important rule: He who speaks first loses.**

In most situations, a response like those I presented above will either get the employer to name a salary range or put the subject to rest until the proper time. However, let's suppose you run into a clever, demanding interviewer who insists you disclose your salary expectations before telling you what he or she is willing to pay. Here is what I suggest:

Farr's Salary Negotiation Rule 2

Know, in advance, the probable salary range for similar jobs in similar organizations.

Chapter 5

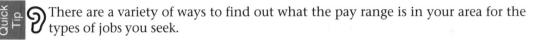

There are a variety of ways to find out what the pay range is in your area for the types of jobs you seek.

For example, the *Occupational Outlook Handbook* provides pay rates for about 250 major jobs. You can find this book at most libraries or online at www.careerOINK.com. Or you can use one of the many free online salary comparison sites, such as www.salary.com. This site allows you to enter your job title and location to see what similar jobs pay in that area. It also allows you to compare cost of living in various areas and other interesting details. Another option is simply calling up people in these jobs, or those who hire people with similar skills, to find out pay ranges in your area.

Let's say that in the previous example you figure the employer's range to be somewhere between $32,000 and $37,000. That is a wide range, but you could then say: "I was looking for a salary in the mid to upper thirties."

That covers a lot of territory! It would include from $32,000 to $39,000 a year or so. You can use the same strategy for any salary bracket you may be considering. For example, if you wanted $38,000 a year and their range might be $35,000 to $43,000, you could say "A salary in the mid-thirties to low-forties." This technique is called "bracketing" and is the basis of the third salary negotiation rule:

Farr's Salary Negotiation Rule 3

Always bracket your stated salary range to begin within their probable salary range and end a bit above what you expect to settle for.

If you are offered the job, you are likely to get offered more than they (or you) may have originally been willing to consider. Which brings me to the last rule:

Farr's Salary Negotiation Rule 4

Never say no to a job or salary offer either before it is made or within 24 hours afterward.

Perhaps you think it impossible to say no before an offer is made, but I have seen it done many times. Let's say that, in a first interview, the question of salary does come up. If you were hoping to get a minimum salary of $35,000 a year and the interviewer mentions that she is hoping to pay $33,000, you just might show some disappointment. You might even say something like, "Oh no, I couldn't consider that!" and if you did, that would be the end. Before you were even offered the job, you turned it down.

However, suppose that particular job turned out to be (if you had only hung around to find out more) the perfect job for you in all respects except the salary. You may have been delighted to take it. Suppose also that the employer (if only he had gotten to know the delightful person you are) found you to be the kind of person to hire even if it took a few extra dollars—say $2,000—to get you. In either case, you would strike a bargain.

For this reason, NEVER give a hint that the salary mentioned is not acceptable to you. You might say, instead, something like this:

> *"That is somewhat lower than I had hoped but this position does sound very interesting. If I were to consider this, what sorts of things could I do to quickly become more valuable to this organization?"*

Remember that a discussion of salary is not necessarily a job offer.

Do not let an employer eliminate you from consideration unless and until you get a firm job offer. If you are not sure, ask "Is this a job offer?" If it is, and if the pay they offer is low, say something like,

> *"Thank you for the offer. The position is very much what I want in many ways and I am delighted at your interest. This is an important decision for me and I would like some time to consider your offer."*

Even if their offer is an insult, do not break their office furniture and stamp out. Be nice, because any job offer is good for your ego when you get to turn it down—and this employer may refer you to other opportunities. At worst, you can call them tomorrow and say:

> *"I am flattered by your job offer but feel that it would not be fair of me to accept. The salary is lower than I would like and that is the one reason I cannot accept it. Perhaps you could reconsider your offer or keep me in mind for future openings that might allow me to be worth more to you?"*

Even as you say no, leave the door open for negotiation. If the employer wants you, he or she may be willing to meet your terms. It happens more often than you might imagine.

Comments on these answers:

Do not use this salary negotiation example as a technique to get a higher wage. Understand that once you say no to an offer, the deal is off. You must be willing to lose that job forever.

Problem Question #6: "How Does Your Previous Experience Relate to the Jobs We Have Here?"

Analysis of the question:

This is another direct question that requires a direct response. It relates to Employer Expectation 3 (credentials) and your response will be very important if you have created a good impression up to this point. This question does require you to overcome any weaknesses your background might present when you are compared to other job seekers. Here are some typical stumbling blocks:

✓ You are just out of school and have limited experience in this career

✓ This is your first job or you have not worked for a period of time

✓ Your prior work experience is not a match for the tasks required in this job

✓ Your previous level of responsibility was lower or higher than this job requires

✓ You have had several jobs, but no clear career direction

✓ You do not have the educational or other credentials many other applicants might have

A strategy to use in answering the question:

Lead with your strengths. If it is obvious that other job seekers might have more education, more years of experience, or whatever qualifications you lack, acknowledge that, and then present your strengths. Use the standard Three-Step Process to answering a problem question. Again, your JIST Card often will provide a starting point.

Sample answer #1:

"As you know, I have just completed an intensive program in the area of information technology (or whatever). In addition, I have over three years work experience in a variety of business settings. That work experience included managing a small business during the absence of the owner. I learned to handle money there and a variety of basic accounting tasks. I also inventoried and organized products worth over six hundred thousand dollars. These experiences helped me understand the importance of good information technology systems in a business setting. While I am a recent information technology graduate, my previous business experience allows me to understand how to use what I have learned in practical and effective ways. My educational experience was very thorough and I have over 300 hours of interactive computer time as part of my course work. Because I am new, I plan to work harder and will spend extra time as needed to meet any deadlines."

Comments on this answer:

This response emphasizes transferable skills (knowledge of accounting procedures) and adaptive skills (meeting deadlines and working hard). This is necessary to counter a lack of previous work experience in the information technology area. In this situation, what was learned in school is also very important and should be emphasized as the equivalent of "real" work.

Sample answer #2:

"In my previous position I used many of the same skills that are needed to do this job well. Even though it was in a different industry, managing a business requires the types of organizational and supervisory skills that I possess. Over the past seven years I guided my region to become one of the most profitable in our company. Sales expanded an average of 30 percent per year during the years I worked there, and profits rose at a similar rate. Since this was a mature company, such performance was highly unusual. I received two promotions during those seven years and rose to the management level quickly. I was later told that no one had previously achieved this. I am now seeking a challenge in a smaller, growth-oriented company such as yours. I feel my experience and contacts have prepared me for this step in my career."

Comments on this answer:

This response acknowledges that the previous career field differed from the one now being considered but emphasizes prior achievements and success. To accomplish this, all sorts of skills would have had to be used. The response also includes the motivation to move on to the challenge of a smaller organization.

Problem Interview Question #7: "What Are Your Plans for the Future?"

Analysis of the question:

This question really explores your motives for working. It asks whether you can be depended on to stay on at this job and work hard at it.

A strategy to use in answering the question:

As always, your best approach is an honest one. I'm not encouraging you to reveal negative information, but you should be prepared to answer the employer's concern in a direct and positive way. Which issues are of concern to an employer will depend on the details of your background.

For example:

- ✓ Will you be happy with the salary? (If not, might you leave?)
- ✓ Will you want to have a family? (If so, will you quit or cut your hours to raise children?)
- ✓ Do you have a history of leaving jobs after a short period of time? (If so, why won't you leave this one too?)
- ✓ Have you just moved to the area and appear to be a temporary or transient resident? (If so, you probably won't stay here long either, right?)
- ✓ Are you overqualified? (If so, what will keep you from going to a better job as soon as you find one?)
- ✓ Do you have the energy and commitment to advance in this job? (If not, who needs someone without energy and drive?)
- ✓ Might you appear to have some other reason to eventually become dissatisfied? (If so, the employer will certainly try to figure out what it is.)

Any of these reasons, and others, can be of concern to an employer. If your situation presents an obvious problem, use the standard Three-Step Process to answering problem interview questions. If you feel you do not have any problem to defend, use steps #2 and #3 of the Three-Step Process to assure the employer that, in effect, this is precisely the organization you want to stay with, grow with, and do well with—for many years to come.

Sample answer #1:

For a younger person or one just entering a new career:

"I realize I need to establish myself in this field and am eager to get started. I've thought about what I want to do and am very sure my skills are the right ones to do well in this career. For example, I am good at dealing with people. In one position, I provided services to over 1,000 different people a week. During the 18 months I was there, I served well over 72,000 customers and not once did I get a formal complaint. In fact, I was often complimented on the attention I gave them. There I learned that I enjoy public contact and am delighted at the idea of taking on this position for that reason. I want to learn more about the business and grow with it. As my contributions and value to the organization increase, I hope to be considered for more responsible positions."

Comments on this answer:

The employer wants to know that you will stay on the job and work hard for your pay. This response helps the employer feel more comfortable with that concern. (Note that this response could be based on work experiences gained in a fast-food job!)

Sample answer #2:

For a person with work history gaps or various short-term jobs:

"I've had a number of jobs (or one, or have been unemployed) and I have learned to value a good, stable position. The variety of my experiences is an asset because I have learned so many things I can now apply to this position. I am looking for a position where I can settle in, work hard, and stay put."

Comments on this answer:

This would be an acceptable response, but a better one would be a bit longer and include some proof of the job seeker's skills. The ideal place to introduce a story would have been right before the last sentence. Some positions, such as sales-oriented ones, require you to be ambitious and perhaps even a bit aggressive. Other jobs have requirements particular to the career field or specific organization. You can't always predict exactly what an employer might want, but you should have a good idea based on what skills that job requires. A good answer to this question will tell the employer that you have what the position requires. You will simply need to say so.

Problem Interview Question #8: "What Will Your Former Employers (or Teachers, References, Warden, or Keeper...) Say About You?"

Analysis of the question:

This question again refers to Employer Expectation 2. The employer wants to know about your adaptive skills—are you easy to get along with, are you a good worker, etc.? Your former employers and other references may tell of any problems you had—or they may not. As you know, many employers will check your references before they hire you, so if anything you say here does not match what a former employer or other reference says, it could be bad news for you.

A strategy to use in answering the question:

Be certain to discuss your job search plans with former employers. Do the same with anyone else who may be contacted for a reference. Clearly tell them the type of job you now seek and why you are prepared to do well in it. If a previous

Chapter 5

employer may say something negative, discuss this openly with your former supervisor and find out what he or she will say in advance.

If you were fired or resigned under pressure, you can often negotiate what would be said to a prospective employer. Lots of successful people have had personality conflicts with previous employers. If these conflicts are presented openly and in the best light possible, many interviewers are likely to understand. It may also be wise to get a written letter of reference, particularly from a not-too-enthusiastic former employer. They will rarely be brave enough to write you a totally negative letter. The letter may be enough to satisfy a potential employer. Larger organizations often don't allow references to be given, and this may be a great relief to you, if you are worried about a negative reference. Check it out by calling them and finding out their policy.

If possible, use references that will say nice things about you. If your ex-boss won't, find someone who will. Often, an interviewer appreciates an honest response. If you failed in a job, telling the truth is often the best policy. Tell it like it was but DO NOT be too critical of your old boss. If you do, it will make you sound like a person who blames others and does not accept responsibility. If you were partly at fault, admit it, but quickly take the opportunity to say what you learned from the experience.

Sample answer:

"My three former employers will all say I work hard, am very reliable, and loyal. The reason I left my previous job, however is the result of what I can only call a personality conflict. I was deeply upset by this but decided that it was time I parted with my former employer. You can call and get a positive reference, but I thought it only fair to tell you. I still respect my ex-boss and am grateful for the experience I gained at that job. While there, I received several promotions and as my authority increased, there were more conflicts. Our styles were just not the same. I had no idea the problem was so serious because I was so involved in my work. That was my error and I have since learned to pay more attention to interpersonal matters."

Comments on this answer:

This response could be strengthened by the introduction of positive skills along with an example that includes some proof to support them.

Problem Interview Question #9: "Why Are You Looking for This Sort of Position and Why Here?"

Analysis of the question:

The employer wants to know if you are the sort of person who is looking for any job, anywhere. If you are, she or he will not be impressed. Employers look for people who want to do what needs to be done. They rightly assume that such a person will work harder and be more productive than one who simply sees it as "just a job." People who have a good reason to seek a particular sort of position will be seen as more committed and more likely to stay on the job longer. The same is true for people who want to work in a particular organization.

A good thing about this question is that it allows you to present your skills and other credentials for wanting this particular job.

A strategy to use in answering the question:

It is most important that you know in advance which jobs are a good match for your skills and interests. Other chapters in this book will help you clarify your job objective and identify the key skills and other credentials you have to do that job. In responding to this question, mention your motivations for selecting this career objective, the special skills you have that the position requires, and any special training or credentials you have which relate to the position.

The question actually has two parts. The first is "Why this position?" The second is "Why here?" If you have a reason for selecting the type of organization you are considering or have even selected this particular organization as highly desirable, be prepared to explain why. If at all possible, learn as much as you can about the organizations you interview with in advance. Call other people to get details, research online, use the library, ask for an annual report, or whatever else it takes to become informed.

Sample answer:

"I've spent a lot of time considering various careers and I think that this is the best area for me. The reason is that this career requires many of my strongest skills. For example, my abilities in analyzing and solving problems are two of the skills I enjoy using most. In a previous position, I would often become aware of a problem no one had noticed and develop a solution. In one situation, I suggested a plan that resulted in reducing customer returns of leased equipment by 15 percent. That may not sound like much, but the result was an increase in retained leases of over $250,000 a year. The plan

cost about $100 to implement. This particular organization seems to be the type that would let me use similar problem-solving skills. It is well run, growing rapidly, and open to new ideas. Your sales went up 30 percent last year and you are getting ready to introduce several major new products. If I work hard and prove my value here, I feel I would have the opportunity to stay with the business as it grows—and grow with it."

Comments on this answer:

This response uses Prove It nicely. It may have been said by an experienced manager or a sharp office worker.

Problem Question #10: "Why Don't You Tell Me About Your Personal Situation?"

Analysis of the question:

A good interviewer will rarely ask this question so directly. If this question is asked this directly, simply ask the person something like "What is it you would you like to know?" In this way you show them that you have nothing to hide. More often, employers will use casual and friendly conversation to get the information they want. In most cases, the interviewer is digging for information that would indicate you are unstable or undependable. For instance:

What They Ask vs. What They Really Want to Know

The Issue	The Reason
Do you have marital or family troubles?	Missed work, poor performance, poor interpersonal skills
Do you handle money and personal responsibilities poorly?	Theft of property, irresponsible job-related decisions
Do you live in a good, stable home?	Socio-economic bias, renters less stable than owners
How do you use leisure time?	Drinking, socially unacceptable behavior
Do you have young children?	Days off and child care problems
Marital status?	If single, will you stay? If married, will you devote the necessary time?

A strategy to use in answering the question:

There are other issues that may be of concern to an employer. Often, these are based on assumptions the person has about people with certain characteristics. These beliefs are often irrelevant (and some may seem to be in bad taste or even illegal), but if the employer wonders whether you can be depended upon, it is in your own best interest to deal with these doubts. Be aware that even your casual conversation should always avoid reference to a potential problem area. In responding to a question about your personal situation, be friendly but positive. Your objective is to give them the answer that they need to have, not just the one they may seem to ask.

Examples of appropriate answers:

Young children at home:

> *"I have two children, both in school. Child care is no problem because they stay with a good friend."*

Single head of household:

> *"I'm not married and have two children at home. It is very important to me to have a steady income and so child care is no problem."*

Young and single:

> *"I'm not married and if I should marry, that would not change my plans for a full-time career. For now, I can devote my full attention to my career."*

Just moved here:

> *"I've decided to settle here in Depression Gulch permanently. I've rented an apartment and the six moving vans are unloading there now."*

Relatives, upbringing:

> *"I am one of three children. Both of my parents still live within an hour's flight from here and I see them several times a year."*

Leisure time:

> *"My time is family-centered when I'm not working. I'm also active in several community organizations and spend at least some time each week in church activities."*

Chapter 5

Comments on these answers:

While all of these responses could be expanded on, they should give you an idea of the types of approaches you can take with your own answers. The message you want to give is that your personal situation will not hurt your ability to work and, indeed, could help it. If your personal life does disrupt your work, expect most employers to lose patience quickly. It is not their problem, nor should it be.

Handling Obvious and Not-So-Obvious "Problems"

Most job seekers have at least one problem that they fear will cause an employer to respond negatively. Some of these are obvious, that is, they can be seen by an employer during an interview; others are not so obvious but are the sort of thing an employer might not be enthusiastic about. How you handle these or similar problems will depend on the situation. Many employers will not react in the way you expect and will give you a fair chance. They will be interested in your ability to do the job you seek. Your task is to convince them that your problem will not be an issue.

In forming your answer, consider if the problem affects your ability to do the work you seek. If it is a serious limitation or safety hazard, you should consider this in your selection of a position and consider changing your job objective. This does not necessarily mean you need to change careers, but it does mean that you should look for a position where the limitation is not serious. For example, a person with a prison record should not seek a job as a bank teller. A person with seizures should not paint tall houses. A person with back problems should not dig ditches or lift boxes.

Avoid Being Screened Out Early

Assuming your job objective is reasonable, you may continue to be concerned that you won't be seriously considered because of your problem. In such a situation you should use job search techniques that don't require you to reveal it too early.

If the problem is obvious or comes up in the interview, deal with it. Use the standard Three-Step Process to answering an interview question. If the problem is not obvious and won't seriously affect your ability to do the job, don't bring it up. Do not discuss your problem unless you fear you will eventually lose your job if it is found out. Wait until you have received or are negotiating a job offer. Too many job seekers reveal a problem on an application when they could have simply left the space blank. Too many bring up a problem that is not a problem at all in a preliminary interview ("I want you to know, madam, that a great aunt, once removed, had some odd habits.") Save your secret until after they like you and want to hire you and perhaps even then keep it private forever.

Some time ago, I was helping a man to find a job who used a wheelchair. He wanted to work as a dispatcher. This position required use of his voice and his mind but not his legs and was a good job objective for him. Yet employers were often unwilling to hire him and I think the wheelchair probably was an issue. I helped him learn to get interviews by using the phone rather than filling out applications. Employers had no idea he was in a wheelchair until he came for the interview. He was direct about the problem and said he got there and getting to work on time would simply not be an issue with him if he were hired. In fact, he pointed out that having a good job was MORE important to him than to most people and that he intended to make sure that his being in a wheelchair would not be an issue. He then presented his skills and abilities to do the job. His approach forced the employer to focus on his ability to do the job rather than the fact that he was in a wheelchair. He got the job and was still there years later.

Some Topics That Should Not Be an Issue— But Sometimes Are

Employers are people. They often want to know things about your personal situation that you may think they have no right to know. Or perhaps you wonder whether an employer will treat you differently because of your status or some other factor that should not affect your ability to do the job. For example, the following topics are sometimes an issue, even though they shouldn't be.

- ✓ Age
- ✓ Arrest record
- ✓ Disabilities or limitations
- ✓ Being unemployed
- ✓ Being fired
- ✓ High earnings in a previous job
- ✓ Being overweight
- ✓ Gender
- ✓ Race or ethnicity
- ✓ "Too much" education or experience for the position being sought
- ✓ Religion
- ✓ Your plans to have children
- ✓ Recent graduate

I review these and other issues in Chapter 16, always trying to give you a productive way to deal with them. There are laws that are designed to protect you from being treated unfairly in the hiring process and you will learn more about these in Chapter 16. But the more important issue is how you can overcome whatever obstacle may be put before you so that you can get the best job you can handle. That is what this book is really about.

Chapter 5

Some Final Interview Tips

You can't prepare for everything that might happen in an interview, but you will find that interviewing for jobs before they are advertised will be much easier and more comfortable than the traditional interview setting because there is less pressure on the employer to qualify you as a job candidate and less pressure on you to fit a specific job need. But whatever interview you find yourself in, remember to be yourself and tell the employer why she or he should hire you. Tell the truth, present your skills, and tell them why you want this job—and why they should hire you over someone else.

You are now much better prepared to do well in the interview than most job seekers. And, if you read the rest of this book, you will be even better prepared.

Quick Summary

The top 10 problem interview questions are

1. Why don't you tell me about yourself?

2. Why should I hire you?

3. What are your major strengths?

4. What are your major weaknesses?

5. What sort of pay do you expect to receive?

6. How does your previous experience relate to the jobs we have here?

7. What are your plans for the future?

8. What will your former employers (or teachers, if you are a recent student) say about you?

9. Why are you looking for this sort of position and why here?

10. Why don't you tell me about your personal situation?

   ✓ Keep the focus in your answers to questions to job-related topics and avoid getting too deeply into personal issues.

   ✓ Emphasize your strengths and be positive, even when describing a weakness or difficult past work experience.

CHAPTER 6

JIST Cards®—
A Powerful New Job Search Tool

═══Quick Overview

In this chapter, I review the following:

✔ JIST Cards—a powerful job search tool

✔ Seven things a JIST Card does

✔ How to use JIST Cards

✔ Why JIST Cards work so well

✔ Tips for creating JIST Cards

✔ Adapting JIST Cards for use with e-mail and electronic resumes

Many years ago I developed the idea of a small card that presents the basic information an employer needs about a prospective employee. I named them JIST Cards, and they have been used by many thousands of job search programs and individuals since.

Many people find it helpful to think of these as a mini resume or as a special type of business card for job seekers. While both analogies are descriptive, a JIST Card is a far more useful and effective job search tool than a resume and provides more information and impact than a business card.

I have included JIST Cards in the first part of the book because they are such an effective job search tool.

Let's Begin with Your Reaction to One

The best way to understand the impact of a JIST Card is to look at and react to one. I've provided a sample JIST Card on this page but, before you look at it, try to imagine that you are an employer who hires or supervises people with similar skills. While you may or may not have a job opening right now, try to react to the information presented as you would be likely to if you were an employer in a hiring situation. Simply react naturally when you read what follows.

Sandy Zaremba

Voice Message: 232-9213

E-Mail: SandyZ@time.net

Position Desired: General Office/Office Management

More than two years' work experience plus one year of training in office practices. Excellent word processing and language skills; can operate accounting systems including posting to general ledger, get along well with others. Trained and supervised a group of five office staff who handled a 27% increase in business with no additional staff expenses. Meet deadlines and work well under pressure. Good spreadsheet and other computer skills.

Willing to work any hours

Organized, honest, reliable, and hard working

What Was Your Reaction?

Don't get too analytical about this, just note how you reacted as the JIST Card information was presented to you with your "employer" hat on. With that mindset, answer the questions that follow:

1. Do you feel good about this person and how she presented herself? (yes or no)

2. Would you be willing to see her if you had a job opening? (yes, no, or maybe)

3. If she asked, would you be willing to see her even if you did not have a job opening? (yes, no, or maybe)

It's Amazing, But Most People Are Willing to Set Up an Interview with Just 30 Seconds of Information

The odds are good that you reacted positively to this JIST Card. Most people can read a typical JIST Card in fewer than 30 seconds. Yet, in that short period of time, most people react in a positive way to what they read. I know because I constantly survey those who attend seminars I give and over 95 percent react positively to reading their first JIST Card. In fact, most people who read a JIST Card say they would interview such a person—based on just this much information.

A few people do react negatively to the sample JIST Card you just read, saying that it does not present enough information or that the person sounds *too* good. It is true that a JIST Card is not information rich. It certainly does not give enough information to hire someone—but neither does a resume, application, or any other job search tool I know of.

Seven Things a JIST Card Does

My observation is that a JIST Card's brevity is one of its major strengths.

It is the only job search tool I know of that can accomplish all of the following:

1. Creates a positive first impression

2. Provides specific details related to the job seeker's skills and credentials

3. Presents performance-related information in a memorable way

4. Is an effective tool for networking and for generating job leads

5. Predisposes most readers to consider giving the job seeker an interview

6. Provides information that can be presented or read in under 30 seconds

7. Is easy to present in person, by mail, or electronically

A Brief History of How JIST Cards Were First Developed

JIST Cards are clearly a different and nontraditional type of tool in the job search. Before I review why I think they work so well, let me tell you how I originally discovered their power.

I developed JIST Cards in response to a need I saw when running job search programs 30 years ago. Back then there wasn't as much information on job seeking as there is now. In those days sending out resumes, responding to want ads, filling out applications, and getting referrals from state and private employment agencies were the major tools of the job search (and, unfortuately, remain the tools for many uninformed job seekers today). I was running a job search program and noticed that the traditional tools did not work well.

Sending out lots of resumes, for example, netted few responses. Filling out applications was a process that took a lot of time but resulted in few interviews. Furthermore, the jobs available from the employment agencies were depressingly low skilled and entry level. I thought there had to be a better way.

I had been sending job seekers in my program out to knock on potential employers' doors without appointments, and a number of job seekers were getting jobs this way. Most employers they visited were in small businesses that had no human resource department and no applications. The jobs sought (such as auto mechanic, factory worker, and food service worker) did not typically require resumes. So I suggested to the job seekers to leave a 3-by-5 inch card with their name, job objective, and credentials for the job. I also had them include my office phone number, which was professionally answered 24 hours a day. Those first JIST Cards were handwritten.

The reaction was impressive and immediate. Within days, I began to get calls asking for one of my job seekers who had dropped in to see an employer a few days earlier. It seemed that, while the employer did not have an opening at that time, he or she did now. The employer wondered if the person who had dropped in and left the card would call as soon as possible. This happened over and over and a surprising number of people landed jobs as a result. I paid attention to these results and kept track of the data.

As the weeks went by, I began getting calls from employers for job seekers who had dropped in weeks or even months earlier. They now had a job opening and wanted to know if the job seeker who had left the card was still available. Often that individual had already found a job, but I could usually send out someone else. I learned from these employers that they had been impressed by the cards and the people who had left them behind. The employers liked the fact that these job seekers seemed more assertive, were clear about why they wanted this particular type of job, and communicated the skills they had to accomplish it. They also told me that the cards were interesting and, because they didn't know what to do with them, because they did not file easily like a resume or application, they had put them on their bulletin board or just left them on their desks. Weeks later, when they needed someone to fill an opening, those cards were still lying around.

Hmmm. Based on this, I began refining the cards by adding more details related to skills, experience, and credentials. Because they worked so well, I also produced several hundred of the cards for each person in the program so that they could pass them out freely. Phone calls from employers looking for those who had dropped off those early cards came rolling in. I received many good leads this way from contacts others had made, and many job seekers got jobs from these leads. Almost all of these jobs had not been advertised, and nobody using conventional job search methods seemed to be aware of them.

It did not take long for me to know that these cards were a different and very effective new job search tool. I wanted them to have a unique name and used the name of the job search program I developed, called JIST, for Job Information and Seeking Training. And that was how "JIST Cards" were named, in case you wondered. Over the years they have been used by countless people, put into many formats, and adapted for use in many industries and jobs, from entry level to executive and professional. They are used in creative paper and electronic forms in ways I could not imagine when I started using them. And now it is your turn to think of new ways to use JIST Cards in your own job search.

Some Ways You Can Use a JIST Card

JIST Cards can help you get results in a way no other job search tool can. I have seen them posted on a grocery store bulletin board in Texas and on a table at a hairstylist's salon in southern California. I've even had friends tell me they found them under their windshield wiper after going to a movie.

While JIST Cards were originally printed, they have been adapted to be used in electronic form as e-mail attachments and in other ways I'll present to you soon.

Chapter 6

Here are just some of the ways you can use JIST Cards:

✓ **Give to friends and relatives.** The odds are that the people who know you best could not describe what you can do as clearly as the information provided on a JIST Card. Give some cards to the people you know best and ask them to circulate them to others who might know of openings for someone with your skills. Friends and relatives are a major source of job leads, and you can quickly get hundreds of your cards into circulation this way. This can expand your network and increase your results dramatically.

✓ **As a business card.** As with a business card, you can give your JIST Card to almost anyone you meet during the time you are looking for a job. One example was a job seeker who gave a handful of JIST Cards to her insurance agent who put them in the waiting room where customers could see them. This resulted in several phone calls from employers and one job offer. This is an excellent way to equip your network contacts with a tool that they can use to help you.

✓ **As an e-attachment or e-signature.** You can attach your JIST Card like an electronic business card to your e-mails, resumes, and other correspondence. You can use color and fonts to make them appear as interesting or professional as you like.

✓ **Send to an employer before an interview.** Think about it. Send an informal note thanking someone for setting up an interview with you and enclose a JIST Card. You can also do this online as an attachment. You provide just enough information to arouse their interest.

✓ **Enclosed with a thank-you note after an interview or phone contact.** Sending an informal thank-you note is simply good manners. Enclosing a JIST Card is good sense. You will learn that a quick e-mail thank you followed by your formal thank you card sent via regular mail is an effective way to follow up. Include your JIST Card with both these communications. It's just one more way to tell prospective employers about yourself and give them a tool for contacting you. I know that this approach often has resulted in the person sending the thank-you note getting the job, even over those with better credentials.

✓ **Attached to an application.** While completing applications is not an effective job search approach for most people, when you are required to complete one, attaching a JIST Card will allow the viewer to quickly get a positive overall impression. It can't hurt. This is true of online applications as well. A JIST Card will separate you from other candidates.

✓ **Attached to a resume.** Unlike a resume, you can read a JIST Card in 30 seconds. It provides a clear and direct presentation of what you want and what you can do. It can also help give readers a positive perception of you as they get into the details of your resume. Again, if you are sending your resume online or posting it on a Web site, include your JIST Card in electronic form.

✓ **As the basis for a telephone presentation.** With just a few changes, the JIST Card can be easily adapted to use as a telephone script for obtaining interviews. I'll show you how this is done in Chapter 14.

✓ **As a source for answering interview questions.** Small as it is, a well-prepared JIST Card includes key information you can use as the basis for answering interview questions. For example, in response to the question "Why don't you tell me about yourself?" you might say, "You might want to know that I am a hard worker." Then go on to provide an example of a situation where your hard work got results. Or you can select almost any key skill, experience, or accomplishment statement from your JIST Card and use it as the basis for answering many interview questions.

Although the JIST Card is an effective job search tool, I believe that its greatest value is the way it forces us to get to the essence of what we have to offer an employer. It can foster a sense of identity and self-definition that comes through in an interview. I have seen it happen and know this to be true.

People have found very creative ways to use their JIST Cards, and I encourage you to do so as well. I will mention them from time to time elsewhere in this book as a tool to use in combination with other job search techniques, and you will think of other uses that I may not specifically mention.

For example, in Chapter 2, I suggest that you develop a list of groups of people you know, and then use JIST Cards as a potential source of job leads. One such group would be "people I went to school with." With that in mind, consider what might happen if you got the alumni list from your high school or college and sent ten JIST Cards to each person on that list along with a letter asking them to help you out. You can obtain many of these lists easily online and some include e-mail addresses. Send an e-mail to the list and ask them to forward an attached electronic JIST Card to others who might know of an opening. Think about the potential leads and contact possibilities.

Seven Reasons JIST Cards Work So Well

Over the years, I have been continually surprised at how well JIST Cards work and I have some thoughts on why this is true.

1. **They are short:** Because it takes less than 30 seconds to read, a JIST Card typically holds the reader's complete attention without interruption. Resumes, letters, applications, and conversations are unable to do this without distraction or the mind wandering. Because they are short, they are "polite" and to the point in such a way that few will react negatively to the presentation.

2. **They are clear:** A JIST Card communicates its purpose, getting to the point quickly and efficiently.

3. **They create a positive impression:** While a well-done resume or application can also create a positive impression, they take longer to do so and often provide details that can be interpreted negatively (such as not having the "right" credentials, training, or experience). A well-prepared JIST Card includes nothing that could be interpreted negatively and most readers are left with a positive (though admittedly general) first impression.

4. **They foster networking:** Because of their size and brevity, JIST Cards are far more likely to be passed along to another person than a resume or application. For this reason, they become a tool used by others in your network in ways that more traditional approaches never could. JIST Cards generate job leads in the networked job market more effectively than any other job search tool I know of. Put a hundred of them in the right hands, and they do get around in unexpected ways. This is also true when attached electronically to e-mail or other correspondence, which can instantly be forwarded around the country or world.

5. **They are hard to file:** Resumes and applications are filed, thrown away, or lost in a pile. JIST Cards are less likely to be handled that way because of their format. Their small size also makes them easier to put on a bulletin board or in some location where they can be seen. They are also saved in e-contact files or printed for future reference.

6. **They help you to be remembered:** While I have been teaching people about JIST Cards for many years, this is a very big country and they are still new to most employers. The novelty of the format is memorable in itself, but the content of a well-crafted JIST Card is also easily remembered by an employer. This is particularly true when included with a thank-you note. This unique touch tends to help an employer remember (and be positively impressed by) one person or job candidate over another.

7. **They present the essence of what an employer wants to know.** While short, a typical JIST Card is packed with information designed to do the following:

- ✓ Introduce you by name

- ✓ Present various ways to contact you via phone, e-mail, or voice messaging

- ✓ Clearly state your job objective

- ✓ Summarize your key credentials, including relevant training and experience

- ✓ Present the most important skills you have for the job, often including specific examples, accomplishments, and numbers to support your claim to these skills

- ✓ Provide other strong qualities you possess, such as a willingness to relocate or work weekends

- ✓ Summarize important adaptive skills, personality traits, or other characteristics that make you a good choice for the job you seek

- ✓ A well-written JIST Card does not present any negatives that could be used to eliminate you from consideration!

A JIST Card does not replace a resume. Instead, it is a tool to empower you in an immediate and positive way. I think that its proven effectiveness to help you generate leads in the networked job market (the hidden job market) is justification enough for its use.

Tips on Creating Your Own JIST Card

There is no doubt that the JIST Card is an effective tool in the job search. Employers respond positively to JIST Cards and they can be used in ways a traditional resume cannot. But you may also find that they are more difficult to create than they at first appear. The reason for this is the fact that they are sophisticated in their simplicity.

Quick Tip

If you have not done your homework, JIST Cards can be quite difficult to write. For example, you need to have a clear idea of your job objective and the skills that best support it. A number of chapters in this book will help you develop the information a JIST Card requires.

If you need to begin your job search at once, create a basic JIST Card now and update it later, when you have better information.

In order to create a good JIST Card you must know yourself very well, know what sort of positions you are looking for, and be able to sort through your personal information to find the few words that best describe your ability to do that job

Chapter 6

well. If there are several different jobs that you are qualified for and would consider working in, I suggest you make more than one JIST Card. This is also true for your resume. You should have resumes designed for the different types of positions you are considering. It is also essential that every statement on your JIST Card be both accurate and true. Copying someone else's just won't do.

Writing an effective JIST Card may require some time on your part. The tips that follow should help you create each section of the card. As you assemble your own card, ask others for feedback before you create your final version.

The Anatomy of a JIST Card

John Kijek

Message: (219) 637-6643
E-mail: JKijek@time.net

Identification

Contact Information

Position desired: Management position in a small-to medium-size organization.

Job Objective

Skills: B.A. in business plus over five years experience, including promotions to increasingly responsible management positions. Have supervised as many as 12 staff and increased productivity by 27 percent over two years. Was promoted twice in the past three years and have excellent references. Started customer follow-up program that increased sales by 22 percent within 12 months. Get along well with others and am a good team worker. Computer literate.

Skills Summary

Willing to travel and available to work any hours

Hardworking, self-motivated, readily accept responsibility

A JIST Card doesn't contain many details, but consider what John Kijek's card does include:

- ✓ **Identification:** A simple courtesy, John's name is given.
- ✓ **A Way to Be Contacted:** Few employers will write, so a phone number and an e-mail address are provided. A cell number or other way to reach the job seeker quickly can also be provided if appropriate. This approach makes sure that John will get every call.
- ✓ **Related Education and Training:** John's JIST Card includes his education related to the job he desires.
- ✓ **Length of Experience:** John lists his total length of work experience as well as the fact that he was promoted several times in his previous jobs.

✓ **Skills and Accomplishments:** This section tells about John's skills and accomplishments. He mentions key job-related skills, as well as several important transferable skills such as his ability to supervise others and get results. Note that he uses numbers to quantify his accomplishments.

✓ **Preferred Working Conditions:** Saying that he is willing to travel and will work any hours are both positives that indicate he is flexible and willing to do whatever is needed.

✓ **Good Worker Traits:** In the last line, John lists his adaptive skills that would be important to most employers.

What's more, he does all this on a 3-by-5 inch card! If you didn't see it you may not have believed it possible to do all this in such a small format, but there it is.

Suggestions for Completing Each Section of Your JIST Card

Here are brief suggestions for completing each section of your own JIST Card. Plan on writing several drafts before you write your final version.

Your name

Don't use nicknames or initials if possible. Keep it simple and don't include your middle name unless you go by that name.

Phone numbers

Remember that an employer will probably not call you twice, so make sure that you have a phone number that will be answered reliably 24 hours a day. Always include your area code—you never know where your cards will end up.

Some people do not like leaving a message on an answering machine, so include the word "messages" on your JIST Card to make it clear that the caller is not likely to speak with you directly. If you use an answering machine or voicemail service, make sure the message is professional and easy to understand. If children or others at home may answer the phone, train them to answer calls professionally, and be certain that they know how to take good notes. Instruct them to repeat the name and phone number of the caller so that they get it right. Write "cell phone" on your JIST Card if you are have one, so the caller knows he or she may reach you directly in a variety of settings.

E-mail address

Many employers prefer to contact you via e-mail, so include one on your card. Make certain the address you use sounds professional; it may make sense to set up a separate address just for your job search messages.

If you are currently employed, do not use your work e-mail address. Doing so makes you look less professional because no employer would want you to use work time for job hunting. Instead, set up a personal e-mail account through your Internet service provider. Yahoo.com and other sites offer free e-mail addresses, so get one if you need one.

Job objective

Don't be too narrow in your job objective. Avoid job titles by saying "general office" rather than "office manager," "accounting" rather than "controller," or "data processing" rather than "Programmer" if you would consider taking a variety of jobs. If you are more specific in your job objective, try to avoid a job title but give other details. For example, say "management position in an insurance-related business" or "working with children in a medical or educational setting."

Don't limit yourself to entry-level jobs if you have the potential or interest in doing more. If you say "office manager," instead of "office worker," or "business manager" instead of "supervisor," you just might get the better job. If you are not sure of your ability to get a higher paying job, it is still wise to keep your options open. Say "office manager" or "responsible office position," for example.

Other chapters in this book will help you explore career and job possibilities. If you aren't sure of what to include in your JIST Card's job objective, look at that content to help you decide what to include on your JIST Card.

Length of experience

You want to maximize all your experience that supports your job objective. If you are changing careers, have been out of the work world for awhile, or do not have much work experience related to the job you seek, you may want to include other experiences to convince the employer you can do the job. Depending on your situation, here are some examples of what you might include as work-related experience:

Paid Work. You can list any work you were paid to do. Experience related to the job you are seeking is best, and should be emphasized if you have it. However, the work does not have to be similar to the job being sought. Working in a fast-food establishment while you attended school counts, and so does a job in an unrelated career.

Volunteer Work. You can include volunteer work as part of your total experience. This is especially true if you don't have much paid work experience. The fact that you did not get paid for what you did is not all that relevant and does not need to be mentioned at this point.

Informal Work. If your paid work history is weak, you can also include work you did at home or as an unpaid hobby. It is best if this work relates to the job, but it doesn't have to. For example, if you worked on cars at home and want to be an auto mechanic, there is an obvious connection. You may have experience working in the family business or taking care of children.

Related Education and Training. Any formal or informal training or education that might help you should be mentioned. Job-related classes in high school, in the military, in college, or any other setting can be used.

To figure out your total experience, complete the following table. Write either years (or months, if you don't have much experience) in the spaces beside each question.

Your Total Experience Includes:

1. Total paid work experience: _____

2. Total volunteer work experience: _____

3. Total informal work experience: _____

4. Total related education or training: _____

   Total Experience: _____

Other tips for writing your experience statement

Because everyone has a different background, I can't give you a single rule for writing a good experience statement. However, here are some tips for writing your own experience statement.

If you have a great deal of work experience: If part of your work experience is not related to the job you seek, you can omit it. For example, if you have 20 years of experience, but not all of that is relevant, say "Over 15 years of work experience" or include just the experience that directly relates to this job. This keeps the employer from guessing how old you are, should you be concerned about this.

If you don't have much paid work experience: You need to include everything possible. If you have no paid work experience in the field you want to work in, emphasize training and other work experience. For example, "Nearly two years of experience, including one year of advanced training in office procedures."

Remember to include the total of all paid and unpaid work as part of your total experience. Include all those part-time and volunteer jobs by saying "Over 18 months total work experience."

If your experience is in another field: Just mention that you have "Four years work experience" without saying in what.

If you had raises and promotions: If you earned promotions, raises, or have other special strengths, this is the time to say it. For example, "Over seven years of increasingly responsible work experience, including three years as a supervisor. Promoted twice."

Eliminate or combine your statement: Depending on your situation, you can combine your education and training with your experience statements. If a lack of formal training or education might hurt your chances, don't mention it at all. If you have a license, certification, or degree that supports your job objective, you can also combine it with your experience statement. For example: "Four years of experience plus two years of training leading to certification as an Emergency Medical Technician."

Skills and accomplishments section

Think about the skills you have that are most important for the position you want. This is the section where both transferable and job-related skills are mentioned. Use the language of the job to describe the more important skills you possess. Be sure to quantify this with numbers to strengthen your case. For example, instead of saying "computer skills" you might say "proficient in word processing (accurately type 70+ words per minute), spreadsheets, and Internet research." You might mention your ability to use any important job-related equipment, software programs, or other job-related skills you have.

Several chapters in Section 1 of this book can help you identify skills to emphasize in your JIST Card. Chapter 3 does a thorough job in identifying the adaptive and transferable skills you have, while Chapter 9 helps you identify job-related skills and accomplishments.

Be sure to emphasize results. It is too easy to overlook the importance of what you do unless you organize it correctly. Add up the numbers of transactions you handled in a previous job, the money you were responsible for, and the results you obtained. Include numbers to support your results. Here are some examples:

✓ A salesperson might say "Expanded sales territory to include over seven new states and increased sales by $1,500,000."

✓ A person with fast-food experience might write "Handled over 50,000 customer contacts with total sales over $375,000, quickly and accurately." (These figures are based on a five-day week, 200 customers a day for one year, and an average sale of $7.50.)

✓ Someone who ran a small store could say "Responsible for managing a business with over $310,000 in sales per year. Reduced staff turnover by 50 percent by introducing employee training and retention program."

✓ Present a successful fund-raising project as: "Planned, trained, and supervised a staff of six on a special project. Exceeded income projections by 40 percent."

Also include in this section one or more of your transferable skills that are important for that position. A manager might mention "Ability to train and supervise others," and an office worker might add "Professional appearance and pleasant telephone voice." Try to quantify these statements with numbers that support these skills. A warehouse manager might say, "Well-organized and efficient. Have reduced expenses by 20 percent while orders increased by 55 percent."

Preferred working conditions, flexibility, or other positive information

This is an optional section of your JIST Card. You can add a few words to let the employer know what you are willing to do. Do not limit your employment possibilities by saying, "Will only work days" or "No travel." It is better to omit this than to include anything negative. Look at the sample JIST Cards for ideas. Then write your own statement.

Adaptive skills/good worker traits

List three or four of your key adaptive skills. Choose skills that are important in the job you are seeking. You identified these skills in Chapter 3.

JIST Card Writing and Production Tips

The best way to write a JIST Card is to begin with longer versions until your content is acceptable, then edit, edit, edit. When you are working with such a small format, every word has to count. Use short, sentences or bullet statements. Delete any word that does not directly support your job objective. Add more information if your JIST Card is too short.

✓ **Make it error free:** After you have edited your content, have others look at it to help you identify any errors or suggest improvements to consider. Read your card out loud to yourself and others to see how it sounds.

It is amazing how many errors slip onto these little cards. Employers will notice such errors and it will NOT create a positive impression, so make sure your final version is absolutely error free.

✓ **Decide on a size and format:** While a 3-by-5 inch card is a standard format, JIST Cards have been done in many creative formats. For example, they can be made the size of a business card, or folded over to have some information on the cover—like your name, job objective, and contact information—and other details on the inside. Or they could be the size of a thank-you note, or any other creative format that makes sense to you.

Chapter 6

You can include graphics, interesting fonts and colors. E-mail attachments in electronic form have lots of possible format options. You can use your creativity here, but keep in mind you have less than 30 seconds to make the JIST Card impression so you should keep the card design professional, clean, and easy to read. I suggest you start with a simple 3-by-5 inch format so you can begin to use it quickly, and then develop fancier formats later in your job search.

✓ **Use light card stock:** With minor adjustments, you can use your computer printer to print four 3-by-5 size JIST Cards on one standard sheet of 8½-by-11 inch page. Use light card stock in a conservative ivory or off-white color. You can buy this stock at most office supply stores. You can also get special pre-perforated card stock that allows you to print out on 3-by-5 inch card stock and then tear off separate cards.

✓ **Make lots of copies:** If you have a computer and good printer, you can print your JIST Cards yourself. But, even if you do, consider taking your final version to a local print shop and have them print and cut at least a few hundred of the cards. You can also have them photocopied on light card stock for a reasonable price at many quick print shops. Good quality printing is essential to help you make a good impression, so don't use cheap paper or poor-quality printing.

✓ **Consider online business card services:** There are many free and low cost online printing services for business cards that charge only shipping costs. They provide various formats. You supply the text and choose the style of card. To find such a site, do a simple word search for "free business cards" online.

✓ **If you don't have your own computer:** If you don't have your own computer and printer, you still have options. Many print shops can "typeset" your JIST Cards for a modest fee, and it is usually worth the money to get a professional appearance. Many libraries also have computers and printers you can use. If you are not experienced with word processing and basic design, however, I suggest you pay a local print shop to layout and print your JIST Cards.

✓ **Electronic formats:** Many people don't want to open e-mail attachments because they are afraid of viruses. So consider creating a text-based JIST Card that can be included in your e-mail message itself. You can make it look a bit better by adding lines and other simple design elements, or you could include it as a graphic file that is viewed as part of the e-mail, with fancier formats, if you know how to do this.

I have seen a variety of creative formats over the years, including business-sized cards, cards printed on both sides, folded cards with name and phone number on the front and other information inside, different ink colors, fancy printed papers, gold-embossed printing, and other features. I liked some of these approaches but not all, so be as creative as you wish in your design, but do use good taste. Remember that the JIST Card's message is simple, and the design should complement the message and not compete with it.

You might also want to consider coordinating the look of your JIST Card so that it matches your resume and stationery. You can use the same paper colors and textures, same ink color, and similar design elements.

More Tips for Using JIST Cards on the Web

If you are currently employed and do not want your employer to know you are looking, be very careful about putting your information on the Web. You can quickly lose control of what you e-mail or post online, and your current employer can become aware of your search for another job. Consider this as you review the tips that follow, which are less of a problem for people who are unemployed or, for other reasons, not worried about their employers knowing that they are looking for a job.

Create a personal Web site: Most ISP's (Internet Service Providers, such as AOL and MSN) allow you to create a simple personal Web site as well as providing you with an e-mail address. If this service is available to you, this is a great place to post a JIST Card as well as a detailed resume. You can note your personal Web page address on your JIST Card and resume and encourage employers to go there for more information.

JIST Cards or resumes can be created with tools provided by your ISP in HTML (Hyper Text Mark-up Language). This is an inexpensive approach to designing online content and is generally included in monthly Internet account fees. A limitation with this type of simple Web site is that most employers you are not in contact with will not find it unless you arrange to establish links to it from various career or industry-related sites.

Post your information on one or more of the large online employment sources such as Monster.com and Hotjobs: While this is more appropriate for your resume than your JIST Card, you can post both on one or more of the many Web sites that accept them. Most of these postings are free to job seekers and allow employers who are looking for your particular qualifications to find your information. Although these sites are not, by definition, a personal Web site, you are likely to have more unsolicited exposure using this resource than you will when posting your information through your Internet Service Provider because these job sites are referenced through links on many career-related sites and on search engines.

Chapter 6

Create your own Web site: A more complex option is to create your own Web site and include on it your JIST Card, resume, and any other information or samples of your work you think will be of interest to an employer. This option makes sense if you have experience in creating Web sites or have visual skills, such as art, graphic design, video, or Web design that are best demonstrated on such a site.

To create your own Web site you need to register your site name for about $100 a year (go to sites such as www.DomainsNext.com or Register4Less.com to find out how this is done). You will need to know how to use Web page development software to design the site, or pay someone else to do it for you.

But having your own site does have advantages. For one, you can tag key words and register with search engines to allow employers using those search engines to find your Web site. For example, if you are a nuclear engineer residing in the state of Washington, you would tag the words "nuclear," "engineer," and "Washington" as key words. A prospective employer using one of the major search engines such as Yahoo, Google, or Excite and typing in the combination words "nuclear," "engineer," and "Washington" could find your Web site and online resume if you have registered your key words with those sites (however, keep in mind that some levels of registration with search engines do require a fee). Many employers will include area codes in their key word search, so tag your area code in addition to specific skill key words when creating a Web page.

A major limitation to this approach is that there may be hundreds of nuclear engineers in Washington, and you may get lost in the shuffle. However, there are two ways to increase the chances of your information being listed near the top of a search engine's list of nuclear engineers in Washington. First, you can pay a fee to the search engine companies for this service. Second, there are companies who specialize in making sure your key words are listed in the top ten hits. They charge a fee of course, but will get you ahead of the pack.

JIST Cards Work If You Work Them

JIST Cards work best if you have hundreds of them in circulation, so it is essential that you don't just create them, but **use them!** Give them away freely because they will not help you get a job if they sit on your desk. Have a few hundred available at all times and keep some with you to give away as opportunities to do so present themselves. Work up an electronic version that you can cut and paste into your e-mails, plus an e-mail attachment with more sophisticated formatting that can be printed by the receiver. Get some ready to go now, even if the first ones you do are pretty simple; you can create more elaborate ones later. I say this because JIST Cards work so well that you should start using them right away.

More Sample JIST Cards

Here are some more sample JIST Cards. To fit this book's page size, they do not appear as 3-by-5 cards and vary from those for entry-level jobs (for persons just out of school) to those for professionals and other occupations. Study them and feel free to use any ideas here that help you to create your own card.

Thomas Marrin

Cell phone: (716) 223-4705   **E-mail:** tmarrin@techconnect.com

Objective: Business management position requiring skills in problem solving, planning, organizing, and cost management.

Skills: Bachelor's degree in Business Administration and over ten years of management experience in progressively responsible positions. Managed as many as 40 staff and budgets in excess of $6 million a year. Consistent record of getting results. Excellent communication skills. Thorough knowledge of budgeting, cost savings, and computerized database and spreadsheet programs. Enjoy challenges, meet deadlines, and accept responsibility.

Willing to relocate.

Results-oriented, self-motivated, good problem-solving skills, energetic.

Lisa Marie Rhodes

E-mail: MLRhodes@earthlink.net

Phone: (424) 351-5935

Position desired: Internet startup or other Web-based business

Actively involved in intensive computer use and Web site development for more than four years. Familiar with all major software used in designing e-commerce Web sites, including graphics, interactive databases, credit card transactions and SQL, as well as firewall, encryption and other security schemes. Excellent writing, grammar, and design skills. Did entire programming and design of a business-to-business e-commerce site and, over 12 months ago, grew site to annual sales of $780,000 before the company went public.

Will consider contract work.

I work quickly and am persistent in finding solutions to complex problems.

Peter Neely

Messages: (237) 649-1234   *Beeper:* (237) 766-9876

Position: Short or Long-Distance Truck Driver

Background and Skills: Over fifteen years of stable work history including no traffic citations or accidents. Formal training in diesel mechanics and electrical systems. Familiar with most major destinations and have excellent map-reading and problem-solving abilities. I can handle responsibility and have a track record of getting things done.

Excellent health, good work history, dependable.

Sandy Zaremba

Home: (512) 232-7608   **Cell:** (420) 405-9099
Message: (512) 234-7465   **E-mail:** Szare@cpmt.net

Position Desired: General Office/Clerical

Skills: Over two years work experience plus one year of training in office procedures. Keyboard 55 wpm; trained in Word, Excel, and other programs; post general ledger; handle payables, receivables, and most accounting tasks. Good interpersonal skills and team player. Work well under pressure and deadlines.

Willing to work any hours.

Organized, honest, reliable, and hardworking.

Joyce Hua

Home: (214) 173-1659
Cell: (420) 440-2255
E-mail: JHua@del.org

Position Desired: Systems Analyst and Designer

Skills: Over 10 years combined education and experience in DBMS: database systems and design. Competent in programming in C++, Java, and DHTML, and database management on Windows, Linux, and other computer platforms. Extensive PC and network applications experience. Supervised staff as large as seven on special projects and have a record of meeting deadlines. Operations management background, sales, and accounting.

Desire career-oriented position, will relocate.

Dedicated, self-starter, creative problem solver.

Paul Thomas

E-mail: Pthomas@yes.net

Home: (214) 173-1659
Message: (214) 274-1436

Position Desired: Research Chemist, Research Management in a small- to medium-size company

Skills: Ph.D. in Biochemistry plus over 15 years of work experience. Developed and patented various processes having current commercial applications worth over 5 millions of dollars. Experienced with all phases of lab work with an emphasis on chromatography, isolation and purification of organic and biochemical compounds. Specialized in practical pharmaceutical and agricultural applications of chemical research. Have teaching, supervision, and project management experience.

Personal: Married over 15 years, stable work history, results and task oriented, ambitious, and willing to relocate.

Richard Straightarrow

Home: (602) 253-9678   **Answering Service:** (602) 257-6643

E-mail: rstarrow@future.com

Objective: Electronics installation, maintenance & sales

Skills: Four years work experience plus two year A.A. degree in Electronics Engineering Technology. Managed a $500,000/yr. business while going to school full-time, with grades in the top 25 percent. Familiar with all major electronics diagnostic and repair equipment. Hands-on experience with medical, consumer, communications, and industrial electronics equipment and applications. Good problem-solving and communication skills. Customer service oriented.

I do what it takes to get the job done right.

Self-motivated, dependable, learn quickly.

Juanita Rodriquez

Home: (639) 247-1643

Cell: (639) 361-1754

E-mail: Jrod1345@selfserve.net

Position desired: Warehouse Management

Skills: Six years experience plus 2 years of formal business coursework. Have supervised a staff as large as 16 people and warehousing operations covering over two acres and valued at over $14,000,000. Automated inventory operations resulting in a 30 percent increase in turnover and estimated annual savings over $250,000. Working knowledge of accounting, computer systems, time and motion studies, and advanced inventory management systems.

Will work any hours.

Responsible, hardworking, and can solve problems.

Deborah Levy

Home: (213) 432-8064

Cell: (213) 888-7365

Position Desired: Hotel Management

E-mail: Debi21@focus.com

Skills: Four years experience in sales, catering, and accounting in a 300 room hotel. Associate's degree in Hotel Management plus one year with the Boileau Culinary Institute. Doubled revenues from meetings and conferences. Increased dining room and bar revenues by 44 percent. Have been commended for improving staff productivity and courtesy. I approach my work with industry, imagination, and creative problem-solving skills.

Enthusiastic, well-organized, detail-oriented.

Jafar Browning

Home: (846) 299-3643

Pager: (846) 517-4525

E-mail: JMB0928@aol.com

Objective: Sales or business position requiring skills in problem solving, planning, organizing, and customer service.

Skills: Two year's experience, including coursework in business, sales methods, customer service, and business software. Promoted and received several bonuses for performance. Set record for largest single sale exceeding $130,000. Consistent record of getting results. Excellent communication skills. Familiar with database, word processing, and spreadsheet software. Internet literate. Enjoy challenges and accept responsibility.

Willing to relocate.

Results-oriented, good problem-solving skills, energetic.

≡ *Quick Summary*

✓ Things a JIST Card Does: A JIST Card's brevity is one of its major advantages. It is the only job search tool I know of that does all of the following:

1. Creates a positive first impression

2. Provides specific details related to what a job seeker can do

3. Presents performance-related information in a memorable way

4. Provides both an effective tool for generating job leads and for presenting information

5. Predisposes most readers to consider giving the job seeker an interview

6. Provides information that can be presented or read in under 30 seconds, essential for networking

✓ Some Ways You Can Use a JIST Card:

➤ Give to friends and relatives.

➤ As a business card, e-mail attachment, or e-signature.

➤ Send to an employer before an interview.

➤ Enclosed with a thank-you note after an interview or phone contact.

➤ Attached to any electronic correspondence.

➤ Posted on personal Web site or job search sites.

➤ Attached to an application.

➤ Attached to a resume.

➤ As the basis for a telephone presentation.

➤ As a source for answering interview questions.

✓ Reasons JIST Cards Work So Well:

1. They are short.

2. They are clear.

3. They create a positive impression.

4. They are easy to use for networking.

5. They are hard to file.

6. They are memorable.

7. They present the essence of what an employer wants to know.

CHAPTER 7

Organize Your Job Search Time and Follow Up to Get Results

≡≡≡*Quick Overview*

In this chapter, I review the following:

✔ How to set up your job search office

✔ How to organize your contacts

✔ How to create your job search schedule

✔ How to maximize job search efforts while continuing current responsibilities

✔ More planning and scheduling tips

It's amazing, but if you have read the previous chapters in this book, you already know more about finding a job than most people in North America. Of course, having the know-how and carrying out the action plan are two separate things. This chapter will help you develop a job search schedule and other techniques designed to structure your job search as if it were your job. This is important to do, because spending more time on your job search, in an organized way, has been proven to reduce the time it takes to get a new or better position. Using these suggestions can help you cut your job search time in half—and that is the reason I have included this information in the first section of the book.

Your Primary Objective Is to Get Two Interviews a Day

After many years of analyzing what works in the job search process, I have come to one very simple conclusion:

The more interviews you get, the sooner you will get a job offer.

This is a very simple concept, but accomplishing it seems to be a serious block for most job seekers. I observe that the major problem for most job seekers is that they don't have an organized plan. They muddle through their day without much discipline, spend too few hours actually looking for interviews, and often don't get much accomplished. In fact, the longer they remain unemployed, the less time they are likely to spend each week actually looking for a job. Clearly, this is counter productive.

Quick Fact ▥▥▶ The average job seeker gets about two interviews per week and spends fewer than 15 hours a week on the job search. At that rate, it takes an average of three to five months to find a job. The average length of time it takes to find a job is tracked by the U.S. Department of Labor. When unemployment rates are higher, it typically takes longer to find a job. For most people, three to five months is a much longer job search period than necessary.

The good news is that you don't have to be the average. After all, it's called an average because half of all people get their jobs in less than the average time.

The Two Most Important Things You Can Do to Decrease the Time Needed to Find Your Next Job

Quick Advice ☑ While it may seem almost too simple, the research indicates there are two things you can do that are likely to decrease how long it takes to get your next job:

1. Spend more time actually looking for work each week.

2. Get at least two interviews each day throughout your job search if you are unemployed, and 2–3 a week if you are under-employed.

Quick Reminder

With the new definition of an interview I am using in this book, getting those two interviews a day is quite possible. Remember, an interview can now include any face-to-face contact with a person who hires or supervises people with your skills—whether or not that person has a job opening at the moment.

While getting two interviews a day is most difficult for someone conducting a traditional job search, the methods I propose make it quite possible. If you do this one thing, there is a fairly simple arithmetic that begins to work to your advantage.

The Arithmetic of Getting Two Interviews a Day

2 interviews a day x 5 days a week = 10 interviews a week

10 interviews a week x 4 weeks = 40 interviews a month

Contrast this with the fact that the average job seeker gets fewer than one or two interviews a WEEK and takes three to five months to get a job. Two interviews a week for three months means it takes the average job seeker 24 to 40 interviews to get a job. Yet I suggest you get 40 interviews in just one month. Which job search approach is likely to work better? When you do the math, it's easy to understand how people using my approach cut their job search time by more than half.

The fact is that one secret of job search success is to devote as much time and energy to *getting* a job as you will to keeping it once you have found it. In a very real sense, getting a job *is* a job. If you approach it in this way, you are much more likely to get a job in less time. It's simple arithmetic.

Set Up Your Job Search Office

To organize your job search as if it were a job, you need a place where you can work. Usually, this will be a place in your home that you set aside as your job search office. In this section I discuss some essentials you should have to set up this office.

Even if you don't have the luxury of a home office, it is important that you set up a place where you can conduct your job search work without interruption. It is important that you concentrate on your job search work; so if you have children or other at-home responsibilities, arrange for someone else to take care of them during your "office hours." Ask for cooperation from all family members to avoid interference during your job search time.

Sometimes you'll meet with resistance. Usually if you have some system in place to reward others for respecting "your" time, they will agree, as this becomes a win-win for all. You can also look forward to the "ice cream" or "playing a game," reward, which will help you focus on getting your job seeking work done.

It is best to select a place where you can safely leave your materials and equipment so that you won't have to set up your work space every day. At the very least, you will need a table or desk to write on, a chair, and enough space to store your materials and computer or other equipment.

Basic Materials and Equipment

As you work on your job search, you will find a variety of reference materials, office supplies, and other things to help you get your work done. Here are the basics:

✓ **A telephone.** It is essential that you have access to a telephone throughout your job search. If you don't have one, set up your office in the home of a friend or relative who does.

✓ **A computer and printer**. You could conduct your job search without a computer, but it is an important tool you should have if at all possible. Your printer must create good-quality output for resumes and letters. New printers are cheap, so be sure your print output looks professional. Keep a spare ink or toner cartridge on hand, as well as good quality papers for resumes and correspondence.

✓ **Erasable ball-point pens.** I prefer black or blue ink pens, and erasable ones are helpful in correcting errors, say, on an application form.

✓ **Legal pads or other note pads.** Use these for notes and contact lists.

✓ **3-by-5 inch cards.** These can be used in a variety of ways to keep notes on each contact, write to-do notes, notes after an interview, or to organize for follow up.

✓ **A 3-by-5 inch card file box with dividers to organize your index cards.**

✓ **Thank-you notes and envelopes.**

✓ **Multiple copies of your resumes and JIST Cards.**

✓ **Business-size envelopes.** Get ones that match your resume paper if possible, as they create a better impression.

✓ **Postage stamps.** Keep a good supply of these on hand at all times.

✓ **The phone book.** Though you can get this information online, a copy of the local directory will be useful for a variety of tasks.

✓ **Calendars, planning or schedule book, PDA** (a pocket-sized "personal digital assistant"), or other electronic scheduling system.

✓ **A copy of this book**, of course.

Chapter 7

If You Don't Have a Computer

If you don't have access to a computer at home, consider buying one; new ones are increasingly inexpensive, and if money is tight, look into buying a used one. All you really need is a simple system with word processing software and a modem for Internet access.

If you really can't afford a computer, most libraries can provide free Internet access and some have computers and printers you can use.

Note this Exception: For the increasingly few who are not computer literate, this may not be the time to buy one because learning to use a computer can become a big distraction. You can get resumes done professionally at many print shops, or ask a friend to do it for you. I'll provide more details for non-computer alternatives in this and other chapters.

Organize Your Contacts and Follow Ups

By using the job search methods you have learned so far, you can quickly develop hundreds of contacts. Keeping track of them will be more than your memory can handle, and you will quickly become disorganized unless you develop a system to keep track of them.

The most important thing is that you need to develop, and then consistently use, some method to keep track of your contacts and appointments. Simple paper systems that are actually used are much more effective than sophisticated computer systems that are not.

Computerized Systems

Computer scheduling systems can be very helpful but are not essential. My earliest attempts at organizing job search contacts involved putting one page per contact in a three-ring binder. This was better than the notes I had been putting on a bulletin board to remind me to follow up on things. Review the suggestions that follow, and then adapt them to work well in your own situation.

Contact-management software

There are a variety of commercially-available contact-management software packages that are designed to assist salespeople and others to follow up on contacts. Most allow you to enter information about a contact (including name, address, and phone numbers) and then make notes related to each. These programs typically allow you to enter a follow up date for an electronic reminder to take action in some way as that date approaches. Many allow you to create form letters that can be modified and sent as needed, to sort contacts by your own criteria, and to assist you in other helpful contact-management tasks.

You will find these types of programs at virtually any software store, and they can be quite useful if you have access to a computer and are reasonably computer literate.

Personal digital assistants

A variety of manufacturers make these pocket-size computers and most come with scheduling software that allows you to create contact files, set up follow up dates and times, and handle similar tasks. They often allow you to use add-ons that offer a variety of other features, including word processing, street address mapping, calculations, and so on.

I use a PDA that allows me to update my contact information, write notes, and set up appointments or reminders on my PC, then update files on the PDA with the same information. It chimes at a time I set to remind me to do something, like leave for an interview. It also allows me to transfer files (like a JIST Card or resume) via infra-red signal to a similar PDA and many other useful things. These small machines can be very helpful in organizing your job search.

Quick Tip
If your budget is tight, go to www.palm.com. This is a site that sells reconditioned PDAs.

Resume and job search software

You can find a variety of commercially developed resume and job search software at book and software stores and Web sites. There is also some free "shareware" software you can find by entering "job search software" or similar phrases in your browser's search engine.

Resume software typically provides you with a step-by-step format for writing an acceptable resume, along with format and design templates and sample resumes. There are also software packages designed to organize your job search schedule, provide interviewing tips, and other options. Some of these packages are available as online editions for a fee, and some Web sites provide similar software for free download, although the free stuff is often of limited value.

Simple Paper Contact Management Systems Work Well, Too

There is something to be said for simplicity, and the paper system I describe here has evolved over many years of experience and works just fine. If you don't have a computer, it will serve the purpose. Even if you have computerized contact management and scheduling systems, I encourage you to read what follows. Doing so will help you adapt the principles I present here to get the most out of your computerized systems.

Job lead cards

Look at the following 3-by-5 inch card. It shows the kinds of information you can keep about each person who helps you in your job search.

Organization: Mutual Health Insurance

Contact Person: Anna Koch   **Phone:** 701-355-0216

Source of Lead: Uncle Ben   **E-mail:** Anna_Koch@healthnet.com

Notes: 4/10—called. Anna, on vacation, left message and sent e-mail with JIST Card. Call back 4/15.

4/15—interview set 4/20 at 1:30. 4/20—Anna showed me around. (friendly people). After visit I sent e-mail thank-you plus paper thank you note and JIST Card. Call back 5/1—5/1 second interview set for 5/8 at 9 a.m.!

You can hand write the same kind of information on a blank 3-by-5 inch card. You should create one card for each person you contact during your job search. Include anyone who gives you a referral, interviews you, or who is a potential employer or job contact. Add brief notes on the cards each time you talk with this contact to help you remember important details for your next encounter.

Organize your contact cards in a card file box

Most stationery stores have small boxes made to hold 3-by-5 inch cards. They also have tabbed dividers for these boxes, with room to write on the tabs. Buy an inexpensive card file box and enough dividers to set up a box divider for each day of the month, numbering them 1 through 31. Once this has been done, file each completed Job Lead Card under the date when you want to follow up. Here are some examples of how this system can be used.

Example 1: You get the name of a referral to call, but you can't get to it right away. You create a Job Lead Card and file it under tomorrow's date.

Example 2: You call someone from a referral source, but the person is busy this week and tells you to call back in two weeks. You file the Job Lead Card under the date that's exactly two weeks in the future.

Example 3: You get an interview with a person who doesn't have any openings currently, but he gives you the name of someone else who might. Send the original contact a thank-you note, then file the card under tomorrow's date if you can't follow up on the new lead today. When you reach the referral the next day, create a new card for that person and file it as needed, then file the original contact's card under a date a few weeks in the future. Now both contacts are in your system.

At the beginning of each week, review all the Job Lead Cards you filed for the week. On your weekly schedule, list any interviews or follow-up calls you promised to make on a particular time and date. At the beginning of each day, pull the Job Lead Cards filed under that date and list them on your Daily Contact Sheet (described in the following section) for that day.

As you contact more and more people in your job search, the number of people you file away for future follow-up will increase. You will develop more and more new networking leads as you follow up with people you've already contacted one or more times in the past. This is a situation where the turtle wins, for a steady and consistent approach really can generate more leads than more "sophisticated" methods. As you develop your network of contacts, it will become increasingly clear to you how important it is to have an organized system to keep track of them.

While following up is a simple concept, it does work. Remember that most people get their jobs from people they know and following up allows you to maintain these contacts in a more effective way. Once you have contacted someone, it often pays to send that person a thank-you note and then stay in touch with him or her repeatedly throughout your job search.

 Following up makes a difference and is one of the most effective ways of getting a job.

Use a daily job search contact sheet

To help you organize your daily activities, I have found that it helps to create a simple list of people you plan on contacting each day. You can create this simple form on regular lined sheets of paper. The sheet has columns as in the following example:

Daily Contact Sheet

Date _____

Contact/ Organization	Referral source	Phone/ E-mail	Notes	JL Card
Angela Alvarez, Unified Transport	Bill Theobard	cell: 786-7608 aalv@ut.com	call after 10	
Frank Pardillo, NOW Trucking	Angela Alvarez Angela's ex boss	298-6342 x 139 Frank@ntruck.com		

Quick Advice

☑ I suggest that you list at least 20 people or organizations to contact before you begin to make any phone calls each day.

Use any source to get these leads—referrals, Job Lead Cards from your card file box, potential contacts from the Internet or *Yellow Pages,* jobs listed in the newspaper want ads, warm contacts you have not yet called, and any other legitimate lead or contact. Check the Job Lead Card column on the form if you have made a card for that contact.

Establish and Stick to a Job Search Schedule

At work, I have a variety of ways that I schedule my time so that I set priorities and get high priority tasks done. When you are out of work, you don't have the structure you take for granted at work. You need to create this structure for your job search, beginning with the basics, such as how many hours a week you plan to work on your job search.

I know that setting a daily schedule may seem too basic a task to worry about, but trust me on this: Doing what I suggest in this section is important. Having a detailed schedule made out in advance makes it far more likely that, come next Tuesday, you will be productively involved in getting interviews rather than goofing off. Writing this schedule down often makes it happen.

If you are under-employed, you can't spend as much time on the job search as I suggest in this section, so adapt the approach to fit what you can do. Whatever your situation, I know that you will want to put things off, particularly things you don't like to do.

So consider scheduling your most-resisted activities early in the day. Also, if you have to choose to do one thing and not another, make sure you do the thing that is most likely to get the best results.

Begin with a Weekly Job Search Schedule

Here are five simple steps that will help you to get started in setting up your job search as a job.

Step 1: Decide how many hours per week to look

How many hours per week do you plan to spend looking for a job?

In most cases, I recommend at least 25 hours per week for a person who is looking for full-time work. An active job search is difficult work, and 40 hours per week is too much for many people. Because the average job seeker spends fewer than 15 hours per week actively looking for work, 25 hours per week is a big improvement.

Whatever you decide is fine, but you should realize that the less time you spend, the longer you are likely to be unemployed.

Write here the number of hours per week you plan to spend looking for a job: _____

Step 2: Decide which days to look

Decide which days each week you will use to look for work. Because most businesses are open Monday through Friday, consider saving these days for contacting employers. Use weekends and evenings to revise your resumes, research employers on the Web, catch up on correspondence, develop new leads, and other tasks. In the first column of the following form, check the days you plan to use for your job search. Don't mark in the other columns yet.

Weekly Planning Worksheet

Day	Number of Hours	Time
_____ Monday	_____	_____
_____ Tuesday	_____	_____
_____ Wednesday	_____	_____
_____ Thursday	_____	_____
_____ Friday	_____	_____
_____ Saturday	_____	_____
_____ Sunday	_____	_____
Total No. Hours/Week	_____	

Step 3: Decide how many hours per day to look

Decide how many hours you will spend looking for work on each of the days you selected on the Weekly Planning Worksheet. For example, if you selected Mondays, you may decide to spend five hours each Monday looking for work. You would then write "5" in the "Number of Hours" column on the form. Do this with all the days you checked until the total equals or exceeds the number of hours per week you listed in Step 1.

Step 4: Decide what times each day to look

Using the same Weekly Planning Worksheet, use the remaining "Time" column to list the times you will use each day to look for work. For example, if you decided to spend six hours each Monday looking for work, you might decide to begin at 8:00 a.m. and work till noon (4 hours), take an hour off for lunch, then work from 1:00 to 3:00 p.m. (2 hours). If you are underemployed, you might use your lunch hour to interview (confidentially) and from 5:00 to 8:00 in the evening to write e-mails and call your networking leads. Complete this section of the worksheet now, even though you may be resisting doing this.

Step 5: Transfer your job search schedule to a calendar

Transfer your schedule to a paper calendar or electronic scheduling system, and include the days and times you scheduled each day of each week to look for a job. A regular paper calendar sheet will do for this, allowing you to see your basic schedule for an entire month at a glance. I've provided a generic calendar page for you to use, although you would be better off using a larger calendar sheet with the correct preprinted dates on it.

If you prefer to use a calendar software program, look for features that allow you to print your calendar out in weekly or monthly formats, and that allow you to make changes and print revised versions easily. Try using different colors to code different types of activities such as research, interviews, and follow-up calls so you can see what the next day's activities are at a glance.

I used to use a "Day Timer" brand planning book that could fit into a pocket or purse—Franklin and other brands are similar. These types of schedule books are VERY helpful for scheduling daily appointments and to-do lists. I took mine everywhere for years and would have no idea of what my schedule would be, or how to contact someone, without it. They are superior in some ways to computerized systems and are very sensible alternatives to more expensive electronic schedulers.

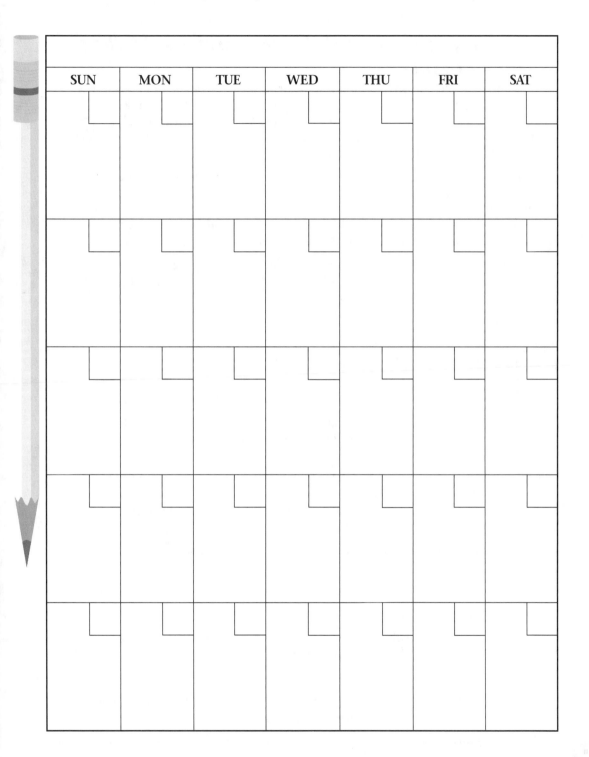

SUN	MON	TUE	WED	THU	FRI	SAT

Chapter 7

Develop a Daily Job Search Schedule That Gets Results

You have decided now what days and hours each week to spend on your job search. To get the most out of your time, you should also decide, in advance, what you will do during each hour of the days that you have scheduled. A specific daily plan is needed, because having one in advance increases the chances that you will use your time most effectively.

After much experimentation, I have developed a simple daily schedule that will work well for most people. It emphasizes setting up interviews in the morning and going to interviews in the afternoon. This is the same basic daily activity schedule I developed for use in structured job search programs where participants achieved dramatic reductions in the time it took to get their next job.

Of course, this schedule is for someone who is unemployed and looking for work full-time. You will have to adapt it if you are currently working, going to school, or have other responsibilities that do not allow for a full-time job search. Look this schedule over carefully and adapt it to fit your needs.

A RECOMMENDED DAILY JOB SEARCH SCHEDULE

7:00 a.m.	Get up, shower, dress, and eat breakfast.
8:00 to 8:15 a.m.	Organize your job search office, review schedule for interviews or promised follow-ups, update daily schedule as needed.
8:15 to 9:00 a.m.	Review Job Lead Cards and old leads for follow-up, develop new leads from want ads, warm contact lists, and all other sources. Check e-mail for job search-related mail, complete Daily Contact Sheet.
9:00 to 10:00 a.m.	Make new and follow-up phone calls and e-mails to get interviews and referrals.
10:00 to 10:15 a.m.	Take a break.
10:15 to 11:00 a.m.	Make more phone calls and send more e-mails.
11:00 to Noon	Make follow-up calls, send follow-up notes, e-mails, and resumes as needed.
Noon to 1:00 p.m.	Lunch break.
1:00 to 3:00 p.m.	Go on interviews, cold contacts in the field, research for interviews online or at library.

Of course, you can adapt the schedule that I recommend to meet your own needs. It is, after all, your schedule.

The important thing is to pay attention to the principles involved as they have been used successfully by many thousands of people. For example, my recommended schedule encourages you to use the telephone as a primary tool for developing job leads because it is quite effective. The sample schedule also creates blocks of time that get you out of your job search office into the real world. It also helps you to resist the natural inclination to sit home and feel sorry for yourself.

Avoid wasting time in your job search schedule by looking at and responding to unrelated e-mail. During the day, stay focused on job search activities and leave personal e-mail to the evening and weekends.

Additional Planning and Scheduling Tips

Remember that we have redefined what counts as an interview. An interview now includes seeing people who hire people like you but don't necessarily have a job opening. With this in mind, consider the following additional tips in creating a job search schedule that will work best for you.

✔ *Set a Daily Objective for Interviews*

Your goal should be to get at least two interviews per day, every day. Remember that because we redefined what an interview is, they are now easier to get. Many people get more than two interviews per day if they use the techniques I suggest.

The recommended daily schedule would be different if you are looking for jobs out of your area. Travel is costly, so if you get one interview in a distant location, focus your efforts on getting more interviews on the same side of town or in the same distant location during that same time frame.

✔ *Expect to Get Rejected*

While I haven't met many normal people who handle rejection well, the job search process requires that you seek or even welcome rejection. I say this because...

The more you get rejected, the closer you are to getting a good job offer.

One example of how seeking rejection pays off is in making cold contact phone calls. After many years of experience in running job search programs, I know that you will need to make 10 to 15 of these calls to get one interview. While that sounds like a lot of rejection, and it is, most people can make that many calls in an hour. That means that two hours of calls can result in two interviews. The calls that don't get you an interview are often friendly and rarely unfriendly, so the rejection you experience is really no big deal if you are prepared for it.

 You can and should set up a reward system for the number of rejections you get. For example, if you get 15 rejections in one day, that means you did your work. Reward yourself. There is a principle involved here that says that success is simply failure turned inside out, so persevere.

✔ Make Phone Calls, Send E-mails, Be Active

You won't get a job by reading job search books or working on your resume. Save those activities for weekends, evenings, and other times. During the day, concentrate on active job search methods that result in setting up interviews.

✔ Stick to Your Schedule

When possible, arrange interviews at times other than those you planned to spend in your job search office. In my suggested daily schedule, I leave each afternoon open for interviewing and for cold contacts in the field. Job search office hours in the mornings focus on setting up interviews. Blocking your time use in simple ways such as this will help you do what you need to get done without losing your focus. But, of course, be flexible to schedule an interview when an employer is available, even if this is somewhat disruptive to your ideal schedule. Plan to take care of your personal business after your job search office hours too.

✔ Don't Get Discouraged

Looking for a job is hard work, so take time for breaks and take time to take care of yourself. It's easy to get discouraged, but find a way to keep a positive attitude and keep getting interviews.

Unemployment is a good time to reflect on what is really important in life, and most people learn that it is other people that matter most to them. Don't lose contact or reject support from others, because they often want to help you in your job search. The best antidote to unemployment is meaningful work, so find a way to get out there and find someone to hire you. Even if you are underemployed for awhile, you will probably handle that better than being unemployed. Chapter 17 has additional tips on coping with unemployment, should you want more information on this.

Now You Know How to Find a Job, But...

You now know far more than the average job seeker about finding job leads and getting interviews. With what you know now, you are more likely to go out and find a job in less time.

There are some other things for you to learn that will be of great value to you in your job search. For example:

✓ Do you know precisely the kind of job you want? Most people have only a general idea, but you should have a more specific sense of what would be the best job for you.

✓ Will you be able to handle the tough interview questions you will be asked? Perhaps not as well as you might. Spending more time improving your interviewing skills will likely result in more and better job offers.

✓ Do you have a specific plan on how to spend your time each day of your job search? Very few people do. Make sure that you don't just read this chapter but actually set up a system to schedule your job search time to get the best results.

I thought a lot about what advice to include in the first section of this book. I wanted to give you quick advice that would most likely help you get a better job in less time. I did this so that you could begin your job search without delay, tomorrow if necessary. For many people, the advice in this section may be all you need. But there is more you can learn, and that is what is provided in the rest of this book. This content covers a variety of topics and is designed to prepare you for the job search in three ways:

1. First, by helping you to understand yourself better. Knowing who you are, what you have done, and what you are good at are important things to know for a variety of reasons.

2. Once you explore yourself, you then need to consider what it is you want in a job. Not just any job should do; you should seek one that is a good "match" for you in a variety of ways.

3. When you have figured out the type of job you want, then—and only then—should you begin your job search. And when you do start looking for a job, you can benefit greatly from learning more about job seeking techniques such as interviewing, making phone contacts, writing resumes, using the Internet, organizing your time, and related topics. The rest of this book will focus on job search methods that work.

You now know enough about finding job leads to go out and find one in less time.

Chapter 7

I hope you go out and find a great job before you finish this book. It happens all the time.

In Conclusion

The final lessons I can offer as I end this section are these:

Trust yourself. No one will ever understand you better than you will. So, once you are reasonably sure of the right thing to do, just go ahead and do it.

Decide to do something worthwhile. Whether it is raising a family or saving the whales, look for something you can do that is special, lasting, and valuable.

Work well. All work is worth doing, so put your energy into it and do it as well as you are able.

Enjoy life. There is always something to marvel at if you look for it.

Say thank you. Many people will help you throughout your life, in large and small ways. Let them know you appreciate them by sending them thank-you notes, thank-you e-mail, or simply saying thanks next time you meet. The more you give, the more you seem to get in return.

Quick Summary

✓ The more interviews you get, the sooner you will get a job offer.

✓ The average job seeker gets about two interviews per week and spends fewer than 15 hours a week on the job search. At that rate, it takes an average of three to four months to find a job. For most people, that is much longer than it needs to be.

✓ As an alternative to the normal and ineffective job search, I suggest two things:

1. Spend more time on actually looking for work.

2. Get at least two interviews each day throughout your job search.

✓ To organize your job search as if it were a job, you need a place where you can work. Usually, this will be a place in your home that can be set aside as your job search office.

✓ Basic materials and equipment include: A computer and Internet access; a telephone; erasable ball-point pens; lined paper or note pads; 3-by-5 inch cards and a 3-by-5 inch card file box with dividers; thank-you notes and envelopes; multiple copies of your resumes and JIST Cards; business-sized envelopes; postage stamps; the *Yellow Pages* phone book; the Internet *Yellow Pages;* calendars and planning or schedule book; access to a good printer; and a copy of this book, of course.

✓ Contact-management software is designed to help you follow up on personal contacts. Most allow you to enter information about a contact including name, address, phone numbers, and e-mail and then make notes related to each. You can keep the same kind of information on blank 3-by-5 inch cards and set up a job lead card box.

✓ To help you organize your daily activities, create a daily contact sheet, listing the people you plan to contact for the day. Complete one of these forms each day. List **at least 20** people or organizations to contact before you begin any phone calls that day. Use any source to get these leads.

✓ Establish and stick to a job search schedule. Five simple steps that will help you get started in setting up your job search as a job are:

Step 1: Decide how many hours per week to look. I recommend at least 25 hours per week if you are unemployed and 10 hours per week if you are underemployed.

Step 2: Decide which days to look.

Step 3: Decide how many hours per day to look.

Step 4: Decide what times each day to look.

Step 5: Transfer your job search schedule to a calendar.

✓ Develop a daily job search schedule. My recommended schedule creates blocks of time that allow you daily changes in activities that include getting into the real world. This helps you resist the natural inclination to sit home and feel sorry for yourself.

SECTION 2
More on Career Planning and Job Search

Labor Market Information Can Help You Make Better Career Decisions

≡≡≡≡Quick Overview

In this chapter, I review the following:

- ✔ Important labor market trends and issues to consider in planning your career and looking for a job
- ✔ The changing and more diverse workforce
- ✔ What you should know about the unemployed
- ✔ The real cost of unemployment
- ✔ How often people change jobs and careers
- ✔ Competition you will face in the job market
- ✔ Major trends in industry and job groups
- ✔ The importance of small employers
- ✔ Why getting more training and education is so important
- ✔ The importance of computer and technology skills
- ✔ How career planning and job seeking skills can give you a competitive edge

If you like facts and data, this chapter should be one of your favorites. It provides a thorough review of labor market trends and how this relates to your career planning and job search. This is an important chapter because it forms a basis for understanding the suggestions I make in the rest of this book.

This was one of the more difficult chapters in this book to write because there has been so much change in the labor market that affects how we look for work and plan our careers, yet few people are aware of how outdated their concepts are. I hope this chapter helps you to understand how you need to act in today's labor market and how, if you've been in the workforce for many years, the job search game has changed.

How the Labor Market Has Changed in Recent Years

Traditionally, most people just take a job that is close to home or is one of the first ones that is offered to them. Most people don't think much about personal satisfaction or long-term career options. They go to school, take the first job they can get, and either stay there for years or look for a better one after awhile and then stay in that job for a long time.

Instead of planning their careers, many people just allow things to happen in a pretty random way. This approach worked pretty well for a lot of people in the past, and it still does for some people now. But depending on "luck" instead of a more thorough career planning approach is no longer wise. A more thoughtful approach to what you do and do not want to do in your career is likely to result in good decisions and good, instead of bad, "luck."

There are a variety of reasons why it is harder now to luck into a good career than it was in the past. Some of the major changes that have an impact on your job prospects include the following:

✓ A growing labor force, with more people looking for jobs than ever before

✓ More frequent job changes

✓ More frequent career changes

✓ Less long-term security with any one organization

✓ Rapid technological change, requiring ongoing training and education

✓ Fewer low-skill jobs offering good pay

✓ Rapid growth in jobs requiring postsecondary technical training or education

✓ Loss of manufacturing jobs to other countries

✓ Long and short-term economic cycles that result in businesses closing, expanding, and contracting, causing many people to look for new jobs on a regular basis

For those who are unprepared, these changes can spell economic and personal disaster. New economic survival skills are needed for our new economy, and you ignore them only at your peril.

Remember, change presents both problems and opportunities. While there are a variety of labor market changes that can harm the unprepared, the new labor market realities also create opportunities for those who look for them. In fact, there are many ways you can take advantage of the current job market—if you know how.

I've spent quite a bit of time looking at labor market data and research and have searched out those things I think are most important for you to understand. This chapter presents these concepts, along with tips on how you can use them to your advantage in your career planning and job search.

Important Labor Market Issues to Consider in Your Career Plans

There is an enormous amount of information on labor market data and trends. You probably don't know much about this data, but there are thousands of research reports, books, technical papers, news articles, and government publications, and truckloads of data available in print and on the Web. A variety of government agencies collects, analyzes, and distributes information on every major job and industry from every corner of the country. The federal Census Bureau, Department of Labor, Department of Education, and other agencies have staffs, data collection programs, and publications routinely gathering, working on, and disseminating employment information. States, provinces, city, county, and local governments do the same for their areas. Hundreds of privately funded associations, endowments, foundations, companies, not-for-profit agencies, news media, individuals, and authors do similar research in specialized areas.

I've sifted through this labor market information to provide the bits that can help you most in understanding how the labor market works. Some of it can help you make practical decisions, such as selecting an industry that pays better than another. Other information is there to inform you of major trends that may apply directly to you.

This is a complex labor market, and the decisions you make now will have a major impact on your future earnings, career satisfaction, and success. So let's spend a little time to cover some of the major labor market trends you will face in the years to come. I suggest you underline or highlight facts you want to remember and think about how you can use what I present here to better your employment situation now or in the future.

Note that most of the data in this chapter comes from the U.S. Department of Labor's Bureau of Labor Statistics or from the U.S. Census Bureau. I have included additional comments on the source of the data at the end of the chapter, if you are interested.

You Are Working in a Larger and More Diverse Workforce

Millions of new workers have poured into the job market in the past several decades, rapidly increasing the size and diversity of our workforce. Fortunately, our economy has created enough new jobs to absorb most or all of these workers. The result is that our rate of unemployment has not increased substantially for most of these years.

Because you are part of this new workforce, let's take a closer look at what has been going on and how you fit into this rapidly expanding labor market. In this section I'll look at the impact of increased numbers of workers and then take a look at how the diversity of our workforce may affect job seekers.

The job search has become more competitive

During the 1980s, the number of people in our workforce increased at an astounding rate of almost 30 percent. Since then, our labor market has continued to expand, although at a less rapid pace. With large numbers of additional workers pouring into the workforce, the competition for available openings has become fierce.

Our economy's ability to create large numbers of new jobs has kept the unemployment rate at moderate levels for many years. The increase in new workers has resulted in larger numbers of people being out of work at any given time. With more workers looking for jobs at any given time, the competition has become more intense for some jobs and will likely remain so in the future.

The Number of People Working Continues to Increase

(Non-institutionalized persons 16 years or older available and looking for work)

	Number in workforce	Number increase	Percent increase
1960	70,000,000		
1970	83,000,000	13,000,000	19
1980	107,000,000	24,000,000	29
1990	126,000,000	19,000,000	18
2000	143,000,000	17,000,000	13
2010 (projected)	160,000,000	17,000,000	12

A number of forces have an impact on the growth in the number of people working. Among the more important factors are more women in the workforce, immigration adding many new workers, the large number of Baby Boomers, and the boomers' children entering the workforce.

We are an increasingly diverse workforce

We are a diverse workforce, consisting of a mix of people of various ages, genders, races, and other characteristics. As a result of increased cultural acceptance of our diversity and a variety of fair employment laws, more jobs are open for all of us based on our qualifications to do the job rather than our cultural or ethnic status. Ten or twenty years is not a long timeframe for most of us, but those who remember as far as forty years ago and earlier can probably tell you how many employment barriers have come down since then.

Let's take a closer look at some of these changes and what they may mean to you.

Employment Trends by Gender

The data that follows show some interesting trends you probably are not aware of. The first set of data shows the number of men in the workforce from 1971 through 2002. The number of men in the workforce has gone up steadily over these years along with increases in the population overall. From 1971 through 2002, the number of men in the workforce increased by 26 million men, an increase of 50 percent during this time.

Of all men 16 and older, the percent in the workforce has been pretty stable, decreasing only slightly. Some of this decrease is the result of people living longer after they retire and of higher percentages of young men being in school before entering the workforce.

Men in the Workforce, 16 Years and Older		
	Number in workforce	*Percent of all men*
1971	52,000,000	79.1
1980	61,000,000	77.4
1990	69,000,000	76.4
2000	76,000,000	74.8
2002	78,000,000	74.1

The employment situation for women has been dramatically different. Look at the data that follows, and you will see substantial differences from the data for men during this same time period. One of the most striking differences is a more rapid increase in the number and percent of women working. From 1971 through 2002, the number of women in the workforce more than doubled, from 32 million to 67 million. This is a growth rate of more than 100 percent for this time-frame, compared to 50 percent for men. In 1971, only 43.4 percent of all women were in the workforce, compared to almost 80 percent of men. By 1980, more than half of all women were in the workforce, and the percentage kept climbing to almost 60 percent by 2000.

Women in the Workforce, 16 Years and Older		
	Number in workforce	Percent of all women
1971	32,000,000	43.4
1980	45,000,000	51.5
1990	57,000,000	57.5
2000	66,000,000	59.9
2002	67,000,000	59.6

A higher percentage of men are in the workforce than women, but the difference has narrowed and will narrow further in the years to come. The U.S. Department of Labor projects a 12 percent overall increase in the number of workers in the ten-year period ending in 2010, with the number of women workers increasing 15 percent while the number of men workers increases by only 9 percent. That may not seem like a big difference, but one way to look at this is that the growth rate for women is 67 percent higher than for men during this same time period.

The large increase in the number and percentage of working women is one of the reasons the overall workforce has increased. This trend has also resulted in more competition for jobs, particularly in areas where women have increased their presence, such as in business management and professional occupations.

Employment Trends by Age

The labor force is projected to grow by about 12 percent in the ten-year period ending 2010, but there are distinctly different patterns of growth rates when broken down by the age of workers.

The large number of Baby Boomers—those born from 1946 through 1964—has had and will continue to have a major impact on the labor force. The age group with the largest increase in workers is those aged 55 to 64. These are Baby

Boomers, as are those in the 45 to 54 age range. The only age group that is projected to decline is the 35 to 44 group, which is the result of Baby Boomers progressing into the next age group. As the Baby Boomers move toward retirement, and with the average lifespan increasing and the age of retirement shifting to 70 or later, they swell the percent of workers 65 and older to more than twice the growth rate of the total labor force.

Labor Force Change by Age, Projected Through 2010

	Number increase	Percent increase
16 to 24	3,366,000	15
25 to 34	2,553,000	8
35 to 44	−3,849,000	−10
45 to 54	6,316,000	21
55 to 64	7,230,000	52
65 and older	1,242,000	30
Overall increase, all ages		12

The large increase in the numbers of older and more experienced workers and the relatively small growth in the numbers of younger workers will have several results. First, younger workers will find it more difficult to move into middle management and some other positions occupied by more experienced workers. Older workers will have similar difficulty competing for these positions because many others in their own age group will compete for them as well. Younger workers, though, will be in shorter supply and this situation will create opportunities for those who look for them.

Employment Trends by Race and Hispanic Origin

Please note that the government publications I have used to research this chapter use the terms white, black, and Hispanic, and other races to refer to Caucasian, African-American, and those of Hispanic, Asian, or other origin. I have continued the use of these terms here for consistency.

I think there is still too much emphasis among employers on someone's origins or other characteristics that workers can't change over their credentials and abilities. But we are fortunate to live in a country where cultural restrictions based on race, religion, gender, ethnicity, and similar characteristics have been minimized as a matter of law and good sense.

To monitor how certain groups are faring in the labor market, the government does collect data based on race and Hispanic origin. And their data shows some changes in our workforce that are worthy of note here.

It should come as no surprise that "white" people make up most of the workforce, just as they do for the population as a whole. But the percentage of white workers as a part of the total workforce has been decreasing and is expected to continue to decrease.

The data that follows shows a projected decrease of 4 percent, to 69 percent of the total, of white workers in the ten-year period ending in 2010. This may not sound like a large decrease but the numbers these percentages represent are quite large. Looking at it this way, the white workforce will increase by just over six million workers during this time while the combined black, Hispanic, Asian, and other minorities workforce is projected to increase by almost eleven million. This means that the combined "minority" workforce is growing almost twice as fast as the white workforce.

As you can see in the table that follows, the largest number of new workers is of Hispanic origin. This group is also projected to grow at a very rapid rate of 36 percent during this time. This growth is occurring as a result of the large number of recent immigrants to the United States, as well as high birth rates among this group. The Asian and other group, which includes American Indians and some Pacific Islanders, makes up a small percentage of the workforce, but is growing at the most rapid pace, projected at 37 percent. The number of black workers is projected to grow at a faster than average rate of 17 percent during this time, but these workers will soon be outnumbered by those with Hispanic origins.

I don't think any of this should make much difference to you as you plan your career and seek a job, other than the impact there will be from a larger number of workers overall and the competition they will present. However it may be that those who can speak more than one language may have an easier time finding some jobs.

Labor Force Growth by Race and Origin 2000/2010

	Percent of workforce		Percent growth	Number increase
	2000	2010		
White, non-Hispanic	73	69	6	6,156,000
Black, non-Hispanic	11	12	17	2,784,000
Hispanic origin (any race)	11	13	36	5,579,000
Asian and other, non-Hispanic	5	6	37	2,339,000

The labor market data indicate that we in the United States are already a diverse workforce and project that we will become more so in the years to come. Our workforce on average is becoming more predominantly female, older, and more racially and ethnically diverse. The question for you to consider is how you might benefit from these changes. Don't let stereotypes restrict your thinking to doing "men's work" or "women's jobs" or limit your options in other ways. More doors are open for all people, so pick the best ones for you and just go ahead in and look around.

Unemployment Is Unpleasant and Expensive, So Minimize Its Impact

A natural consequence of more people coming into the workforce is that more people are also likely to be unemployed at any given time. That seems obvious enough, but this is a different issue from the unemployment rate, a figure that is frequently mentioned in the news. Because you are HIGHLY likely to experience unemployment yourself, on multiple occasions, you need to know more about this matter than the headlines reveal.

NEW JOBS ARE REQUIRED TO ABSORB NEW WORKERS

Millions of additional workers have been added to the workforce in the past ten years, and millions more are projected to be added in the years to come. Unless new jobs are created to absorb them, the unemployment rates will increase rapidly and keep going up.

For example, the workforce is projected to grow about 12 percent over the next ten years. If no new jobs were created during this time, the unemployment rate would increase by that 12 percent to a total of 18 percent or so. That would be an enormous number of people out of work, almost one in five workers.

Fortunately, additional new jobs have been created over the past decades to absorb the large increase in the number of workers. Most of these new jobs have been created by small employers, and this is likely to continue (more about small employers later in this chapter).

This fact will have an impact on your career planning, because you have a good chance of working in a job or industry niche that did not exist ten years ago, or with an employer who created the job you're applying for in the recent past. To find these new jobs and employers, your job search will require you to look in new places and use different methods than you may have used in the past.

The Unemployment Rate and Why People Are Unemployed

Over time, the national unemployment rate goes up and the unemployment rate goes down. The highest unemployment rate in recent history was back in the recession of 1983 when it soared to over 10 percent for a brief time. In the late 1960s and 1990s the unemployment rate dipped to about 4 percent. Most of the time, however, the unemployment rate averages in the 5 to 7 percent range.

There has always been a lot of attention given to the unemployment rate. As you would expect, when the unemployment rate is "low" most people think that is a good thing and when it is "high" that is a bad thing. Politicians brag about their economic policies if the rate goes down or get blamed if it goes up.

The National Unemployment Rate Should Make Little Difference to You

The problem with all this emphasis on the unemployment rate is that it really shouldn't matter much to you. There are a variety of reasons why I make this statement.

Local conditions: A national average rate of unemployment may have little to do with what is going on where you live. The unemployment rate may be much higher or lower there than the national average. More importantly, the local unemployment rate will not tell you how hard or easy it is to find a particular type of job. For example, there may be VERY few jobs open for those in manufacturing in your area even while there is a shortage of applicants for people in the health-care field. This could be the result of a local company laying off lots of workers with similar skills, too many college graduates in an area to employ them all (which is often the case in college towns), or the melt-down of an industry with a strong local presence (such as when the "dot.com" crash occurred in Silicon Valley). Positive growth can also occur in a region that is not at all reflective of the growth pattern found in other areas. Any of these conditions can make the local situation very different from the national one.

There are always some job openings: The fact is that there are almost always some job openings in any region, in times of low and high unemployment. The people who find them are those who go out and look for them, not the ones worrying about the unemployment rate.

THERE IS ONLY ONE UNEMPLOYMENT RATE THAT MATTERS: YOURS

I've often observed that unemployed people, and many of those who interact with them, use a "high" unemployment rate as an excuse for not finding a job. "Why bother looking," they say, "since it is so bad out there?"

Indeed, why bother? I've heard lots of excuses for being out of work, but a high unemployment rate is not a particularly good one. The only rate of unemployment that really matters to you is your personal unemployment rate.

Your Personal Unemployment Rate Is the Only One That Matters

If you are out of work and want a job, your personal rate of unemployment is 100 percent.

If you are working in a job that is acceptable to you, your personal rate of unemployment is 0 percent.

That's it; your personal rate of unemployment is the only unemployment rate that should really matter to you.

A Closer Look at Those Unemployment Statistics

I mentioned earlier that the unemployment rate itself is a bit misleading, because it does not tell the entire story. Here are some additional details that will help you understand this point more clearly.

More people are out of work during each year than is shown in the unemployment rate: At the end of 2002, 67 percent of those 16 and older worked or looked for work during the year, and the unemployment rate at the end of that year was 5.8 percent. But a study by the Census Bureau indicates that almost 10.5 percent of this group experienced one or more bouts of unemployment during the course of the year. Another way to look at this is to understand that more than 10 percent of the workforce is unemployed at some point during each year.

The unemployment rate does not include everyone: The "Percent Unemployed, by Reason Unemployed" table that follows shows the breakdown of the overall unemployment rate by "reasons for unemployment." This data is what is included in the unemployment rate released by the U.S. government. The numbers are from the third quarter of 2003, when the overall unemployment rate was 6.1 percent. I calculated the percent each of the subgroups represents as a percentage of the total unemployment figure. For example, job losers make up 3.4 percent of the unemployment rate but 56 percent of the total of all unemployed.

Percent Unemployed, by Reason Unemployed		
	Percent of the national unemployment rate	*Percent of those counted as unemployed*
Job losers	3.4 percent	56 percent of total
Job leavers	.5 percent	8.8 percent of total
Reentrants	1.7 percent	28.5 percent of total
New entrants	.4 percent	7.1 percent of total
Total unemployment rate: 6.1 percent		

Most people, when they think about who is unemployed, think in terms of people who have lost their jobs. But the unemployment rate includes subcategories of the unemployed that many would not consider. This unemployment figure also excludes some unemployed people who most WOULD consider unemployed.

To give you a better understanding of this concept, let's start with a brief review of the numbers used in the chart above.

In general, people are classified as unemployed if they meet all of the following criteria:

✓ They had no employment during the reference week

✓ They were available for work at that time

✓ They made specific efforts to find employment sometime during the 4-week period ending with the reference week.

Persons laid off from a job and expecting recall need not be looking for work to be counted as unemployed. Given these criteria, only about half of the people included in the unemployment rate, the job losers, are "unemployed" in the traditional sense.

Here are the groups of people counted as unemployed in the national statistics:

✓ **Job losers:** 55.6 percent of the total. Most of these are the people we typically think of as being "unemployed" because they did not leave their jobs voluntarily. But a subgroup of this group includes those on temporary layoff: 12.1 percent of the total. These include people who have been laid off from their jobs and expect to return after a period of time. They often receive compensation during this time, and most do not actively seek work while they wait to be called back.

✓ **Job leavers:** 8.8 percent of total unemployed. This includes people who left their jobs voluntarily, for a variety of reasons.

✓ **Reentrants:** 28.6 percent of the total unemployed. This includes people who left the civilian workforce for a variety of reasons but who are now looking for work again. Reasons for leaving include raising children, going to school, military duty, caring for an older relative, attending a training program, and so on.

✓ **New entrants:** 7.1 percent of the total unemployed. These are people who are entering the workforce for the first time. Many are young people still in school looking for part time jobs or recent graduates looking for their first full-time positions.

Some argue that some or all of the reentrants, new entrants, job leavers, and those on temporary layoffs should be excluded from the unemployment rate. If you excluded all of these people, that would eliminate all but 43.5 percent of the unemployed from the unemployment numbers released by the government. That would reduce a 6.1 percent unemployment rate to an unemployment rate of just 2.65 percent. That seems pretty low, I admit, and a more realistic number would be likely to be somewhat higher, but a reasonable argument can be made that the real "unemployment rate" is lower than is typically given.

But wait, there is more! The government EXCLUDES from the unemployment rate large numbers of people who "marginally attached" to the labor market. They include several subgroups including those employed in part-time jobs because they cannot find full-time jobs and "discouraged workers." These are people who say they want to work but who have not actively sought work within the past four weeks because they do not believe there are jobs available for them for a variety of reasons.

If you add these unemployed people to the same 6.1 percent I have been using as an example, the unemployment rate would jump another 3.9 percent to an even 10 percent unemployment rate.

I know all this is probably more than you want to know about the unemployment rate the U.S. government releases. I present this information to help you understand that the unemployment rate you hear so much about is not what most people think it is. It is a complex number that can be interpreted in a variety of ways and is a compromise in what it does and does not include.

A more important point I want to make is to reinforce that the only unemployment rate that should matter to you is your personal unemployment rate, which is either 0 percent or 100 percent. Each of the people who are or are not included in the unemployment rate is an individual, and each has a situation that differs from all the others. I hope all of this helps you understand that whatever the national or local unemployment rates are, sitting around and waiting is not the way to get your personal unemployment rate to zero. Don't become a "discouraged worker" who says he or she wants to work but does not actually go out and look for a job. From the government's point of view, these folks are not really unemployed, because they are not looking. Behavior, or lack of it, counts; if you don't look for a job you are not likely to find one.

Unemployment Rates by Age, Gender, Race, Hispanic Origin, and Family Status

Being unemployed is a solitary experience, and statistics just don't apply to individuals. Even so, you may find it of interest that unemployment statistics do change based on various sociological factors. For example, information later in this chapter shows a direct relationship between higher levels of education and lower levels of unemployment. People who make more money also tend to take longer to find a job than those whose earnings are lower. Higher-earning individuals also tend to be older, so you have to ask whether it is age or earnings that result in a longer or shorter job search, or both?

Women, on average, experience fewer bouts of unemployment than men and tend to find jobs more rapidly when they need to. Is that because they accept lower paying jobs than men? Or is it because women tend to be in service sector jobs, where the job growth has been, while more men have been in the goods producing sector? Do women earn less than men with comparable levels of education because they are women? Or do women earn less because they have fewer years in the labor force than men of the same age and educational level?

There has been a great deal of research into these questions, but the answers in some cases remain unclear. The government provides data on all sorts of situations, and I present a few of the more interesting ones here.

Unemployment Rates by Age

Fewer young people are in the workforce because many are in school or transitioning to work. Their unemployment rates are also high because they change jobs for a variety of reasons. As they age and become more stable their participation rates increase and unemployment rates decrease.

From age 25 to 54, the percent of workers in the labor market and their unemployment rates tend to be pretty stable. From age 54 on, participation rates begin to drop and continue to drop rapidly. Fewer than half of those aged 60 to 64 are in the workforce, and only 5 percent of those aged 75 and older. The unemployment rates of these older workers remains comparatively low, and many who lose their jobs at these ages simply retire.

Unemployment Rates by Age		
	Percent in workforce	Percent unemployed
16 to 19	39.6	16.5
20 to 24	69.0	9.7
25 to 34	78.8	5.9
35 to 44	80.3	4.6
45 to 54	78.8	4.0
55 to 59	68.0	3.8
60 to 64	48.5	4.0
65 to 69	25.1	3.8
70 to 74	13.4	4.0
75 and older	5.0	2.6

Employment and Unemployment Rates by Race and Gender

Labor force participation rates are pretty consistent for white, black, and Hispanic workers, but the differences in unemployment rates are significant. Hispanic men have significantly higher labor force participation rates than white or black male workers, and black women have higher labor force participation than white or Hispanic women. Black men have higher unemployment rates than black women or than any other group. You can guess at the reasons for these statistics being as they are, and you may or may not be correct for a given individual.

Unemployment Rates by Race and Gender				
	Total	White	Black	Hispanic
By Race				
Percent in workforce	66.6	66.8	64.8	69.1
Percent unemployed	5.8	5.1	10.2	7.5
By Gender				
Men in workforce, 20 years and over	76.3	76.7	72.1	83.6
Percent men unemployed	5.3	4.7	9.5	6.4
Women in workforce, 20 years and over	60.5	60.0	64.4	59.5
Percent women unemployed	5.1	4.4	8.8	7.2

Employment and Unemployment Rates of Families

Data on the employment status for families shows similar trends to those of the workforce as a whole. The data below shows that Hispanic families have the highest percent of one or more family members in the workforce, and black and Hispanic families have higher rates of unemployment. The second part of the data table shows the percent of parents in the labor force by their gender and the age of their youngest natural child. As you can see, a very high percentage of fathers are in the workforce. As with the workforce as a whole, a lower but still high percentage of mothers are in the workforce, with more than half of all mothers whose youngest child is younger than three working outside of the home.

Employment Rates of Families				
	All Families	*White*	*Black*	*Hispanic*
With one or more in the workforce	82.4	82.6	79.0	86.5
With one or more unemployed	7.8	7.0	13.1	11.2
	Percent in workforce		*Percent unemployed*	
	Men	*Women*	*Men*	*Women*
With children under 18	94.3	71.8	4.0	5.7
With children 6 to 17	93.3	78.2	3.6	4.6
With children under 6	95.5	63.7	4.5	7.4
	Percent in workforce		*Percent unemployed*	
Mothers with own children under 3 years old	55.4		8.0	

The Duration of Unemployment

The average length of unemployment goes up as the unemployment rate increases. Over the years, the average length of unemployment is most often in the range of 12 to 18 weeks. But the average length of unemployment should have little meaning to you as an individual.

For example, the mean number of weeks unemployed (where half are unemployed more and half are unemployed less) was 6.8, even though the average number of weeks unemployed was 16.6 for the same time period. The reason is that some people are unemployed far longer than the average for all workers. And, while about 35 percent of all workers find jobs within 5 weeks, almost 20 percent remain unemployed after 26 weeks. Keep in mind that this data does not include "discouraged workers," those who were unemployed but not actively looking. If these workers were included, the average number of weeks unemployed would be significantly higher.

The data that follows shows the number of weeks unemployed by reason for unemployment, and the experience differs significantly in some situations. For example, only 5.5 percent of those on temporary layoff remain unemployed at the end of 26 weeks, versus 25.1 percent of permanent job losers. The second section of the chart shows unemployment by age and gender. Young workers tend to find jobs more rapidly, leaving fewer than 20 percent unemployed by the end of 14 weeks and 8.7 percent at the end of 26 weeks. One reason for these numbers is that these workers tend to take lower-paying and entry-level jobs that are easier to obtain. Men and women over 20 have very similar experiences in their length of unemployment.

Duration of Unemployment in Weeks

All workers, average (mean) duration, in weeks: 16.6

All workers, median duration, in weeks: 6.8

Duration of Unemployment by Reason and Age, in Weeks

	Less than 5	5 to 14	15 to 26	27 and over
All workers	34.5	30.8	16.3	18.3
On temporary layoff	51.6	32.9	10.1	5.5
Permanent job loser	24.5	28.5	21.9	25.1
Completed temp jobs	34.7	31.1	16.6	17.7
Job leavers	40.5	32.6	13.3	13.6
Reentrants	35.1	31.3	14.6	19.0
New entrants	37.2	32.3	13.7	16.8
Age 16-19, both sexes	46.8	33.5	11.0	8.7
Men 20 and older	31.9	30.4	17.2	20.6
Women 20 and older	33.0	30.2	17.4	19.4

The High Cost of Being Unemployed

Some people enjoy the freedom of unemployment. That is often true for those temporarily laid off, because they get financial benefits to replace much of their lost income. And there are others who are content to run out their unemployment compensation and "take time off" without much worry. Most people, however, do not enjoy their time unemployed, and one of the big reasons has to do with the loss of income and related stress.

For all of us who need the income from gainful employment and worry if we don't have it, the task is very simple: to get an acceptable job as soon as possible because we need the money.

Think about it. At its simplest level, the time you spend unemployed is very expensive. Even at modest salary levels, the lost income adds up to thousands of dollars. You are likely to be unemployed a number of times over your working life; this means that the average cost of looking for work could add up to be enough to buy a very nice car, a big yacht, or even a house.

Here is some arithmetic to help you see how much unemployment might cost you. The average worker 16 and older earns $609 per week (about $32,000 a year). If the worker is unemployed, say, 15 weeks, that would be $9,135 in lost wages. Then add lost benefits at about 15 percent of wages to get to $10,505. That is enough to buy a pretty decent used car, or a trip to Europe. And that is for just one unemployment experience. If you change jobs on an average of every 3.7 years (more on this later) during your entire work life of about 40 years, your total cost of unemployment would be $113,568, in today's dollars. Of course, your personal experience is likely to differ, but my point is that unemployment will cost you a lot of money.

QUICK COST OF UNEMPLOYMENT PER $10,000 OF INCOME

Quick Fact ▷ For each $10,000 of annual income, your cost of being unemployed (if your job search lasts 15 weeks) is $2,877 plus lost benefits of an additional 15 percent, for a total of $3,309. To get the cost of one bout of unemployment, just multiply $3,309 by each $10,000 in income you are likely to lose per year.

Annual income	Your cost of being unemployed	Annual income	Your cost of being unemployed
15,000	$4,963	40,000	$13,236
20,000	$6,618	45,000	$14,891
25,000	$8,272	50,000	$16,545
30,000	$9,967	60,000	$19,854
35,000	$11,581	70,000	$23,163

Even worse than the financial cost of an extended job search are the long-term consequences of poor career planning: unhappiness, loss of self-esteem, missed promotions, and other problems. If it takes dollars and cents to convince you of the value of learning more effective job seeking skills, I hope you are now convinced.

You Are Likely to Change Jobs and Careers

My father retired from an organization where he had worked for almost 30 years. He had several jobs before this and then never looked for another job for 30 years. It was a Fortune 500 company, and, believe it or not, they gave him a gold watch when he retired. That wasn't all that unusual a situation for people who retired in past decades, because they tended to stay with an organization for many years.

It's different today. People change jobs and careers more often than in the past. Let's take a closer look at what this means to you.

The Number of Years with the Same Employer

Most people have more than one job during their work lives, but exactly how many? The Department of Labor's most recent survey of "employee tenure" found that workers had been with the same employer an average of 3.7 years. Young people, as the data that follows shows, have shorter average times on the job. This should come as no surprise because older workers tend to stay on the job as they settle into their careers and family lives.

To get some idea of the total number of jobs people work at over a lifetime, I created the last two columns in the table that follows. In the "average number jobs" column, I divided the duration of employment into the years that data covered. For example, workers age 16, 17, 18, and 19 have an average tenure of .7 years for each of these four years. Divide .7 into 4, and you get 5.7 jobs they would have held, on the average, for those four years. I used the same process for the other age ranges up to age 54. In the "total jobs held" column I added the totals for each age bracket onto the previous total for a cumulative total in the 45 to 54 years age bracket.

This process may overstate the number of jobs held by some, but gives a useful way to see how many jobs the average person may hold during their working years. While people change jobs less frequently as they age, the number of jobs they hold is greater than most people think.

More on Career Planning and Job Search **209**

Number of Jobs by Age

While job tenure gives some indication of the number of jobs people hold, it is an estimate. A more accurate measure was done in a longitudinal study by the U.S. Department of Labor titled "Number of Jobs Held, Labor Market Activity, and Earnings Growth among Younger Baby Boomers: Results from More Than Two Decades of a Longitudinal Survey." It found that this group held an average of 9.6 jobs from age 18 to 36. As you would expect, some within the group had more jobs than others, with 17 percent having 15 or more jobs, and 18 percent having zero to four jobs. Men in this group had an average of 9.9 jobs while women had 9.3 jobs.

Tenure and Total Jobs by Age

By age, all workers	Number years with current employer	Average number jobs	Total jobs held
16 to 19 years	.7	5.7	5.7
20 to 24 years	1.2	4.2	9.9
25 to 34 years	2.7	3.7	13.6
35 to 44 years	4.6	2.2	15.8
45 to 54 years	7.6	1.3	17.1
55 to 64 years	9.9	1.0	
65 years and over	8.7		

Average tenure, all workers, all ages .... 3.7 years

Average tenure, 25 years and over .... 4.7 years

This study did not include the job changing histories of younger or older workers but supports the numbers I calculated in the "Tenure and Total Jobs by Age" table above.

Combined Factors of Age and Gender in Job Tenure

Women have less tenure with the same employer than men at all ages, much of this the result of their coming in and out of the workforce while raising children. The exception is for working women age 65 and above, who are beyond the child-rearing age.

Job Tenure by Age and Gender

	Number years with current employer	
Age	Men	Women
20 to 24 years	1.3	1.1
25 to 34 years	2.9	2.5
35 to 44 years	5.1	4.3
45 to 54 years	9.1	6.5
55 to 64 years	10.2	9.6
65 years and over	8.1	9.5

Other interesting facts regarding tenure include the following:

✓ Some workers do not change jobs often: About 30 percent of workers age 25 and over had been with their current employer for 10 or more years, including more than half of those 55 and over.

✓ Tenure increases with age: While 70 percent of teens had tenure of one year or less, only 10 percent of those 55 and over had tenure of less than one year.

✓ Government workers change jobs less often: The median tenure for workers in government jobs was twice that of people working in the private sector, partially due to the relatively older average age of government workers.

✓ Average tenure varies by type of job: Managerial and professional workers had the highest tenure, while those in service jobs had the lowest.

You Will Also Change Careers

Not only are you likely to have a number of different jobs, but you are also likely to make one or more major career changes during your work life. A career change is a change in the type of work you do. While a job change involves moving from one employer to another—and doing a similar job for both—a career change is a more substantial change.

For example, if you waited on tables in a restaurant when going to school, then got a job as a medical technician when you graduated, that would be a change in career (as well as a change in employer, of course). A career change is when you change your work from one occupational group to another, as when a teacher leaves the educational system and becomes a real estate agent.

These examples are pretty clearly changes in careers, but other situations are not so clear-cut. For example, if you get promoted to be the manager of a workgroup, but continue to do many of the things you did before you were promoted, is this a career change? When an Air Force pilot retires from the military and starts flying planes for an airline, is this a career change? Is it a career change when a woman leaves her job at a daycare center to raise children? Or what about a tile worker who starts his own business installing tile?

This lack of clarity is why the Department of Labor has not attempted to research this matter. As a result, no one knows for sure how many careers a person is likely to have, but some experts estimate that the average person will change careers three to five times during their work lives, which seems like a reasonable estimate to me.

This means that the average person can expect ten or more job changes and three to five career changes during their working years. That is a lot of change, and it is an important reason why you need to know more about how to change jobs and plan your career. Learning more about career planning and job seeking will help you over and over again.

Which makes me think this book could be worth more to you than you had previously imagined.

The Demand for Most Jobs Is Expected to Grow, but So Will the Competition

Overall, the number of jobs is projected to grow by about 15 percent by 2010. In general, occupations that require post-secondary through college training and education are projected to grow more rapidly than jobs that require less. But the growth rates among occupational groups are not even; some jobs will grow much more rapidly than others, and some will decline.

Following are projections for you to consider. For the ten years ending in 2010, all major job groups are expected to grow but "professional and related" jobs are projected to grow the most rapidly. This is a large group of jobs that includes the fields of architecture, engineering technical trades, art and design, entertainment, media and communications, community and social service, computer and mathematical, education, legal , life science, social science, health diagnoses and treatment, jobs involving health technologists and technicians, and others. Most of these jobs require technical or other postsecondary training or a college degree.

Growth in Jobs by Category		
	Number of jobs	Projected percent increase
Total new jobs, all occupations	22,160,000	15.2
Management, business, and financial	2,115,000	13.6
Professional and related	6,952,000	26.0
Service	5,088,000	19.5
Sales and related	1,852,000	11.9
Office and administrative support	2,171,000	9.1
Farming, fishing, and forestry	51,000	3.6
Construction and mining	989,000	13.3
Installation, maintenance, and repair	662,000	11.4
Production (factory)	750,000	5.7
Transportation and material moving	1,530,000	15.2

Within some of these major job groups, the competition for specific jobs can be substantial. For example, Physical Therapist is an occupation that is projected to grow faster than average, and the average pay is $54,810, making this a very attractive job. As a result, many people have been attracted to the occupation, and admission to the college programs that prepare Physical Therapists have become extremely competitive. While getting a Physical Therapist job has been easy in the recent past, the increasing number of new graduates has resulted in a tight job market in some areas of the country.

Another example is in management jobs of all kinds, where the large number of experienced baby boomers and the increased access of these jobs to women make it more difficult for all workers to attain these jobs. Some who were qualified for these jobs in the past will not get them now, because there simply are not enough of them to go around.

Some Industries and Sectors Grow Faster Than Others

The data that follows shows the projected growth in number of people employed in various industries in the ten-year period ending 2010. The table also gives you information on the percent of the workforce within each industry and industry group.

While this is a lot of data to absorb, it relates to some things you should consider in making your career plans. As you look at the data, notice that it is organized into two major groups consisting of "goods-producing industries" and "service-producing industries." Within these two major groups are subgroups of related industries. I'll note some trends and make observations following the data table.

Projected Growth by Industry		
	Percent of workforce employed	Percent growth
ALL INDUSTRIES	**100**	**16.4**
GOODS-PRODUCING INDUSTRIES	**20.9**	**6.2**
Agriculture, mining, and construction	**7.1**	**12.3**
Agricultural production	0.8	−2.5
Agricultural services	0.8	38.6
Construction	5.0	12.3
Mining and quarrying	0.2	−14.0
Oil and gas extraction	0.2	−7.3
Manufacturing	**13.8**	**3.1**
Aerospace manufacturing	0.4	18.9
Apparel and other textile products	0.5	−16.3
Chemical manufacturing, except drugs	0.5	−4.5
Drug manufacturing	0.2	23.8
Electronic equipment manufacturing	1.2	6.6
Food processing	1.3	−3.0
Motor vehicle and equipment manufacturing	0.8	8.6
Printing and publishing	1.2	−0.2
Steel manufacturing	0.2	−21.6
Textile mill products	0.4	−5.4
SERVICE-PRODUCING INDUSTRIES	**79.1**	**19.1**
Transportation, communications, and public utilities	**5.2**	**17.9**
Air transportation	1.0	24.9
Cable and other pay television services	0.2	50.6

	Percent of workforce employed	Percent growth
Public utilities	0.6	4.9
Radio and television broadcasting	0.2	9.7
Telecommunications	0.9	12.2
Trucking and warehousing	1.4	21.9
Wholesale and retail trade	**22.7**	**12.8**
Department, clothing, and accessory stores	3.0	4.2
Eating and drinking establishments	6.1	18.3
Grocery stores	2.3	5.6
Motor vehicle dealers	0.9	11.9
Wholesale trade	5.2	11.1
Finance, insurance, and real estate	**5.6**	**9.1**
Banking	1.5	−1.5
Insurance	1.8	6.4
Securities and commodities	0.6	20.3
Services	**37.9**	**27.0**
Advertising	0.2	32.5
Amusement and recreation services	1.3	34.5
Childcare services	0.5	41.9
Computer and data processing services	1.6	86.2
Educational services	8.8	13.6
Health services	8.3	25.5
Hotels and other lodging	1.4	13.3
Management and public relations services	0.8	42.2
Motion picture production and distribution	0.2	28.7
Personnel supply services	2.9	49.2
Social services, except childcare	1.6	42.3
Government	**7.6**	**6.9**
Federal government	1.4	−7.6
State and local government	5.6	11.5

This data shows some important things to consider in your career planning. Here are some highlights.

Goods-Producing and Manufacturing Industries—These industries manufacture, grow, build, or mine something, and it is the industry group people think of when they refer to "manufacturing" jobs. I often hear that the number of these jobs is declining, but the fact is that they are not. Goods-producing industries are actually projected to increase, although not as rapidly as the average for all industries. Even jobs that are in the "manufacturing" industry group are projected to increase slightly, although some industries within this group are projected to reduce the number of people they employ. Reasons for decline are sometimes related to technological improvements that automate functions and reduce the need for workers. Other industries, such as "apparel and other textile" are projected to have fewer jobs as a result of foreign competition. Overall, more goods-producing and manufacturing industries are projected to increase than decrease. Only 14 percent of all workers work in manufacturing jobs and the percentage, although not the actual number of workers, is projected to decrease in the future.

Service-Producing Industries—Almost 80 percent of all employment is in this major sector, and this is where much of the future growth is projected to occur. Only two industry groups are expected to decline: banking and federal government. Banking employment is expected to decrease as mergers and automation make this industry more efficient. Federal government jobs are also expected to decease due to budget cuts and as more tasks are picked up by private contractors and state and local governments. All other industries in this large group are expected to increase their employment. As you look through the list, note that some industries are growing much more rapidly than average. Computer and data processing services (86 percent), cable and other pay television services (51 percent), personnel supply services (49 percent), and management and public relations services (42.2 percent) are among the most rapidly growing industries.

Services Industries—People often confuse the subgroup of "services" industries with the much larger "services-producing industries" group or with the completely different occupational group called "service occupations." Service occupations (not industries) include jobs such as food preparation and serving, building and grounds cleaning, protective service jobs such as correctional officers and firefighters, personal care jobs such as childcare workers and barbers, and healthcare jobs such as dental assistants and pharmacy aides. As a result of this confusion, I often hear things like "low paying service industry jobs like fast-food workers are replacing more highly paid jobs like manufacturing." Well, these are two different things entirely because you really can't compare industry groups with occupational groups.

In fact, the industries that make up the services industry subgroup are quite large and together account for 38 percent of the workforce. Many of the jobs in this industry subgroup pay well and are also expected to grow much more rapidly (at 27 percent) than the average for all industries, with all but one, hotels and lodging, expected to grow more rapidly than average.

Government Employment—Governments are a major employer, employing 7.6 percent of the workforce. I believe the actual number is considerably higher if you were to include all government-funded positions such as teachers, social workers, non-for-profit workers, and many others that are counted as being in other industry subgroups. And, of course, there is the sizeable number of people in the military plus the millions working in defense contract positions and in jobs providing services or products to various government entities. Government positions at the federal level are expected to decrease slightly but that loss is projected to be more than offset by increases in state and local government jobs.

Services-producing Industries Have Accounted for Virtually All Growth

While recent data on the increase or decline in industries or occupations seem minor, the information can be quite significant over a long period of time. Before the industrial revolution, for example, more than 50 percent of the workforce in this country worked on farms. Now, less than 2 percent of our workforce is involved in farming, yet we have more and better food than ever and enough left over to export. Just as with farming, many believe that more efficient factories and improved technologies result in more and better goods being produced by fewer workers. If so, this would be similar to what became of all the farm workers: Improved technologies reduced the percent of the workforce required to create what we need. While this is a bit oversimplified, the fact is that most of the growth in employment over recent decades has been in the services-producing industries and not in the goods-producing industries.

The data that follows shows the number and percent growth in employment from 1979 through 2010. During this time, the number of jobs in the services-producing industries doubled while those in the goods-producing industries increased by only 12 percent.

Long-Term Employment Growth in Service and Goods-Producing Industries

Number of People Employed, in Millions

	1979	1992	2000	2010 (projected)
Service-producing	63	84.7	105.9	126.1
Goods-producing	26.5	23.1	27.9	29.7

Total Growth, 1979 to 2010 (projected)

	Number	Percent
Service-producing	63.1	100
Goods-producing	3.2	12

Opportunities will remain in all industries, including manufacturing, government, agriculture, and other slow-growth or no-growth industries. This is a very large country, and even small industries that are declining will have openings for well-trained people. What is clear, however, is that this is NOT your grandfather's economy. Almost all of the net new jobs have been created outside of manufacturing, and this trend is likely to increase.

Most Job Opportunities Are with Small Employers

Large employers employ a lower percentage of workers than in the past. For example, the FORTUNE 500, consisting of the country's 500 largest employers, decreased the number of people they employed by more than 25 percent between 1980 and the mid 1990s, and the number of people they employ continues to decline. These large employers employed 18 percent of the workforce at the beginning of this time but decreased their employment to about 10 percent by the mid 1990s.

This dramatic decrease occurred during a time when millions of new jobs were being created. Where did all those new jobs come from? Small employers.

The data that follows comes from the current edition of the U.S. Department of Labor's Bulletin 2541. It shows the percent of all workers employed in organizations of different sizes. This data shows that smaller employers, those with 249 or fewer workers, now employ more than 70 percent of the workforce.

Employment by Size of Establishment

Establishment size by number workers employed	Percent of all workers employed
1 to 4	5.9
5 to 9	8.1
10 to 19	10.7
20 to 49	16.3
50 to 99	12.8
100 to 249	16.4
250 to 499	9.6
500 to 999	7.2
1,000 or more	13.2

An economist named David Burch researched the job-generating ability of various sized businesses. His conclusion was that the smallest companies, those with 20 or fewer employees, are responsible for creating as many as 80 percent of the net new jobs that are added to our economy. Similar conclusions have been reached by other researchers.

While larger employers will remain an important source of employment, small businesses are more important to our economy than ever before. Smaller employers cannot be ignored as a major source of employment opportunities. Job search methods that work well with these employers should be used to more effectively find the many jobs that exist.

Education and Training Are Increasingly Important

The earnings information that follows is from the Census Bureau and shows the average earnings for major occupational groups. Look this information over—do you notice any trends? While the exact numbers change slightly over time, what is clear is that some types of jobs pay better than others. Why is this so?

Average Earnings for Major Occupational Groups

Management: **$70,800**

Business and Financial Operations: **$50,580**

Computer and Mathematical: **$60,350**

Architecture and Engineering: **$56,330**

Life, Physical, and Social Science: **$49,710**

Community and Social Services: **$34,190**

Legal: **$69,030**

Education, Training, and Library: **$39,130**

Arts, Design, Entertainment, Sports, and Media: **$39,770**

Healthcare Practitioners and Technical: **$49,930**

Healthcare Support: **$21,900**

Protective Service: **$32,530**

Food Preparation and Serving: **$16,720**

Building and Grounds Cleaning and Maintenance: **$20,380**

Personal Care and Service: **$21,010**

Sales and Related: **$28,920**

Office and Administrative Support: **$27,230**

Farming, Fishing, and Forestry: **$19,630**

Construction and Extraction: **$35,460**

Installation, Maintenance, and Repair: **$34,960**

Production: **$27,600**

Transportation and Material Moving: **$26,570**

Education and Earnings Are Closely Related

It is common sense: People who work in food preparation earn less money than people who work in management or legal occupations. The reason is that the higher-paying jobs require higher level skills and more training and education.

There is a clear relationship between level of education and earnings, but most people don't realize how substantial the differences are as the education level of an individual increases. Following are the earnings by level of education as recently released by the U.S. Department of Labor. I calculated the dollar and percent premium of pay over those who dropped out of high school.

Earnings for Full-Time Workers Ages 25 and Older, by Educational Attainment

Education level	Earnings per year	Earnings premium over high school dropouts	Percent earnings over high school dropouts
Some HS, no degree	21,400		
HS diploma/GED	28,800	7,400	35
Some college, no degree	32,400	11,000	51
Associate degree	35,400	14,000	65
Bachelor's degree	46,300	24,900	116
Master's degree	55,300	33,900	158
Doctorate	70,500	49,100	229
Professional degree	80,200	58,800	275

When you look at the numbers, it's very clear that additional education pays off at all levels. A high school graduate earns $7,400, or 35 percent more than the average high school dropout. A four-year college graduate earns almost $17,500 more than a high school graduate. This means that, over a decade, a college graduate will earn about $175,000 more than someone with a high school diploma. That is enough to make a big difference in lifestyle and more than enough to pay off any cost of the education itself. Over a 40-year worklife, the difference in earnings is staggering. The average college graduate will earn well over a million dollars more than a high school graduate, after inflation is considered. I don't know about you, but many people would consider that to be a lot of money.

Some Have High Earnings at All Levels of Education

Average earnings can be misleading, because half earn more and half earn less than the average. For example, some high school dropouts earn much more than the average for college graduates.

The data below shows the percentage of those with earnings over certain thresholds. The original data was presented by the Department of Labor in weekly earnings of $600 and $1,000 a week, and I converted this to annual compensation. The first column, $31,285 per year, approximates the average annual earnings for all workers, while the second is about two thirds higher than the average.

Higher Earners by Level of Education

	Percent earning over $600/week ($31,285/year)	Percent earning over $1,000/week ($52,143/year)
Less than 4 years of high school	6.0	0.6
4 years of high school	11.9	1.5
1 to 3 years of college	19.4	3.6
4 years of college	34.9	10.3
5 or more years of college	47.9	18.5
All levels of education average	19.5	4.8

As you can see, some people with high school educations or less do earn more than the average for college graduates, but about 98 percent of them earn less. Some better-paying jobs for high school graduates include supervisors of retail salespersons, restaurant cooks, police and sheriff's officers, supervisors of construction and mining workers, electricians, and carpenters. While these jobs do not require advanced education, they do require substantial on-the-job training or considerable academic proficiency and talent. So advanced education is not required for economic success but more training or education greatly increases your chances.

The data that follows shows some interesting trends in the growth of occupations requiring different levels of education or training. The bold text gathers groups of these into more general categories so I could show the percent of jobs that involve each major group.

For example, only 3 percent of the jobs requires a master's degree and above, and another 17 percent requires a four-year college degree. The "projected percent growth" column shows the projected growth rate in jobs for the various levels for the ten-year period ending in 2010, and the "number job openings" column shows the total number of job openings projected for the same period.

Employment Growth by Level Education and Training

	Projected percent growth	Number job openings
Master's, doctoral, and first professional degree (3 percent of the workforce)		
First professional degree	25	321,000
Doctoral degree	24	407,000
Master's degree	23	301,000
Bachelor's degree or bachelor's or degree plus work experience (17 percent of the workforce)		
Bachelor's or higher degree plus work experience	19	1,312,000
Bachelor's degree	23	3,284,000
Associate degree or postsecondary vocational award (8 percent of the workforce)		
Associate degree	32	982,000
Postsecondary vocational award	18	1,539,000
Related work experience or long-term on-the-job training (16 percent of the workforce)		
Work experience in a related occupation	11	2,044,000
Long-term on-the-job training	8	2,417,000
Short or moderate-term on-the-job training (56 percent of the workforce)		
Moderate-term on-the-job training	11	5,322,000
Short-term on-the-job training	14	16,598,000

The average growth rate for all occupations is projected to be 15 percent during this time (the average growth rate for workers is projected at 12 percent). What is most significant is that all jobs requiring postsecondary training or education are projected to grow more rapidly than average, and all jobs requiring less education are projected to grow more slowly than average.

While having a college degree is clearly a good thing, jobs requiring a two-year associate degree are growing the fastest of all, and many of these jobs are in high wage medical and other technical areas.

More Education or Training Does Not Guarantee Success

Most people will earn more as they increase their level of education or training, but success is not guaranteed. This is particularly true for those entering the job market with new credentials.

For example, the outlook for those with four-year college degrees is quite good, with jobs requiring this degree projected to grow faster than the average for all jobs.

While the long-term projections for college graduates are quite good, there are other things to consider to fully understand these projections. For one thing, about 20 percent of the college grads in the workforce are either unemployed (about 3 percent) or are holding jobs not typically held by college grads (about 17 percent). Some of those counted as "underemployed" choose to be so, while they attend graduate school or spend their time in other ways, but many were simply unable to find better jobs due to competition.

Another factor is that, while a large number of jobs requiring grads are projected to open up each year, there will be even more new and returning grads joining the labor force each year. That means that the demand, though high, will be exceeded by the supply, which is even higher.

The bottom line here is that while a college degree is of great value, it will not guarantee success in the job market any more than it has in the past. About one in five new grads will initially have to accept jobs that are not typically held by grads, although many will do better over time. Eventually, more than 90 percent of new graduates are expected to find jobs typically held by college graduates.

The same is true at all levels of training and education. This reinforces my observation that career planning is more important than ever. For those considering additional education, it is vital to know in advance which degrees and occupations offer the best opportunities for employment.

Trade and Technical Training Are Alternatives to a College Degree

More education clearly pays off in the job market, but it should be noted that college is not the only route to higher earnings; many trade, technical, sales, and other fields offer similar opportunities to those without a college degree. A well-trained plumber, auto mechanic, chef, computer repair technician, police officer, tool and die maker, or medical technologist can do quite well in our economy.

These and many other occupations require one to two years of specialized training, and some apprenticeship programs allow for on-the-job training.

Outstanding people in sales, small business, management, self-employment, and other activities can still do quite well without a college degree, although more education is often required to compete for the better positions.

There is plenty of glamour in occupations that are growing rapidly, but many jobs will continue to become available in occupations that are growing slowly or even declining. Jobs will become available to replace those who retire or leave for other reasons, and opportunities will exist in virtually all areas for those with superior abilities, motivation, and preparation.

More Education Pays Off in Less Unemployment, Too

It is clear that education and training pay off in higher average earnings as a result of higher demand in the job market. Look at the data that follows to see how unemployment rates go down as educational attainment goes up. People with more education not only earn more money, they also experience lower unemployment rates. Over time, this combination gives an even more substantial economic advantage to those with higher levels of training or education.

Unemployment Rates by Level of Education or Training

	Percent unemployed
College graduates	3.0
Some college, associate's degree, other	4.7
High school graduates, no college	5.1
Less than a high school diploma	9.1

Grads Tend to Marry Grads, Resulting in Even Higher Income

While most employment data relates to individuals, there is another interesting consideration: People tend to marry those with similar backgrounds. So, for example, a person with a college degree is more likely to marry another person with a college degree or with post-secondary training and education.

The impact of this on family income is greater than you might think for a variety of reasons. For example, those with more education not only tend to earn more money but they are also more likely to be in the labor market. About 85 percent of women and 95 percent of men with college degrees are in the labor market, as compared to about 75 percent of male high school dropouts and less than 50 percent of female high school dropouts.

Another factor in family income is that women at all levels of education and training tend to earn less than men. As a result, families with women heads of households have the lowest earnings of all family situations.

What this means is that married couples with higher levels of education or training tend to have substantially higher family incomes. The one-two punch of significantly lower earnings and lower labor market participation has profound effects on family income. Men and women with little education who are single heads of households are likely to have a particularly bleak economic future.

Computer and Technology Skills Are Essential

Most people understand it is important to know how to use a computer, but here is some information to support just how important it is. For example, a recent study from Olsten Temporary Services found that over 90 percent of office workers and clerical support staff are required to have computer skills to be considered for employment. That shouldn't be any surprise to people who work in those jobs, because computers are now an integral part of the office environment.

For years, many professionals and managers seemed immune from needing to know much about computers. Even recently, I've heard several brag that they didn't do simple word processing or spreadsheet work. Just a few years ago, only 30 to 40 percent of employers required professionals and managers to be computer literate. However, things have changed. Now, 80 percent of professionals and 85 percent of middle managers are required to be computer literate. Even 74 percent of senior managers are expected to have computer skills, compared to only 36 percent just a few years ago.

This is the most dramatic change in the workplace in decades. Millions of people who have lost their jobs in the recent past do not have the level of computer skills most jobs now require. New entrants to the labor market who have good computer skills are often hired over more experienced workers who have not kept up with technology.

Other studies indicate that computer skills pay a premium of 36 to 50 percent in higher wages for those with similar education. This can give a distinct competitive edge to young people who have good computer skills, and some research indicates that this is the case.

Seven Things You Should Do to Get Ahead

I spent a lot of time finding the data to include in this chapter and presenting it in what I hope has been a reasonably interesting way. Here are seven things I hope you will consider doing for yourself, based on the data in this chapter as well as your own good common sense.

1. Upgrade Your Job Skills and Keep Doing It

Too many people think that once they get their "credentials" they are set for life. Not so. No matter how much education or training you already have, you will need more to move ahead in your present job or even to keep it. It is increasingly important for people in all occupational areas to keep learning new things.

New technologies have revolutionized the way many people work. If you are unfamiliar with a new technology that might affect your job, consider going back to school or in some other way learning what you need to stay current. Constantly look for ways to apply new techniques to your own job to increase your productivity. Finish that degree you have always wanted to get. Sign up for any relevant training related to your job. Be willing to try out new things. It is no longer enough to "put in your time" because the world will surely continue to change around you. Become a person that is needed in your workplace and industry. The more skills you have, the more likely that you will have job security and advancement.

INCREASE YOUR COMPUTER LITERACY

Quick Tip

Computer literacy is essential for success in most jobs, and it is most important that you continue to stay up to date. Here are some tips:

Use a computer often. Look for ways to use a computer to make your work and personal life more productive, and use it every day.

Get more education. If you are in school, take as many information technology courses as possible, and use a computer for as many tasks as you can. Most school career services centers will train you on programs that are in demand in the workforce. There are also many low-cost adult education programs that will help you keep up with changing technologies.

Upgrade your computer knowledge and skills. Plan on continually upgrading your computer knowledge and skills by taking classes, reading information technology magazines, learning and using new software programs, using the Internet often, and any other computer-related activity you can think of—even if you have to spend your leisure time doing so. In today's labor market, advanced computer skills are expected and essential.

---

2. Avoid the "Boxes" in Your Life

Most people separate their life activities into the three major categories of play, learning, and work. One way they do this is by age, emphasizing play as the major activity for young children, learning and being educated for youth, working for adults and, finally, retirement and a return to playing again.

Richard Bolles, in a book titled *The Three Boxes of Life,* defined these three activities—playing, learning, and working—as the three boxes that too many people use to limit themselves. Instead, he suggests we should strive to incorporate playing, learning, and working into all aspects of our lives. Working, for example, can also be playing as well as an ongoing learning experience. Ideally, that is what good career and life planning should help you achieve—a balance between leisure, learning, and working rather than a separation. Many companies are realizing this as well and have increased productivity by providing a spirit of "play" in the workplace.

3. Incorporate Life Planning into Your Job Search

Your current priority may be to find your next job. That is a worthy objective, and this book will show you a variety of techniques to accomplish that. Before you begin the search, however, take more time to define clearly what, precisely, you want and need from a job. Be certain to consider how that job might help you go where you want to go with your life. It will be time well spent.

Good career planning is extremely important, but it should be done in the context of what you want to do with your life. How can you, for example, incorporate elements of pleasure and learning into your next job?

4. Develop Your Lifelong Skills

You are likely to change jobs and careers again and again during your life. The job skills you have now will need to be continually upgraded. This makes it increasingly important for you to know what you are particularly good at doing and develop those skills throughout your life. This book will help you identify these special skills and talents. As you mature and your interests change, you will choose to develop new skills or emphasize existing ones in different ways. As you do, look for ways to emphasize your strengths and present them in new and creative ways.

5. Consider Small Organizations

More and more of us work in smaller organizations. Over time, an increasing number of us will spend at least part of our working lives working in (or starting up) a small business. Smaller organizations offer excellent opportunities for young people to gain experience and for more experienced workers to apply their skills. What is more, smaller organizations are now just as secure, on the average, as larger ones and will become increasingly important as a source of jobs in the future. If working in a small organization is a new idea to you, consider it.

6. Do Things You Enjoy Doing

Earning a living can be a difficult task. Over the years I have done many things that I did not enjoy but did them anyway so that I could "earn a living." What I have learned is that having fun, having meaningful relationships, and finding satisfaction and meaning from what we do with our lives is what life is all about. So look for joy in your life and your job, and for some meaning in your life's work.

7. Learn More about Career Planning and Job Seeking Skills

I hope I have presented a few things in this chapter that interest you and, more importantly, motivate you to learn more about career planning and your search for a job. The stakes are very high for you, both in money and in personal satisfaction.

I know there is a lot to think about, and it may all seem a bit overwhelming to make a decision to go in one career or education direction over another. But there are a couple things that I would like you to remember as you leave this chapter:

1. Spend more time exploring your career and education options. Now and in the future, your options are enormous. This is a very good thing, so keep looking and keep learning.

2. Decide to use more effective job search methods. The cost of being unemployed or underemployed is enormous, so promise yourself to learn more about—and use—more effective approaches to getting a good job in less time.

While much of this book encourages you to use active job search methods, here is one more tidbit:

New hires are more likely to stay on a job if recruited though inside sources instead of ads or employment agencies. This conclusion is from researchers at The Ohio State University, led by professor John Wanous, who analyzed data from 28 studies of 39,000 employees.

Long-term success increases by 25 percent or more when new employees are referred by former employees, current employees, and internal postings. This is the reason why most employers prefer to not advertise their jobs: They make better hires by waiting for people to be referred by people the employer can trust.

These two topics, career planning and job search, are what this book is about. I hope this chapter helps motivate you to learn more.

≡≡ Quick Summary

✓ The labor market has changed in recent years: People change jobs and careers more often, there is a larger, more competitive labor force, there has been significant technological change, there are less good paying low-skills jobs, and a loss of manufacturing jobs to other countries.

✓ We have a larger, more diverse workforce with increases in women in the workforce being especially significant.

✓ There is a large segment of older workers because of the Baby Boomer phenomenon, and because people are retiring later in life.

✓ There is a wide variety of statistics about unemployment rates; however, personally you will either be 100 percent employed or 0 percent employed at any point in time. Do not let a period of high unemployment rates deter you from getting out and actively searching for your next job.

✓ Some industries grow faster than others.

✓ Small employers have become a significant force in the employment picture.

✓ Education and training are becoming even more important to your ability to get a job and earn good money, though they don't always guarantee success.

✓ Trade and technical training have become an alternative to a four-year college degree.

✓ Computer skills have become vital for success in many jobs today.

✓ Seven things you should do to get ahead:

   1. Upgrade your job skills and keep doing it

   2. Avoid the "boxes" in your life

   3. Incorporate life planning into your job search

   4. Develop your lifelong skills

   5. Consider small organizations

   6. Do things you enjoy doing

   7. Learn more about career planning and job seeking skills

Comments on the Data Used in This Chapter

Most of the data I use in this chapter comes from various print and online reports from the U.S. Department of Labor's Bureau of Labor Statistics or the Census Bureau. I used the most recent data I could find and, with few exceptions, used annual rather than monthly data to avoid short term distortions. The DOL takes a while to process data, which means that the most recent data available at the time of this writing was about a year old. In some cases, the data came from special reports that are not frequently updated, so some of the data is older by a year or two. This is just the way it is. Labor market data typically changes slowly and the point made by the data does not change much over time.

You may also notice what appear to be inconsistencies in the various data I present, such as different growth projections for the same timeframe. These are probably not errors, but the result of different reports organizing similar information in different ways. For example, the overall projected growth for the labor force is 12 percent while the number of jobs is projected to grow 15 percent. Some tables present data for people age 25 and older, while others present data for all workers 16 and older. I try to use data that makes the most sense in its context and often note these differences along with the data, though I know that it can be a bit confusing.

If you want the newest data, you can often find it somewhere on the www.bls.gov site, though it will usually be presented as part of a big table of numbers in a much less clear way than I present it in this chapter.

CHAPTER 9

Document Your Experience and Accomplishments

≡≡≡Quick Overview

In this chapter, I review the following:

✔ How your accomplishments can reveal your skills

✔ How to complete the Life Experience Worksheets

✔ The Education and Training Worksheets

✔ The Job and Volunteer Worksheet

✔ The Other Life Experiences Worksheet

✔ How You See Yourself (and How Others See You) Worksheet

✔ Key accomplishments and skills to tell an employer about

Chapter 3 helped you identify your key adaptive and transferable skills. This chapter builds upon that earlier chapter by carefully reviewing your past experiences to identify specific situations where you have developed or used these skills. This chapter also helps you to identify job-related skills you've gained from a variety of experiences.

Having a more thorough knowledge of what you are good at and how you developed these skills through experience can be of great value in your job search. For example, it will allow you to answer interview questions much more effectively, select or research a job objective, write a better resume, and get a better job in less time than those who are not as well prepared.

Even so, this is not an exciting or interesting chapter to complete. It will take time to work through the information-gathering forms and do other somewhat tedious tasks. I wish I could make this more fun but I just don't know any other way for you to gather and reflect on this important information. So I suggest you just begin, and slog your way through it, knowing that the payoff is likely to be improved self-knowledge—and a clearer sense of where you want to go in your career.

Emphasize Your Accomplishments

Saying you accomplished something is not the same as saying you did something well. So, as you complete the information in this chapter, remember the situations where you felt some joy or sense of accomplishment. Identify the skills you were using when you experienced these feelings.

 Understand that an "accomplishment" could be something small—something only you know about.

For example, perhaps you never won an award or do not consider yourself outstanding in any particular way. But let's say that you figured out how to make an unauthorized announcement over your school's public address system, releasing everyone early on the last day of school in your senior year. (An action for which you did not get an award but that was quite creative.) Or, that you collected more canned food for the homeless than anyone else in your homeroom. Think about it. Almost every month of your life there is something that you accomplish. These accomplishments are the basis for identifying your skills.

Here is an example of what one person selected as an accomplishment. I listed to the right of her story some of the skills needed to do what she described.

An Activity Presented as an Accomplishment

Presented in the normal way, this same activity could be seen as a relatively meaningless part-time summer job—or it could show something more. The "story" is on the left and the skills it demonstrates are listed on the right.

Activity: "Worked at a concession stand"

Accomplishment	Skills Needed
"Last summer my cousin got ill and could not run his concession at the city fair. Even though I had never run a concession before, I bought the supplies and handled all the details in time to open the stand the first day with only one day's notice! There are usually two people who run the stand, but without help I ran it myself. I served over 5,000 customers that week and took in over $20,000. That is an increase of 36 percent over last year. Because I bought supplies wholesale and in quantity, the profits were 50 percent over last year, too. I worked 12-hour days but always opened on time."	Accepts responsibility Risk taker Problem solver Meets deadlines Good scheduler, prioritized Efficient, fast effective Good customer contact Interpersonal skills Gets results! Budgets money and time Good negotiator Saves money Hard worker Responsible

Do you see how one accomplishment, once you analyze it, can help reveal your skills? John Crystal, a pioneer in career planning, developed this way of analyzing skills many years ago. The approach simply starts with any activity where you felt a sense of accomplishment, where you felt you did something particularly well *and* you enjoyed doing it.

It does not matter if you are the only one who knows about the accomplishment. Simply write down, in as much detail as you can, what you remember about each accomplishment. Then go back over each story and look for the skills you used. A pattern of similar skills being used again and again will usually develop in the things you do well and enjoy doing. These are probably the skills you are particularly good at and enjoy using most.

Chapter 9

The Life Experience Worksheets

As you complete the various worksheets that follow, keep in mind that you are looking for skills and accomplishments. Pay special attention to those experiences and accomplishments that you really enjoyed—these often demonstrate skills that you should try to use in your next job. When possible, quantify your activities or their results with numbers. Employers can relate more easily to percentages, raw numbers, and ratios than to quality terms such as "more," "many," "greater," "less," "fewer," and so on.

For example, saying "presented to groups as large as 200 people" has more impact than "did many presentations."

In some cases, you may want to write a draft on a separate sheet of paper before completing the form in this book. Use an erasable pen or pencil on the worksheets to allow for changes. In all sections, emphasize the skills and accomplishments that best support your ability to do the type of job you are most likely to seek.

Education and Training Worksheet

We spend many years in school and learn more lessons there than you might at first realize. For example, in our early years of schooling we acquire basic skills that are important in most jobs: getting along with others, reading instructions, and accepting supervision. Later on, courses become more specialized and relevant to potential careers.

This worksheet helps you review all your education and training experiences, even those that may have occurred years ago. Some courses may seem more important to certain careers than others. But keep in mind that even the courses that don't seem to support a particular career choice can be an important source of skills.

If you need more space than these worksheets provide, please feel free to complete your notes on additional sheets as needed.

Elementary Grades

While few employers will ask you about these years, jot down any highlights of things you felt particularly good about; doing so may help you identify important interests and directions to consider for the future. For example, note:

✓ Subjects you did well in that might relate to the job you want

✓ Extracurricular activities/hobbies/leisure activities

✓ Accomplishments/things you did well (in or out of school)

High School Experiences

These experiences will be more important for a recent graduate, less so for those with college, work, or other life experiences. But, whatever your situation, what you did during these years can give you important clues to use in your career planning and job search.

Name of school(s)/years attended:

_____

Subjects you did well in or might relate to the job you want:

_____

_____

_____

Extracurricular activities/hobbies/leisure activities:

_____

_____

_____

Accomplishments/things you did well (in or out of school):

_____

_____

_____

_____

_____

College Experiences

If you graduated from a two or four year college or took college classes, what you learned and did during this time will often be of interest to an employer. If you are a new graduate, these experiences can be particularly important because you have less work experience to present. Emphasize here those things that directly support your ability to do the job. For example, working your way through school shows that you are hard working. If you took courses that specifically support your job, you can include details on these as well.

(continued)

Chapter 9

(continued)

Name of school(s)/years attended:

_____

Major:

_____

_____

Courses related to job objective:

_____

_____

_____

_____

Extracurricular activities/hobbies/leisure activities:

_____

_____

_____

_____

Accomplishments/things you did well (in or out of school):

_____

_____

_____

_____

_____

_____

Specific things you learned or can do that relate to the job you want:

_____

_____

_____

_____

There are many formal and informal ways to learn, and some of the most important things are often learned outside of the classroom. Use this worksheet to list any additional training or education that might relate to the job you want. Include military training, on-the-job training, workshops, or any other formal or informal training you have had. You can also include any substantial learning you obtained through a hobby, family activities, online research, or similar informal source.

Names of courses or programs/dates taken/any certificates or credentials earned:

_____

_____

_____

_____

_____

_____

Specific things you learned or can do that relate to the job you want:

_____

_____

_____

_____

_____

_____

The Job and Volunteer History Worksheet

Use this worksheet to list each major job you have held and the information related to each. Begin with your most recent job, followed by previous ones.

Include military experience and unpaid volunteer work here, too. Both are work and are particularly important if you do not have much paid civilian work experience. Create additional sheets to cover all of your significant jobs or unpaid experiences as needed. If you have been promoted, consider handling the new position as a separate job from the original position.

(continued)

(continued)

Whenever possible, provide numbers to support what you did: number of people served over one or more years; number of transactions processed; percent sales increase; total inventory value you were responsible for; payroll of the staff you supervised; total budget you were responsible for; and other specific data. As much as possible, mention results using numbers, as well.

Job #1

Name of organization: _____

Address: _____

Job title(s): Employed from: _____ to: _____

Machinery or equipment you used:

_____

_____

_____

Data, information, or reports you created or used:

_____

_____

_____

People-oriented duties or responsibilities to coworkers, customers, others:

_____

_____

_____

_____

_____

Services you provided or products you produced:

_____

_____

_____

_____

_____

Reasons for promotions or salary increases, if any:

_____

_____

_____

_____

_____

Details on anything you did to help the organization, such as increase productivity, improve procedures or processes, simplify or reorganize job duties, decrease costs, increase profits, improve working conditions, reduce turnover, or other improvements. Quantify results when possible—for example, "Increased order processing by 50 percent, with no increase in staff costs."

_____

_____

Specific things you learned or can do that relate to the job you want:

_____

_____

_____

_____

_____

What would your supervisor say about you?

_____

_____

_____

_____

_____

Supervisor's name: _____

Phone number: _____ E-mail address: _____

(continued)

Chapter 9

(continued)

Job #2

Name of organization: _____

Address: _____

Job title(s): Employed from: _____ to: _____

Machinery or equipment you used:

_____

_____

_____

Data, information, or reports you created or used:

_____

_____

_____

People-oriented duties or responsibilities to coworkers, customers, others:

_____

_____

_____

_____

_____

Services you provided or products you produced:

_____

_____

_____

_____

_____

Reasons for promotions or salary increases, if any:

_____

_____

Details on anything you did to help the organization, such as increase productivity, improve procedures or processes, simplify or reorganize job duties, decrease costs, increase profits, improve working conditions, reduce turnover, or other improvements. Quantify results when possible.

_____

_____

Specific things you learned or can do that relate to the job you want:

_____

_____

_____

_____

_____

What would your supervisor say about you?

_____

_____

_____

_____

_____

Supervisor's name: _____

Phone number: _____ E-mail address: _____

Job #3

Name of organization: _____

Address: _____

Job title(s): Employed from: _____ to: _____

Machinery or equipment you used:

_____

_____

_____

(continued)

(continued)

Data, information, or reports you created or used:

_____

_____

_____

People-oriented duties or responsibilities to coworkers, customers, others:

_____

_____

_____

_____

_____

Services you provided or products you produced:

_____

_____

_____

_____

_____

Reasons for promotions or salary increases, if any:

_____

_____

_____

_____

_____

Details on anything you did to help the organization, such as increase productivity, improve procedures or processes, simplify or reorganize job duties, decrease costs, increase profits, improve working conditions, reduce turnover, or other improvements. Quantify results when possible.

_____

_____

Specific things you learned or can do that relate to the job you want:

_____

_____

_____

_____

_____

What would your supervisor say about you?

_____

_____

_____

_____

_____

Supervisor's name: _____

Phone number: _____ E-mail address: _____

Job #4

Name of organization: _____

Address: _____

Job title(s): Employed from: _____ to: _____

Machinery or equipment you used:

_____

_____

_____

Data, information, or reports you created or used:

_____

_____

_____

(continued)

Chapter 9

(continued)

People-oriented duties or responsibilities to coworkers, customers, others:

_____

_____

_____

_____

_____

Services you provided or products you produced:

_____

_____

_____

_____

_____

Reasons for promotions or salary increases, if any:

_____

_____

_____

_____

_____

Details on anything you did to help the organization, such as increase productivity, improve procedures or processes, simplify or reorganize job duties, decrease costs, increase profits, improve working conditions, reduce turnover, or other improvements. Quantify results when possible.

_____

_____

Specific things you learned or can do that relate to the job you want:

_____

_____

_____

_____

_____

What would your supervisor say about you?

_____

_____

_____

_____

_____

Supervisor's name: _____

Phone number: _____ E-mail address: _____

Other Life Experiences Worksheet

Many people overlook informal life experiences as being important sources of learning or accomplishment. This worksheet is here to encourage you to think about any hobbies or interests you have had—family responsibilities, recreational activities, travel, or any other experiences in your life where you feel some sense of accomplishment. Write any experiences that seem particularly meaningful to you below, and name the key skills you think were involved.

Situation 1: _____

Describe situation and skills used:

_____

_____

_____

_____

_____

Specific things you learned or can do that relate to the job you want:

_____

_____

_____

_____

_____

(continued)

(continued)

Situation 2: _____

Describe situation and skills used:

_____

_____

_____

_____

_____

Specific things you learned or can do that relate to the job you want:

_____

_____

_____

_____

_____

Situation 3: _____

Describe situation and skills used:

_____

_____

_____

_____

_____

Specific things you learned or can do that relate to the job you want:

_____

_____

_____

_____

_____

How Do You See Yourself (and How Do Others See You)?

The previous worksheets can give you a good sense of the skills you have. It's useful to try to itemize those skills as a summary exercise. You may be surprised at how you perceive yourself. But you may also be surprised to know that others may see skills or personal characteristics in you that you overlook. For example, you may overlook that you are good with training others, or have excellent communication skills, or some other characteristic or skill that others think important but that you tend to take for granted or overlook.

This worksheet can be used to summarize your own perceptions of your skills, but it can also be used to gather this kind of information from those who know you well. Fill out the worksheet for yourself, trying to be honest about your own perception of your skills. If you like, you can then make copies and give them to close friends, family members, coworkers, teachers, or others who are likely to give you helpful information. As you get their responses, do keep an open mind. You may get some surprising responses that differ dramatically from your own worksheet, indicating areas you could improve on as well as strengths others see in you that you do not. It is possible that you will get negative or unhelpful information and that is the chance you take in asking for someone else's opinion of you. If they are truly trying to be helpful, though, try to fully understand what they are saying by talking it over with them after you get their completed forms.

Please feel free to photocopy this form and use it as it is. You may also re-create the contents in a word processed document and make any changes you want to it, then e-mail or send copies to the handful of people you trust to give you useful responses. Make sure you complete the last part of the form, telling them how to get this information back to you (via fax, mail, e-mail, etc.).

Personal Strengths Evaluation Worksheet

Greatest Strengths

What are my greatest strengths or best qualities I should present to an employer? In other words, what are the most important reasons I should give an employer for hiring me over someone else?

1. _____

Please explain why: _____

_____

(continued)

(continued)

_____

_____

_____

2. _____

Please explain why:

_____

_____

_____

_____

_____

3. _____

Please explain why:

_____

_____

_____

_____

_____

What might I do to increase my chances for long-term career success? Are there any areas where I might improve, or I might tend to overlook as important?

_____

_____

_____

_____

_____

Which words below describe me as an employee? (Circle the five that are most important for you to present to an employer.)

Accomplished	Flexible	Persevering
Accountable	Focused	Polite
Adaptable	Genuine	Principled
Aggressive	Goal Oriented	Problem Solver
Articulate	Good Phone Skills	Proficient
Bottom Line Person	Good Public Speaker	Prudent
Business Hungry	Good Voice	Punctual
Capable	Good with Numbers	Purposeful
Charismatic	Good with People	Quota Driven
Competent	Good with Processes	Rational
Confident	Good with Systems	Relationship Driven
Cooperative	Honorable	Reliable
Creative	Industrious	Respectful
Customer Oriented	Innovative	Results Oriented
Decisive	Independent	Self-motivated
Democratic	Intuitive	Self-confident
Diligent	Likable	Sensible
Effective	Money Oriented	Situational
Efficient	Moral	Steadfast
Eclectic	Multi-task Person	Teachable
Enterprising	Nurturer	Team Player
Enthusiastic	Patient	Timely
Ethical	Peaceful	Trustworthy
Fair Minded	People Person	Value Oriented
Faithful	Perceptive	Visionary

Anything else I should consider about my skills?

_____

_____

_____

Chapter 9

Key Accomplishments and Skills to Tell an Employer About

This chapter gave you the opportunity to examine the job-related skills you have from education, work, and other life experiences. Keep in mind that you use your job-related skills along with your adaptive and transferable skills. For example, you may have good technical skills in automotive mechanics but you are not likely to succeed in that career without the ability to work quickly, get along with others, and be reliable—your adaptive and transferable skills. It is your combination of job related, adaptive, and transferable skills that will be of most importance to an employer.

The activities in this chapter have given you a few more adaptive or transferable skills to add to your list—or more insight into how you use those skills. Now it is time to consider which skills are likely to be most valuable to you and a prospective employer in a work situation. Answering the following questions may help.

Questions for Review

1. What are the most important accomplishments and skills you can present to an employer related to your educational and training experiences?

_____

_____

_____

_____

_____

2. What are the most important accomplishments and skills you can present to an employer related to your paid and unpaid work experiences?

_____

_____

_____

_____

_____

3. What are the most important accomplishments and skills you can present to an employer related to your other life experiences?

_____

_____

_____

_____

_____

If you find that your opinions about the skills you have or want to use on your next job have changed since the earlier chapter on skills, that's okay. These are your lists, and you can do anything you want with them. Feel free to go back and do those activities again as you learn new things—or simply if you change your mind.

Defining your skills and deciding what to do with them is a process that is never completely done. In the next chapter, you will use your "skills knowledge" in a new way to help you define what sort of job you want—even if you already have a job objective.

☰ *Quick Summary*

✓ When reviewing your history, remember the situations where you felt some joy or sense of accomplishment, and identify the skills you were using when you experienced these feelings. Understand that an "accomplishment" could be something small—something only you know about.

✓ One accomplishment, once you analyze it, can help reveal several of your skills. John Crystal, a pioneer in career planning, developed this way of analyzing skills many years ago.

✓ You may find it helpful to identify five or so things that you felt you did particularly well and that you enjoyed doing. When you are done, write down, in as much detail as you can, what you remember about each accomplishment. Then go back over each story and look for the skills you used.

✓ A pattern of similar skills being used again and again will usually develop to reveal the things you do well and enjoy doing. They are usually adaptive or transferable skills.

✓ As you complete the various worksheets, keep in mind that you are looking for skills that you have demonstrated in addition to your accomplishments. Pay special attention to those experiences and accomplishments that you really enjoyed. When possible, include numbers to describe your activities or their results. In other words, quantify your accomplishments.

Chapter 9

✓ Interview people who know you well to find out areas that you may have overlooked about your skills, strengths, and weaknesses. This will keep you from missing something about your qualifications for a job that may be very important.

✓ In this chapter, you had the opportunity to examine the job-related skills you have gained from education, work, and other life experiences. These, plus your adaptive and transferable skills, will be of great importance to an employer.

CHAPTER 10

Define Your Ideal Job

≡Quick Overview

In this chapter, I review the following:

✔ Why a job title is not the same as a job objective

✔ What most people want from work

✔ How to define what you really want to do

✔ The nine components of an ideal job

✔ How to clarify and refine your ideal job objective

If you are reading this chapter, you either: 1) Have a clear job objective or 2) You don't. In either case, this chapter will present important things for you to consider.

People often approach career planning and job seeking with the assumption that they are looking for a particular job title or type of job. This is a sensible approach, but there are reasons why you should consider other factors as well. For example, what industry would you like to work in or with what sorts of people, and in what sort of an organization? The answers to these questions and other questions can be VERY important to you for a variety of reasons, yet are often not given much consideration.

This chapter will help you identify your work preferences in various important areas beyond a simple job title. Completing the activities in this chapter will help you define what would make up the characteristics of an ideal job by exploring what you really want in terms of your values, interests, skills, work environment, and other preferences. While you may accept a position that is less than ideal in some way, your knowing what is most important to you will help you search for a position that comes reasonably close.

Even if you already have a reasonably clear job objective, it is likely that you are overlooking many opportunities in related jobs and industries. This chapter will help you throw a wider net in your search for openings. If your objective is general, this chapter allows you to select details to present to an employer that best support what you want to do in your next job.

Once you define the characteristics of your ideal job, Chapter 11 will help you to explore specific job titles and industries. If you already know the types of jobs you want, this and the next chapter will help you explore career and job alternatives that you may not have considered.

A Job Title Is Not the Same as a Job Objective

Defining your "ideal" job is a tricky business. The U.S. Department of Labor has formal written descriptions for more than 12,000 job titles. This is far too many jobs for you or anyone else to really know well enough to consider. Add to that the many substantial differences among employers and work environments, and the choices quickly become overwhelming. You might be delighted to work in one place (it being all that you could hope for in a great place to work) and entirely miserable working in another. Yet, both could have the same job title and *look* very much the same to a job seeker.

Many people confuse their job objective with a job title, but they are not the same thing at all. For example, if you were looking for a job as an accountant, computer technician, or receptionist, those are job titles. A job objective, however, is more complex and specific to you and your needs.

Here is an example of a job objective: "A position requiring skills in organizing, communicating, and dealing with people. Prefer a small- to mid-size organization engaged in creative activities. Background in office management, skilled in word processing, spreadsheets, Internet research, and other computer operations."

Although it doesn't mention a job title, this is just the sort of thing that a person who has worked as a "receptionist" or other general office position in the past might write on a resume. It mentions skills and preferences without limiting the choices. This approach leaves open a variety of options that would not be called "receptionist," and it also provides more information on what the person wants and is good at doing. This sample job objective would allow this person to do a wide variety of jobs that would not be limited to a specific job title called "receptionist." A few of the many jobs this person might do include office manager, sales associate, customer services representative, business manager, Web site manager, sales associate, and many others.

Most people don't take the time to clarify what they have to offer, or what they want to do. Their resumes often show this lack of clarity by listing a job title without providing information on what they *want* to do. They often present the same lack of clarity in their search for a job by seeking a job title, rather than the type of work, employer, and work environment they prefer. As a result, they often end up being an "accountant" (or whatever) instead of doing something they really want to do.

Employers don't often consider a job seeker for jobs with different titles and responsibilities from those the job seeker has held in the past. Opportunities are lost, and people end up being receptionists, accountants, and computer technicians because that's what they did in the past, but perhaps not what they would prefer to do in the future.

So don't limit yourself by looking for a job title or listing an option-killing job title on your resume. Instead, be clear about what you want and have to offer and seek an employer who will allow you to do a job that fits those interests and skills. Then, let *them* figure out where you would best fit in and the job title they want to give you.

What Most People Want from Work

For most of human history, a high percentage of people were not happy in their jobs. Of course, back then, many people didn't expect to be happy in their work. Work was, well, work, and what enjoyment you had was likely to come from outside of work.

More recently, however, more and more people are looking for both meaning and enjoyment from the same activities they do to earn their livings. While many people still go to work simply to earn a living, many want more. And the good news is that many are finding it.

Money Is Important, But Other Things Are Even More So

A study by the Gallup Poll indicated that 78 percent of those surveyed rated "interesting work" as very important in being satisfied with their jobs. Only one measure, "good health insurance and other benefits," was rated higher. While many people do value making good money (particularly if you don't make enough to live reasonably well), only 56 percent rated "high income" as being very important to them. It's not that money isn't important—it is; it's just that most working people value other things, too.

The table that follows shows nine other things that were rated higher than money:

Many Things Are Rated As More Important Than High Earnings

Factor	Percent of People
Interesting work	78
Job security	78
Opportunity to learn new skills	68
Having a week or more of vacation	66
Being able to work independently	64
Recognition from coworkers	62
Regular hours, no weekends or nights	58
Being able to help others	58
Limiting job stress	58
High income	56

While some of the items listed here are clearly self-serving, such as job security and benefits, most people are pretty reasonable in what they want. In fact, most of the things people want in their work have to do with wanting recognition, opportunity, and other positive values. Still, people are clearly looking for more from their jobs than just making a living.

The following table shows the results of another survey, this one by Louis Harris and Associates, asking people to rate those things they considered to be very important in their work. Again, money comes up as important, but not as important as some other things.

What People Want from Work

Factor	Percentage Rating as Important
A challenging job	82
Good benefits	80
Good pay	74
Free exchange of information	74
Chance to make significant contributions	74
The right to privacy	62

In another survey conducted by Media General Associated Press, working adults were asked to name the one thing they liked most about their work. The responses are listed below along with the percentage who rated each as being most important to them. Once again, notice that money is not in first place.

The One Thing That People Like Most About Their Jobs

Factor	Percentage of People
The work itself	32
People at work	23
Money	12
Hours	7
Benefits	6
Boss	3
Other reasons	17

I have believed for many years that your life situation effects what is most important to you, and, sure enough, there is research to support that belief. In a study asking working people to select the two factors that were most important in their current jobs, there are distinctly different answers based on the level of education. This table presents the results of the survey taken by Research & Forecasts. It asked people to rate various work factors and select their two most important choices. The percentages indicate those who selected each item among their highest two work-related values.

Work Values Differ by Level of Education

	High School Grad or Less	Some College	College Graduate
Percent selecting factor among two most important			
Pay	46	42	29
Amount of independence	31	35	40
Pleasant working conditions	30	23	17
Liking the people at work	29	24	19
Gratifying work	25	32	43
Contribution to the public good	11	14	23
Important career step	10	15	19

As you can see, pay is less important for those with higher levels of education. Average earnings also increase with education, a very important consideration in understanding the varying responses. For people with higher levels of education (and earnings), having independence and gratifying work are the highest rated values, with pay a distant third. However, for those with lower levels of education and earnings, money becomes far more important. No surprise here, it makes sense: Once you are making a decent living, other things become more important. Even for those with lower levels of education and earnings, the research indicates that fewer than half *did not* select pay as one of their top two choices. Over 50 percent of the high school grads or those with less education picked other things as being more important than pay alone.

The research makes it clear that most people rate various measures of personal satisfaction very high in their jobs. The type of work you do and the people you work with are consistently more important to your job satisfaction than pay. For this reason, you would be wise to spend some time considering what you want out of your work before you go out and look for it. That is what this and the next chapter help you do.

Define What You Really Want to Do

The information and activities that follow will help you consider a variety of things that most people don't think about in an organized way. Yet, these very things will make a huge difference to you in your long term career satisfaction and success.

The Nine Most Important Components of an Ideal Job

Many experts have given a lot of thought to the factors a person should consider in selecting a job that is particularly well suited to them. There is a large body of research on predictors for career satisfaction and success, with great differences in opinion on what approach is most valid or factors most important to consider.

Among the more helpful approaches for self-assessment are those that define clusters of related factors to consider in defining the ideal job. While a variety of people have contributed to the process that follows, Bernard Haldane, John Crystal, and Richard Bolles have articulated this approach most clearly in their writings.

The nine factors that follow are adapted from what they and other vocational researchers suggest are the most important things to consider in defining your job objective. Of course, I've added some of my own ideas to the discussion that follows.

1. Skills and abilities	6. Location
2. Interests	7. Special knowledge
3. Personal values	8. Work environment
4. Preferred earnings	9. Types of people you like to work with or for
5. Level of responsibility	

You may have noticed that what is not included in the list is a job title. That can come later, in Chapter 11, after all the other factors are clearly defined.

All of these nine factors are interrelated, so before you can define your ideal job, let's explore each of these factors in more detail.

1. What skills and abilities would you prefer to use?

Knowing what you are good at, and which of these skills you would like to use in your next job, is essential in developing a proper job objective. Chapters 3 and 9 give you a good sense of what skills and abilities you want to use on your next job. Go back now and review those chapters as needed. Think about those skills and abilities that you enjoy using *and* are good at. Then list below the five that you would most like to use in your next job.

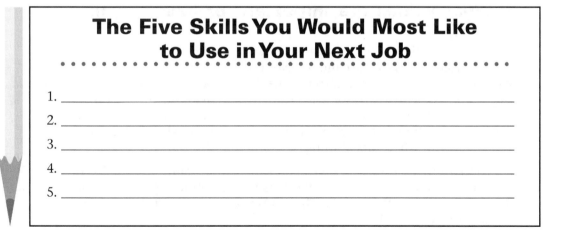

The Five Skills You Would Most Like to Use in Your Next Job

1. _____
2. _____
3. _____
4. _____
5. _____

Chapter 10

2. What interests you?

Many career "tests" or inventories ask you to consider what activities or jobs interest you the most. They organize your responses and then point you to career options or job titles that most closely match your responses. The next chapter helps you to explore specific job titles based on interests and skills, but you already have a general idea of the kinds of things that interest you from working through previous chapters, including Chapter 9, where you summarized a variety of learning, work, and other life experiences.

So consider, in a general way, what sorts of things interest you most. This could be based on courses or training programs you have taken, extra-curricular or similar activities, hobbies or leisure activities, or just things you would like to work into a career if you could. List three to five interests below, emphasizing those things that you would most like to be part of a future career.

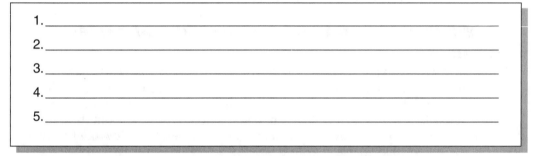

1. _____
2. _____
3. _____
4. _____
5. _____

3. What values are important or have meaning to you?

What are your values? I once had a job where the sole reason for the existence of the organization was to make money. Not that this is necessarily wrong, it's just that I wanted to be involved in things that I could believe in. For example, some people work to help others, some to clean up our environment, and others to build things, make machines work, gain power or prestige, care for animals or plants, or something else. I believe that all work is worthwhile if done well, so the issue here is just what sorts of things are important to you.

The checklist that follows will help you identify what values you would choose from one or more of the values that others have identified as being important or satisfying to them in their work. (This list is adapted from *The World of Work and You*, published by JIST.)

Work Values Checklist

This checklist presents 36 values many people find important in their jobs. Read each value and think about how important each of these things is to you. Then rate each item using the scale below. Put a check mark in the column to the right of each value that best indicates how important that value is to include in your career.

1 = Not important
2 = Important
3 = Very important

	Not Important	Important	Very Important
1. **Help society:** Contribute to the betterment of the world I live in.			
2. **Help other people:** Help others directly, either individually, or in small groups.			
3. **Public contact:** Have lots of daily contact with people.			
4. **Teamwork/work with others:** Have close working relationships with a group; work as a team toward common goals.			
5. **Competition:** Compete against a goal or other people, where there are clear outcomes.			
6. **Make decisions on my own:** Have the power to set policy and determine a course of action.			
7. **Have a pleasant work environment:** Be in a work environment I enjoy.			
8. **Be busy:** Have work that keeps me fully occupied and not bored.			
9. **Power and authority:** Have control over other people's work activities; be a manager or supervisor.			
10. **Influence people:** Be in a position to change other people's attitudes and opinions.			
11. **Work alone:** Do things by myself, without much contact with or supervision by others.			
12. **Knowledge:** Seek knowledge, truth, and understanding.			
13. **Status:** Be looked up to by others at work and in the community or be recognized as a member of an organization whose work or status is important to me.			

(continued)

(continued)

	Not Important	Important	Very Important
14. **Artistic creativity:** Do creative work in writing, theater, art, design, or any other area.			
15. **General creativity:** Create new ideas, programs, or anything else that is new and different.			
16. **Teaching and instructing:** Have a job in which I teach or guide other people.			
17. **Change and variety:** Have job duties that often change or are done in different settings.			
18. **Free time:** Have work that allows me to have enough time for family, leisure, and other activities.			
19. **Quality:** Do work that allows me to meet high standards of excellence.			
20. **Stability:** Have job duties that are predictable and not likely to change over a long period of time.			
21. **Security:** Be fairly sure of keeping my job and not having to worry much about losing it.			
22. **Sense of accomplishment:** Have work that allows me to feel I am accomplishing something worthwhile or important.			
23. **Excitement:** Do work that is often exciting.			
24. **Adventure:** Do work that allows me to experience new things and take some risks.			
25. **Good coworkers:** Have a job where I like my coworkers and supervisor.			
26. **Earnings:** Be paid well compared to other workers.			
27. **Advancement:** Work that allows me to get training, experience, and opportunities to advance in pay and level of responsibility.			
28. **Independence:** Work for or by myself; decide for myself what kind of work I'll do and how I'll do it.			
29. **Location:** Have work that allows me to live in a town or geographic area that matches my lifestyle and allows me to do things I enjoy.			

	Not Important	Important	Very Important
30. **Physical challenge:** Have a job whose physical demands are challenging and rewarding.			
31. **Time freedom:** Have a flexible work schedule that allows me to have control of my time.			
32. **Beauty:** Have a job that allows me to enjoy or that involves sensitivity to or for beauty.			
33. **Friendship:** Have work that develops close personal relationships with coworkers.			
34. **Recognition:** Be recognized for the quality of my work in some visible or public way.			
35. **Moral Fulfillment**: Feel that my work is contributing to a set of moral standards that I feel are very important.			
36. **Community:** Live in a town or city where I can get involved in community affairs.			
Other Values or Preferences: Write other work values or preferences that are very important to you and that you want to include in your career planning.			

Your Most Important Values

Look over the checklist you just completed. Select the five values you would *most* like to include in your career or job and list them below. List them in order of importance to you, beginning with the most important value. These are the values you should consider most when selecting a career or making other important life decisions.

1. _____

2. _____

3. _____

4. _____

5. _____

4. How much money do you want to make—or are you willing to accept?

Earlier in this chapter, I presented some research that indicates that pay is not the most important thing for most people. Even so, many people use pay rates as a primary reason for selecting one career over another, or one job over another.

It's easy to say that money isn't important, but it is. Earnings are particularly important for those starting out and for those with lower incomes. How much you earn is also an issue for most working people.

While money may not be everything, when planning your career or looking for a job, it is important to consider the money issue in advance. Doing so now will help you make a good decision later, when you receive a job offer, and have to balance the money with other factors. For example, would you take a position ideal for you in many ways if the money was a bit less than you wanted?

Quick Case Study

I remember a middle-aged executive who had made over $80,000 per year. He had been unemployed for some time and was quite depressed. When asked what he wanted to earn in his next job, he told me that he wanted to start at about $85,000 but that he really only needed $40,000 per year to maintain his lifestyle now that his kids were grown. He also told me that he and his spouse liked where they lived, did not want to leave, and would settle for less money if they could stay where they were. I suggested he redefine his job objective to include jobs he would enjoy doing and not to screen out jobs paying less than $80,000 per year. With a more flexible approach to his job search, he quickly accepted a job paying $47,000 and loved it. He told me he would never consider going back to what he did before, whatever the salary.

Your Acceptable Pay Range Worksheet

Pay is important, but relative. What you want to earn in your next job and in the future will affect your career choices. You need to consider that some compromise on money is always possible. This is why you should know in advance the pay you would accept, in addition to what you would prefer. Here are a few questions to help you define your salary range:

1. If you found the perfect job in all other respects (or were desperate), what would be the very least pay you would be willing to accept (per hour, week, or year)? _____

2. What is the upper end of pay you could expect to obtain, given your credentials and other factors? _____

3. What sort of income would you need to pay for a desirable lifestyle? (However you want to define this.) _____

4. How much money do you hope to make in your next job?

_____

Many people will take less money if the job is great in other ways—or if they simply need to survive. And we all want more pay if we can get it. Realistically, your next job will probably be somewhere between your minimum and maximum amount. Complete the following to determine a reasonable pay range for your next position.

Reasonable lower end of what you will accept on your next position

_____

Reasonable upper end of pay you can expect on your next job

_____

5. How much responsibility are you willing to accept?

In most organizations, those who are willing to accept more responsibility are also typically paid more. With few exceptions, if you want to earn more, you will have to accept more responsibility and/or get more education. Higher levels of responsibility often require you to supervise others or make decisions that affect the organization. When things don't go well, people in charge are also held accountable for the performance of their area of responsibility. Some people are willing to accept this responsibility and others, understandably, would prefer not to. Decide how much responsibility you are willing to accept and write that in the next worksheet.

Chapter 10

Your Preferred Level of Responsibility

Here are some questions to help you consider how much responsibility you want or are willing to accept in your ideal job.

1. Do you like to be in charge? _____

2. Are you good at supervising others? _____

3. Do you prefer working as part of a team? _____

4. Do you prefer working by yourself or under someone else's guidance?

_____

Jot down where you see yourself, in terms of accepting responsibility for others, and in other ways within an organization.

_____

_____

_____

_____

6. Where do you want your next job to be located—in what city or region?

Narrowing down your job search as much as possible is a good thing to do. One of the factors to consider during your search for a job is where, geographically, you want to work. This could be as simple a decision as finding a job that allows you to live where you are now. This might be because you want to live near your relatives, like where you live and don't want to move, or want to be close to your favorite childcare center. Maybe you are or are not willing to relocate, an important question to consider now, before it comes up in an interview.

There are often good reasons for wanting to stay where you now live, although certain jobs and career opportunities may be limited unless you are willing to move. For example, if you live in a small town, some jobs may exist in small numbers, if at all. If you are willing to leave, you may be able to find jobs with higher overall wages, a larger and more varied job market, or some other advantage. If you decide to stay where you are, there are still geographic issues to consider. How far are you, for example, willing to commute? Would it be more desirable for you to work on one side of town than the other?

When you've looked at all the options, you can make a more informed decision. If you prefer to stay but are willing to move, a good strategy is to spend a substantial part of your job search time looking locally. If you are willing to relocate, don't make the common mistake of looking for a job "anywhere." That sort of scattered approach is both inefficient and ineffective. It is preferable to narrow your job search to a few key geographic areas and concentrate your efforts there.

Keep in mind that the right job in the wrong place is not the right job. A better course of action, before you get desperate, is to define the characteristics of the place you'd like to live.

For example, suppose you would like to live near the ocean, in a mid-sized city, and in a part of the country that has mild winters but does have four seasons. That leaves out a large number of places, doesn't it? Or it may be as simple as wanting to live near your mom. As you add more criteria, there are fewer and fewer places to look and your job search becomes more precise. The more precise you are, the more likely you will end up with what you want. One way to do this is to consider the places you have already lived. Think about what you did and did not like about them. Use a sheet of paper to list the things you did like (on the left side) and did not like (on the right). This may help you identify the things you would like to have in a new place. You should also go to your library or the Internet to research a particular location you are considering or just to learn about the options.

Preferred Geographic Location

Go ahead and write down your preferences for where you prefer your work to be located.

_____

_____

_____

_____

_____

_____

7. What special knowledge or interests would you like to use or pursue?

You have all sorts of prior life experience, training, and education that can help you succeed in a new job. Chapter 9 reviews these in detail, and you might want to look over that material in considering your options.

Perhaps you know how to fix computers, keep accounting records, or cook good food. Write down the things you have learned from schooling, training, hobbies, family experiences, and other formal or informal sources. Perhaps one or more of them could make you a very special applicant in the right setting. For example, an accountant who knows a lot about fashion would be a very special candidate if he or she just happened to be interviewing for a job with an organization that sells clothing, home furnishings, or has another connection to style and fashion.

Formal education, special training, and work experience are obviously important, but leisure activities, hobbies, volunteer work, family responsibilities, and other informal activities can also help define a previously overlooked job possibility.

To help you consider alternatives, use a separate sheet of paper to make a list of the major areas in which you:

1. Have received formal education or training
2. Have learned to do something from prior on-the-job, hobby, or other informal experience
3. Are very interested in, but don't have much practical experience

Once you have made your list, go back and select the areas that are most interesting to you. These could give you ideas for jobs you might otherwise overlook. List your top five choices on the worksheet that follows, beginning with the one that is most important to you.

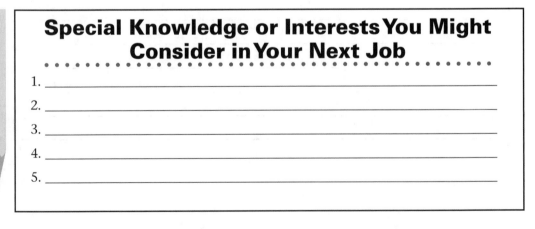

Special Knowledge or Interests You Might Consider in Your Next Job

1. _____
2. _____
3. _____
4. _____
5. _____

If you already have a job objective and it does not include one of your top three choices, don't toss out that job objective yet. For instance, if you are looking for a job as a warehouse manager, but you selected your hobby of making pottery as one of the three, can you think of a possible job combining the two? Perhaps distributing pottery supplies or managing some part of a pottery business would be more your cup of tea than just managing any sort of warehouse.

8. What sort of work environment do you prefer?

I don't like to work in a building without windows, and I do like to get up and move around occasionally. While most of us can put up with all sorts of less-than-ideal work environments, some work environment issues will bother us more than others.

Once again, defining the things you did not like about previous work environments is a good way to help you define what you prefer. Think of all the places you've worked or gone to school and write down the things you didn't like about those environments. Then redefine them as positives, as in the following example. When you have completed the list for each job you've had (use extra sheets if necessary), go back and select the five environmental preferences that are really important to you. Here is one example of such a worksheet to help you get started.

Job: Accountant for the Internal Revenue Service	
Things I Did Not Like About the Workplace	*Environment I Would Like in My Next Job*
too noisy	quiet workplace
no variety in work	lots of variety in work
no windows	my own window
parking was a problem	my own air strip (just kidding)
too much sitting	more activity
not people-oriented	more customer contact
indoors in nice weather	more outside work
too large an organization	smaller organization

Chapter 10

..... Your Preferred Work Environment .....

Write down those things about your work environment that are most important to include in your next job on the lines below. List your most important selection first, followed by others in order of importance.

1. _____

2. _____

3. _____

4. _____

5. _____

---

9. What types of people do you prefer to work with?

An important element in enjoying your job is the people you work with and for. If you have ever had a rotten boss or worked with a group of losers, you know exactly why this is so important. Keep in mind that what someone else defines as a good group of people to work with might not be good for you.

You could argue that there is no way to know in advance the types of people you will end up having as coworkers. However, first impressions work both ways. Your potential employer judges you within the first 30 seconds of a face to face meeting. You can do the same regarding your potential boss and coworkers. This is why it is a good idea to meet with the people you will work with before you accept a position. Ask them questions if you can't get a good read on the type of people they are. If you haven't already given any thought to the subject, the following exercise will help you do just that.

Think about all your past jobs (work, military, volunteer, school, etc.) and your coworkers on those jobs. As in the previous sample worksheet, write down the things you didn't like about your coworkers, and then redefine them into qualities you'd like to see in your work mates. When your list is complete, go back and identify the types of people you would really like to work with in your next job. Then select the five qualities that are most important to you.

Characteristics of the People You Would Prefer to Work With

Write those characteristics below, in their order of importance to you.

1. _____

2. _____

3. _____

4. _____

5. _____

Now You Have a Definition of Your Ideal Job

The activities you just completed will help you more clearly define the preferred characteristics of your next job. One or more of the factors may take considerably more time to resolve than what I could offer in the brief activities I provide in this chapter. Any one of them, if left unresolved, can cause you problems during your search for a job. Even worse, accepting a job that is in major conflict with one or more of these factors can eventually lead to job failure or unhappiness. So spend whatever time is needed to resolve each of the nine factors so that you are clear what you would prefer in your ideal job.

Use this worksheet to help you gather your thoughts and narrow down your job objective as much as is reasonable. Answer each question by including those things you identified as being most important to you in the activities you worked through earlier in this chapter. In some cases, such as the question about skills, you may need to review previous chapters to refresh your memory.

As you complete this worksheet, don't worry about what specific job titles you will be considering; that will be covered in the next chapter. Instead, this worksheet will help you clarify the characteristics to look for in a job that is a good match for you in a variety of ways. Answer each question by including only those two or three things that are most important to you.

The Ideal Job Worksheet

1. What skills or abilities do you most want to use or include in your next job?

Adaptive skills or abilities:

_____

_____

_____

_____

_____

Transferable skills or abilities:

_____

_____

_____

_____

_____

Job-related skills or abilities:

_____

_____

_____

_____

_____

2. What sorts of things interest you that you may want to include or pursue your next job?

_____

_____

_____

_____

_____

3. What values are particularly important for you to include or pursue in your next job?

_____

_____

_____

_____

4. What range of earnings do you expect or would prefer?

_____

5. What level of responsibility would you prefer in your work?

_____

_____

6. What location or geographic characteristics would you prefer?

_____

_____

7. What special knowledge or interests would you like to use or pursue?

_____

_____

_____

_____

8. What type of work environment do you prefer?

_____

_____

9. What types of people would you prefer to work with or for?

_____

_____

Chapter 10

The Three Most Important Things to Include in My Next Job

· ·

After you have completed the preceding worksheet, go back over all your responses and select the three and only three things that are MOST important to include in your next job. Write those three things below.

1. _____

2. _____

3. _____

Once you have assembled the components of your ideal job, consider the possibilities. Your task in the job search is to find a job that comes as close as possible to meeting the criteria you have selected. If you conduct a creative job search, you won't be looking for *a* job but for *the right* job. Of course, you may need to make some compromise between the ideal and what you accept. But the closer you can come to finding a job that meets your preferences, the better that job will be for you. Now, on to the next chapter, where you can explore the possibilities of work, including a job title.

≡ *Quick Summary*

✓ There are thousands of job titles. In addition, there are obvious variables in work environments. You might be delighted to work in one workplace and entirely miserable working in another. However, both jobs could look very much the same to a job seeker.

✓ Many people confuse a job objective with a job title, but they are not the same thing at all. A job objective is more complex and specific to you and your needs. A job objective mentions skills and preferences without limiting the choices. This approach leaves open a variety of options. It also provides more information on what a person wants and is good at doing.

✓ When surveyed, most people do not choose money as their top consideration in a job. Many other factors rate higher in various studies.

✓ The nine components or factors of an ideal job are 1) Skills required, 2) Your interests, 3) Your Values, 4) Preferred earnings, 5) Level of responsibility, 6) Location, 7) Special knowledge, 8) Work environment, 9) Types of people you like to work with or for.

✓ Before beginning your job search, it is essential that you have a clear statement of what sort of job you want and that you know what kinds of skills and experiences are needed to perform that job well.

Identify Specific Industries and Job Titles

≡≡≡Quick Overview

✔ In defining your job objective, consider both types of jobs and industries you want to work in.

✔ Identify industries that suit you.

✔ Complete the Checklist of Industries.

✔ Research your top industry choices.

✔ Identify job clusters within industries.

✔ Research job titles within industries.

✔ Complete the Job Matrix Worksheet to pinpoint a combination of job title, job factors, and industry that best fit your interests.

Most people jump into an education or training program or a job search without much consideration of their true job objective (which I reviewed in the previous chapter). Instead, they often begin and end with a job objective that is poorly formed and that excludes many possibilities. In most cases, they look for a job similar to one they had in the past or that they think is related to their education or training. Rather than analyze what they really want to do, they stick to what they believe they are qualified for.

Many people simply look for any job that will pay them enough to live on. Because they have not done the work to define what they really want, they are very likely to get "a" job rather than work that is a good match for them.

Too many people overlook many job opportunities. They simply go about their careers with very little information about the universe of career and job possibilities that might suit them. They often end up in an educational program that prepares them for work that may or may not suite them, and later find jobs in a haphazard way.

I think that most of us can do better. While I am not suggesting that the process of defining a job objective is a simple one, I do think that there are a few simple things that you can do to help you make better decisions, which are the covered in this chapter

Consider Several Major Variables when Defining a Job Objective

Chapter 10 presented a variety of important factors to consider in defining your ideal job. I will assume that you will now keep those factors in mind as you get more specific in defining your job objective in this chapter.

Remember that, in Chapter 10, you did not define a specific job title. That was intentional on my part, because I want to shake you out of the conventional approach that focuses narrowly on a job title and causes you to overlook far more important matters for your long-term career satisfaction and success.

But it is helpful to have a good idea of what sort of a job you want in terms of job title, as well as where you are most likely to find the job you want. To help you with this, this chapter covers two major topics you should consider in detail before you begin your search for a job:

1. The industry or industries you want to target, and

2. The types of jobs you want to seek

Identify Industries That Interest You

While almost everybody understands the advantage of looking at a certain type of job rather than "any" job, they often overlook the importance of considering various industries. Yet what industry you work in is often as important as what job you choose. Why? There are various reasons, but here are the primary ones:

✓ **Some industries pay better**—Let's say you want to manage some sort of warehouse operation or work in a clerical position. If so, it might help you to know that you are more likely to be paid better in the drug manufacturing industry than in the department or grocery store industries. The same basic job, doing the same basic sorts of things, but one industry pays better. That could end up being a very important difference to you over a period of time.

✓ **Some industries present more risk or less stability**—Some industries routinely hire more people when the economy is strong and lay people off when it is weak. Other industries tend to be more stable in their employment and less affected by short term business cycles. Some industries are growing rapidly, others are declining, and many are changing as the result of technology or other forces. If it is important for you to work in a stable situation where you are less likely to be "laid off," then select a more stable industry.

✓ **Some industries will be more fun for you**—Some industries will simply appeal to you more for a variety of reasons. You could be interested based on your interests, values, previous training or education, or a variety of other factors. Selecting an industry that appeals to you more than another could be as important to you as the job you do.

Checklist of Industries to Consider in More Detail

Following is a list of 42 major industries that cover most of the labor market. Complete the checklist that follows to give you some ideas about what industries you should consider more closely.

The first column lists the industry. The next three columns allow you to decide how interested you are in working in that industry or in learning more about it. Put a check mark into only one of these three columns for each industry. For example, if an industry does not interest you at all, put a check mark in the "No interest" column. If that industry interests you somewhat or you are not sure, put a check mark in the "Somewhat interested" column. It that industry seems very interesting to you, put a check mark in the "Very interested" column.

Industry to consider	No interest	Some-what interested	Very interested
Goods-producing industries			
Agriculture, mining, and construction			
Agricultural production			

(continued)

Chapter 11

(continued)

Industry to consider	No interest	Some-what interested	Very interested
Agricultural services			
Construction			
Mining and quarrying			
Oil and gas extraction			
Manufacturing			
Aerospace manufacturing			
Apparel and other textile products			
Chemical manufacturing, except drugs			
Drug manufacturing			
Electronic equipment manufacturing			
Food processing			
Motor vehicle and equipment manufacturing			
Printing and publishing			
Steel manufacturing			
Textile mill products			
Service-producing industries			
Transportation, communications, and public utilities			
Air transportation			
Cable and other pay television services			
Public utilities			
Radio and television broadcasting			
Telecommunications			
Trucking and warehousing			
Wholesale and retail trade			
Department, clothing, and accessory stores			
Eating and drinking establishments			
Grocery stores			
Motor vehicle dealers			
Wholesale trade			

Industry to consider	No interest	Some-what interested	Very interested
Finance, insurance, and real estate			
Banking			
Insurance			
Securities and commodities			
Services			
Advertising			
Amusement and recreation services			
Childcare services			
Computer and data processing services			
Educational services			
Health services			
Hotels and other lodging			
Management and public relations services			
Motion picture production and distribution			
Personnel supply services			
Social services, except childcare			
Government			
Federal government			
State and local government			

Write in below any other industries that interest you that were not in the checklist above:

_____

_____

_____

Now identify the industries you most want to learn about. The checklist above will help you quickly identify industries you should explore in more detail. Review the checklist and select the five industries that you most want to consider in your job search and write them below.

1. _____

_____

(continued)

Chapter 11

(continued)

2. _____

_____

3. _____

_____

4. _____

_____

5. _____

_____

Learn More About Targeted Industries

Details on each of the industries in the checklist you completed are tracked by the U.S. Department of Labor. As a result, helpful descriptions for each of these industries is provided in a government publication titled *Career Guide to Industries*. A bookstore version of the same publication titled *Career Guide to America's Top Industries* is more readily available in libraries and bookstores. You can also find the descriptions at www.careerOINK.com or at the U.S. Department of Labor's Bureau of Labor Statistics Web site at www.bls.gov under the publications section. A sample description for one of the industries follows.

A Sample Industry Description

What follows is the description for one of the major industries I listed in the industry checklist I provided earlier in this chapter. While the format has been changed to fit this book, it includes all the information found in the *Career Guide to Industries* publication noted above.

I selected the Health Services industry description because it is a large and growing one. It includes information sections including:

✓ Significant points

✓ Nature of the Industry

✓ Working Conditions

✓ Employment

✓ Occupations in the Industry

✓ Training and advancement

✓ Earnings

✓ Outlook

✓ Sources of Additional Information

This particular description was the most current available at the time of this writing. The most recent DOL descriptions use data from previous years, so don't be put off by what looks like older data in the descriptions—it takes a long time for them to collect and analyze the information and this is simply the way they do things. The descriptions are updated every two years, so check for the current publication to get the most recent descriptions for the industries you want to research.

HEALTH SERVICES

Significant Points

✓ Health services is one of the largest industries in the country, with more than 11 million jobs, including the self-employed.

✓ About 13 percent of all wage and salary jobs created between 2000 and 2010 will be in health services.

✓ Nine out of 20 occupations projected to grow the fastest are concentrated in health services.

✓ Most jobs require less than 4 years of college education.

Nature of the Industry

✓ Combining medical technology and the human touch, the health services industry administers care around the clock, responding to the needs of millions of people—from newborns to the critically ill.

✓ More than 469,000 establishments make up the health services industry; all vary greatly in terms of size, staffing patterns, and organizational structures. Two-thirds of all private health services establishments are offices of physicians or dentists. Although hospitals constitute less than 2 percent of all private health services establishments, they employ nearly 40 percent of all workers (Table 1). When government hospitals are included, the proportion rises to 45 percent of the workers in the industry.

(continued)

Chapter 11

(continued)

Health Services Sample Industry Description

Table 1. Percent distribution of wage and salary employment and establishments in private health services, 2000

Establishment type	Establishments	Employment
Total, health services	100.0	100.0
Hospitals, private	1.6	39.3
Offices of physicians including osteopaths	41.1	19.7
Nursing and personal care facilities	4.5	17.9
Offices and clinics of dentists	23.8	6.8
Home healthcare services	3.1	6.3
Offices of other health practitioners	19.2	4.4
Health and allied services, not elsewhere classified	3.3	3.5
Medical and dental laboratories	3.5	2.1

The health services industry includes establishments ranging from small-town private practice physicians who employ only one medical assistant to busy inner city hospitals that provide thousands of diverse jobs. More than half of all non-hospital health services establishments employ fewer than five workers. On the other hand, almost two-thirds of hospital employees were in establishments with more than 1,000 workers.

The health services industry consists of the following eight segments:

Hospitals. Hospitals provide complete healthcare, ranging from diagnostic services to surgery and continuous nursing care. Some hospitals specialize in treatment of the mentally ill, cancer patients, or children. Hospital-based care may be on an inpatient (overnight) or outpatient basis. The mix of workers needed varies, depending on the size, geographic location, goals, philosophy, funding, organization, and management style of the institution. As hospitals work to improve efficiency, care continues to shift from an inpatient to outpatient basis whenever possible. Many hospitals have also expanded into long-term and home healthcare services, providing a continuum of care for the communities they serve.

Nursing and personal care facilities. Nursing facilities provide inpatient nursing, rehabilitation, and health-related personal care to those who need continuous healthcare, but do not require hospital services. Nursing aides provide the vast majority of direct care. Other facilities, such as convalescent homes, help patients who need less assistance.

Offices and clinics of physicians, including osteopaths. Physicians and surgeons practice privately or in groups of practitioners who have the same or different specialties. Group practice has become the recent trend, including clinics, freestanding emergency care centers, and ambulatory surgical centers. Physicians and surgeons are increasingly working as salaried employees of group medical practices, clinics, or integrated healthcare systems.

Home healthcare services. Skilled nursing or medical care is sometimes provided in the home, under a physician's supervision. Home healthcare services are provided mainly to the elderly. The development of in-home medical technologies, substantial cost savings, and patients' preference for care in the home have helped make this once small segment of the industry into one of the fastest growing in the U.S. economy.

Offices and clinics of dentists. Almost one out of every four healthcare establishments is a dentist's office. Most employ only a few workers, who provide general or specialized dental care, including dental surgery.

Offices and clinics of other health practitioners. This segment includes offices of chiropractors, optometrists, and podiatrists, as well as occupational and physical therapists, psychologists, audiologists, speech-language pathologists, dietitians, and other miscellaneous health practitioners. Demand for the services of this industry is related to the ability of patients to pay, either directly or through health insurance. Hospitals and nursing facilities may contract out for these services. This industry also includes alternative-medicine practitioners, such as acupuncturists, homeopaths, hypnotherapists, and naturopaths.

Health and allied services, not elsewhere classified. Among the diverse establishments in this group are kidney dialysis centers, drug treatment clinics and rehabilitation centers, blood banks, and providers of childbirth preparation classes.

Medical and dental laboratories. Medical laboratories provide analytic or diagnostic services to the medical profession or directly to patients following a physician's prescription. Workers may analyze blood, take x rays, or perform other clinical tests. In dental laboratories, workers make dentures, artificial teeth, and orthodontic appliances. Medical and dental laboratories provide the fewest number of jobs in health services.

In the rapidly changing health services industry, technological advances have made many new procedures and methods of diagnosis and treatment possible. Clinical developments such as organ transplants, less invasive surgical techniques, skin grafts, and gene therapy for cancer treatment continue to increase longevity and improve the quality of life for many Americans. Advances in medical technology also have improved the survival rates of trauma victims and the severely ill, who then need extensive care from therapists and social workers, among other support personnel.

Advances in information technology also continue to improve patient care and worker efficiency with devices such as hand-held computers that record notes on each patient. Information on vital signs and orders for tests are electronically transferred to a main database, eliminating paper and reducing record-keeping errors.

Cost containment also is shaping the healthcare industry, as shown by the growing emphasis on providing services on an outpatient, ambulatory basis; limiting unnecessary or low-priority services; and stressing preventive care that reduces the

Chapter 11

(continued)

(continued)

Health Services Sample Industry Description

eventual cost of undiagnosed, untreated medical conditions. Enrollment in managed healthcare programs—predominantly Preferred Provider Organizations (PPOs), Health Maintenance Organizations (HMOs), and hybrid plans such as Point-of-Service (POS) programs—continues to grow. These prepaid plans provide comprehensive coverage to members and control health insurance costs by emphasizing preventive care. Cost effectiveness also is improved with the increased use of Integrated Delivery Systems (IDS). An IDS combines two or more segments of the industry to increase efficiency through the streamlining of functions, primarily financial and managerial. According to a Deloitte & Touche survey, only 48 percent of surveyed hospitals expect to be stand-alone, independent facilities in 2005, as compared with 61 percent in 2000. These changes will continue to reshape not only the nature of the health services workforce, but also the manner in which health services are provided.

Working Conditions

Nonsupervisory workers in private health services averaged 33.1 hours per week in 2000, compared with 34.5 for all private industry. Hours varied somewhat among the different segments of the industry. Workers in home healthcare averaged only 29.5 hours per week; those in nursing and personal care facilities worked 32.6 hours; and hospital workers averaged 35.0 hours.

Many workers in the health services industry are on part-time schedules. Part-time workers made up 15.3 percent of the workforce as a whole in 2000, but accounted for 36.8 percent of workers in offices and clinics of dentists and 18.8 percent of those in offices of physicians. Students, parents with young children, dual job-holders, and older workers make up much of the part-time workforce.

Many health services establishments operate around the clock and need staff at all hours. Shift work is common in some occupations, such as registered nurses. Numerous health service workers hold more than one job, particularly in hospitals and in nursing and personal care facilities.

In 1999, the incidence rate for occupational injury and illness in hospitals was 9.2 cases per 100 full-time workers, compared with an average of 6.3 for the private sector. Nursing and personal care facilities had a much higher rate, 13.5. Healthcare workers involved in direct patient care must take precautions to guard against back strain from lifting patients and equipment, exposure to radiation and caustic chemicals, and infectious diseases such as AIDS, tuberculosis, and hepatitis. Home care personnel who make house calls are exposed to the possibility of being injured in highway accidents, all types of overexertion when assisting patients, and falls inside and outside homes.

Employment

The health services industry provided more than 11 million wage and salary jobs in 2000. Almost one-half of all salaried health services jobs were in hospitals;

another one-third were in either nursing and personal care facilities or offices of physicians including osteopaths. About 91 percent of wage and salary jobs were in the private sector; the remainder, in State and local government hospitals.

In 2000, there were about 383,000 self-employed workers in the health services industry. Of these, more than two-thirds were in offices of physicians, dentists, and other health practitioners. Health services jobs are found throughout the country, but are concentrated in large States, specifically California, New York, Florida, Texas, and Pennsylvania.

Workers in health services tend to be older than workers in other industries. They are also more likely to remain employed in the same occupation due, in part, to the high level of education and training required for many health occupations.

Occupations in the Industry

Health services firms employ large numbers of workers in professional and service occupations. Together, these two occupational groups cover nearly 3 out of 4 jobs in the industry. The next largest share of jobs is in office and administrative support. Management, business, and financial operations occupations account for only 4.9 percent of employment. Other occupations in health services comprise only 2.5 percent of the total (Table 2).

Professional occupations such as physicians and surgeons, dentists, registered nurses, social workers, and physical therapists, usually require at least a bachelor's degree in a specialized field or higher education in a specific health field, although registered nurses also enter through associate degree or diploma programs. Professional workers often have high levels of responsibility and complex duties. They may supervise other workers or conduct research, as well as provide services.

Other health professionals and technicians work in many fast growing occupations, such as medical records and health information technicians and dental hygienists. These workers may operate technical equipment and assist health diagnosing and treating practitioners. Graduates of 1- or 2-year training programs often fill these positions; these jobs usually require specific formal training beyond high school, but less than 4 years of college.

Service occupations attract many workers with little or no specialized education or training. This group includes nursing aides, home health aides, maids and housekeeping cleaners, dental assistants, medical assistants, and personal and home care aides. Service workers may advance to higher level positions or transfer to new occupations, with experience and, in some cases, further education and training.

Most jobs in health services provide clinical services, but there also are many in occupations with other functions as well. Numerous workers in management and administrative support jobs keep organizations running smoothly. Although many

(continued)

Chapter 11

(continued)

Health Services Sample Industry Description

medical and health services managers have a background in a clinical specialty or training in health services administration, some enter these jobs with a general business education.

Each segment of the health services industry employs a different mix of health-related occupations and other workers.

Hospitals. Hospitals employ workers with all levels of education and training to provide a wider variety of services than other segments of the health services industry. About 1 in 4 hospital workers is a registered nurse. Hospitals also employ many physicians and surgeons, therapists, and social workers. About 1 in 5 jobs is in a service occupation, such as nursing, psychiatric, and home health aide, or building cleaning worker. Hospitals also employ large numbers of office and administrative support workers.

Nursing and personal care facilities. More than three-fifths of all nursing facility jobs are in service occupations, primarily nursing, psychiatric, and home health aides. Professional and administrative support occupations are a much smaller percentage of employment in nursing facilities than in other parts of the health services industry. Federal law requires nursing facilities to have licensed personnel on hand 24 hours a day, and to maintain an appropriate level of care.

Offices and clinics of physicians, including osteopaths. Many of the jobs in offices of physicians are in professional and related occupations, primarily physicians and surgeons and registered nurses. A large number of jobs, however, are in office and administrative support occupations, such as receptionists and information clerks, who comprise one-third of the workers in physicians' offices.

Home health care services. More than half of the jobs in home health care are in service occupations, mostly home health aides and personal and home care aides. Nursing and therapist jobs also account for substantial shares of employment in this industry.

Offices and clinics of dentists. More than one-third of the jobs in this segment are in service occupations, mostly dental assistants. The typical staffing pattern in dentists' offices consists of one professional with a support staff of dental hygienists and dental assistants. Larger practices are more likely to employ office managers and administrative support workers, as well as dental laboratory technicians.

Offices and clinics of other health practitioners. Professional and related occupations accounted for about 2 in 5 jobs in this segment, including physical therapists, occupational therapists, dispensing opticians, and chiropractors. Office and administrative support occupations also accounted for a significant portion of all jobs, almost one-third.

Medical and dental laboratories. Professional and related workers account for more than one-third of all jobs in this industry segment, primarily clinical laboratory and radiologic technologists and technicians. Unlike the case in other segments of the health services industry, many jobs also are in production occupations—most notably, dental laboratory technicians.

Health and allied services, not elsewhere classified. This segment of the health services industry employs the highest percentage of professional and related workers, including counselors, social workers, and registered nurses.

Table 2. Employment of wage and salary workers in health services by occupation, 2000 and projected change, 2000–2010
(Employment in thousands)

Occupation	Employment, 2000		Percent change, 2000–2010
	Number	Percent	
All occupations	11,065	100.0	25.5
Management, business, and financial occupations	546	4.9	27.3
Medical and health services managers	167	1.5	34.9
Business operations specialists	87	0.8	19.2
Professional and related occupations	4,975	45.0	26.9
Social workers	110	1.0	37.2
Dentists	86	0.8	13.7
Physicians and surgeons	459	4.1	27.8
Registered nurses	1,774	16.0	25.3
Physical therapists	109	1.0	36.7
Medical and clinical laboratory technologists	133	1.2	18.0
Medical and clinical laboratory technicians	121	1.1	18.9
Dental hygienists	142	1.3	37.1
Radiologic technologists and technicians	159	1.4	23.5
Health diagnosing and treating practitioner support technicians	210	1.9	23.9
Licensed practical and licensed vocational nurses	552	5.0	18.8
Medical records and health information technicians	118	1.1	54.1
Service occupations	3,275	29.6	29.5
Dental assistants	237	2.1	37.8
Home health aides	261	2.4	59.6
Nursing aides, orderlies, and attendants	1,053	9.5	21.7
Medical assistants	301	2.7	59.8
Medical transcriptionists	87	0.8	30.3
Food preparation workers	98	0.9	15.4
Food and beverage serving workers	97	0.9	3.9

(continued)

Chapter 11

(continued)

Health Services Sample Industry Description

Occupation	Employment, 2000 Number	Employment, 2000 Percent	Percent change, 2000–2010
Janitors and cleaners, except maids and housekeeping cleaners	93	0.8	21.9
Maids and housekeeping cleaners	245	2.2	12.4
Personal and home care aides	160	1.4	66.8
Office and administrative support occupations	1,987	18.0	16.0
First-line supervisors/managers of office and administrative support workers	147	1.3	3.3
Billing and posting clerks and machine operators	166	1.5	29.0
Bookkeeping, accounting, and auditing clerks	96	0.9	15.6
Receptionists and information clerks	288	2.6	26.6
Office clerks, general	264	2.4	12.2
Medical secretaries	280	2.5	20.0
Secretaries, except legal, medical, and executive	144	1.3	2.1
Installation, maintenance, and repair occupations	80	0.7	9.8
Production occupations	118	1.1	13.7

NOTE: *May not add to totals due to omission of occupations with small employment.*

Training and Advancement

A variety of programs after high school provide specialized training for jobs in health services. Students preparing for healthcare careers can enter programs leading to a certificate or a degree at the associate, baccalaureate, professional, or graduate level. Two-year programs resulting in certificates or associate degrees are the minimum standard credential for occupations such as dental hygienist or radiologic technologist. Most therapists and social workers have at least a bachelor's degree; physicians and surgeons, optometrists, and podiatrists have significant additional education and training beyond college. Persons considering careers in healthcare should have a strong desire to help others, genuine concern for the welfare of patients and clients, and an ability to deal with diverse people and stressful situations.

The health services industry provides many job opportunities for people without specialized training beyond high school. In fact, 56 percent of the workers in nursing and personal care facilities have a high school diploma or less, as do 25 percent of the workers in hospitals.

Some health services establishments provide on-the-job or classroom training, as well as continuing education. For example, in all certified nursing facilities, nursing aides must complete a State-approved training and competency evaluation program and participate in at least 12 hours of in service education annually. Hospitals are more likely than other segments of the industry to have the resources and incentive to provide training programs and advancement opportunities to their employees. In other segments, staffing patterns tend to be more fixed and the variety of positions and advancement opportunities more limited. Larger establishments usually offer a broader range of opportunities.

Some hospitals provide training or tuition assistance in return for a promise to work for a particular length of time in the hospital after graduation. Many nursing facilities have similar programs. Some hospitals have cross-training programs that train their workers—through formal college programs, continuing education, or in-house training—to perform functions outside their specialties.

Health specialists with clinical expertise can advance to department head positions or even higher level management jobs. Medical and health services managers can advance to more responsible positions, all the way up to chief executive officer.

Earnings

Average earnings of nonsupervisory workers in health services are slightly higher than the average for all private industry, with hospital workers earning considerably more than the average, and those in nursing and personal care facilities and home healthcare services earning less (table 3). Average earnings often are higher in hospitals because the percentage of jobs requiring higher levels of education and training is greater than in other segments. Segments of the industry with lower earnings employ large numbers of part-time service workers.

	Earnings		Weekly
Industry segment	Weekly	Hourly	Hours
Total, private industry	$474	$13.74	34.5
Health services	488	14.75	33.1
Hospitals	577	16.49	35.0
Offices and clinics of medical doctors	507	15.46	32.8
Offices and clinics of dentists	436	15.58	28.0
Offices and clinics of other health practitioners	401	13.15	30.5
Home health care services	367	12.44	29.5
Nursing and personal care facilities	349	10.72	32.6

Table 3. Average earnings and hours of nonsupervisory workers in private health services by industry segment, 2000

Chapter 11

(continued)

(continued)

Health Services Sample Industry Description

As in most industries, professionals and managers working in health services typically earn more than other workers do. Earnings in individual health services occupations vary as widely as their duties, level of education and training, and amount of responsibility (table 4). Some establishments offer tuition reimbursement, paid training, child daycare services, and flexible work hours. Healthcare establishments that must be staffed around the clock to care for patients and handle emergencies often pay premiums for overtime and weekend work, holidays, late shifts, and time spent on call. Bonuses and profit-sharing payments also may add to earnings.

Earnings vary not only by type of establishment and occupation, but also by size. Salaries are often higher in larger hospitals and group practices. Geographic location also can affect earnings.

Table 4. Median hourly earnings of the largest occupations in health services, 2000

Occupation	Health services	All industries
Medical and health services managers	$27.12	$27.10
Dental hygienists	24.70	24.68
Registered nurses	21.56	21.56
Radiologic technologists and technicians	17.25	17.31
Licensed practical and licensed vocational nurses	13.96	14.15
Dental assistants	12.47	12.49
Medical assistants	11.07	11.06
Receptionists and information clerks	10.15	9.63
Nursing aides, orderlies, and attendants	8.83	8.89
Home health aides	8.10	8.23

Unionization is more common in hospitals, although most segments of the health services industry are not heavily unionized. In 2000, 13.8 percent of hospital workers and 10.1 percent of workers in nursing and personal care facilities were members of unions or covered by union contracts, compared with 13.5 percent of all workers in private industry.

Outlook

Wage and salary employment in the health services industry is projected to increase more than 25 percent through 2010, compared with an average of 16 percent for all industries (table 5). Employment growth is expected to account for about 2.8 million new jobs—13 percent of all wage and salary jobs added to the economy over the 2000-10 period. Projected rates of employment growth for the various segments of this industry range from 10 percent in hospitals, the largest and slowest growing industry segment, to 68 percent in the much smaller home healthcare services.

Table 5. Employment of wage and salary workers in health services by industry segment, 2000 and projected change 2000–2010 (Employment in thousands)

Industry segment	Employment, 2000	Percent change, 2000–2010
All industries	133,718	16.5
Health services	11,065	25.5
Hospitals, public and private	4,960	9.8
Offices of physicians including osteopaths	1,973	43.8
Nursing and personal care facilities	1,796	21.9
Offices and clinics of dentists	686	25.6
Home health care services	643	68.0
Offices of other health practitioners	439	46.8
Health and allied services, not elsewhere classified	358	53.6
Medical and dental laboratories	209	29.2

Many of the occupations projected to grow fastest are concentrated in the health services industry. For example, by 2010, employment within the health services industry of personal and home care aides is projected to increase by 67 percent, medical assistants by 60 percent, physician assistants by 57 percent, and medical records and health information technicians by 54 percent.

Employment in health services will continue to grow for a number of reasons. The elderly population, a group with much greater than average healthcare needs, will grow faster than the total population between 2000 and 2010, increasing the demand for health services, especially for home healthcare and nursing and personal care. Advances in medical technology will continue to improve the survival rate of severely ill and injured patients, who will then need extensive therapy and care. In addition, new technologies enable the identification and treatment of conditions not previously treatable. Medical group practices and integrated healthcare systems will become larger and more complex, increasing the need for office and administrative support workers. Also con-tributing to industry growth will be the shift from inpatient to less expensive outpatient care, made possible by technological improvements and Americans' increasing awareness of and emphasis on all aspects of health. Various combinations of all these factors will ensure robust growth in this massive, diverse industry.

Chapter 11

(continued)

(continued)

Health Services Sample Industry Description

Employment growth in the hospital segment will be the slowest within the health services industry, as the segment consolidates to control costs and as clinics and other alternate care sites become more common. Hospitals will streamline healthcare delivery operations, provide more outpatient care, and rely less on in-patient care. Job opportunities, however, will remain plentiful because hospitals employ a large number of people. Besides job openings due to employment growth, additional openings will result as workers leave the labor force or transfer to other occupations. Occupations with the most replacement openings are usually large, with high turnover due to low pay and status, poor benefits, low training requirements, and a high proportion of young and part-time workers, such as nursing, psychiatric, and home health aides. Occupations with relatively few replacement openings, on the other hand, are those with high pay and status, lengthy training requirements, and a high proportion of full-time workers, such as physicians and surgeons.

The fastest growth is expected for workers in occupations concentrated outside the inpatient hospital sector, such as medical assistants and personal and home care aides. Because of cost pressures, many healthcare facilities will adjust their staffing patterns to lower bottom-line labor costs. Where patient care demands and regulations allow, healthcare facilities will substitute lower-paid providers and cross-train their workforce. Many facilities have cut the number of middle managers, while simultaneously creating new managerial positions as they diversify. Because traditional inpatient hospital positions are no longer the only option for many future healthcare workers, persons seeking a career in the field must be flexible and forward-looking.

The demand for dental care will increase due to population growth, greater retention of natural teeth by middle-aged and older persons, and greater awareness of the importance of dental care and ability to pay for services.

For some management, business, and financial operations occupations, rapid growth will be countered by restructuring to reduce administrative costs and streamline operations. The effects of office automation and other technological changes will slow employment growth in office and administrative support occupations but, because the employment base is large, replacement needs will continue to create substantial numbers of job openings. Slower growing service occupations also will have job openings due to replacement needs.

Technological changes, such as increased laboratory automation, will negatively affect the demand for other occupations as well. For example, the use of robotics in blood analysis may limit job growth of medical and clinical laboratory technologists and technicians, although the nature of healthcare precludes wholesale productivity gains in many instances.

Health services workers at all levels of education and training will continue to be in demand. In many cases, it may be easier for job seekers with health-specific training to obtain jobs and advance. Specialized clinical training is a requirement for many jobs in health services and is an asset even for many administrative jobs that do not specifically require it.

Sources of Additional Information

Disclaimer: Links to non-BLS Internet sites are provided for your convenience and do not constitute an endorsement.

For referrals to hospital human resource departments about local opportunities in healthcare careers, contact:

✓ American Hospital Association/American Society for Hospital Human Resources Administrators, One North Franklin, Chicago, IL 60606.

For additional information on specific health-related occupations, contact:

✓ American Medical Association/Health Professions Career and Education Directory, 515 N. State St., Chicago, IL 60610. Internet: http://www.ama-assn.org/ama/pub/category/2322.html

There is also a wealth of information on health careers and job opportunities available through the Internet, schools, libraries, associations, and employers.

Information on the following occupations may be found in the *Occupational Outlook Handbook:* Cardiovascular technologists and technicians; Chiropractors; Clinical laboratory technologists and technicians; Dental assistants; Dental hygienists; Dental laboratory technicians; Dentists; Diagnostic medical sonographers; Dietitians and nutritionists; Emergency medical technicians and paramedics; Licensed practical and licensed vocational nurses; Medical and health services managers; Medical assistants; Medical records and health information technicians; Medical secretaries; Medical transcriptionists; Nuclear medicine technologists; Nursing, psychiatric, and home health aides; Occupational therapist assistants and aides; Occupational therapists; Ophthalmic laboratory technicians; Opticians, dispensing; Optometrists; Personal and home care aides; Pharmacists; Pharmacy aides; Pharmacy technicians; Physical therapist assistants and aides; Physical therapists; Physician assistants; Physicians and surgeons; Podiatrists; Psychologists; Radiologic technologists and technicians; Receptionists and information clerks; Recreational therapists; Registered nurses; Respiratory therapists; Social and human service assistants; Social workers; Speech-language pathologists and audiologists; Surgical technologists; Veterinarians.

Tips for Getting the Most Out of the Industry Descriptions

I won't kid you: Looking stuff up is a pain, and I know you will resist looking up the industry descriptions. I went to the trouble of including an actual sample description here to motivate you to look up and use them. I think if you look over the advice that follows, you will understand how useful these listings can be to you.

Chapter 11

Here are some steps you can take to get the most out of these descriptions:

✓ **Mark them up and write on them:** Circle or underline anything that is particularly important to you, like the pay rates, skills, education, or training required.

✓ **Include important requirements in your interviews and resume:** Later, when you are looking for a job in this industry, include things you underline here that are important to emphasize to an employer. For example, do you have the skills or other characteristics this industry requires? Do you have related interests, experience, training, or education? Can you mention any important industry trends to indicate your knowledge of what is going on in the industry? Jot notes in the margin of strengths you have that could be emphasized at a later time in an interview or resume.

✓ **Pay particular attention to the related jobs:** While some jobs are found in most industries (such as accountants, administrative support, and clerical workers), industry-related jobs are listed at the end of the industry's description. For industries that interest you, you might consider seeking one or more of these jobs. Circle job titles that interest you.

✓ **Consider its pay, growth, and other factors:** I mentioned earlier that some industries pay better than others. Because this is so, consider working in an industry that pays better than average, particularly if you find it of interest. You should also, of course, consider other factors such as industry growth, stability, and other factors. For example, government jobs tend to be more stable than jobs in industries that are more sensitive to changes in the economy.

Identify Specific Job Titles That Interest You

As you have just learned, industries have been thoughtfully organized into logical groupings. Using these groupings and listings allows you to quickly identify industries that seem more interesting than others.

In a similar way, labor market experts have organized jobs and information about jobs into logical groups or clusters. It just so happens that these groupings are VERY helpful for exploring career options or identifying jobs to target in your job search.

Once you identify a job title of interest, the description for that job will help you prepare for an interview, write a better resume, and increase your chances of getting a better job in less time.

Identify Job Clusters Based on Interests

There are a variety of organizational systems that group jobs based on interests, type of job, personality type, and other factors. The better systems make it easy to identify a variety of specific job titles that most closely match your interests and abilities.

One such system was developed by the U.S. Department of Labor and is called the Guide to Occupational Exploration (GOE). Based on extensive research, the GOE organizes all jobs into one of 14 major "Interest Areas." Each Interest Area is then further divided into more specific subgroups of jobs. This system provides a simple and intuitive approach to access more than 12,000 specific job titles, including many that most people would otherwise overlook.

Interest Areas Checklist

Read each interest area carefully. For each area, put a check mark in the column to the right that best describes your level of interest.

Interest Area	Not Interested	Somewhat Interested or Not Sure	Very Interested
Arts, Entertainment, and Media. *An interest in creatively expressing feelings or ideas, in communicating news or information, or in performing.* You can satisfy this interest in several creative, verbal, or performing activities. For example, if you enjoy literature, writing or editing might appeal to you. Do you prefer to work in the performing arts? If so, you could direct or perform in drama, music, or dance. If you especially enjoy the visual arts, you could become a critic of painting, sculpture, or ceramics. You may want to use your hands to create or decorate products. You may prefer to model clothes or develop sets for entertainment. Or you may want to participate in sports professionally as an athlete or coach.			
Science, Math, and Engineering. *An interest in discovering, collecting, and analyzing information about the natural world; in applying scientific research findings to problems in medicine, the life sciences, and the natural sciences; in imagining and manipulating quantitative data; and in applying technology to manufacturing, transportation, mining, and other economic activities.* You can satisfy this interest by working with the knowledge and processes of the sciences. You may enjoy researching and developing new knowledge in mathematics; or maybe solving problems in the physical or life sciences would appeal to you. You may want to study engineering and help create new machines, processes, and structures. If you want to work with scientific equipment and procedures, you could seek a job in a research or testing laboratory.			

(continued)

Chapter 11

(continued)

Interest Area	Not Interested	Somewhat Interested or Not Sure	Very Interested
Plants and Animals. *An interest in working with plants and animals, usually outdoors.* You can satisfy this interest by working in farming, forestry, fishing, and related fields. You may like doing physical work outdoors, such as on a farm. You may enjoy animals; perhaps training or taking care of animals would appeal to you. If you have management ability, you could own, operate, or manage a farm or related business.			
Law, Law Enforcement, and Public Safety. *An interest in upholding people's rights, or in protecting people and property by using authority, inspecting, or monitoring.* You can satisfy this interest by working in law, law enforcement, fire fighting, or related fields. For example, if you enjoy mental challenge and intrigue, you could investigate crimes or fires for a living. If you enjoy working with verbal skills, you might want to defend citizens in court or research deeds, wills, and other legal documents. You may prefer to fight fires and respond to other emergencies. Or, if you want more routine work, perhaps a job in guarding or patrolling would appeal to you. If you have management ability, you could seek a leadership position in law enforcement and the protective services. Many positions in the various military branches are related to this interest and give you the chance to learn technical and leadership skills while serving your country.			
Mechanics, Installers, and Repairers. An interest in applying mechanical and electrical/electronic principles to practical situations by use of machines or hand tools. You can satisfy this interest working with a variety of tools, technologies, materials, and settings. If you enjoy making machines run efficiently or fixing them when they break down, you could seek a job installing or repairing machines such as copiers, aircraft engines, automobiles, or watches. You may prefer to deal directly with certain materials, and could work cutting and shaping metal or wood. Or if electricity and electronics interest you, you could install cables, troubleshoot telephone networks, or repair videocassette recorders. If you prefer routine or physical work in settings other than factories, maybe repairing tires or batteries would appeal to you.			
Construction, Mining, and Drilling. *An interest in assembling components of buildings and other structures, or in using mechanical devices to drill or excavate.* If construction interests you, you can find fulfillment in the many building projects that are undertaken at all times. If you like to organize and plan, you can find careers in management. You can play a more direct role inputting up and finishing buildings by doing jobs such as plumbing, carpentry, masonry, painting, or roofing. You might like working at a mine or oilfield, operating the powerful drilling or digging equipment. There are also several other jobs that let you use your hands.			

Interest Area	Not Interested	Somewhat Interested or Not Sure	Very Interested
Transportation. *An interest in operations that move people or materials.* You can satisfy this interest by managing a transportation service, by helping vehicles stay on their assigned schedules and routes, or by driving or piloting a vehicle. If you enjoy taking responsibility, maybe managing a rail line would appeal to you. If you work well with details and can take pressure on the job, you might consider being an air traffic controller. Or would you rather get out on the highway, on the water, or up in the air? If so, you could drive a truck from state to state, sail down the Mississippi on a barge, or fly a crop duster over a cornfield. If you prefer to stay closer to home, you could drive a delivery van, taxi, or school bus. You can use your physical strength to load freight and arrange it so that it gets to its destination in one piece.			
Industrial Production. *An interest in repetitive, concrete, organized activities most often done in a factory setting.* You can satisfy this interest by working in one of many industries that mass-produce goods, or for a utility that distributes electric power, gas, and so on. You may enjoy manual work, using your hands or hand tools. Maybe you prefer to operate machines. You might like to inspect, sort, count, or weigh products. Using your training and experience to set up machines or supervise other workers might appeal to you.			
Business Detail. *An interest in organized, clearly defined activities that require accuracy and attention to detail, primarily in an office setting.* You can satisfy this interest in a variety of jobs in which you take care of the details of a business operation. You may enjoy using your math skills; if so, maybe a job in billing, computing, or financial record keeping would satisfy you. If you prefer to deal with people, you may want a job in which you meet the public, talk on the telephone, or supervise other workers. You may like to do word processing on a computer, make copies on a photocopier, or work out sums on a calculator. Maybe a job in filing or recording would satisfy you. Or you might want to use your training and experience to manage an office.			
Sales and Marketing. *An interest in bringing others to a particular point of view by personal persuasion, using sales and promotional techniques.* You can satisfy this interest in a variety of sales and marketing jobs. If you like using technical knowledge of science or agriculture, you might enjoy selling technical products or services. Or maybe you are more interested in selling business-related services such as insurance coverage, advertising space, or investment opportunities. Real estate offers several kinds of sales jobs. Perhaps you'd rather work with something you can pick up and show to people. You might work in stores, sales offices, or customers' homes.			

(continued)

Chapter 11

(continued)

Interest Area	Not Interested	Somewhat Interested or Not Sure	Very Interested
Recreation, Travel, and Other Personal Services. An interest in catering to the personal wishes and needs of others, so that they can enjoy cleanliness, good food and drinks, comfortable lodging away from home, and enjoyable recreation. You can satisfy this interest by providing services for the convenience, feeding, and pampering of others in hotels, restaurants, airplanes, and so on. If you enjoy improving the appearance of others, perhaps working in the hair and beauty-care field would satisfy you. You might want to provide personal services such as taking care of small children, tailoring garments, or ushering. Or you may use your knowledge of the field to manage workers who are providing these services.			
Education and Social Service. *An interest in teaching people or improving their social or spiritual well being.* You can satisfy this interest by teaching students, who may be preschoolers, retirees, or any age between. Or if you are interested in helping people sort out their complicated lives, you may find fulfillment as a counselor, social worker, or religious worker. Working in a museum or library may give you opportunities to expand people's understanding of the world. If you also have an interest in business, you might find satisfaction in managerial work in this field.			
General Management and Support. *An interest in making an organization run smoothly.* You can satisfy this interest by working in a position of leadership, or by specializing in a function that contributes to the overall effort. The organization may be a profit-making business, a non-profit organization, or a government agency. If you especially enjoy working with people, you might find fulfillment from working in human resources. An interest in numbers may cause you to consider accounting, finance, budgeting, or purchasing. Or maybe you would enjoy managing the organization's physical resources (for example, land, buildings, equipment, or utilities).			
Medical and Health Services. *An interest in helping people be healthy.* You can satisfy this interest by working on a health-care team as a doctor, therapist, or nurse. You might specialize in one of the many different parts of the body or types of care, or you might be a generalist who deals with the whole patient. If you like technology, you might find satisfaction working with X-rays, one of the electronic methods of diagnosis, or clinical laboratory testing. You might work with healthy people, helping them stay in condition through exercise and eating right. If you like to organize, analyze, and plan, a managerial role might be right for you.			

Your Top Interest Areas

Review each interest area from the previous table, and then write the 3 to 5 areas that interest you the most in the spaces below. Don't worry for now if your selections are practical; just list the interest areas that you most want to know more about, beginning with the area that interests you the most.

1. _____

2. _____

3. _____

4. _____

5. _____

Specific Jobs and Job Groups to Consider Worksheet

This worksheet will help you identify specific groups of jobs and even job titles that you should explore in more detail. Here is some information about what the worksheet includes and some tips for using it well.

✓ **Interest Areas**—Each of the 14 Interest Areas are included in large bold print in the list that follows. Find the Interest Areas you rated among your top five in the Interest Area Checklist you just completed. Then write the number (from 1 to 5) you assigned to that selection in the margin to the right of those Interest Areas.

✓ **Related Work Groups**—Each Interest Area organizes jobs into more specific work groups. Most of the work group names are pretty clear and will give you a good idea of the jobs they include. Review the work group names for the five Interest Areas you selected as most interesting and put a check mark in the box for the work groups you want to explore in more detail.

✓ **Related Major Job Titles**—A list of specific job titles is provided for each Interest Area. These are from a list of about 250 major job titles that are described in a book titled the *Occupational Outlook Handbook*, published in editions by both the U.S. Department of Labor and JIST Publishing. Review these job titles and put a check mark in the box for the job titles you want to learn more about.

(continued)

Chapter 11

(continued)

Arts, Entertainment, and Media
Work Groups ☐ Managerial Work in Arts, Entertainment, and Media ☐ Writing and Editing ☐ News, Broadcasting, and Public Relations ☐ Visual Arts: Studio Art ☐ Visual Arts: Design ☐ Performing Arts, Drama: Directing, Performing, Narrating, and Announcing ☐ Performing Arts, Music: Directing, Composing and Arranging, and Performing ☐ Performing Arts, Dance: Performing and Choreography ☐ Craft Arts ☐ Graphic Arts ☐ Media Technology ☐ Modeling and Personal Appearance ☐ Sports: Coaching, Instructing, Officiating, and Performing

Major Job Titles: ☐ Actors, Directors, and Producers ☐ Advertising, Marketing, and Public Relations Managers ☐ Announcers ☐ Barbers, Cosmetologists, and Related Workers ☐ Broadcast and Sound Technicians ☐ Dancers and Choreographers ☐ Demonstrators, Product Promoters, and Models ☐ Designers ☐ Instructors and Coaches, Sports and Physical Training ☐ Jewelers and Precious Stones and Metal Workers ☐ Musicians, Singers, and Related Workers ☐ News Analysts, Reporters, and Correspondents ☐ Photographers and Camera Operators ☐ Prepress Workers (example: Desktop Publishers) ☐ Public Relations Specialists ☐ Visual Artists ☐ Woodworking Occupations (examples: Woodcarvers, Furniture Designers) ☐ Writers and Editors, Including Technical Writers

Science, Math, and Engineering
Work Groups ☐ Managerial Work in Science, Math, and Engineering ☐ Physical Sciences ☐ Life Sciences: Animal Specialization ☐ Life Sciences: Plant Specialization ☐ Life Sciences: Plant and Animal Specialization ☐ Life Sciences: Food Research ☐ Social Sciences: Psychology, Sociology, and Anthropology ☐ Social Sciences: Economics, Public Policy, and History ☐ Laboratory Technology: Physical Sciences ☐ Laboratory Technology: Life Sciences ☐ Mathematics and Computers: Data Processing ☐ Mathematics and Computers: Data Analysis ☐ Engineering: Research and Systems Design ☐ Engineering: Industrial and Safety ☐ Engineering: Design ☐ Engineering: General Engineering ☐ Engineering Technology: Surveying ☐ Engineering Technology: Industrial and Safety ☐ Engineering Technology: Design ☐ Engineering Technology: General

Major Job Titles: ☐ Accountants and Auditors ☐ Actuaries ☐ Aerospace Engineers ☐ Agricultural and Food Scientists ☐ Architects, Except Landscape and Marine ☐ Atmospheric Scientists ☐ Biological and Medical Scientists ☐ Budget Analysts ☐ Chemical Engineers ☐ Chemists ☐ Civil Engineers ☐ Computer Programmers ☐ Computer Systems Analysts, Engineers, and Scientists ☐ Conservation Scientists and Foresters ☐ Construction and Building Inspectors ☐ Drafters ☐ Economists and Marketing Research Analysts ☐ Electrical and Electronics Engineers ☐ Engineering, Natural Science, and Computer and Information Systems Managers ☐ Engineering Technicians ☐ Geologists, Geophysicists, and Oceanographers ☐ Industrial Engineers, Except Safety Engineers ☐ Landscape Architects ☐ Machinists and Numerical Control Machine Tool Programmers ☐ Materials Engineers ☐ Mathematicians ☐ Mechanical Engineers ☐ Mining Engineers, Including Mine Safety Engineers ☐ Nuclear Engineers ☐ Operations Research Analysts ☐ Petroleum Engineers ☐ Physicists and Astronomers ☐ Psychologists ☐ Science Technicians ☐ Social Scientists, Other ☐ Statisticians ☐ Surveyors, Cartographers, Photogrammetrists, and Surveying Technicians ☐ Urban and Regional Planners

Plants and Animals Work Groups ☐ Managerial Work: Farming and Fishing
☐ Managerial Work: Nursery, Groundskeeping, and Logging ☐ Animal Care and Training ☐ Hands-on Work: Farming ☐ Hands-on Work: Forestry and Logging ☐ Hands-on Work: Hunting and Fishing ☐ Hands-on Work: Nursery, Groundskeeping, and Pest Control

Major Job Titles: ☐ Conservation Scientists and Foresters ☐ Farmers and Farm Managers ☐ Fishers and Fishing Vessel Operators ☐ Forestry, Conservation, and Logging Occupations ☐ Landscape Architects ☐ Landscaping, Groundskeeping, Nursery, Greenhouse, and Lawn Service Occupations ☐ Veterinarians ☐ Veterinary Assistants and Nonfarm Animal Caretakers

Law, Law Enforcement, and Public Safety Work Groups ☐ Managerial Work in Law, Law Enforcement, and Public Safety ☐ Law: Legal Practice and Justice Administration ☐ Law: Legal Support ☐ Law Enforcement: Investigation and Protection ☐ Law Enforcement: Technology ☐ Law Enforcement Security ☐ Public Safety: Emergency Responding ☐ Public Safety: Regulations Enforcement

Major Job Titles: ☐ Adjusters, Investigators, and Collectors ☐ Correctional Officers ☐ Emergency Medical Technicians ☐ Fire Fighting Occupations ☐ Guards ☐ Inspectors and Compliance Officers, Except Construction ☐ Lawyers and Judicial Workers ☐ Paralegals and Legal Assistants ☐ Police and Detectives ☐ Private Detectives and Investigators ☐ Science Technicians (example: Crime Lab Technicians)

Mechanics, Installers, and Repairers Work Groups ☐ Managerial Work in Mechanics, Installers, and Repairers ☐ Electrical and Electronic Systems: Installation and Repair ☐ Electrical and Electronic Systems: Equipment Repair ☐ Mechanical Work: Vehicles and Facilities ☐ Mechanical Work: Machinery Repair ☐ Mechanical Work: Medical and Technical Equipment Fabrication and Repair ☐ Mechanical Work: Musical Instrument Fabrication and Repair ☐ Hands-on Work in Mechanics, Installers, and Repairers

Major Job Titles: ☐ Aircraft Mechanics and Service Technicians ☐ Automotive Body Repairers ☐ Automotive Mechanics and Service Technicians ☐ Blue-Collar Worker Supervisors ☐ Coin and Vending, and Amusement Machine Servicers and Repairers ☐ Computer, Automated Teller, and Office Machine Repairers ☐ Diesel Mechanics and Service Technicians ☐ Electric Power Generating Plant Operators and Power Distributors and Dispatchers ☐ Electronic Home Entertainment Equipment Repairers ☐ Electronics Repairers, Commercial and Industrial Equipment ☐ Elevator Installers and Repairers ☐ Farm Equipment Mechanics ☐ Handlers, Equipment Cleaners, Helpers, and Laborers ☐ Heating, Air Conditioning, and Refrigeration Mechanics and Installers ☐ Home Appliance and Power Tool Repairers ☐ Industrial Machinery Repairers ☐ Line Installers and Repairers ☐ Maintenance Mechanics, General Utility ☐ Millwrights ☐ Mobile Heavy Equipment Mechanics ☐ Motorcycle ☐ Boat, and Small-Engine Mechanics ☐ Musical Instrument Repairers and Tuners ☐ Telecommunications Equipment Mechanics, Installers, and Repairers

(continued)

Chapter 11

(continued)

Construction, Mining, and Drilling Work Groups □ Managerial Work in Construction, Mining, and Drilling □ Construction: Masonry, Stone, and Brick Work □ Construction: Construction and Maintenance □ Construction: General □ Mining and Drilling □ Hands-on Work: Construction, Extraction, and Maintenance

Major Job Titles: □ Blue-Collar Worker Supervisors □ Boilermakers □ Bricklayers and Stonemasons □ Carpenters □ Carpet, Floor, and Tile Installers and Finishers □ Cement Masons, Concrete Finishers, and Terrazzo Workers □ Construction and Building Inspectors □ Construction Equipment Operators □ Construction Managers □ Drywall Installers and Finishers □ Electricians □ Glaziers □ Handlers, Equipment Cleaners, Helpers, and Laborers □ Hazardous Materials Removal Workers □ Insulation Workers □ Material Moving Equipment Operators □ Painters and Paperhangers □ Plasterers and Stucco Masons □ Plumbers, Pipefitters, and Steamfitters □ Roofers □ Sheet Metal Workers and Duct Installers □ Structural and Reinforcing Metal Workers

Transportation Work Groups □ Managerial Work in Transportation □ Vehicle Expediting and Coordinating □ Air Vehicle Operation □ Water Vehicle Operation □ Truck Driving □ Rail Vehicle Operation □ Other Services Requiring Driving □ Support Work in Transportation

Major Job Titles: □ Aircraft Pilots and Flight Engineers □ Air Traffic Controllers □ Blue-Collar Worker Supervisors □ Busdrivers □ Dispatchers □ Flight Attendants □ Handlers, Equipment Cleaners, Helpers, and Laborers □ Material Moving Equipment Operators □ Rail Transportation Occupations □ Taxi Drivers and Chauffeurs □ Truckdrivers □ Water Transportation

Industrial Production Work Groups □ Managerial Work in Industrial Production □ Production Technology: Machine Set-up and Operation □ Production Technology: Precision Hand Work □ Production Technology: Inspection □ Production Work: Machine Work, Assorted Materials □ Production Work: Equipment Operation, Assorted Materials Processing □ Production Work: Equipment Operation, Welding, Brazing, and Soldering □ Production Work: Plating and Coating □ Production Work: Printing and Reproduction □ Production Work: Hands-on Work, Assorted Materials □ Metal and Plastics Machining Technology □ Woodworking Technology □ Systems Operation: Utilities and Power Plant □ Systems Operation: Oil, Gas, and Water Distribution □ Hands-on Work: Loading, Moving, Hoisting, and Conveying

Major Job Titles: □ Apparel Workers □ Bindery Workers □ Blue-Collar Worker Supervisors □ Butchers and Meat, Poultry, and Fish Cutters □ Dental Laboratory Technicians □ Electric Power Generating Plant Operators and Power Distributors and Dispatchers □ Electronic Semiconductor Processors □ Forestry, Conservation, and Logging Occupations □ Handlers, Equipment Cleaners, Helpers, and Laborers □ Industrial Production Managers □ Inspectors, Testers, and Graders □ Jewelers and Precious Stones and Metal Workers □ Machinists and Numerical Control Machine Tool Programmers □ Material Moving Equipment Operators □ Metalworking and Plastics-Working Machine Operators □ Ophthalmic Laboratory Technicians □ Painting and Coating Machine Operators □ Photographic Process Workers □ Precision Assemblers □ Prepress Workers □ Printing Press Operators □ Shoe and Leather Workers and Repairers □ Stationary Engineers □ Textile Machinery Operators □ Tool and Die Makers □ Upholsters □ Water and Wastewater Treatment Plant Operators □ Welders, Cutters, and Welding Machine Operators □ Woodworking Occupations (example: Wood Lathe Operators)

Business Detail **Work Groups** □ Managerial Work in Business Detail □ Administrative Detail: Administration □ Administrative Detail: Secretarial Work □ Administrative Detail: Interviewing □ Bookkeeping, Auditing, and Accounting □ Material Control □ Customer Service □ Communications □ Records Processing: Verification and Proofing □ Records Processing: Preparation and Maintenance □ Records and Materials Processing □ Clerical Machine Operation

Major Job Titles: □ Adjusters, Investigators, and Collectors □ Administrative Services and Facility Managers □ Bank Tellers □ Billing Clerks and Billing Machine Operators □ Bookkeeping, Accounting, and Auditing Clerks □ Brokerage Clerks and Statement Clerks □ Cashiers □ Communications Equipment Operators □ Computer Operators □ Counter and Rental Clerks □ Court Reporters, Medical Transcriptionists, and Stenographers □ Dispatchers □ Employment Interviewers, Private or Public Employment Service □ File Clerks □ Health Information Technicians □ Hotel, Motel, and Resort Desk Clerks □ Human Resources Clerks, Except Payroll and Timekeeping □ Interviewing and New Account Clerks □ Library Assistants and Bookmobile Drivers □ Loan Clerks and Credit Authorizers, Checkers, and Clerks □ Mail Clerks and Messengers □ Office and Administrative Support Supervisors and Managers □ Office Clerks, General □ Order Clerks □ Payroll and Timekeeping Clerks □ Postal Clerks and Mail Carriers □ Prepress Workers □ Receptionists □ Reservation and Transportation Ticket Agents and Travel Clerks □ Secretaries □ Shipping, Receiving, and Traffic Clerks □ Stock Clerks □ Word Processors, Typists, and Data Entry Keyers

Sales and Marketing **Work Groups** □ Managerial Work in Sales and Marketing □ Sales Technology: Technical Sales □ Sales Technology: Intangible Sales □ General Sales □ Personal Soliciting

Major Job Titles: □ Advertising, Marketing, and Public Relations Managers □ Cashiers □ Counter and Rental Clerks □ Demonstrators, Product Promoters, and Models □ Economists and Marketing Research Analysts □ Insurance Sales Agents □ Manufacturers' and Wholesale Sales Representatives □ Public Relations Specialists □ Real Estate Agents and Brokers □ Retail Salespersons □ Retail Sales Worker Supervisors and Managers □ Securities, Commodities, and Financial Services Sales Representatives □ Services Sales Representatives □ Travel Agents

Recreation, Travel, and Other Personal Services **Work Groups** □ Managerial Work in Recreation, Travel, and Other Personal Services □ Recreational Services □ Transportation and Lodging Services □ Barber and Beauty Services □ Food and Beverage Services: Preparing □ Food and Beverage Services: Serving □ Apparel, Shoes, Leather, and Fabric Care □ Cleaning and Building Services □ Other Personal Services

Major Job Titles: □ Barbers, Cosmetologists, and Related Workers □ Busdrivers □ Chefs, Cooks, and Other Kitchen Workers □ Flight Attendants □ Food and Beverage Service Occupations □ Home Health and Personal Care Aides □ Hotel Managers and Assistants □ Hotel, Motel, and Resort Desk Clerks □ Janitors and Cleaners and Institutional Cleaning Supervisors □ Pest Controllers □ Private Household Workers □ Recreation Workers □ Reservation and Transportation Ticket Agents and Travel Clerks □ Restaurant and Food Service Managers □ Retail Salespersons □ Taxi Drivers and Chauffeurs □ Travel Agents

(continued)

Chapter 11

(continued)

Education and Social Service
Work Groups ☐ Managerial Work in Education and Social Service ☐ Social Services: Religious ☐ Social Services: Counseling and Social Work ☐ Educational Services: Counseling and Evaluation ☐ Educational Services: Postsecondary and Adult Teaching and Instructing ☐ Educational Services: Preschool, Elementary, and Secondary Teaching and Instructing ☐ Educational Services: Library and Museum

Major Job Titles: ☐ Adult and Vocational Education Teachers ☐ Archivists, Curators, Museum Technicians, and Conservators ☐ College and University Faculty ☐ Counselors ☐ Education Administrators ☐ Human Resources Clerks, Except Payroll and Timekeeping ☐ Human Service Workers and Assistants ☐ Instructors and Coaches, Sports and Physical Training ☐ Librarians ☐ Library Assistants and Bookmobile Drivers ☐ Library Technicians ☐ Preschool Teachers and Child-Care Workers ☐ Protestant Ministers ☐ Psychologists ☐ Rabbis ☐ Recreation Workers ☐ Roman Catholic Priests ☐ School Teachers—Kindergarten, Elementary, and Secondary ☐ Social Workers ☐ Special Education Teachers ☐ Teacher Assistants

General Management and Support
Work Groups ☐ General Management Work and Management of Support Functions ☐ Management Support: Human Resources ☐ Management Support: Purchasing ☐ Management Support: Accounting and Auditing ☐ Management Support: Investigation and Analysis

Major Job Titles: ☐ Accountants and Auditors ☐ Adjusters, Investigators, and Collectors ☐ Administrative Services and Facility Managers ☐ Budget Analysts ☐ Cost Estimators ☐ Economists and Marketing Research Analysts ☐ Employment Interviewers, Private or Public Employment Service ☐ Financial Managers ☐ General Managers and Top Executives ☐ Government Chief Executives and Legislators ☐ Human Resources, Training, and Labor Relations Specialists and Managers ☐ Insurance Underwriters ☐ Loan Officers and Counselors ☐ Management Analysts ☐ Office and Administrative Support Supervisors and Managers ☐ Property, Real Estate, and Community Association Manager ☐ Purchasing Managers, Buyers, and Purchasing Agents ☐ Receptionists ☐ Secretaries

Medical and Health Services
Work Groups ☐ Managerial Work in Medical and Health Services ☐ Medicine and Surgery ☐ Dentistry ☐ Health Specialties ☐ Medical Technology ☐ Medical Therapy ☐ Patient Care and Assistance ☐ Health Protection and Promotion

Major Job Titles: ☐ Cardiovascular Technologists and Technicians ☐ Chiropractors ☐ Clinical Laboratory Technologists and Technicians ☐ Dental Assistants ☐ Dental Hygienists ☐ Dentists ☐ Dietitians and Nutritionists ☐ Emergency Medical Technicians ☐ Health Information Technicians ☐ Health Service Managers ☐ Home Health and Personal Care Aides ☐ Licensed Practical Nurses ☐ Medical Assistants ☐ Nuclear Medicine Technologists ☐ Nursing and Psychiatric Aides ☐ Occupational Therapists ☐ Occupational Therapy Assistants and Aides ☐ Opticians, Dispensing ☐ Optometrists ☐ Pharmacists ☐ Pharmacy Technicians and Assistants ☐ Physical Therapist Assistants and Aides ☐ Physical Therapists ☐ Physician Assistants ☐ Physicians ☐ Podiatrists ☐ Psychologists ☐ Radiologic Technologists ☐ Recreational Therapists ☐ Registered Nurses ☐ Respiratory Therapists ☐ Speech-Language Pathologists and Audiologists ☐ Surgical Technologists

Your Top Work Groups and Job Titles

Go back and review the Interest Areas that were NOT among your top selections. Quickly review the work groups and job titles listed for each and checkmark any that interests you. (This is worth doing to help you identify jobs you might not have considered otherwise.)

Next, go back and underline any checked work group or job title that is of great interest to you. Select no more than ten work groups and about the same number of job titles. Then write, in order of interest, the five to ten work groups that most interest you below. Then write the five to ten job titles that most interest you, also in order of interest. It's okay if you have fewer than ten work groups or job titles, but you should have at least five of each.

Top Work Groups to Explore	Top Job Titles to Explore
1. _____	1. _____
2. _____	2. _____
3. _____	3. _____
4. _____	4. _____
5. _____	5. _____
6. _____	6. _____
7. _____	7. _____
8. _____	8. _____
9. _____	9. _____
10. _____	10. _____

Get more information on the jobs that interest you most

At this point, you should have a pretty good idea of the types of jobs that interest you most. You now face one of the following two situations:

1. You want to explore your options before deciding.

2. You have a clear idea of the job or type of job you want.

In either case, it's a good idea for you to learn more about the jobs that interest you.

Chapter 11

Three good reasons to research job options

It you are still uncertain about which jobs you will seek, there are obvious reasons for you to learn more about your job options. Doing so will help you eliminate some from consideration and allow others to emerge as the jobs that will best match what you want.

You may also have begun this chapter knowing what sort of job you will seek. That certitude may come as the result of past training, education, work experience, or for other reasons. If this is your situation, you may be thinking that you already know about these jobs and don't need to learn more about them. Not true, for several reasons. By researching various options, you:

✓ **Increase opportunities in your job search by identifying a wider range of job targets**—There are thousands of specialized job titles and you are almost certain to overlook a number of them that would fit your needs very well—if you know about them. Looking up a few job titles is a start, but reviewing all jobs within clusters of similar jobs is likely to help you identify jobs you don't know much about—but which would be good ones for you to consider.

✓ **Improve your interview skills**—Sure, you may think you know what's involved in a particular job, but that is not the same as preparing for an interview. Most people with substantial education, training, and work experience in a particular job do not do a good job of presenting their skills for that job in the interview. People who do their homework by carefully reading a job description and then mentioning key skills that job requires in an interview often get job offers over those with better credentials. Why? Because they do a more convincing job in the interview, they make it easier for an employer to understand why they should hire this job seeker over another.

✓ **Write a better resume**—Knowing the specific skills a job requires allows you to focus on those in your resume and JIST Card.

It is the better-prepared job seeker who often gets the job over those with better credentials. Remember this, and consider doing your "homework" on your job options now, and throughout your job search.

Major sources of work group and job descriptions

While there are hundreds of sources of career information, just a few will give you most of what you need. I've listed this primary resource information here, along with where to find these sources.

Primary Sources of Career Information

Guide for Occupational Exploration (GOE): The third edition of the GOE, published by JIST, is the source of the Interest Areas and related work groups used in the "Specific Jobs and Job Groups to Consider Worksheet." The GOE's system of organizing jobs based on interests was developed by the U.S. Department of Labor. The system is based on substantial research into how people can use their interests to explore career and learning options.

The GOE provides lots of additional information on the Interest Areas and work groups used in the worksheet. For example, the information on each work group includes the types of jobs in that group, sources of training or education needed, related school subjects to pursue, related leisure activities and hobbies, and a complete list of job titles within each work group. Descriptions for the more than 1,000 jobs within the various work groups are also included in the GOE, allowing you to identify very specific job opportunities quickly.

Occupational Outlook Handbook (OOH): The OOH is published by the U.S. Department of Labor and is updated every two years. It provides excellent descriptions for each of the more than 250 major job titles listed in the Specific Jobs and Job Groups to Consider Worksheet. Together, these jobs cover about 86% of the job market. Each job description includes information on the skills required, pay rates, projections for growth, education and training required, working conditions, advancement opportunities, related jobs, and job-specific sources of additional information, including Internet sites. The OOH is available in most schools, libraries, and career counseling centers. *America's Top 300 Jobs* has the same information as the OOH and is more likely to be available for checkout from the library. The *Enhanced Occupational Outlook Handbook*, published by JIST, includes all the OOH text plus brief descriptions for all the O*NET jobs and related job titles from the *Dictionary of Occupational Titles*— a very useful book.

Occupational Information Network (O*NET): This is a database of information maintained by the U.S. Department of Labor. The O*NET database provides specific information on hundreds of data elements for each of more than 1,000 job titles. A book titled the *O*NET Dictionary of Occupational Titles* (published by JIST) provides the only complete printed source of the O*NET descriptions.

Dictionary of Occupational Titles (DOT): This is an older book published by the U.S. Department of Labor that provides brief descriptions for more 12,000 job titles. The government replaced the DOT system with the newer O*NET database, but the DOT's many very specialized job titles are still considered an important career counseling resource for some occupational areas.

Chapter 11

More print and Internet sources of information

A resource appendix at the end of this book lists a variety of books and other print and Internet resources providing job descriptions and other job search resources. Following are a few of the most helpful sources of job titles and descriptions.

CareerOINK: The Web site at www.careerOINK.com is operated by JIST to provide a variety of helpful career information resources including:

✓ Look up of jobs in GOE interesest areas and groups

✓ Self-assessment tools, sample resumes

✓ Quick lookup of the more than 14,000 job descriptions from the OOH, O*NET, and DOT

✓ Military to civilian job cross-reference and many other free resources

Government Web Sites: You can find the OOH job descriptions under the publications section of the U.S. Department of Labor's Bureau of Labor Statistics' Web site at www.bls.gov. Another government site at www.onetcenter.org provides access to the O*NET data base, as well as lots of useful related information.

Focus Your Job Search and Seek the Ideal Job

In this and the previous chapter, I've tried to give you a variety of information and advice to help you define what you want in your next job clearly. Career planning and job search is, however, an imperfect process that requires you to ultimately compromise and take some chances. You are not likely to find the perfect job, because being completely satisfied with anything is not part of the human condition, but the activity that follows can help you define a combination of things to increase the possibility of finding a job that fits you well.

I've suggested previously that you should select one or more jobs and then look for them in organizations or industries where you also have an interest. For example, if you have experience or training to work in accounting and love airplanes, you might consider looking for an accounting-related position in the aircraft manufacturing or airline industry; an airport or a government agency monitoring airline safety; or in an industry that provides materials or services to the aircraft industry. There are many other possibilities you or others might think of if you combined those three elements of job and industry/organization type/interest.

You can do the same thing with some of the ideal job factors you identified in Chapter 10. For example, if you have experience or training in marketing and love to cook in your free time, it may make sense for you to look for a position in a food or restaurant-related industry. Combining a type of job with an industry that interests you can make a lot of sense. In a similar way, you can also combine a type of job with one or more of the factors to define an ideal job. You considered each of these factors in Chapter 10, and they include

1. Skills and abilities

2. Interests

3. Personal values

4. Preferred earnings

5. Level of responsibility

6. Location

7. Special knowledge

8. Work environment

9. Types of people you like to work with or for

The Job Matrix Worksheet that follows will help you "brainstorm" creative combinations of job title and industry as well as job title and the ideal job factors you identified in Chapter 10. Directions for using the Job Matrix Worksheet follow. Give it a try and be creative!

Directions to Complete the Very Quick Job Matrix Worksheet

The Job Matrix has three columns and six rows. You can make your own matrix on separate sheets of paper and include more rows and columns that combine more factors than the ones mentioned in this book. I suggest you not modify the contents until after you understand how the matrix works. Use the matrix I've included in the book to get started; later you can select other job titles, industries, or ideal job factors and use your own matrix worksheets to come up with interesting and creative jobs possibilities.

Step 1: Work Groups or Job Titles

Look at the Job Matrix and notice that it has three columns and six rows. At the top of the three columns are spaces for you to write in specific work group names or job titles. The activities you completed earlier in this chapter have helped you select work groups and specific job titles that interest you. Select three of these groups or titles and write them in the spaces provided at the top of each column in the Job Matrix.

(continued)

(continued)

Step 2: Industries and Ideal Job Factors

Down the left side of the matrix are spaces for you to write. The first two rows provide spaces for you to write in the names of industries that interest you that you identified earlier in this chapter. Write the names of one of these industries in each of the spaces provided in the first three rows of the matrix.

Next, review Chapter 10 and select three of the factors you selected as being most important to include in your next job. (You listed these at the end of Chapter 10.) Write one of these most important factors in the spaces provided in the remaining three rows on the Job Matrix.

Step 3: Be Creative

Now it is time to get creative. Let's say you wrote the job title "Public Relations Specialist" at the top of the first column and "Agricultural Services" in the first row (an industry, because you grew up on a farm and know a lot about this). The box in the upper left corner is where these two items intersect. In that box, write any possible jobs that might combine the job of Public Relations Specialist in the Agricultural Services industry. Can you think of anything? A few obvious combinations might occur to you, like "PR for an agricultural chemical company" or "PR for a government ag program" as well as some that may not be so obvious. Write anything that occurs to you in that box, even if it seems unrealistic or silly.

Then go to the next box, either down or across (whatever makes more sense to you), and repeat the process for a new combination of factors to consider. For example, let's say you wrote "cross country bicycle racing" in the third row down because that is something you love to do in your free time. In that row's first column headed "Public Relations Specialist" can you think of any jobs that would combine those two things? Yep, I can: "PR for a bicycle manufacturer or parts supplier" and "promoting races" and "building interest in cycling by working for a bicycle racing association" for just a few ideas. Repeat this same process for each and every box on your Job Matrix Worksheet, writing any job ideas that combine the two elements that intersect in each box.

Step 4: Identify the Combinations That Make the Most Sense to You

Some job combinations just won't make much sense or will not seem interesting or practical to you. This is your matrix, so ignore those and circle the ones that do make sense to you as possible job targets.

Remember that you can use additional sheets of paper to create additional job matrices to help you consider a variety of options that the sample matrix in this book could not present.

The Very Quick Job Matrix Worksheet

	Work Group or Job Title	Work Group or Job Title	Work Group or Job Title
Top Industry			
Top Industry			
Top Industry			
Ideal Job Factor			
Ideal Job Factor			
Ideal Job Factor			

(continued)

(continued)

Step 5: Go Out and Find Those Job Opportunities

Some of the combinations you come up with may seem unreasonably difficult to find. But, if a combination interests you, you might be surprised at how well you might be received by an employer who needs someone with that odd combination of interests. For example, if you were to enter "amateur bicycle racing association" in your Web browser, you will find a variety of interesting Web sites of organizations and businesses that are very much involved in this sort of activity. Among them is www.usacycling.org, a variety of regional clubs, a site that links to bicycle racing clubs around the world, bicycle racing parts suppliers, and other related sites.

Each of these sources provides the opportunity for you to reach out and make contacts. And many of them will employ people in a variety of jobs. Find the right people in these settings and many of them will be happy to help you. Some will give you job leads, some will teach you about what they do and where someone like you might fit in the field, many will accept e-mail and a resume from you, and a few will be willing to interview you.

If you really want a job involved with bicycle racing in some way (or in a variety of other improbable combinations of things that interest you), there are real opportunities. And, if you think about it, if you were an employer in the bicycle racing industry who needed someone with public relations, accounting, warehousing, sales, or any other job-related skills, wouldn't you rather hire someone who really loves bicycle racing? Yes, you would, and that will be your competitive edge, if you seek the right jobs for the right reasons.

Sample Content from Major Career References

I've included sample job descriptions and other excerpts from major career reference books here so you can better understand how useful that information can be to you. These books are revised on a regular basis, so ask for the most current editions at your library.

I mentioned earlier that much of the information in these books is available for free on the Internet. But understand that much of the best information is NOT available on the Internet, because few authors and publishers are willing to spend the years and substantial money to develop information then give it away for free. A good site to check out for career information is www.careerOINK.com.

It is run by JIST, the people who publish more career reference books than anyone (and who publish *The Very Quick Job Search*), and it includes much of the information in the books mentioned here for free.

Also check out the appendix at the end of this book that lists other sources of information, including other books and Web sites that provide similar information.

Some things you can learn from the job descriptions:

It is important to read the descriptions of the jobs that interest you for a variety of reasons. Here are the most important ones; by reading job descriptions you can:

- ✓ **Explore career alternatives:** The jobs are arranged into logical clusters, so finding those that interest you is quite easy. You can quickly find out more about a job and also learn about other jobs that you may have overlooked.

- ✓ **Get help deciding on education or training:** Too many people decide to obtain job-related training or education without knowing much about the job they will eventually seek. Reviewing the job descriptions will help you learn more about an occupation BEFORE you enroll in an education or training program.

- ✓ **Identify the skills and other characteristics needed for the job you want:** You can look up a job that interests you and the descriptions will tell you the transferable and job-related skills and abilities it requires. Assuming that you have these skills, you can then emphasize them in your resume and interviews.

- ✓ **Find skills from previous jobs to support your present objective:** Look up descriptions for jobs you have had in the past. A careful reading will help you to identify skills you used that can be transferred and used in the new job. Even "minor" jobs can be helpful in this way. For example, if you waited on tables while going to school, you would discover that doing this requires the ability to work under pressure, deal with customers, work quickly, have good communication, and many other skills. If, for example, you were now looking for a job as an accountant, you can see how transferable skills used in an apparently unrelated past job (such as waiting on tables) really can be used to support your ability to do another job.

- ✓ **Identify related job targets:** All of the major career references provide a way to identify other jobs that are closely related to the one that interests you. Because the jobs are listed within clusters of similar jobs, you can easily browse adjacent descriptions of similar jobs that you may have overlooked. All of this information gives you options to consider in your job search, as well as information to include in your resume's job objective.

Chapter 11

✓ **Prepare for interviews:** Before an interview, carefully review the job description and you will be much better prepared to emphasize your relevant key skills. You should also study jobs you have held in the past and identify activities you performed there that are needed in the new job.

✓ **Find out the typical salary range, trends, and other details:** The descriptions will help you to know what pay range to expect, as well as many other details about the job and trends that are affecting it. But note that your local pay and other details can differ significantly from the national information provided.

From the Guide for Occupational Exploration

The GOE provides information on 158 Work Groups arranged within the 14 Interest Areas presented earlier in this chapter. The first major section of the book presents information on each of these Interest Areas and the Work Groups within them. The information that follows is for the first work group in the Arts, Entertainment, and Media Interest Area. It provides a variety of information on the work group to help you decide if it is a good match for you, including skills required; related hobbies, leisure activities, and school subjects; education or training required; and titles of major jobs within this group.

The second part of the GOE provides brief descriptions for each of the more than 1,000 jobs it lists in the various Work Groups. A sample copy of one of these job descriptions follows the sample Work Group information.

The GOE is a very easy book to use and this chapter has already helped you to select the Interest Areas and Work Groups to explore in more detail.

Sample GOE Work Group description (reduced from actual size)

Part 1. GOE Interest Areas and Work Groups _____

14.07 Patient Care and Assistance

Workers in this group are concerned with the physical needs and welfare of others. They may assist professional workers. These workers care for people who are very old, very young, or have handicaps, frequently helping people do the things they cannot do for themselves. Jobs are found in hospitals, clinics, day-care centers, nurseries, schools, private homes, and centers for disabled people.

What kind of work would you do?

Your work activities would depend on your job. For example, you might

- Assist patients to walk.
- Administer medication as directed by a physician or nurse.
- Demonstrate and assist patients in bathing, dressing, and grooming.
- Measure and record vital signs.
- Sterilize equipment and supplies, using germicides, a sterilizer, or an autoclave.
- Serve meals and feed patients who need assistance.
- Collect samples, such as urine, blood, and sputum, from patients for testing and perform routine laboratory tests on samples.

What things about you point to this kind of work?

Is it important for you to

- Have work where you do things for other people?
- Never be pressured to do things that go against your sense of right and wrong?
- Have steady employment?

Have you enjoyed any of the following as a hobby or leisure-time activity?

- Applying first aid in emergencies as a volunteer
- Chauffeuring special groups such as children, older people, or people with disabilities
- Driving an ambulance as a volunteer
- Helping conduct physical exercises for people with disabilities

- Helping people with disabilities take walks
- Nursing sick relatives and friends
- Serving as a volunteer in a fire department or emergency rescue squad

Have you liked and done well in any of the following school subjects?

- Patient and Health Care
- Pathology
- Health
- Nursing Care
- Psychology
- Nutrition
- Human Growth and Development

Are you able to

- Listen to and understand information and ideas presented through spoken words and sentences?
- Communicate information and ideas in speaking so others will understand?
- Tell when something is wrong or is likely to go wrong?
- Read and understand information and ideas presented in writing?
- Exert maximum muscle force to lift, push, pull, or carry objects?

Would you work in places such as

- Hospitals and nursing homes?
- Doctors' and dentists' offices and clinics?
- Schools and homes for people with disabilities?
- Elementary schools?
- High schools?
- Factories and plants?
- Colleges and universities?

What skills and knowledges do you need for this kind of work?

For most of these jobs, you need these skills:

- Service Orientation—actively looking for ways to help people
- Active Listening—listening to what other people are saying and asking questions as appropriate
- Social Perceptiveness—being aware of others' reactions and understanding why they react the way they do

---

(continued)

(continued)

14 Medical and Health Services

These knowledges are important in most of these jobs:

- Customer and Personal Service—principles and processes for providing customer and personal services including needs-assessment techniques, quality service standards, alternative delivery systems, and customer satisfaction evaluation techniques
- Medicine and Dentistry—the information and techniques needed to diagnose and treat injuries, diseases, and deformities

What else should you consider about this kind of work?

Some workers in this group, such as practical nurses and home health aides, often work in temporary or part-time jobs.

There are usually many openings for well-trained newcomers in this field. Many of these jobs are with places operated by federal, state, or local governments. You may have to pass a civil-service test to qualify for some of them. The outlook is mostly very good because of job turnover and the growing health-care needs of a graying population.

If you take a job caring for someone in that person's home, you might have to be on duty 24 hours a day. People who work for places that provide around-the-clock patient care usually have to work evening or night shifts and weekends. An advantage of some of

these jobs is that they include room and board as part of the wages.

Some of these jobs involve close physical contact with people. Workers may have to help lift, bathe, groom, or feed people.

Additional schooling is necessary to advance to higher-level work.

How can you prepare for jobs of this kind?

Occupations in this group usually require education and/or training ranging from 30 days to more than two years. Employers usually require that applicants have a high school education or its equal. Coursework in health, first aid, English grammar, and speech for interpersonal communication is useful. Hospitals, community agencies, colleges, and public vocational schools offer training courses for many of these jobs. The average program requires about one year to complete. Some jobs in this group require state licenses.

Hospitals and clinics provide on-the-job training for many of these jobs. This training usually includes classroom instruction, demonstration of skills and techniques, and practice. The length of training depends on the job.

Interest and experience in home management, child care, or adult care provide a good background for working with aged, blind, or very young people.

SPECIALIZED TRAINING

JOBS	EDUCATION/TRAINING	WHERE OBTAINED
14.07.01 Patient Care and Assistance		
All in Patient Care and Assistance	Medical Terminology; Math Computing (Fractions and Decimals)	High school, volunteer work at a hospital or health-care facility
29-2053.00 Psychiatric Technicians	Psychiatric/Mental Health Services Technician	Trade/technical school, hospital, two-year college, four-year college, military (Army, Navy, Air Force)
29-2061.00 Licensed Practical and Licensed Vocational Nurses	Practical Nurse (L.P.N. Training)	Trade/technical school, hospital, two-year college, four-year college, military (Army)
31-1011.00 Home Health Aides	Nurse Assistant/Aide; Custodial, Housekeeping, and Home Services Workers and Managers; Elder Care Provider/Companion; Homemaker's Aide; Home Health Aide; Health Aide	On the job, vocational school
31-1012.00 Nursing Aides, Orderlies, and Attendants	Nurse Assistant/Aide; Home Health Aide; Health Aide	On the job, vocational school, hospital, military (Army, Navy, Air Force)

(continues)

Sample GOE Job Descriptions

Part 2. The Job Descriptions_____

therapy assistant, perform only delegated, selected, or routine tasks in specific situations. Duties include preparing the patient and the treatment area. **Education:** Moderate-term O-J-T. **Occupational Type:** Social. **Job Zone:** 2. **Average Salary:** $21,870. **Projected Growth:** 43.7%. **Occupational Values:** Social Service; Moral Values; Security; Supervision, Human Relations; Achievement; Coworkers; Working Conditions. **Skills Required:** Speaking; Instructing. **Abilities:** Oral Expression; Oral Comprehension. **Interacting with Others:** Assisting and Caring for Others; Communicating with Other Workers; Establishing and Maintaining Relationships. **Physical Work Conditions:** Indoors; Special Uniform; Standing; Using Hands on Objects, Tools, Controls.

31-9011.00 Massage Therapists

Massage customers for hygienic or remedial purposes. No other data currently available.

14.07.01 Patient Care and Assistance

29-2053.00 Psychiatric Technicians

Care for mentally impaired or emotionally disturbed individuals, following physician instructions and hospital procedures. Monitor patients' physical and emotional well-being and report to medical staff. May participate in rehabilitation and treatment programs, help with personal hygiene, and administer oral medications and hypodermic injections. **Education:** Associate degree. **Occupational Type:** Social. **Job Zone:** 3. **Average Salary:** $20,890. **Projected Growth:** 10.9%. **Occupational Values:** Social Service; Coworkers; Supervision, Human Relations; Company Policies and Practices; Security; Activity; Compensation. **Skills Required:** Social Perceptiveness; Service Orientation; Active Listening; Problem Identification; Speaking; Reading Comprehension. **Abilities:** Problem Sensitivity; Oral Expression; Oral Comprehension. **Interacting with Others:** Assisting and Caring for Others; Communicating with Other Workers; Establishing and Maintaining Relationships. **Physical Work Conditions:** Indoors; Special Uniform; Standing.

29-2061.00 Licensed Practical and Licensed Vocational Nurses

Care for ill, injured, convalescent, or disabled persons in hospitals, nursing homes, clinics, private homes, group homes, and similar institutions. May work under the supervision of a registered nurse. Licensing required. **Education:** Postsecondary vocational training. **Occupational Type:** Social. **Job Zone:** 3. **Average Salary:** $26,940. **Projected Growth:** 19.7%. **Occupational Values:** Social Service; Coworkers; Achievement; Ability Utilization; Activity; Security; Social Status. **Skills Required:** Service Orientation; Information Gathering; Active Listening; Reading Comprehension; Problem Identification. **Abilities:** Oral Expression; Oral Comprehension. **Interacting with Others:** Assisting and Caring for Others; Communicating with Other Workers. **Physical Work Conditions:** Indoors; Special Uniform; Standing; Using Hands on Objects, Tools, Controls; Diseases/Infections; Common Protective or Safety Attire.

31-1011.00 Home Health Aides

Provide routine, personal healthcare, such as bathing, dressing, or grooming, to elderly, convalescent, or disabled persons in the patient's home or in a residential care facility. **Education:** Short-term O-J-T. **Occupational Type:** Social. **Job Zone:** 1. **Average Salary:** $16,250. **Projected Growth:** 58.1%. **Occupational Values:** Social Service; Moral Values; Security; Achievement; Independence; Variety. **Skills Required:** Service Orientation; Social Perceptiveness. **Abilities:** Oral Comprehension; Static Strength; Oral Expression. **Interacting with Others:** Assisting and Caring for Others; Establishing and Maintaining Relationships. **Physical Work Conditions:** Indoors; Standing; Sitting.

31-1012.00 Nursing Aides, Orderlies, and Attendants

Provide basic patient care under direction of nursing staff. Perform duties such as feeding, bathing, dressing, grooming, or moving patients, or changing linens. **Education:** Short-term O-J-T. **Occupational Type:** Social. **Job Zone:** 2. **Average Salary:** $16,620. **Projected Growth:** 23.8%. **Occupational Values:** Social Service; Moral Values; Coworkers; Activity; Security; Supervision, Human Relations; Supervision, Technical. **Skills Required:** Service Orientation; Active Listening; Social Perceptiveness. **Abilities:** Oral Comprehension; Oral Expression; Static Strength; Arm-Hand Steadiness; Near Vision; Written Comprehension; Information Ordering. **Interacting with Others:** Assisting and Caring for Others; Establishing and Maintaining Relationships; Communicating with Other Workers. **Physical Work Conditions:** Indoors; Special Uniform; Diseases/Infections; Standing; Common Protective or Safety Attire; Walking or Running.

31-1013.00 Psychiatric Aides

Assist mentally impaired or emotionally disturbed patients, working under direction of nursing and medical staff. **Education:** Short-term O-J-T. **Occupational Type:** Social. **Job Zone:** 2. **Average Salary:** $22,170. **Projected Growth:** 7.7%. **Occupational Values:** Social Service; Coworkers; Security; Activity; Supervision, Human Relations; Moral Values. **Skills Required:** Active Listening; Speaking; Reading Comprehension; Social Perceptiveness; Judgment and Decision Making. **Abilities:** Oral Expression; Problem Sensitivity; Oral Comprehension. **Interacting with Others:** Assisting and Caring for Others; Establishing and Maintaining Relationships. **Physical Work Conditions:** Indoors; Special Uniform; Walking or Running; Standing; Using Hands on Objects, Tools, Controls; Diseases/Infections; Sitting.

14.08.01 Health Protection and Promotion

21-1091.00 Health Educators

Promote, maintain, and improve individual and community health by assisting individuals and communities in adopting healthy behaviors. Collect and analyze data to identify community needs prior to planning, implementing, monitoring,

More on Career Planning and Job Search **319**

Chapter 11

From the Occupational Outlook Handbook

I've included one job description from the current edition of the *Occupational Outlook Handbook* that was available at the time of this writing. The data on job growth and earnings it refers to in the text is a few years old by the time it is processed and published by the government, but don't be turned off by that as it is essentially accurate.

I selected a sample job description that fits into the GOE work group used previously. This allows you to see how different the descriptions are. The OOH covers about 250 major jobs, while the GOE includes about 1,000 job descriptions, including many more specialized ones that are not described in the OOH or are included along with several other jobs in the OOH. As a result, the OOH descriptions are more detailed and use fewer and less compact lists than the descriptions in the GOE.

Quick Tip A good way to approach this is to start with the GOE, then go to the OOH to read descriptions of jobs that are of greatest interest.

Sample OOH Job Description

Licensed Practical and Licensed Vocational Nurses

(O*NET 29-2061.00)

Significant Points

- Training lasting about 1 year is available in about 1,100 State-approved programs, mostly in vocational or technical schools.
- Nursing homes will offer the most new jobs.
- Job seekers in hospitals may face competition as the number of hospital jobs for LPNs declines.

Nature of the Work

Licensed practical nurses (LPNs), or licensed vocational nurses (LVNs) as they are called in Texas and California, care for the sick, injured, convalescent, and disabled under the direction of physicians and registered nurses. (The work of *physicians and surgeons* and *registered nurses* is described elsewhere in the *Handbook*.)

Most LPNs provide basic bedside care. They take vital signs such as temperature, blood pressure, pulse, and respiration. They also treat bedsores, prepare and give injections and enemas, apply dressings, give alcohol rubs and massages, apply ice packs and hot water bottles, and monitor catheters. LPNs observe patients and report adverse reactions to medications or treatments. They collect samples for testing, perform routine laboratory tests, feed patients, and record food and fluid intake and output. They help patients with bathing, dressing, and personal hygiene, keep them comfortable, and care for their emotional needs. In States where the law allows, they may administer prescribed medicines or start intravenous fluids. Some LPNs help deliver, care for, and feed infants. Experienced LPNs may supervise nursing assistants and aides.

LPNs in nursing homes provide routine bedside care, help evaluate residents' needs, develop care plans, and supervise the care provided by nursing aides. In doctors' offices and clinics, they also

Licensed practical and licensed vocational nurses take vital signs such as temperature, blood pressure, pulse, and respiration.

may make appointments, keep records, and perform other clerical duties. LPNs who work in private homes also may prepare meals and teach family members simple nursing tasks.

Working Conditions

Most licensed practical nurses in hospitals and nursing homes work a 40-hour week, but because patients need around-the-clock care, some work nights, weekends, and holidays. They often stand for long periods and help patients move in bed, stand, or walk.

LPNs may face hazards from caustic chemicals, radiation, and infectious diseases such as hepatitis. They are subject to back injuries when moving patients and shock from electrical equipment. They often must deal with the stress of heavy workloads. In addition, the patients they care for may be confused, irrational, agitated, or uncooperative.

Employment

Licensed practical nurses held about 700,000 jobs in 2000. Twenty-nine percent of LPNs worked in nursing homes, 28 percent worked in hospitals, and 14 percent in physicians' offices and clinics. Others worked for home healthcare services, residential care facilities, schools, temporary help agencies, or government agencies; about 1 in 5 worked part time.

Training, Other Qualifications, and Advancement

All States and the District of Columbia require LPNs to pass a licensing examination after completing a State-approved practical nursing program. A high school diploma, or equivalent, usually is required for entry, although some programs accept candidates without a diploma or are designed as part of a high school curriculum.

In 2000, approximately 1,100 State-approved programs provided practical nursing training. Almost 6 out of 10 students were enrolled in technical or vocational schools, while 3 out of 10 were in community and junior colleges. Others were in high schools, hospitals, and colleges and universities.

Most practical nursing programs last about 1 year and include both classroom study and supervised clinical practice (patient care). Classroom study covers basic nursing concepts and patient-care related subjects, including anatomy, physiology, medical-surgical nursing, pediatrics, obstetrics, psychiatric nursing, administration of drugs, nutrition, and first aid. Clinical practice usually is in a hospital, but sometimes includes other settings.

LPNs should have a caring, sympathetic nature. They should be emotionally stable because work with the sick and injured can be stressful. They also should have keen observational, decision making, and communication skills. As part of a healthcare team, they must be able to follow orders and work under close supervision.

Job Outlook

Employment of LPNs is expected to grow about as fast as the average for all occupations through 2010 in response to the long-term care needs of a rapidly growing elderly population and the general growth of healthcare. Replacement needs will be a major source of job openings, as many workers leave the occupation permanently.

Employment of LPNs in nursing homes is expected to grow faster than the average. Nursing homes will offer the most new jobs for LPNs as the number of aged and disabled persons in need of long-term care rises. In addition to caring for the aged and disabled, nursing homes will be called on to care for the increasing number of patients who have been discharged from the hospital but who have not recovered enough to return home.

LPNs seeking positions in hospitals may face competition, as the number of hospital jobs for LPNs declines. An increasing proportion of sophisticated procedures, which once were performed only in hospitals, are being performed in physicians' offices and clinics, including ambulatory surgicenters and emergency medical centers, due largely to advances in technology. As a result, employment of LPNs is projected to grow much faster than average in these places as healthcare expands outside the traditional hospital setting.

Employment of LPNs is expected to grow much faster than average in home healthcare services. This is in response to a growing number of older persons with functional disabilities, consumer preference for care in the home, and technological advances, which make it possible to bring increasingly complex treatments into the home.

Earnings

Median annual earnings of licensed practical nurses were $29,440 in 2000. The middle 50 percent earned between $24,920 and $34,800. The lowest 10 percent earned less than $21,520, and the highest 10 percent earned more than $41,800. Median annual earnings in the industries employing the largest numbers of licensed practical nurses in 2000 were as follows:

Personnel supply services	$35,750
Home health care services	31,220
Nursing and personal care facilities	29,980
Hospitals	28,450
Offices and clinics of medical doctors	27,520

Related Occupations

LPNs work closely with people while helping them. So do emergency medical technicians and paramedics, social and human service assistants, surgical technologists, and teacher assistants.

Sources of Additional Information

For information about practical nursing, contact:
➤ National League for Nursing, 61 Broadway, New York, NY 10006. Internet: **http://www.nln.org**
➤ National Association for Practical Nurse Education and Service, Inc., 1400 Spring St., Suite 330, Silver Spring, MD 20910.
➤ National Federation of Licensed Practical Nurses, Inc., 893 US Highway 70 West, Suite 202, Garner, NC 27529-2597.

From the O*NET Dictionary of Occupational Titles

The O*NET DOT is a big book that provides the only printed source of information on the more than 1,000 jobs that are kept in the U.S. Department of Labor's database. It uses an organizational structure that organizes jobs into groups of related jobs. These groupings are different from the ones used in the GOE but the table of contents makes it pretty easy to find the jobs that interest you.

© JIST Works

More on Career Planning and Job Search

Chapter 11

I've included one page from the table of contents to show you how the jobs are organized into groups.

Because of the large number of jobs, each O*NET description has to be carefully constructed so that it provides a lot of useful information in a compact space. One of the ways this was accomplished was by using some codes and terms in the descriptions that are described in the book but are not self-explanatory when you look at a description. I included a sample job description from the book on page 324; here are a few brief notes to help you interpret some of those codes:

- ✓ **O*NET number:** This number allows the job to be cross-referenced to a variety of other occupational information systems.

- ✓ **Knowledge, Abilities, and Skills:** These are pretty clear, I think, in that they refer to knowledge, abilities, and skills that this job requires. The description lists only the characteristics that are rated as most important for that job. These entries will help you to know what characteristics you need to succeed in the job and things to emphasize in an interview or resume.

- ✓ **GOE Group:** This allows you to cross-reference the Guide for Occupational Exploration, review the information on the Work Groups that are most closely related to this job, and identify related job titles to consider.

- ✓ **Instructional Programs:** This lists the "Classification of Instructional Programs" training or education programs and code numbers that are often used to provide specific job-related training or education needed for the job. The "Knowledge" entries in the description will also give you a good idea of the types of courses that will help you prepare for the job—and that you should emphasize in your interview and resume.

- ✓ **Related DOT Job/s:** This lists one or more (sometimes many more) related job titles that you can look up in the *Dictionary of Occupational Titles*.

Sample O*NET Table of Contents Page

Chapter 11

Sample O*NET Job Description

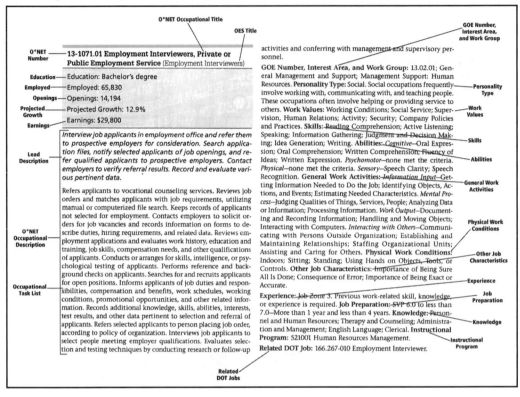

Quick Summary

✓ It's important that you consider both the industry you want to work in and the types of jobs you want, not just a particular job title, to identify your job objective.

✓ You should identify industries that suit you in regard to their pay scales, their stability, and how much you'd enjoy working in them.

✓ Use a variety of publications and online sources to get information about industries and jobs that interest you.

✓ Identify job clusters within industries that fit your career goals.

✓ Research the top jobs and industries that you have selected to identify a broad group of target jobs, improve your interview skills, and write a more targeted resume.

✓ The Job Matrix Worksheet helps you find the places where your desired industry, job title, and job factors (such as personal values and work environment) intersect.

CHAPTER 12

Quick Tips on Writing— and Getting Results from—Your Resume

There is entirely too much emphasis placed on the resume in the job search. If you are looking for a job where an employer will expect you to have a resume, write one, but the problem is that many people believe that a resume should be used to get interviews. That is a very old-fashioned idea.

Unfortunately, too many people write resume and job search books that provide bad advice. Their idea of the job search is the traditional one, where a job is advertised and people are screened in or out of an interview based on an application or a resume. In that context, the advice is to send out lots of great-looking resumes (that will somehow stand out from the others) and get you an interview.

The Internet has not really changed the "more resumes are better" game, it has only added a new tool. The Internet allows you to put your resume on one of the large resume-posting sites and, in theory, allow thousands of employers to find you.

While that approach makes sense from the recruiting manager's point of view, it is not a helpful mindset for you to adopt. It encourages you to be passive and completely dependent on someone else to evaluate your merits without ever meeting you. Because most people now work for smaller employers who don't have a personnel department, the passive and traditional approach of sending in an unsolicited resume, via mail, e-mail or some other method, just does not make good sense.

Even where there *is* a human resource office and a traditional interview/screening situation, you would be far better off calling up or e-mailing the person who is most likely to supervise you at a company and asking for an interview. How could it hurt? While others are dutifully (and passively) sending in their resumes to the personnel department, you have made direct contact and have a shot at an interview.

So a legitimate question might be "Why have a resume at all?" Some job search authors have argued that resumes are not needed in the job search. My opinion is that most people should have a resume, because employers expect them and they can be a useful tool in your job search. My concern is about how you use your resume in your job search. I'll present both sides of the resume argument in this chapter, along with tips on writing and using a superior resume.

This chapter presents the basics of how to both create and use a resume in your job search. It should be enough information for most people to write a superior resume and, more importantly, use it to best effect.

If you want more resume-writing advice, there are many good resume books available, including some I've written: *America's Top Resumes for America's Top Jobs*, *The Quick Resume and Cover Letter Book,* and *Same-Day Resume.* Check out the appendix at the back of this book for additional Web, book, and other resources.

What Is a Resume?

Of course you know what a resume is. But let's start at the beginning and examine what a resume is more closely and consider what it can and cannot do as your first step in creating one.

A "resume" is the term most often used to describe a piece or two of paper that contains a summary of your life's history. The idea is to select those specific parts of your past that support the contention that you can do a particular job well.

Most often, the paper or electronic form of the resume presents you to prospective employers who, based on their response to the resume, may or may not grant you an interview. The resume, along with the application form, is the tool employers use most to screen job seekers.

Some People Say You Don't Need a Resume at All

Despite the popularity of resumes, some job search experts say that you don't need one. They point out research showing the very low response rates from sending out lots of unsolicited resumes and the poor results experienced by those who post resumes on the Internet. They also present a variety of other reasons why resumes are not that important; some of these reasons make a lot of sense.

Some Reasons Why Resumes Are Not Considered Essential

Here are some of the good arguments against the resume as an essential tool in your job search:

1. Resumes aren't good job search tools.

   It's true; resumes don't do a good job of getting you an interview. When used in the traditional way, your resume is far more likely to get you screened out. There are better ways to get in to see people, and many of these methods are presented throughout this book.

2. Some jobs don't require resumes.

   Employers of office, managerial, professional, and technical workers often want the details provided by a resume. But for many jobs, particularly entry-level, trade, or unskilled positions, resumes aren't typically required at all.

3. Some job search methods don't use resumes.

   Many people get jobs without using a resume at all. In most cases, they get interviews because they are already known to the employer or are referred to them by someone who does. While a resume might help in these situations, they are not required.

4. Some resume experts call a resume by another name.

   Richard Lathrop, for example, advises you not to use a resume at all in his book, *Who's Hiring Who?* Instead, he advises you to use his "Qualifications Brief." Bernard Haldane, author of *Career Satisfaction and Success*, suggests that you use his "Professional Job Power Report" instead of a resume. And there are other names, including "Curriculum VITA," "Employment Proposal," and others. In all their forms, however, they are really various types of resumes.

Some Good Reasons Why You SHOULD Have a Resume

In my opinion, all things considered, there are more good reasons to have a resume than not:

1. Employers often ask for resumes.

   This alone is reason enough to have a resume. If an employer asks for one, why have excuses?

2. Resumes help structure your communications.

   A good resume requires you to clarify your job objective, select related skills and experiences, document accomplishments, and write it all down in a short format. Doing these things are all very worthwhile activities and are essential steps required in the job search, even if you don't use a resume at all.

3. If used properly, a resume can be an effective job search tool.

   A well-done resume presents details of your experiences efficiently and in a way that helps an employer to refer to them as needed. It can also be used as a tool to present the skills you have to support your job objective and to present details that are often not solicited in a preliminary interview. When used appropriately, a well-done resume can help you conduct an effective job search campaign.

How Do You Use a Resume?

"Send out your resume to lots of strangers or post it on the Web and, if it is good enough, you will get lots of job offers"—and other fairy tales

I've made the point in this book before that your objective in your job search is to get a good job; your objective is NOT to create a great resume.

That's right. Contrary to the advice of many resume and job search experts, writing a dynamite or perfect (or whatever) resume will rarely get you the job you want. THAT will happen only following an interview, with the occasional odd exception. Therefore, the task in the job search is to get interviews and to do well in them, and sending out lots of resumes to people you don't know—and other traditional resume advice—is a lot of BALONEY (or, if you prefer, bologna).

I hope this doesn't upset you. It's simply the truth. That is why I suggest that you do a *simple* resume early in your job search. This approach allows you to get on with getting interviews rather than sitting at home working on a better resume. Later, as time permits, you can create a more sophisticated resume. In the meantime, you can use the basic but perfectly acceptable one you write today to start looking for a job tomorrow.

The rest of this chapter presents my approach to writing and using resumes, an approach I've refined over many years of thinking and research. It will present an approach designed to help you get a better job in less time, not to write and design the world's greatest resume (as if such a thing exists). While other job seekers are reading resume books by resume book authors who suggest you spend weeks writing and worrying about your resume, you will be out getting interviews.

Four Tips for Using a Resume Effectively

At best, a resume will help you get an interview. However, there are better ways of getting one—as you've learned in earlier chapters of this book. Here is a quick review of how to use your resume to its best effect:

1. Get the interview first.

   With few exceptions, don't send an unsolicited resume. It is almost always better to directly contact the employer by phone, by e-mail, or in person. Then send your resume after you schedule an interview, so that the employer can read about you before your meeting.

2. Send your resume after an interview.

   Send a thank-you note after an interview and enclose a JIST Card or resume—or both. (JIST Cards are covered in Chapter 6.)

3. Give resumes to people you know.

   Give or e-mail copies of your resume (and JIST Card) to everyone in your growing job-search network. They can pass or e-mail them along to others who might be interested.

4. If all else fails, use traditional techniques.

   If you can't make direct contact with a particular prospective employer, send your resume in the traditional way. An example would be answering a want-ad with only a box number for an address. However, if that's all you do, don't expect much to happen.

Quick Tip

Whatever you do, honesty is the best policy. Many people lie on their resumes and claim credentials they don't have, hoping that no one will find out. Many organizations now verify this information, sometimes long after a person is hired.

I have always found that it is best to avoid lying, but that does not mean that you have to present negative information! Make sure that everything you put in your resume *supports your job objective* in some direct way! If you really can do the job that you want, someone will probably hire you because you can. And not telling lies will allow you to sleep better at night.

A Big Problem with Resumes Is That Everyone Is an Expert

A resume is one of those things that almost everyone seems to know more about than you do. If you were to show your resume to any three people, you would probably get three different suggestions on how to improve it. One person might tell you that you really only need a one-page resume ("And how come no references are listed?") and then e-mail them to thousands of employers from a list you buy on the Web. Another will tell you that, of course, you should have listed all your hobbies plus the fact that you won the spelling bee in sixth grade, right in front of the whole school. The third may tell you that your resume is boring and that the way to get attention is to print your resume, with red ink, on a brown paper bag.

So, one of the problems with resumes is that everyone is an expert but few agree. This means that *you* will have to make some decisions about how you do your resume. Fortunately, I'll help.

GUIDELINES FOR WRITING A SUPERIOR RESUME

Here are some basic guidelines you should follow when you develop your resume. They aren't rules exactly, but you should carefully consider each of these suggestions as each is based on many years of experience and, I think, makes good common sense.

Keep It Short

Opinions differ on this, but one or two pages is a good range for most resumes. If you are seeking a managerial, professional, or technical position—where most people have lots of prior experience—two or three pages is the norm. In most cases, a resume longer than two pages will not be read by a busy person. Shorter resumes are often harder to write, but are more often read.

Eliminate Errors

I am always amazed how often an otherwise good resume has typographical, grammar, or punctuation errors. Your resume simply can't have any errors! Find someone who is good at proofreading and ask that person to review yours, if necessary. Then run it through a spell checker, and review it again.

Make It Look Good

You surely know that your resume's overall appearance will affect an employer's opinion of you. Is it well laid out? Is it "crisp" and professional looking? Does it include good use of "white space"? Major word processing programs have attractive resume design templates that allow you to simply enter text into a professionally-formatted template. Even resumes sent via e-mail as HTML text can include some attractive elements (more on this later).

Use Technology Tools

It is essential to use a computer to prepare your resume and create electronic files for e-mailing and pasting into online job applications. If you don't have access to a computer or high-quality printer have someone else print or produce your resume for you. And be certain to obtain a copy on disk so that you can update, edit, and e-mail your resume throughout your job search.

You can use any word processing program to prepare your resume. Because Microsoft Word is the most commonly used program I recommend that you use it, if possible, particularly if you plan to use the Internet and e-mail extensively during your search.

(continued)

Chapter 12

(continued)

Get Professional Help if You Need It

There are many resume writing and design services available online. Do a simple search on a search engine site such as google.com or yahoo.com; you will be amazed at the resources you will locate. Major resume posting and other sites often have or link to resume writing help sites. If you need more personalized help, I suggest you use the resume-writing services of professionals who belong to the Professional Association of Resume Writers (www.PARW.com) or the National Resume Writer's Association (www.NRWA.com). Both groups provide certification for members and require them to adhere to a code of ethics. Their Web sites include a list of members, all of whom can be contacted via e-mail.

You can also have your resume word processed and "designed" at local secretarial services and smaller print shops, as well as nationwide chains such as Kinko's. They will charge a modest fee for this service but can make your resume look quite professional with attractive formatting and sharp laser printing.

Get Good-Quality Copies

Good-quality photocopies of resumes are widely used and accepted. If you do have your own computer and high-quality printer, individually prepared and printed resumes can present a better appearance and, of course, allow you to target your resume to a particular job or employer. While laser printers create a crisper image, good-quality inkjet output is also perfectly acceptable.

You can also take your resume to most small print and photocopy shops and have them print a few hundred copies for a reasonable price. However you produce them, it is important that you keep plenty of them on hand. You can produce targeted resumes and cover letters individually for important job prospects as the need arises.

Use Quality Paper

Using quality paper for your resume is important. Never use cheap paper like those typically used for photocopies. Most copy machines will copy your resume content onto good quality paper, so get your own paper supply if necessary. Most print shops and office supply stores have a selection of papers, and you often can get matching envelopes. Although most resumes are printed on white paper, I prefer an off-white (ivory) paper. You could use other light colors such as light tan, blue, or gray, but I do not recommend red, pink, or green tints.

Papers also come in different qualities, and you can see the difference. Ones that include cotton fibers, for example, have a richer texture and a quality "feel" that is appropriate for the professional look you should use in a resume.

Stress Accomplishments and Use Action Words

Most resumes are boring. In yours, don't simply list what your duties were, emphasize what you got done! Make sure that you mention the specific skills you have to do the job, as well as any accomplishments and credentials. Even a simple resume can include some of these elements, as you will soon see. Look over the list of "Action Words and Phrases" and sample resumes in this chapter for ideas.

Write from the Employer's Point of View

As you write your resume, consider what the employer needs to know about your skills, experience, education, and accomplishments. What would you want to know about a person if you were hiring them? For example, would you want to know they won the 6th grade speech contest—or that they have excellent oral and written communication skills? Would you want to know they belonged to a sorority or fraternity, or would you rather know they have excellent interpersonal skills? Would you want to know they have four years experience in a convenience store, or that they have four years of inside sales and marketing experience for a nationwide corporation and were responsible for handling large amounts of cash?

Target everything you write to meet the needs of the job you want. For example, if you worked in a chemical laboratory performing high-pressure liquid chromatography analysis and are looking for the same sort of job now, write "Proficient in performing high-pressure liquid chromatography analyses." If you want to obtain a job in a medical laboratory working with different equipment, you may present the same experience as "Proficient in performing highly sensitive chemical/biological analyses."

Don't Be Humble

Like an interview, your resume is no place to be humble. If you don't communicate what you can do, who will?

Make Every Word Count

Write a long rough draft and then edit, edit, edit. If a word or phrase does not support your job objective, consider dropping it.

(continued)

(continued)

Write It Yourself

While I expect you to use ideas and even words or phrases you like from the sample resumes in this book, it is most important that your resume represent you, and not someone else. Present your own skills in your resume, and support them with your own accomplishments. If you do not have good written communication skills, it is perfectly acceptable to get help from someone who does. Just make sure your resume ends up sounding like you wrote it.

Break Some Rules

This will be your resume, so you can do whatever makes sense to you: There are few rules that can't be broken in putting together your own resume. In this book, you will learn about the different types of resumes and see a few basic examples. Remember that it is often far more useful to you to simply have an acceptable resume as soon as possible—and use it in an active job search—than to delay your job search while working on a better resume. A better resume can come later, after you have created a presentable one that you can use right away.

The Three Major Types of Resumes

To keep this simple, I will discuss only three types of resumes. There are other, more specialized types, but these three are generally the most useful.

The Chronological Resume

The word "chronology" refers to a sequence of events in time, and the primary feature of this type of resume is the listing of jobs you've held from the most recent backward. This is the simplest type of resume and is a useful format if used properly. This type of resume works best when you've had a long, steady work history and promotions that you want to showcase.

The Skills or Functional Resume

Instead of listing your experience under each job, the skills resume clusters your experiences under major skill areas. For example, if you are strong in communication skills, under that major heading you could list a variety of supportive experiences from different jobs, school, or volunteer situations. You would also present several other major skill areas.

This approach would make little sense, of course, unless you had a job objective that *required* these skills. For this reason and others, a skills resume is harder to write than a simple chronological resume. If you have limited paid work experience, are changing careers, or have not worked for awhile, a skills resume may be a clearly superior approach to help you present your strengths and avoid displaying your weaknesses.

The Combination, or Creative, Resume

Elements of chronological and skills resumes can be combined in various ways to improve the clarity or presentation of a resume. For example, if you have a good work history that supports your current job objective, you could start with a Skills section that supports the skills needed in the job you want, and then include a shorter chronological Work Experience section that presents the essential elements of your work history. Or you could begin with a summary of your work history, in chronological order, followed by a review of the key skills you have to do the job, or some other creative combination that presents you well.

There are also creative formats that defy any category but that are clever and have worked for some people. I've seen handwritten resumes (usually *not* a good idea); unusual paper colors, sizes, and shapes; resumes with tasteful drawings and borders; and lots of other ideas. Some of them were well done and well received, others were not.

ELECTRONIC RESUMES

The Internet requires that you adapt the content of your paper resume to an electronic version that is better suited for transmitting online or posting to resume databases that can be searched by potential employers. While you can attach a copy of you resume to an e-mail as a word processed file (allowing it to be printed out to look just like your paper resume), many employers want your resume submitted in special formats. Because electronic resumes have become so prevalent today, I'll cover them at the end of the chapter in more detail.

Begin with a Basic Chronological Resume You Can Write in an Hour

Keeping things simple has its advantages. This section shows you how to create a basic chronological resume in about an hour. While the resulting resume can certainly be improved, it has the distinct advantage of letting you get on with your job search right away. Later, as time permits, you can revise a better one.

The biggest advantage of a chronological resume is that it is easy to do. It works best for those who have had several years of experience in the same type of job they are seeking now, because a chronological resume will clearly display your recent work experience. If you are changing careers, have been out of the workforce, or do not have much paid work experience related to the job you want, a skills or functional resume, presented later in this chapter, might be a better choice.

Most employers prefer chronological resumes—even those that are basic and lack excitement—provided that they are neat and error free. You can use it early in your job search while you work on a more sophisticated resume. The goal here is to get an acceptable resume together quickly so that you won't be sitting at home worrying about your resume instead of out looking for a job.

Following are two examples of chronological resumes. The information and format of the first are quite basic, but the approach works well enough in this situation because Judith is looking for a job in the same career field and has a good job history. The Instant Resume Worksheet later in this chapter will help you write the content for this type of basic resume in about an hour.

In the second example, Judith's basic resume is improved, with a number of added features. Note especially the more descriptive job objective, the "Skills and Qualifications" section, and the added details of her accomplishments and skills in both the "Education" and "Work Experience" sections. Although the improved resume would take most people longer than an hour to create, it uses the basic chronological approach and could be completed by most people in just a few hours.

A Basic Chronological Resume Sample

Judith J. Jones

115 South Hawthorne Avenue
Chicago, Illinois 66204
(312) 653-9217 (home)
email: jj@earthlink.com

JOB OBJECTIVE

Desire a position in the office management, accounting, or administrative assistant area. Prefer a position requiring responsibility and a variety of tasks.

EDUCATION AND TRAINING

Acme Business College, Lincoln, Illinois
Graduate of a one-year business program.

U.S. Army
Financial procedures, accounting functions.

John Adams High School, South Bend, Indiana
Diploma, business education.

Other: Continuing education classes and workshops in business communication, computer spreadsheet and database programs, scheduling systems, and customer relations.

EXPERIENCE

2001-present—Claims Processor, Blue Spear Insurance Co., Wilmette, Illinois. Handle customer medical claims, develop management reports based on spreadsheets I created, exceed productivity goals.

2000-2001—Returned to school to upgrade my business and computer skills. Took courses in advanced accounting, spreadsheet and database programs, office management, human relations, and new office techniques.

1998-2000—E4, U.S. Army. Assigned to various stations as a specialist in finance operations. Promoted prior to honorable discharge.

1996-1998—Sandy's Boutique, Wilmette, Illinois. Responsible for counter sales, display design, cash register and other tasks.

1994-1996—Held part-time and summer jobs throughout high school.

PERSONAL

I am reliable, hard working, and good with people.

Chapter 12

An Improved Chronological Resume Example

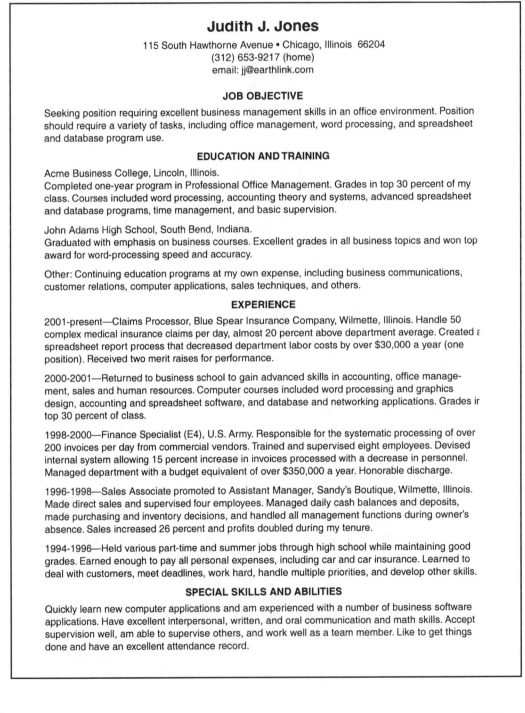

Judith J. Jones

115 South Hawthorne Avenue • Chicago, Illinois 66204
(312) 653-9217 (home)
email: jj@earthlink.com

JOB OBJECTIVE

Seeking position requiring excellent business management skills in an office environment. Position should require a variety of tasks, including office management, word processing, and spreadsheet and database program use.

EDUCATION AND TRAINING

Acme Business College, Lincoln, Illinois.
Completed one-year program in Professional Office Management. Grades in top 30 percent of my class. Courses included word processing, accounting theory and systems, advanced spreadsheet and database programs, time management, and basic supervision.

John Adams High School, South Bend, Indiana.
Graduated with emphasis on business courses. Excellent grades in all business topics and won top award for word-processing speed and accuracy.

Other: Continuing education programs at my own expense, including business communications, customer relations, computer applications, sales techniques, and others.

EXPERIENCE

2001-present—Claims Processor, Blue Spear Insurance Company, Wilmette, Illinois. Handle 50 complex medical insurance claims per day, almost 20 percent above department average. Created a spreadsheet report process that decreased department labor costs by over $30,000 a year (one position). Received two merit raises for performance.

2000-2001—Returned to business school to gain advanced skills in accounting, office management, sales and human resources. Computer courses included word processing and graphics design, accounting and spreadsheet software, and database and networking applications. Grades in top 30 percent of class.

1998-2000—Finance Specialist (E4), U.S. Army. Responsible for the systematic processing of over 200 invoices per day from commercial vendors. Trained and supervised eight employees. Devised internal system allowing 15 percent increase in invoices processed with a decrease in personnel. Managed department with a budget equivalent of over $350,000 a year. Honorable discharge.

1996-1998—Sales Associate promoted to Assistant Manager, Sandy's Boutique, Wilmette, Illinois. Made direct sales and supervised four employees. Managed daily cash balances and deposits, made purchasing and inventory decisions, and handled all management functions during owner's absence. Sales increased 26 percent and profits doubled during my tenure.

1994-1996—Held various part-time and summer jobs through high school while maintaining good grades. Earned enough to pay all personal expenses, including car and car insurance. Learned to deal with customers, meet deadlines, work hard, handle multiple priorities, and develop other skills.

SPECIAL SKILLS AND ABILITIES

Quickly learn new computer applications and am experienced with a number of business software applications. Have excellent interpersonal, written, and oral communication and math skills. Accept supervision well, am able to supervise others, and work well as a team member. Like to get things done and have an excellent attendance record.

Writing the Major Sections of a Chronological Resume

An Instant Resume Worksheet follows these tips. The tips help you complete each section of that resume worksheet. I suggest you read one section of the tips below, then complete that part of the resume worksheet. You may also want to refer to previous chapters of this book to remind you of key skills, accomplishments, or other details to include when completing the Instant Resume Worksheet.

The heading section

Do not write the word "Resume" at the top of the page. This is unnecessary, because it's perfectly clear that this is a resume.

The identification section

This section consists of your name, your address, your phone numbers, and your e-mail address.

Name

You want to present a professional image, so avoid using a nickname. But don't feel you must spell out your entire first, middle, and last name; in most cases, use just your first name, optional middle initial, and last name.

Address

Don't abbreviate anything, such as Street to St., and do include your ZIP code. If you might move during your job search, ask a relative, friend, or neighbor if you can temporarily use their address to handle your mail. As a last resort, arrange for a mailbox at the post office. Forwarded mail will be delayed, which can cause you to miss an opportunity. If you plan to move to a new city during your job search, get a local address at the new location so that you appear to be settled there.

Phone numbers

An employer is likely to phone you rather than write to you. For this reason, it is essential that your resume provide a phone number that is reliably answered during the day. There are several ways to accomplish this:

✓ **Use an answering machine or voice-mail service.** These are inexpensive and reliable ways to be sure you don't miss messages. Use a professional-sounding message for incoming callers to hear. Consider how a prospective employer would react to your message, and let that be your guide.

✓ **List an alternative phone number or two.** If you have a cell phone, consider using it as your primary contact number. Many resumes will list a home number and an alternative phone number such as a work, cell phone, or pager number. You can list the number of a reliable relative or friend who will answer your calls if your home number is busy or unanswered. It is best to designate these numbers as "home" or "messages" or "answering service" so that an employer will know what to expect. Don't include a work number unless it gives direct access to your phone and is not picked up by others when you are not there. And be ethical and discreet about not using your employer's time for your job search.

Make sure that anyone likely to answer your home phone is trained on how to handle messages from employers. And on your resume, always include your area code: You never know who will be calling—or from where.

E-mail address

Many employers prefer to e-mail you rather than call, so include an e-mail number if at all possible. Check your e-mail account every day so you can quickly respond to any employer contact. And don't use an unprofessional sounding e-mail address like "big.alice@getserious.com" You can obtain free e-mail accounts from providers such as Hot Mail and Juno. With these accounts, you'll have access from any Internet-connected computer and can keep your job search correspondence separate from messages that go to your regular e-mail account.

You should now complete the Identification section of the Instant Resume Worksheet on page 346.

The job objective statement

You don't have to use a job objective statement on a chronological resume. Many (if not most) of the resumes in Part 2 don't lead off that way. What they all do, however, is clearly answer the employer's question "Who are you and what can you do for me?" Many include a Summary or Profile or other introductory section instead of an objective. If you're writing a skills/functional resume, a Job Objective statement becomes more important because it is less obvious from looking at your resume what job you want.

It's difficult to write a job objective that does not exclude you from jobs you would consider without sounding as if you would be willing to do just about anything. But including a clear, focused objective is quite helpful to people reading your resume.

I see lots of job objectives that emphasize what the person *wants* but don't provide information on what the person *can do*. For example, an objective that says "Interested in a position that allows me to be creative and offers adequate pay and advancement opportunities" is *not* a good objective at all. Who cares? This objective (a real one that someone actually wrote) displays a self-centered, "gimme" approach that will turn off most employers.

Look through the following examples of simple but useful job objectives. Most provide some information on the type of job the writer is seeking, as well as the skills he or she offers. The best ones avoid a narrow job title and keep options open to a wide variety of possibilities within a range of appropriate jobs.

SAMPLE JOB OBJECTIVES

✓ A responsible general office position in a busy, medium-sized organization.

✓ A management position in the warehousing industry. Position should require supervisory, problem-solving, and organizational skills.

✓ Computer programming and/or systems analysis. Prefer an accounting-oriented emphasis and a solutions-oriented organization.

✓ Medical assistant or secretary in a physician's office, hospital, or other health services environment.

✓ Responsible position requiring skills in public relations, writing, and reporting.

✓ An aggressive and success-oriented professional, seeking a sales position offering both challenge and growth.

✓ Desire position in the office management, secretarial, or clerical area. Position should require flexibility, good organizational skills, and an ability to handle people.

If you are custom-writing your resume for a specific position, you can cleverly say something like "To obtain a position as (insert position title being sought here) with the (insert employer name here)."

More on Career Planning and Job Search **341**

I've included a Job Objective Worksheet on page 357. Go ahead and complete it now, along with the Job Objective section on the Instant Resume Worksheet on page 346. You should complete these worksheets even if you choose not to use an objective on your resume. You will find that writing an objective focuses your thoughts and helps you to identify relevant skills and accomplishments when you are writing the rest of your resume.

Education and training section

Recent graduates should put their educational credentials toward the top of their resumes, because they represent the more substantial part of their experience. More experienced workers typically place their education toward the end of their resumes, because their work experience is typically more important to stress.

You can drop the education section entirely if it doesn't support your job objective or if you don't have the educational credentials typically required for the position. This is particularly true if you have lots of work experience in your career area. Some job seekers fear being "over qualified" for positions they are willing to accept and intentionally leave out their more advanced credentials. Usually, though, you should emphasize the most recent and/or highest level of education or training that relates to the job.

Look at the sample resumes later in this chapter for ideas. Then, on a separate piece of paper, rough out your education and training section. After you edit it to its final form, write it on the Instant Resume Worksheet on page 346.

Honors and awards

If you have received any formal recognition or awards that support your job objective, you can mention them either in a separate resume section or in the work experience, skills, education, or personal sections.

Work, military, and volunteer experience section

This section of the resume provides the details of your work history. If you have had significant work history, list each job along with details of what you accomplished and any special skills you used. Emphasize only those skills that directly relate to the job objective you have stated on your resume.

USE ACTION WORDS AND PHRASES

Use active rather than passive words and phrases throughout your resume. The following list includes many good examples of the types of words to include. Look at the sample resumes later in this chapter for additional ideas.

Administered	Implemented	Presented
Analyzed	Improved	Promoted
Controlled	Increased productivity	Reduced expenses
Coordinated	Increased profits	Reviewed
Created	Initiated	Researched
Designed	Innovated	Scheduled
Developed	Instructed	Set priorities
Diagnosed	Led	Solved
Directed	Managed	Supervised
Established policy	Modified	Trained
Expanded	Negotiated	Troubleshot
Guided	Organized	
Headed	Planned	

Previous job titles

Remember that you can modify the title you had to more accurately reflect your responsibilities. For example, if your title was "sales clerk" but you frequently opened and closed the store and were often left in charge, you might use the more descriptive title "night sales manager." Check with your previous supervisor if you are worried about this, and ask if he or she would object. If you were promoted, you can handle the promotion as a separate job—and make sure that you mention the fact that you were promoted.

Previous employers

Provide the organization's name, city, and the state or province in which it is located. A street address or supervisor's name is not necessary; you can provide those details on a separate sheet of references.

Employment dates

If you have large gaps in your employment history that are not easily explained, use full years (rather than months and years) to avoid emphasizing the gaps. If you have a significant period of time during which you did not work, did you

Chapter 12

do anything else that could explain it in a positive way? School? Travel? Raising a family? Self-employment? Even if you mowed lawns and painted houses for money while you were unemployed, that counts as self-employment. It's much better than saying you were unemployed for a significant period of time.

Professional organizations

If you belong to job-related professional groups, it's worth mentioning, particularly if you are (or were) an officer or are active in some other way. Mention any accomplishments or awards.

Personal information section

Years ago, resumes traditionally included things such as your height, weight, marital status, hobbies, leisure activities, and other personal trivia. My advice is to not include this sort of information. Earlier I advised you to make every word count—if it does not support your job objective, delete it. The same goes for personal information.

There are situations in which relevant extracurricular activities or hobbies can help you; if so, go ahead and use them. Look at the sample resumes and decide for yourself.

Although a personal section is optional, I sometimes like to end a resume on a personal note. Some of the sample resumes provide a touch of humor or playfulness as well as selected positives from outside school and work lives. This is also a good place to list significant community involvement, a willingness to relocate, or personal characteristics an employer might like. Keep it short, and make it relate in some way to your job objective.

Turn now to the Instant Resume Worksheet on page 351 and list any personal information you think is appropriate.

References section

It is not necessary to include the names of your references on your resume. There are better things to do with the precious space. It's not even necessary to state "references available upon request" at the bottom because that is obvious. If employers want them, they know they can ask you for them.

It *is* important to talk to your references in advance. Pick people who know your work as an employee, volunteer, or student. Your references do not have to be your supervisors or employers; they can be anyone who can speak about your work-related abilities. Make sure your references will say nice things about you by asking them just what they will say. Push for any negatives, and don't feel hurt if you get some. Nobody is perfect. Hearing about negatives up front gives you a chance to take someone off your list before he or she can do you any damage.

When you know who to include, list them on a separate sheet with a heading like "Employment References for (insert your name)." Include names, titles addresses, phone numbers, e-mail addresses, and details of why these people are on your list. You can also mention here, if it is true, that your references are "excellent," along with any helpful details such as "responsible for promoting me to a supervisory position."

Be aware that some employers are not allowed by their organization to give references. I have refused to hire people who probably had good references but whose past employers would not give me any meaningful information. If your references are restricted in giving phone or e-mail references, ask them in advance to write a letter of reference that you can photocopy as needed. Written letters of reference are a good idea to have anyway, so you might want to ask for one.

Keep copies of the list plus any letters of recommendation and provide them when they are asked for. Do not attach them to your resume unless you are asked to do so.

The Instant Resume Worksheet

On the Instant Resume Worksheet, list your most recent job first, followed by each previous job. Use additional sheets as needed to cover *all* your significant jobs or unpaid experiences. You can treat any significant volunteer or military experience as you would any job.

Whenever possible, provide numbers to support what you did: the number of people served over one or more years, the number of transactions processed, the total inventory value you were responsible for, the payroll of the staff you supervised, the total budget you managed, and so on. As much as possible, demonstrate results using numbers such as a percentage increase in sales. Specific results support your ability and lend credibility to your resume.

Emphasize your accomplishments! Think about the things you accomplished in jobs, school, the military, and other settings. Emphasize these things, even if this seems like bragging.

Many of the sample resumes include statements about accomplishments to show you how this is done. When writing about your work experience, be sure to use action words. Quantify what you did and provide evidence that you did it well. Take particular care to mention skills that directly relate to doing the job you want.

Use separate sheets of paper to write rough drafts of your resume. Edit it so that every word contributes something. When you're done, transfer your statements to the Instant Resume Worksheet on page 348.

Chapter 12

The Instant Resume Worksheet

Directions: This worksheet will help you organize the information you need to complete a simple chronological resume. It also provides the basis for a skills resume. Write rough drafts for each of the more complicated sections that follows. Then complete the form with wording that's close to that you want to use in your resume.

Identification

Name: _____

Home address: _____

_____

Phone number and description (if any): _____

Alternative phone number and description: _____

Alternative phone number and description: _____

E-mail address: _____

Job Objective

_____

_____

_____

Education and Training

Begin with the highest level or most recent.

Graduate Degree

(Skip this section if you have not attended a master's or doctorate program.)

Institution name: _____

City and state/province (optional): _____

Degree or certificate earned: _____

Relevant courses, awards, achievements, and experiences: ____

_____

_____

_____

_____

College/Post-High School Training

Institution name: _____

City and state/province (optional): _____

Degree or certificate earned: _____

Relevant courses, awards, achievements, and experiences: _____

_____

_____

_____

_____

_____

High School

This is usually not included unless it is the highest educational level you have attained.

Institution name: _____

City and state/province (optional): _____

Degree or certificate earned: _____

Relevant courses, awards, achievements, and experiences: _____

_____

_____

_____

_____

_____

Armed Services Training and Other Training or Certification

_____

_____

_____

_____

_____

(continued)

(continued)

Specific things you can do as a result: _____

_____

_____

_____

Work, Military, and Volunteer Experience

Begin with your most recent job.

Name of organization: _____

Address: _____

Phone number: _____

Dates employed: _____

Job title(s): _____

Supervisor's name: _____

Details of any raises or promotions: _____

_____

_____

Machinery or equipment you handled: _____

_____

_____

Special skills this job required: _____

_____

_____

List what you accomplished or did well: _____

_____

_____

_____

Next most recent job.

Name of organization: _____

Address: _____

Phone number: _____

Dates employed: _____

Job title(s): _____

Supervisor's name: _____

Details of any raises or promotions: _____

_____

_____

_____

Machinery or equipment you handled: _____

_____

_____

_____

Special skills this job required: _____

_____

_____

_____

List what you accomplished or did well: _____

_____

_____

_____

Next most recent job.

Name of organization: _____

Address: _____

(continued)

Chapter 12

(continued)

Phone number: _____

Dates employed: _____

Job title(s): _____

Supervisor's name: _____

Details of any raises or promotions: _____

_____

_____

_____

Machinery or equipment you handled: _____

_____

_____

_____

Special skills this job required: _____

_____

_____

_____

List what you accomplished or did well: _____

_____

_____

_____

Next most recent job.

Name of organization: _____

Address: _____

Phone number: _____

Dates employed: _____

Job title(s): _____

Supervisor's name: _____

Details of any raises or promotions: _____

_____

_____

_____

Machinery or equipment you handled: _____

_____

_____

_____

Special skills this job required: _____

_____

_____

_____

List what you accomplished or did well: _____

_____

_____

_____

If you need space for more jobs, attach additional sheets.

Professional Organizations

_____

_____

_____

_____

Personal Information

_____

_____

_____

_____

Write Your Basic Resume Now

At this point, you should have completed the Instant Resume Worksheet. Carefully review dates, addresses, phone numbers, spelling, and other details of the information it contains. The Worksheet can now be used as a guide for preparing a better-than-average chronological resume.

Use the examples of simple chronological resumes in this chapter as the basis for creating your own chronological resume. Additional examples of skills resumes are included later in this chapter, and you should look them over for ideas for writing and formatting your own.

Remember that your initial objective is not to do a wonderful, powerful, or creative resume. That can come later. You first need to have an acceptable resume, one that can be used tomorrow to begin an active job search. So keep it simple and set yourself a tight deadline for having a simple resume together so that the lack of one does not become a barrier to your job search.

Once you have your resume written, put the information you have collected in the form of a resume. If you do not have a computer or are not a good typist, I suggest that you have someone else type or word process your resume for you. But whether you do it yourself or have it done, CAREFULLY REVIEW IT ONCE MORE for typographical and other errors that may have slipped in. Then, when you are certain that everything is correct, make corrections to produce the final version.

Write a Skills/Functional Resume in Less Than a Day

Even though it takes a bit longer to write a skills (or functional) resume, the format has some advantages that might make it worth your time.

Why Consider Using a Skills Resume?

In its simplest form, a chronological resume is little more than a list of job titles and other details. Many employers look for people with successful histories in jobs similar to the open position. If you are a recent graduate or have little prior experience in the career you now want, you will find that a simple chronological resume emphasizes your lack of related experience rather than your ability to do the job.

A skills resume avoids these problems by highlighting what you have done—under a heading such as "Specific Skills"—rather than listing the jobs you have held.

If you hitchhiked across the country for two years, a skills resume won't necessarily display this time as a gap in your employment record. Instead, you could now say, "Traveled extensively throughout the country and am familiar with most major market areas." That could be a useful experience for certain positions.

Because it is a tool that can hide your problem areas, many employers do not like the skills resume. And a skills resume is probably not the best format for a wide-scale search that includes mass mailing (or e-mailing) your resume to potential employers and responding to want ads and online postings. But if you plan to pursue the active, targeted job search I recommend in this book, a skills resume will let you "put your best foot forward" for each opportunity you encounter. And if you have a problem that a traditional chronological resume highlights, a skills resume might help get you the opportunity to meet with a prospective employer rather than be screened out.

If your work history is short or sporadic, you should consider doing a skills resume, even though it does take a bit more work to create a good one.

A Sample Skills Resume

Following is an example of a basic skills resume for a recent high school graduate whose only paid work experience has been in a fast-food restaurant. A skills resume is a good choice here because it allows the writer to emphasize her strengths without emphasizing that her work experience is limited.

Although the sample format is simple, it presents the writer in a positive way. Because her employment will be at the entry level in a nontechnical area, an employer will be more interested in her basic skills—those that can transfer from things she has done in the past—than in her job-specific experiences. The work experience she has is a plus. Also notice how she presents her gymnastics experience as "Hardworking."

Lisa M. Rhodes

813 Evergreen Drive
Evansville, IN 47715
lisamrhodes@aol.com
Home: (812) 643-2173   Message: (812) 442-1659

Job Objective

Sales-oriented position in a retail or distribution business.

Skills and Abilities

Communications: Good written and verbal presentation skills. Use proper grammar and have a good speaking voice.

Interpersonal: Able to accept supervision and get along well with co-workers. Received positive evaluations from previous supervisors.

Flexible: Willing to try new things and am interested in improving efficiency on assigned tasks.

Attention to Detail: Like to see assigned areas of responsibility completed correctly. Am concerned with quality, and my work is typically orderly and attractive.

Hardworking: Have worked long hours in strenuous activities while attending school full-time. During this time, I maintained above-average grades. At times, I was working as many as 65 hours a week in school and other structured activities.

Customer Contacts: Have had as many as 500 customer contacts a day (10,000 per month) in a busy retail outlet. Averaged lower than a .001% rate of complaints and was given the "Employee of the Month" award in my second month of employment.

Cash Sales: Handled over $2,000 a day ($40,000 a month) in cash sales. Balanced register and prepared daily sales summary and deposits.

Education

Graduate of Harrison High School. Took advanced English and other classes. Member of award-winning band. Excellent attendance record. Superior communication skills. Graduated in top 30% of class.

Other

Active gymnastics competitor for four years. This experience taught me discipline, teamwork, and how to follow instructions. I am ambitious, outgoing, and willing to work.

Postscript to the Sample Skills Resume

This is a real resume, for a real person, though the name and details are fictionalized. A few years have gone by since I first wrote it, and I thought you might be interested in how this person turned out. Lisa went on to college; dropped out after three years with no clear career or life direction; took a customer service job; learned computer applications software on the job; and after several jobs and promotions with the same employer is now a well-paid network administrator and Web site developer. With all her experience since this first resume, Lisa's resume now would be quite different. But it is interesting that many skills she emphasized in her early resume are used in her current job.

How to Write a Skills Resume

The skills resume includes a number of sections that are similar to those in a chronological resume. Here I will discuss only the sections that are substantially different: the "Job Objective" and "Skills and Abilities" sections. Refer to the material earlier in this chapter about chronological resumes for information on sections that are common to both types of resume.

Don't be afraid to use a little creativity in writing your own skills resume. You are allowed to break some rules in this format, if it makes sense to do so.

The job objective statement for a skills resume

Although a simple chronological resume does not require a career objective, a skills resume does. Without a reasonably clear job objective, it is not possible to select and organize the key skills you have to support that objective.

You should carefully construct your job objective statement. To see some examples of job objective statements, refer to "Sample Job Objectives" earlier in this chapter.

Tips for writing a good job objective

The job objective you write should meet your specific needs. But here are some general things to consider when you write it.

1. **Avoid job titles.** Job titles such as "receptionist" or "marketing analyst" can involve very different activities in different organizations. If your resume says your objective is to be a receptionist, you will probably not be considered for such jobs as "office manager" or "marketing assistant," even though you could do them. For this reason, it is best to use broad categories of jobs rather than specific titles, so that you can be considered for a wide variety of positions related to the skills you have. For example, instead of "receptionist," you could say "responsible office-management or clerical position," if that's what you would really consider and are qualified for.

More on Career Planning and Job Search **355**

Chapter 12

2. **Define a "bracket of responsibility" to include the potential for up-ward mobility.** Although you might be willing to accept a variety of jobs related to your skills, you should definitely include jobs that require higher levels of responsibility and pay. The example above would allow the candidate to be considered for an office-management position as well as for office support and clerical jobs. In effect, you should define a "bracket of responsibility" in your objective that includes the range of jobs you are willing to accept. This bracket should include the lower range of jobs you would consider, as well as those that require higher levels of responsibility, up to and including the most responsible job you think you could handle. Even if you have not been given those higher levels of responsibility in the past, many employers will consider you for them if you have the skills to handle them.

3. **Include your most important skills.** What are the most important skills needed for the job you want? Include one or more of these in your job objective statement. The implication is that if you are looking for a job that *requires* "organizational skills," then you must have those skills. Of course, your interview (and resume) should give evidence that you have those skills, by providing specific examples.

4. **Include specifics only if they really matter to you.** If you have substantial experience in a particular industry (such as "computer-controlled machine tools") or you have a narrow, specific objective that you *really* want (such as "art therapist with the mentally handicapped"), it's okay to say so. But you should realize that narrowing your alternatives might keep you from being considered for other jobs for which you qualify. Still, if that's what you want, it's worth pursuing. I would, however, encourage you to have a second, more general objective ready, just in case.

5. **Research the job you want.** Read descriptions of your target job. Then emphasize in your resume the skills you have that are mentioned in these descriptions. The *Occupational Outlook Handbook (OOH),* created by the U.S. Department of Labor, provides brief descriptions of more than 250 major jobs, and I recommend it as a good source of information. You can find this book in library reference sections and bookstores, as well as on the Department of Labor's Web site at www.dol.gov. Another book, *America's Top 300 Jobs,* provides the same information as the *OOH,* but libraries are more likely to allow you to check it out.

Use the Job Objective Worksheet

Use the following worksheet to help you construct an effective and accurate job objective statement for your resume.

The Job Objective Worksheet

Directions: Complete each of the following items. When you're done, you'll have a better idea of what to include in your resume's job objective statement.

1. **What sort of position, title, and area of specialization do you want?** Write the type of job you want, just as you might explain it to someone you know.

   _____

   _____

   _____

2. **Define your bracket of responsibility.** Describe the range of jobs you would accept, from the minimum up to those you think you could handle if you were given the chance.

   _____

   _____

   _____

3. **Name the key skills you have that are important in this job.** Describe the two or three key skills that are particularly important for success in the job that you are seeking. Select one or more of these that you are strong in and that you enjoy using. Write it (or them) here.

   _____

   _____

   _____

4. **Name any specific areas of expertise or strong interest that you want to use in your next job.** If you have substantial interest, experience, or training in a specific area and want to include it in your job objective (remembering that it might limit your options), write it here.

   _____

   _____

   _____

(continued)

Chapter 12

(continued)

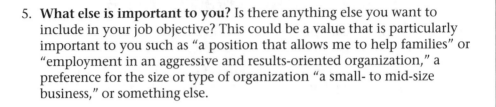

5. **What else is important to you?** Is there anything else you want to include in your job objective? This could be a value that is particularly important to you such as "a position that allows me to help families" or "employment in an aggressive and results-oriented organization," a preference for the size or type of organization "a small- to mid-size business," or something else.

_____

_____

_____

Finalize your job objective statement

Most employers are impressed by candidates who are very clear about the jobs they want and why they want them. Few interviews end well unless the interviewer is convinced that you really want the job and have the skills to do it. For that reason it is essential to have a clear job objective.

Once you've determined that, you can go out and get interviews for jobs that closely approximate what you want. In interviews, support your interest in the job by presenting the skills and experiences you have and the advantages you present over other candidates. It sounds simple enough—and it can be—as long as you are clear about what job you want to do and are well organized about finding it.

The skills section

This section of your skills resume can also be called *Areas of Accomplishment, Summary of Qualifications, Areas of Expertise and Ability,* or something similar. Look through the sample resumes later in this chapter for other ideas.

Whatever you call it, this section is what makes a skills resume different from a chronological resume. To construct it, you must carefully consider which skills you want to emphasize. You should feature skills that are essential to success on the job you want and skills that are your particular strengths. You probably have a good idea of which skills meet both criteria, but you may find it helpful to review Chapter 3 to help you identify these skills.

Note that many skills resumes emphasize skills that are not specific to a particular job. These types of skills are known as *transferable skills.* For example, the skill of being well organized is important in *many* jobs. In your resume, you should provide specific examples of situations or accomplishments that show you have that skill. This is where you bring in examples from previous work or other experiences.

Key skills list

Here are the key skills for success in most jobs. If you have to emphasize some skills over others, these are ones to consider (if you have them, of course).

The Basics	**Key Transferable Skills**
Accept supervision	Able to instruct others
Computer and Internet Literate	Manage money and budgets
Get along with coworkers	Manage people
Get things done on time	Meet deadlines
Good attendance	Deal with the public
Hard worker	Negotiate effectively
Honest	Organize/manage projects
On time	Comfortable with public speaking
Productive	Possess written communication skills

In addition to these types of skills, most jobs require skills that are specific to that particular job. For example, an accountant needs to know how to set up a general ledger, use accounting software, and develop income and expense reports. These skills are called *job-specific* skills and are quite important in qualifying for a job.

 Check out the Web site www.careerOINK.com to get thorough descriptions of all major jobs, including those from the *Occupational Outlook Handbook* and other government sources. CareerOINK is a free site developed by JIST Publishing.

Find the job titles you want to consider, print those descriptions, circle key skills they require, and emphasize those skills in your resume.

Identify your key skills

Your resume should emphasize skills that are particularly important for the job you want. Include any other job-specific skills or other skills you have that you think are important to communicate to an employer relative to the job you want. Write at least three, but no more than six, of these most important skills on the following lines:

1. _____

2. _____

3. _____

4. _____

5. _____

6. _____

Chapter 12

Prove your key skills

Now, write each of the preceding skills on a separate piece of paper. Then write any particularly good examples of when you used each skill. If possible, you should use work situations, but you can also use volunteer work, school activities, or any other life experience. Whenever possible, quantify the example by including numbers to support those skills such as money saved, increased sales, or other measures. Emphasize results you achieved and accomplishments.

The following is an example of what one person wrote for a key skill. It might give you ideas on how you can document your own skills.

AN EXAMPLE OF A KEY SKILL

Key Skill: Meeting Deadlines—I volunteered to help my social organization raise money. I found out about special government funds, but the proposal deadline was only 24 hours away. I stayed up all night and submitted the proposal on time. We were one of only three groups whose proposals were approved, and we were awarded over $100,000.

Edit your key skills proofs

Go over each "proof sheet" from the preceding exercise and select the proofs you think are particularly valuable in supporting your job objective. You should have at least two proofs for each skills area. After you have selected your proofs, rewrite them using action words and short sentences. Delete anything that is not essential. Edit each of your proofs until they are clear, short, and powerful. You can then use these statements in your resume, modifying them as needed to fit that format.

Here is an edited version of the preceding skill statement in a form that's appropriate for a resume.

KEY SKILL REWRITE

Key Skill: Meeting Deadlines—On 24-hour notice, submitted a complex proposal that successfully obtained over $100,000 in funding.

TIPS FOR FINE-TUNING YOUR RESUME

Before you make a final draft of your skills resume, look over the sample resumes at the end of this chapter for ideas on content and format. Several of them use interesting techniques that might be useful for your particular situation. Also keep in mind the following tips:

✓ If you have a good work history, a brief chronological listing of jobs is a helpful addition to your skills resume. When you add this listing, your resume becomes a combination-format resume, which combines the best of a chronological resume and a skills/functional resume.

✓ If you have substantial work history, begin the resume with a summary of your total experience, which provides the basis for details that follow.

✓ Remember that this is your resume, so do what you think is best.

✓ Trust your own judgment, and be willing to break a few rules if you think it will help you.

✓ Write the draft content for your resume on separate sheets of paper or on a computer.

✓ Rewrite and edit until the resume communicates what you really want to say about yourself and communicates to an employer why they should hire you over someone else.

✓ Once you have your resume "done," print the "final" copy on your computer printer and ask someone else to review it for typographical and other errors. If someone else is word-processing your resume, have them print you a "final" copy and have it reviewed by a third person, again, for any errors you might have overlooked.

✓ When you are sure that your resume contains no errors (and only then), have multiple copies of the final version printed or photocopied for distribution.

Five Examples of Skills Resumes

Look over the five sample resumes that follow to see how others have adapted the basic skills format to fit their own situation. These examples are based on real resumes (though their names and other details are not real), and I have included comments to help you understand details that may not be apparent. The formats and designs of these sample resumes are intentionally basic and can be done with virtually any word processor.

Chapter 12

Sample Skills Resume 1: A Career Changer with a New Degree

The next page presents the resume of a career changer. After working in a variety of jobs, Darrel went to school and learned computer programming. The skills format allows him to emphasize the business experiences in his past to support his current job objective. There is no chronological listing of jobs, and no dates are given for his education, so it is not obvious that he is a recent graduate with little formal work experience as a programmer.

Darrel does a good job of presenting his previous work experience and includes numbers to support his skills and accomplishments. Even so, the relationship between his previous work and current objective could be improved. For example, collecting bad debts requires discipline, persistence, and attention to detail—the same skills required in programming. And, although he is good at sales, how does this relate to programming?

To correct this, he might consider modifying his job objective to include the use of his sales skills (such as selling technological services) or emphasizing other skills from his previous work experience. Still, his resume is effective and does a decent job of relating past business experience to his ability to be an effective programmer in a business environment.

A career changer's JIST Card

The following sample JIST Card accompanies the first resume example. This nifty job search tool is covered in more detail in Chapter 6.

Darrel Craig   (412) 437-6217
Message: (412) 464-1273
E-mail: DarrelCraig@aol.com

Position Desired: PROGRAMMER/SYSTEMS MANAGEMENT

Skills: Over 10 years of combined education and experience in data processing, business, and related fields. Programming ability in Linux, C++, Java, and VBA. Knowledge of various database and applications programs in networked PC, Mac, and mainframe environments. Substantial business experience, including accounting, management, sales, and public relations.

Dedicated, self-starter, creative, dependable, and willing to relocate.

Skills resume for a career changer with a new degree

Darrel Craig

**Career
Objective**

Challenging position in programming or related areas that would best utilize expertise in the business environment. This position should have many opportunities for an aggressive, dedicated individual with leadership abilities to advance.

**Programming
Skills**

Include functional program design relating to business issues, including payroll, inventory and database management, sales, marketing, accounting, and loan amortization reports. In conjunction with design, proficient in coding, implementation, debugging, and file maintenance. Familiar with distributed network systems, including PCs and Macs, and working knowledge of DOS, Linux, C++, Java, and VBA.

**Areas of
Expertise**

Interpersonal communication strengths, public relations capabilities, innovative problem-solving and analytical talents.

Sales

A total of nine years of experience in sales and sales management. Sold security products to distributors and alarm dealers. Increased company's sales from $16,000 to over $70,000 per month. Creatively organized sales programs and marketing concepts. Trained sales personnel in prospecting techniques while also training service personnel in proper installation of security alarms. Result: 90% of all new business was generated through referrals from existing customers.

Management

Managed security alarm company for four years while increasing profits yearly. Supervised office, sales, and installation personnel. Supervised and delegated work to assistants in accounting functions and inventory control. Worked as assistant credit manager, responsible for over $2 million per month in sales. Handled semi-annual inventory of five branch stores totaling $10 million dollars and supervised 120 people.

Accounting

Balanced all books and prepared tax forms for alarm company. Eight years of experience in credit and collections, with emphasis on collections. Collection rates were over 98% each year, and was able to collect a bad debt in excess of $250,000 that the company deemed "noncollectable."

Education

School of Computer Technology, Pittsburgh, PA
Business Application Programming/TECH EXEC—3.97 GPA

Robert Morris College, Pittsburgh, PA
Associate degree in Accounting, Minor in Management

2306 Cincinnati Street, Kingsford, PA 15171 (412) 437-6217
Message: (412) 464-1273   E-mail: DarrelCraig@aol.com

More on Career Planning and Job Search **363**

Sample Skills Resume 2: A Resume That Incorporates Chronological Elements

Peter lost his factory job when the plant closed. He picked up a survival job as a truck driver, and now he wants to make this his career. It allows him to earn good money, and he likes the work.

Notice how his resume emphasizes skills from previous experiences that are essential for success as a truck driver. This resume uses a combination format: It includes elements of both a skills and chronological resume. The skills approach allows him to emphasize specific skills that support his job objective, and the chronological listing of jobs allows him to display his stable work history.

The miscellaneous older jobs that Peter had are simply clustered together under one grouping because they are not as important as more recent experience—and because doing this conceals his age. For the same reasons, he does not include dates for his military experience or high school graduation, nor does he separate them into different categories, such as "Military Experience" or "Education." They just aren't as important in supporting his current job objective as they might be for a younger person.

An unusual element here is Peter's statement about his not smoking or drinking, although it works, as do his comments about a stable family life.

Peter also has a version of this resume in which the job objective includes supervision and management of trucking operations. He added a few details to the content to support this objective. When it made sense, he used the other version.

He got a job with a small long-distance trucking company driving a regular route, and now he supervises other drivers.

Skills resume that incorporates chronological elements

Peter Neely

203 Evergreen Road
Houston, Texas 39127
PNDriver@hotmail.com
Messages: (237) 649-1234   Beeper: (237) 765-9876

POSITION DESIRED: Truck Driver

Summary of Work Experience:	Over 20 years of stable work history, including substantial experience with diesel engines, electrical systems, and truck driving.

SKILLS

Driving Record/ Licenses:	Chauffeur's license, qualified and able to drive anything that rolls. No traffic citations or accidents for over 20 years.
Vehicle Maintenance:	I keep correct maintenance schedules and avoid most breakdowns as a result. Substantial mechanical and electrical systems training and experience permit many breakdowns to be repaired immediately and avoid towing.
Record Keeping:	Excellent attention to detail. Familiar with recording procedures and submit required records on a timely basis.
Routing:	Knowledge of many states. Good map-reading and route-planning skills.
Other:	Not afraid of hard work, flexible, get along well with others, meet deadlines, responsible.

WORK EXPERIENCE

1998–Present	CAPITAL TRUCK CENTER, Houston, Texas Pick up and deliver all types of commercial vehicles from across the United States. Am trusted with handling large sums of money and handling complex truck-purchasing transactions.
1988–1998	QUALITY PLATING CO., Houston, Texas Promoted from Production to Quality Control. Developed numerous production improvements resulting in substantial cost savings.
1986–1988	BLUE CROSS MANUFACTURING, Houston, Texas Received several increases in salary and responsibility before leaving for a more challenging position.
1982–1986	Truck delivery of food products to destinations throughout the South. Also responsible for up to 12 drivers and equipment-maintenance personnel.
Prior to 1982	Operated large diesel-powered electrical plants. Responsible for monitoring and maintenance on a rigid schedule.

OTHER

Four years of experience in the U.S. Air Force operating power plants. Stationed in Alaska, California, Wyoming, and other states. Honorable discharge. High school graduate, plus training in diesel engines and electrical systems. Excellent health, love the outdoors, stable family life, nonsmoker and nondrinker.

Sample Skills Resume 3: A Resume for Someone with Limited Work Experience

This resume uses few words and lots of white space. It looks better, I think, than more crowded resumes. I would like to see more numbers used to indicate performance or accomplishments. For example, what was the result of the more efficient record-keeping system she developed? And why did she receive the Employee-of-the-Month awards?

Andrea does not have substantial experience in her field, having held only one job. For this reason, the skills format allows her to present her strengths better than a chronological resume would.

Because she has formal training in retail sales and is a recent graduate, she could have given more details about specific courses she took or other school-related activities that support her job objective. Even so, her resume does a good job of presenting her basic skills in an attractive format.

Resume for someone with limited work experience

ANDREA ATWOOD
3231 East Harbor Road
Grand Rapids, Michigan 41103
atwood@juno.com

Home: (303) 447-2111   Message: (303) 547-8201

Objective: A responsible position in retail sales.

Areas of Accomplishment:

Customer Service	Communicate well with all age groups. Able to interpret customer concerns to help them find the items they want. Received six Employee-of-the-Month awards in three years.
Merchandise Display	Developed display skills via in-house training and experience. Received Outstanding Trainee award for Christmas toy display. Dress mannequins, arrange table displays, and organize sale merchandise.
Stock Control and Marking	Maintained and marked stock during department manager's six-week illness. Developed more efficient record-keeping procedures.
Additional Skills	Operate cash register and computerized accounting systems. Willing to work evenings and weekends. Punctual, honest, reliable, and hardworking.
Experience:	Harper's Department Store Grand Rapids, Michigan 1995 to present
Education:	Central High School Grand Rapids, Michigan 3.6/4.0 grade-point average Honor Graduate in Distributive Education
	Two years of retail sales training in Distributive Education. Also took courses in business writing, computerized accounting, and word processing.

Sample Skills Resume 4: A Template-Based Format

Linda's resume is based on one included in David Swanson's *The Resume Solution*. It shows the resume style that he prefers, using lots of white space, short sentences, and brief but carefully edited narrative.

The format for this resume is based on a resume template that is provided with a popular word-processing program. Most word-processing programs provide several predetermined resume design options that include various typefaces and the use of other simple but effective format and design elements. Other resumes in this book have used similar templates, and this approach makes formatting a resume much easier, although sometimes it can be challenging to make your unique information fit into the constraints of a template.

Linda's resume is short but presents good information to support her job objective. It is based on the principle of "less is more."

A resume with a template-based format

6673 East Avenue
Lakeland, California, 94544

(415) 555-1519 (leave message)
lindamwinston@aol.com

Linda Marsala-Winston

Objective

Copywriter, Account Executive in Advertising or Public Relations Agency

Experience

1999–Present   Great River Publishing   Southridge, WA
Copywriter

- Developed copy for direct-mail catalogs featuring collectible items, for real estate developments, and for agricultural machinery and equipment.

1996–1999   *Habitat* Magazine   Southridge, WA
Writer

- Specialized in architecture, contemporary lifestyles, and interior design.

1994–1996   Fullmer's Department Store   San Francisco, CA
Sales Promotion Manager

- Developed theme and copy for grand opening of new store in San Francisco Bay area.

1991–1994   Mehari, Inc.   Los Angeles, CA
Fabric Designer

- Award-winning textile designer and importer of African and South American textiles.

Education

1991   University of California   Berkeley, CA

- B.A., English.
- 30 hours of graduate study in Journalism.

1994   California State University   Fresno, CA

- M.A., Guidance and Counseling.

Professional Membership

San Francisco Women in Advertising

Chapter 12

Sample Resume 5: A Combination Format

This is one of those resumes that is hard to put into a category—it is neither a skills nor a chronological resume, but combines elements of both. Remember that I have suggested you can break any rule you want to in putting together your own resume—if you do so for a good reason. Thomas' resume does break some rules, but he does so for good reasons, and the resume presents him well.

Thomas has kept his job objective quite broad and does not limit it to a particular industry or job title. Because he sees himself as a business manager, it does not matter much to him what kind of business he works in, although he prefers a larger organization, as his job objective indicates.

His education is toward the top of his resume because he considers it a strength. His military experience, although not recent, is also listed toward the top because he also felt that would help him. Note how he presented his military experience using civilian terms such as annual budgets and staff size, things that are easy to relate to a business environment.

Thomas has many years of experience with one employer, but he lists each job he held there as a separate one. This allows him to provide more details about his accomplishments within each job and also clearly points out that he was promoted. This nicely shows his progression to increasingly responsible jobs.

A resume that uses a combination format

THOMAS R. MARRIN
80 Harrison Avenue
Baldwin, New York 11563
Answering Service: (716) 223-4705
Email: tom_marrin@optonline.net

OBJECTIVE:

A middle/upper-level management position with responsibilities including problem solving, planning, organizing, and budget management.

EDUCATION:

University of Notre Dame, B.S. in Business Administration. Course emphasis on accounting, supervision, and marketing. Upper 25% of class. *Additional training:* Advanced training in time management, organizational behavior, and cost control.

MILITARY:

U.S. Army–2nd Infantry Division, 1990 to 1993. 1st Lieutenant and platoon leader–stationed in Korea and Fort Knox, Kentucky. Supervised an annual budget of nearly $4 million and equipment valued at over $40 million. Responsible for training, scheduling, and activities of as many as 40 people. Received several commendations. Honorable discharge.

BUSINESS EXPERIENCE:

Wills Express Transit Co., Inc.—Mineola, New York

Promoted to Vice President, Corporate Equipment—1998 to Present

Control purchase, maintenance, and disposal of 1,100 trailers and 65 company cars with $6.7M operating and $8.0M capital expense responsibilities.

- Scheduled trailer purchases, 6 divisions.

- Operated 2.3% under planned maintenance budget in company's second-best profit year while operating revenues declined 2.5%.

- Originated schedule to coordinate drivers' needs with available trailers.

- Developed systematic Purchase and Disposal Plan for company car fleet.

- Restructured Company Car Policy, saving 15% on per-car cost.

(continued)

Chapter 12

(continued)

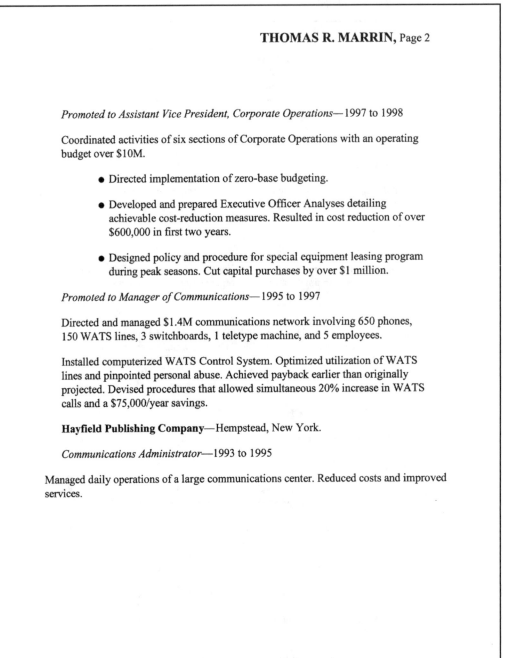

THOMAS R. MARRIN, Page 2

Promoted to Assistant Vice President, Corporate Operations—1997 to 1998

Coordinated activities of six sections of Corporate Operations with an operating budget over $10M.

- Directed implementation of zero-base budgeting.

- Developed and prepared Executive Officer Analyses detailing achievable cost-reduction measures. Resulted in cost reduction of over $600,000 in first two years.

- Designed policy and procedure for special equipment leasing program during peak seasons. Cut capital purchases by over $1 million.

Promoted to Manager of Communications—1995 to 1997

Directed and managed $1.4M communications network involving 650 phones, 150 WATS lines, 3 switchboards, 1 teletype machine, and 5 employees.

Installed computerized WATS Control System. Optimized utilization of WATS lines and pinpointed personal abuse. Achieved payback earlier than originally projected. Devised procedures that allowed simultaneous 20% increase in WATS calls and a $75,000/year savings.

Hayfield Publishing Company—Hempstead, New York.

Communications Administrator—1993 to 1995

Managed daily operations of a large communications center. Reduced costs and improved services.

Electronic, Scannable, and E-mail Resumes: How to Adapt Your Resume for an Electronic Job Search

Most of the previous tips for writing and designing a resume assume you will be printing it on paper. Because you are likely to also need to submit your resume in electronic form, you will need to adapt your paper version for this format. Even if you pursue a targeted job search as I've recommended—and therefore don't need to e-mail your resume to thousands of recruiters or companies—you should use the Internet to make your job search easier and faster.

It is important to understand that the content of electronic resumes differs little from their printed versions. This means that most of the work you do to create a print version of your resume can be used in an electronic version as well. The differences are primarily in how these documents are formatted. While your printed resume can be creative with different fonts, colors, sizes, and text positioning, most electronic resumes are necessarily simple and plain.

Here are a few tips on using the Internet as it relates to your resume.

- ✓ **Research.** The Internet is a vast resource where you can find information on companies, industries, job descriptions, salaries, and just about anything else you can think of. Use the Internet to compile and narrow down your target list of companies. Check these companies' Web sites for language you can use in your resume and cover letter or to see what relevant jobs they might have posted.

- ✓ **Speedy communication.** After you talk with a potential employer, you can quickly e-mail your resume and avoid regular mail delays. You can immediately apply online for a job at one of your target companies and, if your skills fit, could be interviewing the next day.

- ✓ **Follow-up.** Mass e-mailing to people you don't know is not a good way to conduct your search. But once you've established contact, e-mail is often the preferred method of communication with many businesspeople.

You'll need to create at least two different file formats for your electronic job search:

- ✓ **Word-processing file.** This is the original format you used to create your resume. If you used Microsoft Word, in many cases you can safely send your resume as an attachment to your e-mail message. Most employers and recruiting firms that receive your resume will be able to open, view, download, print, and file your MS Word resume.

Chapter 12

If you have used a different word-processing program, try to save or convert your resume file to a Word-compatible format, if you know how to do so; or you can simply create a universal-format text resume, as described below.

In some instances you will be required to "cut and paste" your resume into an online application, or you might be responding to a job posting that states "no attachments." In each of these cases, a text version will be required.

✓ **Text file.** If you can use a Rich Text format (RTF) to save your resume, do so, because this preserves most of the formatting you have included in your word-processed resume. As an option, ASCII Text (Text Only or Plain Text is the usual term used when saving a file to this format) is a plain-text file format that can be read by all computers using the Windows operating system. This kind of file cannot include formatting such as bold type, bullet points, or graphics. But the most important part of your resume—the content—will come through perfectly.

✓ **PDF file.** An optional format to consider is the PDF format, created by using the Adobe Acrobat program. The full Acrobat program (as opposed to the free reader program) allows you to save a word-processed document in a format that can be read no matter what software applications a person has, as long as they have the Acrobat reader. (This reader is available for free on a wide variety of Web sites, including www.adobe.com.) The benefit of this format is that it retains all formatting, and is essentially a picture of your word-processed resume that is easily open, read, and printed by anybody. However, you cannot paste a PDF file in an online form as you can with a text-only file format.

Converting Your Resume to Text Format

Here's how to create a Text file from your word-processed resume:

1. Open your resume file.

2. Using the "Save As" function, give the file a new name and choose the "Rich Text," "Text Only," "Plain Text," or "ASCII text" option.

3. Close the file.

4. Now reopen the new file and you'll see that a transformation has taken place. Your formatting has disappeared, bullets have turned into asterisks, and the font has been changed to Courier.

5. Review your resume to see if there are any obvious glitches or formatting problems. For example, sometimes apostrophes get turned into a funny assortment of characters, tabs disappear, or square bullets change into question marks. With an ASCII resume, you can use only standard "typewriter" symbols (such as asterisks) as accents and graphics.

6. Add extra line breaks and blank lines if necessary for readability. Don't worry about how long your resume is or whether it fits nicely onto a page.

7. If you have used a column format, you might have to reposition some text so that it aligns properly.

8. Save the file—it will be saved with an ".rtf" or ".txt" file extension rather than the standard ".doc" that is used for MS Word files.

Using Your Text File in Your Electronic Job Search

This new text file now becomes your e-mail and online application resume. Here's how to use it:

✓ **When applying for a job online:** If you are applying for a job listed on a company's Web site, you will usually be asked to "paste your resume here." To do this, open your Text file resume, choose "Select All," then "Copy." Switch back to the Web site, place your cursor in the appropriate text box in the form, and enter the "Paste" command (Ctrl+V). Your text resume will automatically flow into the box.

Some online resume forms only allow for a certain number of words or characters (usually 250 words). If this is the case, you should use the word processor's word count function to determine and adjust, if necessary, the length of your resume so that you can create a version to fit the required length.

✓ **When responding to an ad that states "no attachments."** Paste your Text resume into the body of your e-mail message, directly after a short cover letter. Use the subject line of your e-mail to say something relevant about yourself and/or the job you're applying for, for instance: "Re: CUSTOMER SERVICE JOB #459-A, 4 yrs. experience, customer ratings near 100%."

Following are two versions of the same resume—first in a traditional word-processed format, then transformed into a text file.

Chapter 12

A traditional resume

Meredith Gordon

617-243-5540
meredith@netcom.com
25 Edgeview Drive, Stoneham, MA 02180

GOAL	**Pharmaceutical Sales**
SUMMARY OF QUALIFICATIONS	• **SALES AND COMMUNICATION SKILLS:** Successful sales and customer service experience... proven communication abilities (listening, speaking, presenting)... strong problem-solving skills... ability to establish rapport with diverse individuals. • **HEALTH/WELLNESS KNOWLEDGE:** Degree in Health Education and Promotion... internship experience communicating health issues to city employees and the public. • **PERSONAL ATTRIBUTES:** Self-motivated and energetic... possess strong planning, organizational, and time management skills... professional in appearance and demeanor...enthusiastic, energetic, sincere, and hard working.

EDUCATION

Bachelor of Science in Health Education and Promotion, June 2002
Salem State University, Salem, Massachusetts

Internship: City of Salem Health Department, January–June 2002

- Assisted health educators in planning and carrying out various health education programs for more than 500 city employees as well as members of the community.
- Wrote, edited, designed, and coordinated printing and distribution of a monthly health newsletter distributed to all city employees.
- Prepared and delivered educational presentations on topics such as stress and safety.
- Attended and participated in professional meetings with health education staff.
- Provided staff support for tobacco and cardiovascular disease-prevention programs.
- Compiled a comprehensive list of smoke-free restaurants in Essex County.

EXPERIENCE

Front Desk/Customer Service Representative: Nauticus Fitness Center, Stoneham, MA, 2001–Present

- Provide customer-focused assistance to visitors and members; answer questions about programs, schedules, and referrals to health care providers located in the facility.
- Present program benefits and promote program registration.
- Recognized for problem-solving skills and ability to deliver customer satisfaction.

Sales Associate: Fitness Gear, Peabody, MA, 2000-Present

- Consistently earn commissions and incentives for sales performance as measured against monthly objectives.
- Personally set daily, weekly, and monthly goals and self-monitor performance.
- Completed sales training with emphasis on promoting product benefits.

ADDITIONAL QUALIFICATIONS

Computer Skills: MS Word, Excel, PowerPoint, Outlook, Internet applications.
Activities: Competitive tennis league.

A traditional resume converted to a text resume

```
Meredith Gordon
617-243-5540
meredith@netcom.com
25 Edgeview Drive, Stoneham, MA 02180

========================================
GOAL:  Pharmaceutical Sales

========================================
SUMMARY OF QUALIFICATIONS

* SALES AND COMMUNICATION SKILLS:  Successful sales and customer service
experience... proven communication abilities (listening, speaking, presenting)...
strong problem-solving skills... ability to establish rapport with diverse
individuals.
* HEALTH/WELLNESS KNOWLEDGE:  Degree in Health Education and Promotion... internship
experience communicating health issues to city employees and the public.
* PERSONAL ATTRIBUTES:  Self-motivated and energetic... possess strong planning,
organizational, and time management skills... professional in appearance and
demeanor...enthusiastic, energetic, sincere, and hard working.

========================================
EDUCATION

Bachelor of Science in Health Education and Promotion, June 2002
Salem State University, Salem, Massachusetts

INTERNSHIP: City of Salem Health Department, January-June 2002
* Assisted health educators in planning and carrying out various health education
programs for more than 500 city employees as well as members of the community.
* Wrote, edited, designed, and coordinated printing and distribution of a monthly
health newsletter distributed to all city employees.
* Prepared and delivered educational presentations on topics such as stress and
safety.
* Attended and participated in professional meetings with health education staff.
Provided staff support for tobacco and cardiovascular disease-prevention programs.
* Compiled a comprehensive list of smoke-free restaurants in Essex County.

========================================
EXPERIENCE

Front Desk/Customer Service Representative:  Nauticus Fitness Center, Stoneham, MA,
2001-Present
* Provide customer-focused assistance to visitors and members; answer questions
about programs, schedules, and referrals to health care providers located in the
facility.
* Present program benefits and promote program registration.
* Recognized for problem-solving skills and ability to deliver customer
satisfaction.

Sales Associate:  Fitness Gear, Peabody, MA, 2000-Present
* Consistently earn commissions and incentives for sales performance as measured
against monthly objectives.
* Personally set daily, weekly, and monthly goals and self-monitor performance.
* Completed sales training with emphasis on promoting product benefits.

ADDITIONAL QUALIFICATIONS
* Computer Skills:  MS Word, Excel, PowerPoint, Outlook, Internet applications.
* Activities: Competitive tennis league.
```

What Is a Scannable Resume?

It is important to understand that some large companies and most resume data-base sites do not want paper resumes and will scan any paper resumes they receive to remove all your resume's formatting and leave only the words. If you send them your resume in a PDF, rich text, or other electronic form, they will run it through software to convert your resume into text and only text. That allows them to put the content of your resume into a database form that can be easily searched by employers to find combinations of key words that they are looking for. For this reason, you should consider creating a "scannable" version of your resume that will work well in for this situation.

Following are some tips to consider in creating such a resume. While doing this will increase your chances of an employer selecting you over others, do remember that many thousands of other resumes will be in the same database, so your chances of being selected are slim unless you have very specialized credentials.

1. **Contain the right words that match the employer's queries (known as "key words").** Key words are simply words that an employer or company uses to define the most important qualifications for a job they're trying to fill. Key words typically are nouns ("sales," "accounting," "customer satis-faction," "Bachelor's degree") rather than verbs ("increased," "achieved," "initiated") or adjectives ("successful," "excellent," "dynamic").

   If you have held jobs similar to the one you're seeking, your resume probably contains the right key words. You can learn more key words from job descriptions for similar jobs, and you might want to add some of these to your resume to increase your chances of being "found" in a key-word search.

   If you are looking for a position unlike anything you've ever done before, your resume might not be found by a key-word search. But if this is your circumstance, you're probably not looking for a job by these mass-application means, anyway.

2. **Be readable by scanning software.** What is considered "scannable" can vary dramatically from company to company. Advanced scanning soft-ware can read a variety of formats and font variations, but simple scan-ners will have trouble with anything out of the ordinary. For best results, use a simple, unadorned format, eliminate bold and italic type, remove bullets, and eliminate graphics. Place all text at the left margin, and use at least 11-point type.

   You can remove all potential scanning problems by sending your resume electronically, by e-mail or through a Web site application form. Your text or word-processed resume can enter the database directly, without having to pass through a physical scan.

And if you prefer to send a hard-copy resume to be scanned, simply use the text version of your resume. It is 100 percent scannable.

Tips to Make Your Electronic Resume Stand Out

While electronic resumes are generally dull and uniform looking, here are a few tips that can help make your electronic resume a bit more presentable.

✓ Use white space to separate the sections of the resume. Leave two or three blank spaces between the major sections defining your experience, skills, education, and other sections.

✓ Capitalize your name and the major sections of the resume to set them apart. Do not overuse capitalization or nothing will stand out.

✓ Limit your line length to 60–65 characters and perform hard returns at the end of each line so your lines do not automatically wrap and create odd looking lines of text when the employer views it.

✓ Because real bullets are a graphic element that can't be used in electronic resumes, insert pseudo bullets that will reproduce accurately in text-only files by using the: "+", "*", or "#" keys.

Quick Summary

✓ A "resume" is the term most often used to describe a piece or two of paper summarizing your life's history. The idea is to select those specific parts of your past that support you doing a particular job well. Most often, the paper then presents you to prospective employers who, based on their response to the paper, may or may not grant you an interview. Along with the application form, it is the tool employers use most to screen job seekers.

✓ Your objective should be to get a good job, not to do a great resume. Trying to get an interview by sending out dozens of resumes is usually a waste of stamps. Do a *simple* resume early in your job search. This approach allows you to get on with getting interviews rather than sitting at home working on a better resume. Contrary to the advice of many resume and job search "experts," writing a perfect resume will rarely get you the job you want. Interviews (not resumes) get jobs.

✓ For a variety of reasons, many career professionals suggest that resumes aren't needed at all. Resumes don't do a good job in getting you an interview. When used in the traditional way, your resume is far more likely to get you screened out.

Chapter 12

✓ Some resume experts call a resume by another name, such as "Qualifications Brief," "Professional Job Power Report," "Curriculum VITA," "Employment Proposal," and other terms. In all their forms, they are really various types of resumes.

✓ All things considered, there are more good reasons to have a resume than not: Employers often ask for resumes. Resumes help structure your communications. A well-done resume presents details of your experiences efficiently and in a way that an employer can refer to as needed. It can also be used as a tool to present the skills you have to support your job objective and to present details that are often not solicited in a preliminary interview.

✓ Quantify your experience and achievements in a resume whenever possible.

✓ Four tips for using a resume effectively: 1. Get the interview first. (Don't send an unsolicited resume. It is better to directly contact the employer by phone or in person. Then send your resume after you schedule an interview, so that the employer can read about you before your meeting.) 2. Send your resume after an interview. 3. Give resumes to people you know. 4. If all else fails, use traditional techniques.

✓ Types of Resumes:

> The Chronological Resume: The primary feature of this type of resume is the listing of jobs held from the most recent backwards. This is the simplest of resumes and can be a useful format if used properly. The big advantage of a chronological resume is that it is easy to write. It works best for those who have had several years of experience in the same type of job they are seeking now. This is because a chronological resume will clearly display your recent work experience.

> The Skills or Functional Resume: Rather than listing your experience under each job, the skills resume style clusters your experiences under major skill areas. This approach would make little sense, of course, unless you had a job objective that required these skills. For this reason and others, a skills resume is harder to write than a simple chronological resume. If you have limited paid work experience, are changing careers, or have not worked for awhile, a skills resume may be a clearly superior approach to help you present your strengths and avoid displaying your weaknesses.

> The Combination or Creative Resume: Elements of chronological and skills resumes can be combined in various ways to improve the clarity or presentation of a resume. There are also creative formats that defy any category but that are clever and have worked for some people.

➤ Most employers will find a chronological resume perfectly acceptable (if not exciting), providing it is neat and has no errors. You can use it early in your job search while you work on a more sophisticated resume. The important point here is to get an acceptable resume together quickly so that you won't be sitting at home worrying about your resume instead of out looking for a job.

✓ In writing about your work experience, use action words and emphasize what you accomplished. Quantify what you did and provide evidence that you did it well. Take particular care to mention skills that would directly relate to doing well in the job you want. Think about the things you accomplished in jobs, school, military, and other settings.

✓ Use the Instant Resume Worksheet in this chapter to create a usable resume quickly. Use the examples of simple chronological resumes in this chapter as the basis for creating your own chronological resume. Follow the "Guidelines for Writing a Superior Resume" presented in this chapter, to keep it short, simple, positive, and professional.

✓ While a simple chronological resume does not absolutely require a career objective, a skills resume does. Without a reasonably clear job objective, it is not possible to select and organize the key skills you have to support that job objective.

✓ While the job objective you write should meet your specific needs, here are some tips to consider in writing it: Avoid job titles. Define a "bracket of responsibility" to include the possibility of upward mobility. Include your most important skills. Include specifics if these are important to you.

✓ The Job Objective Worksheet in this chapter can help you construct a well-stated, clear, accurate job objective. This is important because most employers will be impressed with someone who is very clear about the job they want and why they want it. Few interviews end well unless the interviewer is convinced that you want the job available and have the skills to do it reasonably well.

✓ Before you make a final draft of your skills resume, look over the sample resumes at the end of this chapter for ideas on content and format. Several of them use interesting techniques that may be useful for your particular situation. Also, keep in mind the tips presented in this chapter for fine-tuning your resume before submitting it.

✓ When working with electronic resumes that you send as e-mail attachments or post online, be aware that if you save your word-processed file in certain formats the resume will either not be readable by some people, or will lose some formatting. Plain Text or Rich Text formats are able to be read by many common software programs.

Chapter 12

✓ Some companies use scanning software to turn your resume into text that they can search for key words, so include important terms and phrases in both hard copy and electronic versions of your resume.

Cover Letters, Thank-You Notes, E-mail, and Other Job Search Correspondence

≡Quick Overview

In this chapter, I review the following:

✔ Guidelines for writing superior cover letters

✔ Why a brief cover letter is best

✔ How to write cover letters to people you know

✔ How to write cover letters to people you don't know

✔ Cover letter key words

✔ What a cover letter MUST include

✔ What to avoid in a cover letter

✔ Tips on when and why to send thank-you notes

✔ Sample cover letters, thank-you notes, etc.

✔ How to use e-mail and snail mail for cover letters and thank-you notes

The first part of this chapter provides advice on writing cover letters and includes various samples. I've tried to keep this basic, with an emphasis on letters that are sent after you have made some sort of personal contact with an employer. That's because letters—just like resumes—won't get you a job offer.

Writing a simple cover letter is pretty easy. Once you know how it's done, you should be able to write one in about 15 minutes or so.

During the course of an active job search, you will probably send out a variety of correspondence in electronic or paper formats. These types of miscellaneous written communications used during a job search are often overlooked in job search books. Thank-you notes are an example of correspondence that can make a big difference to you during your search for a job if used well. These and similar forms of written communications are the focus of the second part of this chapter.

Just as resumes can be sent in paper or electronic form, so can other job search-related correspondence. All of the advice on topics like "cover letters" is easily adapted to situations appropriate for e-mail. I'll try to provide e-mail-related tips as I go, but much of what I say about corresponding on paper can be easily adapted to work for correspondence sent on the Internet.

When and How to Write a Good Cover Letter

As with resumes, a big mistake with cover letters is to use them as part of a passive job search campaign in which you send out lots of unsolicited resumes. This is true with resumes sent as e-mail attachments, because what you say in your e-mail is a form of cover letter as well. In either case, I suggest that cover letters are best used *after* you have made some personal contact with a potential employer. This contact can be by phone, via e-mail, or in person.

It is not appropriate to send a resume to someone without explaining why. That is why an introductory letter, e-mail, or note should be attached to your resume. The traditional way to handle this is to provide a letter *along with* your resume—a cover letter. Depending on the circumstances, the letter would explain your situation and ask the person who receives it for some specific action, consideration, or response.

Entire books discuss the art of writing cover letters. Some authors go into great detail on how to construct "powerful" cover letters. Some suggest that a cover letter can replace a resume by providing information specifically targeted to the person receiving it. While these ideas have merit, my objective here is to give you a simple, quick review of cover letter basics that will meet most needs.

While many situations require writing a formal cover letter, there are many others where a simple note or e-mail will do. Additional information on notes and e-mail are provided later in this chapter.

Only Two Groups of People Will Receive Your Cover Letters

If you think about it, you will send a resume and cover letter to only two groups of people:

✓ People you know.

✓ People you don't know.

While I realize this sounds simplistic, it's true. And this observation makes it easier to understand how you might structure your letters to each group. But before I show you some useful and effective cover letters, let's first review some basics regarding writing cover letters in general.

SEVEN QUICK TIPS FOR WRITING A SUPERIOR COVER LETTER

No matter who you are writing to, virtually every good cover letter—paper or e-mail—should follow these guidelines:

1. Write to Someone in Particular

NEVER send a cover letter to "To whom it may concern" or use some other impersonal opening. We all get enough junk mail and e-mail; if you don't send your letter to someone by name, it will be treated like junk mail. (The only exception to this is when you respond to a "blind ad" for a job that does not include a specific person to send it to. In these situations, you can address your cover letter "Hiring Authority" or "Hiring Representative.")

2. Make Absolutely NO Errors

One way to offend people quickly is to misspell their names or use incorrect titles. If you have any question, call and vilify the corectly spalding of of their nime and other detales before you send the latter. (Hey! Did you catch those erears?) Review your letters carefully to be sure that they do not contain any typographical, grammatical, or other errors.

3. Personalize Your Content

I've never been impressed by form letters of any kind, and you should not use them. Those computer-generated letters that automatically insert a name never fool anyone, and I find cover letters done in this way offensive. While I know some resume and cover letter books recommend that you send out lots of these "broadcast letters" to people you don't know, I suggest that doing so wastes time and money. If you can't personalize your letter in some way, don't send it.

(continued)

More on Career Planning and Job Search **385**

(continued)

4. Present a Good Appearance

Your contacts with prospective employers should always be professional, so buy good quality stationery and matching envelopes. Use papers and envelopes that match or complement your resume paper. The standard paper size (8½ x 11) is typically used, but you can also use the smaller Monarch-size paper (3⅞ x 7½) with matching envelopes. For colors, I prefer white, ivory, or light beige.

Cover letters are rarely handwritten anymore, and employers expect them to be word processed or typed (without error!), with excellent print quality.

Use a standard letter format that complements your resume type and format. Most word-processing software provides templates or "wizards" to automate your letter's format and design. I used such templates to create the formats for the sample letters used in this chapter.

And don't forget the envelope! It should also be carefully done, without abbreviations or errors.

5. Provide a Friendly Opening

Begin your letter with a reminder of any prior contacts and the reason for your correspondence now. If there is a position available now, mention the position that interests you and how you heard about it. The examples will give you some ideas for how this can be handled.

6. Target Your Skills and Experiences to the Organization, Position, or Recipient

To do this well, you must know something about the organization or person with whom you are dealing. Present any relevant background that may be of particular interest to the person you are writing. Because your resume is attached, you don't need to repeat what is in there, although you can emphasize important points or add details that are not in your resume. Support your accomplishments with numbers if possible.

7. Close with an Action Statement

Don't close your letter without clearly identifying what you will do next. I do not recommend that you leave it up to the employer to contact you, because that doesn't guarantee follow-up. *Your objective is to get an interview or some other meaningful contact, so ask for this as appropriate.* Close on a positive note and let the employer know that you desire further contact.

Quick Reference While many situations require writing a formal letter, a simple note will do in many instances (for example, when you know the person you are writing to). Additional information on informal notes appears in the next chapter.

Quick Tip Using a few simple techniques, it is possible to make the acquaintance of all sorts of people. That's why I say that it wastes time and money to send your resume or cover letter to strangers—it is relatively easy to make direct contact.

The section later in this chapter titled "Writing Letters to People You Don't Know" provides details on how to make contact with people you haven't met before, and I recommend that you read more about this.

SURVEY FINDS THAT COVER LETTERS ARE IMPORTANT

It should come as no surprise that many employers find cover letters helpful. In a survey by HRnext/BenefitsNext, Human Resource managers (mostly from larger companies) were asked, "How important is the cover letter in an application?" They were given five choices for their responses and here is what they said:

✓ 7% indicated they are "Very important, it can clinch a job"

✓ 39% indicated "It's among the important factors"

✓ 22% indicated "It depends on the job"

✓ 19% indicated "It's important only if it's awful"

✓ 12% indicated "We don't even look at cover letters"

Another way to look at this is that 68% of these employers find that cover letters are important for at least some jobs and another 19% said that they don't help much but that a bad one can hurt you. Keep in mind, however, that this was a survey of people working in larger organizations who screen many applicants. Smaller employers get far fewer resumes and cover letters and are likely to pay more attention to a cover letter. This is even more so if you send them to employers who you have made some personal connection with or who may not be actively screening applicants. In these situations, a well written letter or e-mail with your resume attached will be much more important.

USE SNAIL MAIL PLUS E-MAIL

Quick Tip

If it makes sense to correspond via e-mail, do so. But people who get a lot of e-mail may not follow up, or can easily delete your message—particularly if they don't know you. So, for employment situations that do interest you, consider following up your e-mail by sending a paper resume and cover letter. Doing this is likely to get you more attention than just sending e-mail, and that's a good thing.

Writing Cover Letters to Someone You Know

It is always best if you know the person to whom you are writing. As I have said elsewhere, any written correspondence is less effective than personal contact, so the ideal circumstance is to send a resume and cover letter after having spoken with or e-mailed the person directly.

For example, it is far more effective to first call someone who has advertised in the paper than to simply send a letter and resume. You can come to know people through their listing in the *Yellow Pages*, personal referrals, e-mail, and other ways. You may not have known them yesterday, but you can get to know them today.

So, for the purposes of teaching you good job search principles, I'll assume you have made some sort of personal contact before sending your resume. This assumption about prior contact can include hundreds of variations, but I will review the most important ones and let you adapt them to your own situation.

Writing Cover Letters to People You Know

There are four basic situations when you might send cover letters to people you know, and each one requires a different approach. The situations are presented below, along with an explanation. I'll provide sample cover letters for each situation later.

The four types of cover letters illustrate an approach that can be used in getting interviews, which, of course, is the real task in the job search. Look at the samples for each type of cover letter and see how, in most cases, they assume that personal contact has been made before the letter and resume were sent.

THE FOUR TYPES OF COVER LETTERS TO PEOPLE YOU KNOW

Situation #1. An interview is scheduled, and a specific job opening may interest you. In this case, you have already arranged an interview for a job opening that interests you, and the cover letter or e-mail should provide details of your experience that relate to the specific job.

Situation #2. An interview is scheduled, but no specific job is available. This is a letter or e-mail you will send for an interview with an employer who does not have a specific opening for you now, but who might in the future. This situation provides fertile ground for finding job leads where no one else may be looking.

Situation #3. After an interview takes place. Many people overlook the importance of sending a letter after an interview. This is a time to say that you want the job (if that is the case, say so) and to add any details that show why you think you can do the job well.

Situation #4. No interview is scheduled, yet. There are situations where you just can't arrange an interview before you send or e-mail a resume and cover letter. For example, you may be trying to see a person whose name was given to you by a friend, but that person is on vacation. In these cases, sending a good cover letter and resume will allow any later contacts to be more effective.

Sample Cover Letters Addressed to People You Know

The following are sample cover letters for the four preceding situations. Note that they use different formats and styles to show you the range of styles that are appropriate. Each one addresses a different situation, and each incorporates all of the cover letter writing guidelines presented earlier in this chapter.

Remember that a resume will accompany each of these letters and the resume will include phone numbers, e-mail addresses, and other details that may not be included in the letters.

Sample Cover Letter: Pre-Interview, for a Specific Job Opening

Comments: This writer called first and arranged an interview—the best approach of all. Note how this new graduate included a specific example of how he saved money for a business by changing its procedures. He happened to gain his experience working with lots of people while working as a waiter but does not mention that here because doing so is not to his advantage for the job he now seeks. Note also how this letter includes skills such as "hard worker" and "deadline pressure" that I reviewed in Chapter 9 of this book.

Richard Swanson
113 So. Meridian Street
Greenwich, Connecticut 11721
March 10, 20XX

Mr. William Hines
New England Power and Light Company
604 Waterway Blvd.
Parien, Connecticut 11716

Mr. Hines:

I am following up on the phone call we had today. After getting the details on the position you have open, I am certain that it is the kind of job I have been looking for. A copy of my resume is enclosed providing more details of my background. I hope you have a chance to review it before we meet next week.

My special interest has long been in the large-volume order processing systems that your organization has developed so well. While in school, I researched the flow of order processing work for a large corporation as part of a class assignment. With some simple and inexpensive procedural changes I recommended, processing time was reduced by an average of three days. For the number of transactions involved, this one change resulted in an estimated increase in interest revenues of over $35,000 per year.

While I am a recent graduate from business school, I have considerable work experience for a person of my age. I have worked in a variety of jobs dealing with large numbers of people and deadline pressure. My studies have also been far more hands-on and practical than those of most schools, so I have a good working knowledge of current business systems and procedures. I am computer literate and have used software including various spreadsheet, word processing, and accounting systems. In addition, I have used the Internet for research and promotion and handled Web page administration. I also have a track record of cutting costs and increasing profits, including a past position where I helped to increase profits more than 20 percent. As someone who has worked my way through school, I am used to hard work and handling a variety of tasks.

I am most interested in the position you have available and am excited about the potential it offers. I look forward to seeing you next week. If you need to reach me before then, you can call me at (973) 299–3643 or e-mail me at rswanson@msn.net.

Sincerely,

Richard Swanson

Sample Cover Letter/E-mail: Pre-Interview, No Specific Job Opening

Comments: This letter indicates that the writer first contacted the employer via e-mail and set up an interview as the result of someone else providing the employer's name. The writer explains why she is moving to the city and asks for help in making contacts there. While no job opening exists here, she is wise in assuming that there might be one in the future. Even if this is not the case, she asks the employer to think of others who might have a position for someone with her skills. Assuming that the interview goes well and the employer gives her names of others to call, she can then follow up with them.

ANN MARIE ROAD
616 Kings Way • Minneapolis, MN 54312

February 10, 20XX

Mrs. Francine Cook
Park-Halsey Corporation
5413 Armstrong Drive
Minneapolis, Minnesota 56317

Dear Mrs. Cook,

When Steve Marks suggested I contact you via e-mail, I had no idea you would be so helpful. I've already followed up with several of the suggestions you sent me in your e-mail and am now looking forward to meeting with you next Tuesday. The resume I've enclosed will give you a better sense of my qualifications. Perhaps it will help you think of other people in organizations that may be interested in my background.

The resume does not say why I've moved to Minneapolis, and you may find that of interest. My spouse and I visited the city several years ago and thought it a good place to live. He has obtained a very good position here, and based on that, we decided it was time to commit ourselves to a move.

As you can see from my work experience, I tend to stay on and move up in jobs, so I now want to more carefully research the job opportunities here before making a commitment. Your help in this task is greatly appreciated.

Feel free to contact me at (834) 264-3720 if you have any questions; otherwise, I look forward to meeting with you next Tuesday.

Sincerely,

Anne Marie Road

P.S. My e-mail address is amfurn@movingtarget.com, and my cell phone is (763) 585-0025.

More on Career Planning and Job Search **391**

Sample Cover Letter: After an Interview

Comments: This letter shows you how you might follow up after an interview and make a pitch for solving a problem—even when no job formally exists. In this example, the writer suggests that she can use her skills to solve a specific problem that she uncovered during her conversations with the employer. While it never occurs to many job seekers to set up an interview where there appears to be no job opening, many jobs are created as a result of such interviews.

3233 Hawthorn Drive
Port Charlotte, Florida 81641
April 10, 20XX

Ms. Christine Massey
Import Distributors, Inc.
417 East Main Street
Atlanta, Georgia 21649

Dear Ms. Massey,

I know you have a busy schedule, so was delighted that you arranged a time to see me so quickly. While I know you don't have a position for someone with my skills at this time, your organization is just the sort of place I would like to work. As we discussed, I like to be busy with a variety of duties, and the active pace I saw at your company is what I seek.

Your ideas on increasing business sound innovative to me. I've thought about the customer service problem and would like to discuss a possible solution with you. I will work out a draft of procedures and bring it with me when we meet or send it to you, if you prefer. These procedures can be used with the computers your staff already has and would not require any additional cost to implement.

Whether or not you have a position for me in the future, I appreciate the time you have given me already. An extra copy of my resume is enclosed for your files, or to pass on to someone else.

Let me know if you want to discuss the ideas I presented earlier in this letter. I can be reached at any time on my cell phone at (942) 267-1103. I will e-mail you next week, as you suggested, to keep you informed of my progress.

Sincerely,

Sandra Kijek
skijek@netnet.net

Sample Cover Letter: No Interview Is Scheduled

Comments: This letter explains why the person is looking for a job and presents additional information that would not normally be included in a resume. Note that the writer had obtained the employer's name from the membership list of a professional organization, an excellent source of job leads. Also note that the writer stated that he would call again to arrange an appointment. While this letter is assertive and might turn off some employers, others would be impressed with his assertiveness and be willing to see him. Note: Look at Chapter 6 for an example of a JIST Card.

Justin Moore
8661 Bay Dr.
Tempe, AZ 27317
827-994-2765   e-mail jmoore72@aol.com
January 5, 20XX

Doris Michaelmann
Michaelmann Clothing
8661 Parkway Blvd.
Phoenix, AZ 27312

Ms. Michaelmann:

Perhaps you remember my sending you an e-mail a week ago, along with a copy of my resume. I have also called a few times while you were in meetings. Since I did not want to delay contacting you, I decided to write you this letter.

I am a member of the American Retail Clothing Association and got your name from our membership directory. I am contacting local members to ask their help in locating a suitable position. I realize you probably do not have a position open for someone with my skills but ask you to do two things on my behalf.

First, I ask that you consider seeing me at your convenience within the next few weeks. Though you may not have a position available for me, you may be able to assist me in other ways. And, of course, I would appreciate any consideration for future openings. Second, you may know of others who have job openings now or might possibly have them in the future.

While I realize that this is an unusual request and that you are quite busy, I do plan on staying in the retail clothing business in this area for some time and would appreciate any assistance you can give me in my search for a new job.

My resume is attached for your information along with a "JIST Card" that summarizes my background. As you probably know, Allied Tailoring has closed, and I stayed on to shut things down in an orderly way. Despite their regrettable business failure, I was one of those who was responsible for Allied's enormous sales increases over the past decade and have substantial experience to bring to any growing retail clothing concern, such as I hear yours is.

I will contact you next week and arrange a time that is good for us both. Please feel free to contact me at any time regarding this matter.

Sincerely,

Justin Moore

Writing Cover Letters to People You Don't Know

If it is not practical to directly contact a prospective employer via phone or some other method, it is acceptable to send a resume and cover letter. This approach makes sense in some situations, such as if you are moving to a distant location or responding to a blind ad offering only a post office box number or e-mail address.

The approach of sending out "To Whom It May Concern" letters and e-mails by the hundreds is discussed elsewhere in this book and is not recommended. However, there are ways to modify this "shotgun" approach to be more effective. Try to find something you have in common with the person you are contacting. For example: "In doing some networking, I came across your company. Based on what I learned, I'd enjoy the opportunity to discuss my background and how it is a good fit for your company." By mentioning this link, your letter then becomes a personal request for assistance. Look at the letters that follow for ideas.

The first two sample cover letters address unfamiliar people. Note that both writers "zeroed in" on location as the common link.

Several of the letters that follow use design templates that come with a widely used word processing program. Using these design templates can give your letters a professional look and allow you to focus on what you are saying rather than how your letter looks.

Sample Cover Letter: No Interview Is Scheduled

Comments: Responding to a want ad puts you in direct competition with the many others who will read the same ad, so the odds are not good that this letter would get a response. The fact that the writer does not yet live in the area is another negative. Still, I believe that you should follow up on any legitimate lead you find. In this case, someone who is available to interview right away is likely to be hired for the position. But a chance exists that, with good follow-up, another position will become available. Or the employer might be able to give the job seeker the names of others to contact.

---

12 Lake Street
Chicago, Illinois 60631
January 17, XXXX

The Morning Sun
Box N4317
2 Early Drive
Toronto, Ontario R5C IS3

Re: Receptionist/Bookkeeper Position

As I plan on relocating to Toronto, your advertisement for a Receptionist/Bookkeeper caught my attention. Your ad stated yours is a small office and that is precisely what I am looking for. I like dealing with people, and in a previous position had over 5,000 customer contacts a month. With that experience, I have learned to handle things quickly and pleasantly.

The varied activities in a position combining bookkeeping and reception sound very interesting. I have received formal training in accounting methods and am familiar with accounts receivable, accounts payable, and general ledger posting. I am familiar with several computerized accounting programs and can quickly learn any others that you may be using.

My resume is enclosed for your consideration. Note that I went to school in Toronto and I plan on returning there soon to establish my career. Several members of my family also live there and I have provided a local phone number, should you wish to contact me. Please contact me as soon as possible, because I plan on being in Toronto in the near future and would like to speak with you about this or future positions with your company. I will call you in the next few weeks to set up an appointment, should I not hear from you before then.

Thank you in advance for your consideration in this matter.

Sincerely,

John Andrews

P.S. You can reach me via e-mail at johnjandrews@cincore.com or leave a phone message at 587.488.3876.

Sample Cover Letter: No Interview Is Scheduled

Comments: This is another example of a person conducting a long-distance job search using names obtained from a professional association. This letter also explains why he is leaving his old job and includes positive information regarding his references and skills that would not normally be found in a resume. John asks for an interview even though there may not be any jobs open now and also asks for names of others to contact.

July 10, XXXX

Mr. Paul Resley
Operations Manager
Rollem Trucking Co.
I-70 Freeway Drive
Kansas City, Missouri 78401

Mr. Resley:

I obtained your name from the membership directory of the Affiliated Trucking Association. I have been a member for over 10 years, and I am very active in the Southeast Region. The reason I am writing is to ask for your help. The firm I had been employed with has been bought by a larger corporation. The operations here have been disbanded, leaving me unemployed.

While I like where I live, I know that finding a position at the level of responsibility I seek may require a move. As a center of the transportation business, your city is one I have targeted for special attention. A copy of my resume is enclosed for your use. I'd like you to review it and consider where a person with my background would get a good reception in Kansas City. Perhaps you could think of a specific person for me to contact?

I have specialized in fast-growing organizations or ones that have experienced rapid change. My particular strength is in bringing things under control, then increasing profits. While my resume does not state this, I have excellent references from my former employer and would have stayed if a similar position existed at its new location.

As a member of the association, I hoped that you would provide some special attention to my request for assistance. I plan on coming to Kansas City on a job-hunting trip within the next six weeks. Prior to my trip I will call you for advice on who I might contact for interviews. Even if they have no jobs open for me now, perhaps they will know of someone else who does.

My enclosed resume lists my phone number and other contact information should you want to reach me before I call you. Thanks in advance for your help on this.

Sincerely,

John B. Goode
Treasurer, Southeast Region
Affiliated Trucking Association

John B. Goode

312 Smokie Way   Nashville, Tennessee 31201

More Sample Cover Letters and Tips

I've included additional sample cover letters that address a variety of situations and use a variety of formats and approaches. Some use graphics and others use formats that are based on letter design templates included in a major word processing program.

The letters from Patricia Dugan and Douglas Parker are based on samples from David Swanson's book, *The Resume Solution.* Professional resume writer Rafael Santiago in Papillion, Nebraska, provided the letter by Marquita Lipscomb that features interesting design elements and formats. And professional resume writer Michael Robertson in Alexandria, Virginia, provided Jane Maeyers' letter. The remaining letters came from various books I have written in the past.

I hope that these samples give you ideas for writing your own cover letters. Once you get the hang of it, you should be able to write a simple cover letter in about 15 minutes. Just keep in mind that the best cover letter is one that follows you having set up an interview. Anything else is just second best, at best.

Sample Cover Letter: No Interview Is Scheduled

947 Cherry Street
Middleville, Ohio 01234
October 22, 20XX

Mr. Alfred E. Newman, President
Alnew Consolidated Stores, Inc.
1 Newman Place
New City, OK 03033

Dear Mr. Newman:

I am interested in the position of national sales director, which you recently advertised in the *Retail Sales and Marketing* newsletter.

I am very familiar with your company's innovative marketing techniques, as well as your enlightened policy in promoting and selling environmentally sound merchandise nationwide. I have been active for some time now in environmental protection projects, both as a representative of my current employer and on my own. I recently successfully introduced a new line of kitchen products that exceeds federal standards, is environmentally safe, and is selling well.

The enclosed resume outlines my experience and skills in both sales and marketing in the retail field. I would like to meet with you to discuss how my skills would benefit Alnew Consolidated Stores. I will contact you soon to request an interview for current or future positions and may be reached at (513) 987-6543 or by e-mail at Redding@reddinghome.com.

Thank you for your time and consideration.

Sincerely,

Robin Redding

Sample Cover Letter: Pre-Interview, No Specific Job Opening

LISA MARIE FARKEL   3321 East Haverford Road
Baldwin, North Carolina 12294
Email: lfarkel@dotcom.net
Phone: 400-541-0877
Fax: 400-541-0988

March 15, 20XX

Mr. Howard Duty
WXLC TV
10212 North Oxford Avenue
Halstead, South Carolina 124567

Dear Mr. Duty:

Thank you for agreeing to meet with me at 3:00 p.m. on March 23rd to talk about job opportunities for broadcast technicians. Although I understand that you have no openings right now, I'm enclosing my resume to give you some information about my training and background.

You will see that I have worked on both up-to-date and older equipment. Working part time for a small station, I've learned to monitor, adjust, and repair a variety of equipment, including both the newer automated and computerized items as well as the older ones. Keeping a mix of older and newer equipment working smoothly has required me to learn many things and has been an invaluable experience. At Halstead Junior College, I have become the person to call if the new, state-of-the-art audio and video equipment does not perform as it should.

I look forward to graduating and devoting all my time and energy to my career. Your help is greatly appreciated, particularly your invitation to spend more time observing field operations during your live election coverage.

Sincerely,

Lisa Marie Farkel

P.S. I found your Web site and was VERY impressed that you did most of the work on it. You may be interested to know that I also have created a Web site for our college TV station. If you have time, you can find it at ncstate.edu.WNCSTV—I'd like your feedback!

Enclosure: resume

Sample Cover Letter: No Interview Is Scheduled

<u>JANE MAEYERS</u>
123 Alexandria Drive
Alexandria, Louisiana 71409
(318) 443-0101
E-mail: Maeyers@alexandria.net

October 23, 20XX

Attention: Ms. Brenda Barnes
Coordinator of Student Activities
Screening Committee
Coldgate University
Campus Box 7
Emporia, Kansas 66801

<u>RE: Position as Coordinator of
Student Activities Organization & Special Events,
or related position</u>

Dear Screening Committee:

I have planned, developed, supervised, taught, and successfully completed numerous tasks assigned to me in my 10 years of experience as a recreation specialist. Now I'm ready to apply the same expertise and principles of hard work in starting a productive and challenging career as Coordinator of Student Activities Organization & Special Events, or a related position, with your organization. Because this position matches my interests, qualifications, and work and education experience, I can be a productive and valuable coordinator from day one.

The resume enclosed also outlines all the details of my career background as a recreation specialist. With these credentials and my belief in quality hard work, I will make a significant contribution to Coldgate University.

I am looking forward to working with your organization and would appreciate the opportunity to discuss employment opportunities with you soon.

Please inform me by letter or call (318) 443-0101 to arrange a time when we can meet at your convenience. I can also be contacted via email at Maeyers@alexandria.net. Thank you for your time and consideration.

Sincerely,

Jane Maeyers

Sample Cover Letter: No Interview Is Scheduled

6345 Highland Boulevard
Minneapolis, Minnesota

June 28, 20XX

Mr. James A. Blackwell
Vice President, Engineering
Acme Revolving Door Company
New Brunswick, Pennsylvania 21990

Dear Mr. Blackwell:

I graduated from the University of Minnesota this spring with a 3.66 grade average and a Bachelor of Science Degree in Mechanical Engineering.

Your company has been highly recommended to me by my uncle, John Blair, the Pennsylvania District Governor for Rotary, International. He has appreciated your friendship and business relationship over the years and has advised me to forward my resume. My own reading in business publications has kept me aware of the new products that Acme has marketed. Also, I recently visited your excellent Web site and was impressed with the variety of materials you produce.

My objective is to design mechanical parts for a privately owned company that enjoys an excellent reputation and that conducts business internationally.

I hope that I may take the liberty of calling your office to see if we might meet to discuss possible opportunities with Acme. I plan to be in Pennsylvania toward the end of next month, and this might provide a convenient time to meet, if your schedule permits.

Sincerely,

Patricia Dugan
(612) 555-3445
PDugan775@neverland.net

Sample Cover Letter: Pre-Interview, for a Specific Job Opening

1768 South Carrollton Street
Nashville, Tennessee 96050
May 26, 20XX

Ms. Karen Miller
Office Manager
Lendon, Lendon, and Sears
Suite 101, Landmark Building
Summit, New Jersey 11736

Dear Ms. Miller:

Enclosed is a copy of my resume that describes my work experience as a legal assistant. I hope this information will be helpful as background for our interview next Monday at 4 p.m.

I appreciate your taking time to describe your requirements so fully. This sounds like a position that could develop into a satisfying career. And my training in accounting—along with experience using a variety of computer programs—seems to match your needs.

Lendon, Lendon, and Sears is a highly respected name in New Jersey. I am excited about this opportunity and I look forward to meeting with you.

Sincerely,

Richard Wittenberg

Sample Cover Letter: No Interview Is Scheduled

B

ALBAROSA BARTON
12603 SOUTH 33RD STREET
OMAHA, NEBRASKA 68123
PHONE (402) 292-9052
FAX (402) 393-0099
EMAIL ALBAROSA@OFCORPS.COM

March 30, 20XX

YALE BUSINESS SERVICES
Alexander Bell, Director of Human Resources
1005 Denver Street, Suite 1
Bellevue, Nebraska 68005-4145

Dear Mr. Bell:

I am enclosing a copy of my resume for your consideration and would like to call your attention to the skills and achievements in my background that are most relevant.

I am an achiever, with four years of experience as a highly successful administrator. I've always set high standards and consistently achieved my goals. I've served in the United States Air Force as an Administrative Specialist/Assistant. I acquired my training through the excellent programs the Air Force provides. I am highly motivated and would be a dynamic IT administrator for whatever company I represent.

I am confident in my administrative abilities and have already proven myself in the areas of NT network administration and ERP implementation.

I look forward to hearing from you soon and having the opportunity to discuss your needs and plans.

Cordially,

ALBAROSA BARTON

Sample Cover Letter: No Interview Is Scheduled

4550 Parrier Street
Espinosa, California 44478

September 11, 20XX

Mr. Craig Schmidt
District Manager
Desert Chicken Shops
Post Office Box 6230
Los Angeles, California 98865

Dear Mr. Schmidt:

My resume (enclosed) outlines my four years of successful experience as a fast food manager with a nationwide network of restaurants. I graduated from a Restaurant Management curriculum at Harman University with a 3.75 GPA in 2000.

I have been impressed with the rapid growth and exceptional quality of product and service for which Desert Chicken has become well known. This is the kind of organization I hope to work for now.

My experience includes positions as cook, night manager, assistant manager, and manager for my current employer.

I will call your office in a few days to see if we might schedule a convenient time to meet and discuss some areas of mutual interest.

Thanks very much for your consideration.

Sincerely,

Douglas Parker
dparker@west.com

Enclosure

Sample Cover Letter: No Interview Is Scheduled

Are You Understaffed?

Meet Marquita! "An Experienced Administrative Assistant If I Ever Met One!"

MARQUITA IS:
Creative
Intelligent
Honest
Quick to Learn
Willing to Learn
Resourceful

QUALIFIED ... STRONG PEOPLE BACKGROUND AND PEOPLE SKILLS IN:
Knowing When and How to Ask Questions
Handling Complaints
Motivating Others
Knowing When to Listen

I am looking for full-time administrative work and will provide you with top-notch, quality support. If you are looking for the best, why not give me a call?

Marquita M. Lipscomb

1005 Denver Street—Bellevue, Nebraska 68005—(402) 733-0200

Sample Cover Letter: No Interview Is Scheduled

Apartment A35
4085 Larchmont Road
Seattle, Washington 97033

September 1, 20XX

The Seattle News
Box N9142
1414 East New York Street
Seattle, Washington 97002

Your advertisement for an Administrative Assistant could have been written with me in mind. I have had three years' experience in a busy office where time management, communication skills, and ability to deal with all kinds of people are vital.

Directing support staff, writing customer service letters, and preparing monthly, quarterly, and yearly sales reports are my responsibilities. I regularly use computer software packages to track and maintain our sales revenues and customer mailing lists. I am proficient in word processing, database, and spreadsheet software on both Mac- and PC-based computers and frequently use the Internet for research. My communication skills are excellent, and I can work on multiple tasks and still meet deadlines.

For your consideration, I have enclosed a resume that more completely describes my education and experience. I look forward to meeting with you soon.

Sincerely,

Susan Deming

(555) 555-3221 cell phone
susandeming@email.net

Sample Cover Letter: No Interview Is Scheduled

JLM

LOOKING FOR A HUMAN RESOURCES MANAGER?

ONE WITH A HIGHLY SUCCESSFUL TRACK RECORD?

If you are, please take a look at me.

➤ Twenty-four years' experience in the United States Air Force ... from vehicle operator and dispatcher ... to Vehicle Operations Manager in seven U.S. and foreign locations.

➤ A proven track record in training and development as a driver's school instructor, successfully training 90 students per month ... initiated in-house training programs for dispatchers, improving customer service and self-motivation in the trainees.

➤ Innovative and creative ... like challenge and enjoy bringing order from chaos and improving techniques and technologies.

➤ A skilled manager ... over a 24-year period have managed six 60-personnel operations ... excellent job of handling yearly budgets averaging $800,000+.

➤ Ideas that work ... with documented results showing successful accomplishments of varied operational projects.

➤ An established reputation ... known for being a highly motivated achiever of even the most difficult operations and management tasks.

My personal characteristics include a high level of dedication to work ... strong personal values of honesty and integrity ... excellent professional training ... professional appearance and manner ... even tempered and handle stress well.

Want to hear more? I've enclosed my resume and would like the opportunity to further discuss how I can be a successful member of your team. Call me.

Sincerely,

James L. Miller

Enclosure

JAMES L. MILLER
15689 South 25th Street
Omaha, Nebraska 68123
Phone: (402) 291-5046
E-mail: OmahaJames@NBnet.com

A Powerful and Often Overlooked Job Search Tool: The Thank-You Note

While resumes and cover letters get the attention, thank-you notes often get results. That's right—sending thank-you notes reflects both good manners and good job search sense. When used properly, they can help you make a positive impression with employers that more formal correspondence often can't.

So, in just a few pages, here are the basics of writing and using thank-you notes, an often overlooked but surprisingly effective job search tool.

The Three Times When You Should Definitely Send Thank-You Notes

Thank-you notes get results. They are a social tradition that is more intimate and friendly than more formal and manipulative business correspondence. I think that is one of the reasons they work so well—people respond well to those who show good manners and say thank you. Here are some situations when you should use them, along with sample notes to show you how it's done.

Right after the call or interview send an e-mail thank-you note and follow this up with a handwritten thank-you note two days later. The hard copy is important as they will need to open it and you will have their attention for another 30 seconds. This matters.

Before an interview

There are some situations when you can send a less formal note before an interview. In some cases, you can simply thank someone for being willing to see you. Depending on the situation, enclosing a resume could be a bit inappropriate. Remember, this is supposed to be sincere thanks for their help and not an opportunity to assert yourself.

Sample Thank-You Note #1

April 5, 20XX

Cynthia Vernor,

Thanks so much for your willingness to see me next Wednesday at 9:00 a.m. I know that I am one of many who are interested in working with your organization and appreciate the opportunity to meet you, and learn more about the position.

I've enclosed a JIST Card that presents the basics of my skills for this job and will bring a copy of my resume to the interview. Please call me if you have any questions at all.

Sincerely,

Bruce Vernon

Enclose a JIST Card with your thank-you notes. You can find samples of them in Chapter 6. They fit well into a thank-you note sized envelope and they provide key information an employer can use to contact you. JIST Cards also provide key skills and other credentials that will help you create a good impression. And, of course, the employer could always forward the card to someone else who might have a job opening for you.

After an interview

One of the best times to send a thank-you note is right after an interview. Consider sending an e-mail immediately after the interview, then follow up with a mailed thank-you note. There are several reasons for this, in my opinion:

1. Doing so creates a positive impression. The employer will assume you have good follow-up skills, to say nothing of good manners.

2. It creates yet another opportunity for you to remain in the employer's consciousness at an important time.

3. Should they have buried, passed along, or otherwise lost your resume and previous correspondence, sending a thank-you note and a corresponding JIST Card provides one more chance for them to find your number and call you.

For these reasons, I suggest you send a thank-you note right after the interview and certainly within 24 hours. The following is an example of such a note.

Sample Thank-You Note #2

August 11, 20XX

Dear Mr. O'Beel,

Thank you for the opportunity of interviewing for the position you have available in the production department. I want you to know that this is the sort of job that I have been looking for and am enthusiastic about the possibility of working for you.

I am not just saying this. I have been searching for just such a position and believe that I have both the experience and skills to fit nicely into your organization and be productive quickly. I am also able to start immediately.

Thanks again for the interview, I enjoyed the visit.

Sara Hall

Quick Tip

Send a thank-you note as soon as possible after an interview or meeting. This is when you are freshest in the mind of the person who receives it and are most likely to create a good impression.

Whenever anyone helps you with your job search

Send a thank-you note to anyone who helps you during your job search. This includes those who give you referrals, people who provide advice, or simply those who are supportive of you during your search for a new job. I suggest you routinely enclose one or more JIST Cards in these notes because the recipient can then give them to others who may be in a better position to help you.

Sample Thank-You Note #3

October 31, 20XX

Debbie Childs
2234 Riverbed Avenue
Philadelphia, PA 17963

Ms. Helen A. Colcord
Henderson and Associates, Inc.
1801 Washington Blvd., Suite 1201
Philadelphia, PA 17963

Dear Ms. Colcord,

Thank you for sharing your time with me so generously yesterday. I really appreciated talking to you about your career field.

The information you shared with me increased my desire to work in such an area. Your advice has already proven helpful as I have an appointment to meet with Robert Hopper on Friday.

In case you think of someone else who might need a person like me, I'm enclosing another resume and JIST Card.

Sincerely,

Debbie Childs

Seven Quick Tips for Writing Thank-You Notes

Here are some brief tips to help you write your thank-you notes.

Use quality paper and envelope

Use quality note paper with matching envelopes. Most stationery stores have thank-you note cards and envelopes in a variety of styles. Select a note that is simple and professional, avoiding cute graphics and sayings. A simple "Thank You" on the front will do. For a professional look, match your resume and thank-you note papers by getting them at the same time. I suggest off-white and buff paper colors.

Handwritten or typed is acceptable

The tradition with thank-you notes is that they are handwritten. If your handwriting is good, it is perfectly acceptable to write them. If not, they can be word processed or typed. But avoid making them appear too formal.

Use a formal salutation

Unless you already know the person you are thanking, don't use their first name. Write "Dear Ms. Pam Smith," or "Ms. Smith," or "Dear Ms. Smith," rather than the less formal "Dear Pam." Include the date.

Keep the note friendly and informal

Keep your note short and friendly. This is not the place to write "The reason you should hire me is…" Remember, the note is a thank you for what *they* did, not a hard-sell pitch for what *you* want. And make sure it does not sound like a form letter; one way to do this is to reference a specific topic that came up during your interview. As appropriate, be specific about when you will next contact them. If you plan to meet with them soon, still send a note saying you look forward to the meeting and thanking them for the appointment. And make sure that you include something to remind them of who you are and how to reach you, because your name alone may not be enough for them to recollect you.

Sign it

Sign your first and last name. Avoid initials and make your signature legible.

Send it right away

Write and send your note no later than 24 hours after you make your contact. Ideally, you should write it immediately after the contact, while the details are still fresh in your mind. Always send a note after an interview, even if things did not go well. Better yet, send a thank-you e-mail and then a mailed thank-you note. They can't hurt.

Enclose a JIST Card

Depending on the situation, a JIST Card is often the ideal enclosure to include with a thank-you note. It's small, soft-sell, and provides your phone number, should the employer wish to reach you. It is both a reminder of you, should any jobs open up, and a tool to pass along to someone else. Attaching a JIST Card to your e-mail allows the recipient to quickly forward it to others, too. For your paper notes, make sure your notes and envelopes are big enough to enclose an unfolded JIST Card.

More Sample Thank-You Notes

I've included a few more samples of thank-you notes and letters. They cover a variety of situations and will give you ideas on how to write your own. Notice that they are all short, friendly, and typically mention that the writer will follow up in the future—a key element of a successful job search campaign.

Also note that several are following up on interviews where no specific job opening exists, yet. As I've mentioned elsewhere, getting interviews before a job opening exists is a very smart thing to do. All of these examples came from David Swanson's book titled *The Resume Solution* and are used with permission.

Chapter 13

April 22, 20XX

Dear Mr. Nelson,

Thank you so much for seeing me while I was in town last week. I appreciate your kindness, the interview, and all the information you gave me.

I will call you once again in a few weeks to see if any openings have developed in your marketing research department's planned expansion.

Appreciatively,

Phil Simons

Answering machine: (633) 299-3034

Email: philsimons@mindspeed.net

September 17, 20XX

Mr. Bill Kenner
Sales Manager
WRTV
Rochester, Minnesota 87236

Dear Mr. Kenner:

Thank you very much for the interview and the market information you gave me yesterday. I was most impressed with the city, your station, and with everyone I met.

As you requested, I am enclosing a resume and JIST Card, and have requested that my ex-manager call you on Tuesday, the 27th, at 10:00 a.m. to provide you with a reference.

Working at WRTV with you and your team would be both interesting and exciting for me. I look forward to your reply and the possibility of helping you set new records next year.

Sincerely,

Anne Bently

Mr. William Boysen
1434 River Drive
Polo, Washington 99656

October 14, 20XX

Dear Bill,

I really appreciate you recommending me to Alan Stevens at Wexler Cadillac. We met yesterday for almost an hour and we're having lunch again on Friday. If this develops into a job offer, as you think it may, I will be most grateful.

Enclosed is a copy of a reference letter by my summer employer. I thought you might find this helpful.

You're a good friend, and I appreciate you thinking of me.

Sincerely,

Dave

July 26,20XX

Dear Ms. Bailey,

Thank you for the interview for the auditor's job last week.

I appreciate the information you gave me and the opportunity to interview with John Petero. He asked me for a transcript, which I am e-mailing to you today separately.

Working in my field of finance in a respected firm such as Barry Productions appeals to me greatly.

I appreciate your consideration and look forward to hearing from you.

Sincerely,

Dan Rehling

May 21, 20XX

Mrs. Sandra Waller
Yellow Side Stores
778 Northwest Boulevard
Seattle, Washington 99659

Dear Ms. Waller:

Thank you so much for the interview you gave me last Friday for the Retail Management Training Program. I learned a great deal and know now that retailing is my first choice for a career.

I look forward to interviewing with Mr. Daniel and Ms. Sobczak next week. For that meeting, I will bring two copies of my resume and a transcript, as you suggested.

Enclosed is a copy of a reference letter written by my summer employer. I thought you might find it helpful.

Sincerely,

Elizabeth Duncan

March 22, 20XX

Dear Ms. Samson:

Thanks for talking with me by phone today. You made me feel at ease!

I appreciate you granting me an interview appointment and will look forward to meeting you in your office at 10:00 a.m. on Tuesday, March 29.

I will bring my design portfolio with me. Thanks again.

Sincerely,

Bradley Kurtz

Other Job Search Correspondence

Besides thank-you notes and JIST Cards, there are a variety of other communications you can send to people during the course of your job search. Following are some brief comments about some of them.

Follow-up Letters after an Interview

After an interview, to solve a problem, or to present a proposal, you might wish to send some follow-up correspondence. I have already shown you some examples of letters and notes that were sent following an interview. In some cases, a longer or more detailed letter would be appropriate. The objective here would be to provide additional information or to present a proposal.

The sample letter from Sandra Kijek included earlier in this chapter is an example of a follow-up letter that suggests a specific proposal. In some cases, you could submit a much more comprehensive proposal that would essentially justify your job. If there were already a job opening available, you could submit an outline of what you would do if hired. If there was no available job, you could submit a proposal that would create a job, and state what you would do to make hiring you pay off.

In writing such a proposal, it is essential that you be specific in telling them what you would do and what results these actions would bring. For example, if you proposed you could increase sales, how would you do it and how much might profits increase? Tell the employer what you could accomplish and they may just create a new position for you. It happens more often than you probably realize.

Whatever the situation, your post-interview letter should present any concerns the employer may have had with you during the interview in positive light. For example, if the employer voiced concern over a lack of specific experience, you would address his concern by stating you are a quick study, self-motivated, and detail-oriented. Once you have put their concerns to rest, it is always advisable to reinforce your interest in the job (if that is the case). A statement like, "After hearing more about the job, I am even more certain my skills and education will be beneficial to your company. I am eager to begin working for you and will call next Tuesday to inquire about the hiring decision."

Enclosures

In some cases, you may want to include something along with other correspondence, such as a sample of your writing. This can be appropriate, although I advise against sending too much material unless the employer requests it. Never send originals of anything unless you are willing to lose them. Assume, in all cases, that what you send will be kept.

Post-it™ Notes

You have surely seen and used those little notes that stick on papers, walls, and other things. They can be useful when used to point out specific points on attachments, to provide additional details, or simply to indicate who the materials are coming from. Use just one or two of them to avoid a cluttered look.

To Anyone Who Helps You in Your Job Search

As I mentioned in the thank-you note section, you should consider sending notes or letters to anyone who helps you in your job search. This includes those who simply give you the name of someone else to contact, speak with you on the phone, or corresponded via e-mail. Besides being good manners, such a note provides you with an opportunity to do two other things:

1. Give them additional information about you via an enclosed resume and JIST Card (that they can pass along to others)

2. Help to keep your needs in their consciousness

While this list of advantages should look suspiciously like those I presented on cover letters, it's worth repeating here.

 Anyone can become part of your job search network and can help you. Staying in touch—and giving them tools such as a JIST Card—allows them to help you in ways that are difficult to anticipate in advance.

A List of References

Once an employer begins to get serious, the person doing the hiring may want to contact your references as part of a final screening process. To make this easier for them, I suggest that you prepare a list of people to contact. This list should include the complete name, title, organization, address, phone number, and e-mail address for each person. You should also include information about how each one knows you. For example, note that Mr. Rivera was your immediate supervisor for two years.

Be sure to inform those on your list that they may be contacted and asked to provide references. In some cases, you should take the time to prepare them by sending them information on the types of jobs that you now seek, a current resume, JIST Card, and other details about your job objective. If there is any question whether they would provide you with a positive reference, discuss this in advance so that you know what they are likely to say about you. If it is not positive, consider dropping them from your list.

Letters of Reference

Many organizations fear lawsuits as the result of giving out negative information regarding an ex-employee. For this reason, it can often be difficult for a prospective employer to get meaningful information on someone they are considering. This is one reason I recommend that you request previous employers and other references to write you a letter that you can submit to others if asked to do so. If the letters are positive, the advantages should be clear. Even if the letter is negative, at least you now know that there is a problem with this reference. Depending on the situation, you might contact this previous employer and negotiate what they will tell those who contact them. Of course, you should never volunteer a negative letter of reference.

Unsolicited Letters Requesting an Interview or Other Assistance

Once more, I want to discourage you from doing this as a primary technique. Even though many job search books recommend sending out lots of unsolicited letters and resumes—or posting them on various Internet job banks—the evidence is overwhelming that this does not work for most people. The rare exception is if your skills are very much in demand. In most cases, you would still be far better off to simply pick up the phone and ask for an interview.

I do think that sending a letter or e-mail to people with whom you share a common bond, such as alumni or members of a professional group, can be reasonably effective. This is particularly so if you are looking for a job in another city or region and send a letter asking them to help you by giving you names of local contacts. Several of the sample cover letters included in this chapter provide examples of those using this very technique which can work, particularly if you follow up by phone or e-mail.

How to Use E-mail and Snail Mail for Cover Letters and Thank-You Notes

Many hiring managers prefer correspondence via e-mail. It's quick, easy, and free. E-mail is instantaneous. The employer will receive your e-mail seconds from the time it is sent. Therefore, if the timeline on hiring is short, e-mail would be an advantage over snail mail.

When you are interviewed and the employer gives you his or her card with an e-mail address, it is generally acceptable to correspond via e-mail. However, if you have a formal cover letter or thank-you note template and send these as e-mail attachments, make sure they are in a universal format such as Microsoft Word, WordPerfect, Rich Text, Adobe PDF, or HTML and always mention the format of your letter in your e-mail message. A statement such as, "I have attached a cover letter/thank-you note in Word 2000 format. Should you have any problems receiving it in this format, contact me immediately" works in most cases. If you are ever in doubt about whether an employer can open your attachments, you should directly type the cover letter or thank-you note in the body of your e-mail.

While the mail service has considerably improved since the Pony Express days, it still takes a day or two to send and receive a cover letter or thank-you note locally. While this often looks more formal than e-mail letters, it may not be received in time for consideration. Consider the advantages and disadvantages of each. Essentially it boils down to speed versus formality.

Quick Summary

✓ As with resumes, a big mistake with cover letters is to use them as part of a passive job search campaign in which you send out lots of unsolicited resumes.

✓ Cover letters are best used after you have made some personal contact with a potential employer by phone or in person, rather than as a replacement for direct contact.

✓ The seven guidelines for writing superior cover letters are

1. Write to someone in particular

2. Make absolutely no errors

3. Personalize your content

4. Present a good appearance

5. Provide a friendly opening

6. Target your skills and experiences

7. Define the next step

✓ Ask for the interview.

✓ Base your cover letters on the samples in this chapter, taking into account whether you know the recipient or not.

✓ While resumes and cover letters get the attention, thank-you notes often get results. Sending thank-you notes shows both good manners and good job search sense. When used properly, they can help you make a positive impression with employers that more formal correspondence often can't.

✓ In this chapter, you learn the basics of writing and using thank-you notes— that often overlooked but surprisingly effective job search tool. Send a thank-you note 1) before an interview, 2) after an interview, and 3) any time someone helps you in your job search. And ASK for the job or the next step.

✓ There are a variety of miscellaneous types of correspondence, (including follow-up letters, letters of reference, proposals, etc.) that you can send to people during the course of your job search. These types of communication can help you to make a good impression, and most importantly, can help you find (or create) the job you want.

CHAPTER 14

Use the Phone and E-mail to Get Lots of Interviews

≣≣≣Quick Overview

In this chapter, I review the following:

✔ Why using the telephone can be both a very effective and very efficient job search method

✔ Using e-mail to support your phone calls in an effective way

✔ How to use your JIST Card as a basis for a phone interview

✔ The five parts of an effective phone script

✔ Tips for completing your phone script

✔ Tips for making cold contacts—calling people you don't know

✔ Tips for making warm contacts—calling people you know

✔ How to get the interview

✔ How to have a successful phone interview

✔ What recruiters do and you can do for yourself—the hidden method of marketing

✔ How to overcome phone phobia

This chapter shows you some very effective ways to use the telephone and e-mail to find job openings and set up interviews.

You may be wondering why you need to use the phone at all, when e-mail is so much simpler. I use e-mail a lot and it is true that it is a very helpful tool. I am for using whatever works, so what I am suggesting here is that you use both e-mail and the phone in your job search, as well as written forms of communication.

When to use the Phone and When to Use E-mail

E-mail is a wonderfully efficient way to communicate. It offers a variety of advantages that a phone cannot, including:

It is more convenient—You can send e-mail any time you want and the recipients can chose to deal with messages as they chose. It does not interrupt people as a phone call can.

You can attach files—You can attach a copy of your resume, JIST Card, or anything else you want.

You can forward it to others—Your e-mailed resume or message can be easily forwarded by the recipient to others who might be interested, along with a note from them to consider you.

It's fast—There are no delays as there are when mailing or transferring papers within an organization.

It's free—You incur no long distance phone charges and no mailing costs.

Some people prefer e-mail—I am one of many who prefer getting work-related e-mail instead of phone calls in most situations. The reason is that phone calls interrupt what I am doing, while someone sending me e-mail allows me to deal with them in a more controlled and time-efficient way. I get so many phone calls from telemarketers and other nuisance calls that I will often let incoming calls whose numbers I don't recognize (via caller ID) go to voicemail. Many employers also prefer e-mail, particularly from people they don't know, and some will insist that you communicate with them only via e-mail.

You probably already know all this and may also prefer to use e-mail yourself. Even so, I think you should primarily use the phone during your job search.

Why the Telephone Remains a Superior Contact Method

The advantages of e-mail are real and I encourage you to use e-mail in appropriate ways throughout your job search. But there are some very good reasons you should also use the telephone as a primary way to contact potential employers:

E-mail is easily ignored and deleted—One of e-mail's advantages to the recipient is also its disadvantage to you. E-mail allows employers to ignore a message until they chose to deal with it. A busy person may wait days before responding, quickly view and put it aside for a "later" response, or simply delete it as junk e-mail from someone they don't know. Think of e-mail as a locked car, sitting in your driveway. You don't think much about it until you want to use it.

Phone calls get a bit more attention—A phone call, however, is more like the car alarm going off—far more likely to get your attention or at least get you to wonder why it is going off. I know, e-mails can get attention. But you have to remember that most e-mail users get LOTS of junk mail and learn to quickly delete anything that looks like it comes from someone they don't know. Attachments to e-mail are particularly dangerous to open, because they can contain viruses. So, unless your e-mail is to someone you know, it has a good chance of being ignored or deleted. We all get junk phone calls too, of course, but almost everyone will at least listen to voicemail before deleting it—which is more attention than most e-mail gets. And calling someone presents to possibility of getting to them in a more direct, personal way.

A phone call provides a different and more interactive experience—If you prepare well, a direct phone contact allows you to have an impact that an e-mail simply can't. Even if you get to the potential employer's voicemail, a well-done presentation will at least be listened to. If you do get through to the potential employer, a phone conversation allows you to interact with that person in a more personal and natural way. They will hear your voice, ask you questions in real time and get your responses, experiencing your verbal communication skills. An interactive phone call also allows you to react to what's being said and allows them to make a decision to see or not see you in an interview, or to follow up in some other way.

It is harder to say no to you in person—Phone calls provide an experience that is closer to being "face to face." It is a much more personal interaction and one where you both have the opportunity to interact, react to questions and tone of voice, and correct misunderstandings. If you ask the employer to set up a time to see you, you are also much more likely to succeed than you would be in asking the same thing in an e-mail. This assumes, of course, that they "like" how you come across in the phone call.

So Use Both Telephone and E-mail

Keep in mind that my objective is to help you to get interviews. Making direct contacts with employers is one of the most effective job search methods there is. Phone techniques can be most effective when combined with e-mail use in intelligent and appropriate ways.

In fact, many job seekers get more interviews by using the phone than by any other method.

For example, you can

- ✓ Call people you already know to get interviews or referrals without delay
- ✓ Follow up by calling leads you initially get from want ads or the Web, when the only initial contact provided is via e-mail

✓ Stay in touch with prospective employers and with people in your network who might hear of openings

✓ Make cold calls to employers whose names you get from the *Yellow Pages* and the Internet

...and many other combinations of uses I will review in this chapter. These basic and simple-to-use techniques can make a big impact on how many job leads you get. Many people have used these methods to get two or more job interviews in just a few hours of work each day.

Overcome Phone Phobia

The truth is that using e-mail is less threatening than calling for most job seekers. Many people find the assertive phone techniques I present in this chapter intimidating. True, making phone calls to people you don't know really is more difficult than sending the same people e-mails. Most people are worried about making such phone calls and they find all sorts of reasons to avoid making them. Why? Because they, and probably you, fear making a fool of yourself and being rejected.

Think about why sending e-mail is easier than making a phone call to a potential employer. Really. It is the same reason people want to find their jobs on the Internet rather than go out and knock on doors and call people up. It is safer and far less likely to result in a direct and personal situation where you would feel humiliated and rejected. But is avoiding more challenging situations really worth it if doing so prolongs your job search? I think not. So try to face your fears and let the logical part of you help overcome your resistance to using the phone.

Using the telephone combined with e-mail is one of the most efficient ways of looking for work. You don't spend time traveling, and you can contact a large number of people in a very short time. In one morning, for example, you can easily make personal contact with more than 20 employers—once you learn how.

Most phone calls take only a minute or so. And most employers don't mind talking to a person they might be interested in hiring.

Making these calls does require you to overcome some shyness. But once you get used to it, phone calls are really quite easy to make. And making direct contacts by phone is often necessary to effectively follow up on an initial contact you had to make by e-mail.

Using the phone is, then, an important skill you need to help you get a job. I suggest that you start by making calls to people you know—your warm contacts. Then call the people they refer you to. This network of people is often happy to help you. Even people you pick from the *Yellow Pages* will usually treat you well.

Quick Tip

The experience of thousands of job seekers is that very few potential employers will be rude to you. And after all, if you do encounter somebody who is rude, you probably wouldn't want to work for that sort of person anyway.

Sample Phone Contact Based on JIST Card Content

You first read about JIST Cards in Chapter 6 and it may have occurred to you then that your JIST Card can be used as the basis for what you say in a job search phone call. Remember Sandy Zaremba's JIST Card from Chapter 6? I used the content of her JIST Card to create the script for a phone call. As you read the text that follows, imagine you are an employer who hires people with these skills.

Hello, my name is Sandy Zaremba. I am interested in a general office or office management position. I have more than two years of work experience plus one year of training in a variety of office and office management procedures. I have excellent word processing and language skills, am experienced with a variety of accounting systems and procedures, and get along well with others. I also trained and supervised a group of five office workers who handled a 27% increase in sales with no additional staffing expense. I have a track record of meeting deadlines, work well under pressure, and have good spreadsheet and other computer skills. I am willing to work any hours, am organized, honest, reliable, and hard working. When may I come in for an interview?

How did you react to this phone call?

If you were an employer, how would you feel about a person who called you with this approach? If you needed a worker like this, would you give this person an interview?

_____

_____

_____

_____

Just as with the JIST Card, most people say that this phone script makes a positive impression. Most people say they would give Sandra an interview if they had an opening. Not everyone, but most. Because of this typical reaction, reading a phone script based on your JIST Card proves to be a very effective way to use the telephone in your job search.

Chapter 14

A Review of Some Key Concepts

In reading this chapter, there are two key concepts that you need to keep in mind.

1. First, it is essential that you remember the new definition of an interview:

An interview is any face-to-face contact with a person who hires or supervises people with your skills—even if there is no job opening now.

This concept is important because you will often be calling or e-mailing people who don't have a job opening at this time, or who may not even know of any job openings for someone with your skills. In spite of this, there are opportunities you can find in these situations, and you must train yourself to be alert to them.

2. The second thing to keep in mind is that there are many ways to find job leads.

In an earlier chapter, I grouped various methods into either making contacts with people you know (also called *warm contacts*) and techniques for making contacts with people you don't know (or *cold contacts*).

The nice thing about using the phone and e-mail is that you can use them with most job search approaches. For example, you can use them to help contact and stay in touch with people you know (and the people they refer you to) as well as to make cold contacts with people you don't know.

Because it is easier and less threatening to use the phone and e-mail with people you know, much of what follows emphasizes cold contacts with people you don't know. Using the phone and e-mail to make cold contacts is a very effective approach and learning how to do this will also help you in communicating with warm contacts.

Use Your JIST Card as the Basis for a Phone Script

It just so happens that the content of your JIST Card makes a very nice basis for a presentation that you make by phone. JIST Cards were covered in Chapter 6 and, if you've written one, it will help you greatly in getting the most out of this chapter.

The Transformation from JIST Card to Phone Script

Read the following example to see how one person used the content of his JIST Card to develop a phone script. As you read the phone script that follows, imagine that you are an employer who hires people with these skills. Would you be interested in interviewing this person?

John Kijek
Cell phone/messages: 219-232-9213
E-mail: jkijek@time.net

Position Desired: Management position in a small to medium sized organization

Skills: B.A. degree in business plus over five years experience in increasingly responsible management positions. Supervised up to 12 staff and increased productivity 27%. Promoted twice within three years and have excellent references. Initiated sales follow up program resulting in 22% sales increase within 12 months. Get along well with others and am a good team worker.

Willing to travel and will work any hours

Hard working, self-motivated, willing to accept responsibility

---

Anatomy of a Phone Script

As with a JIST Card, a telephone script is separated into different sections. The five parts of a phone script are identified in the sample below.

Introduction

Position

Hello, my name is John Kijek. I am interested in a management position in a small to medium-sized organization. I have a degree in business, plus over five years' experience in increasingly responsible management positions. I have supervised as many as 12 staff whose productivity increased by 27 percent over two years. During a three-year period, I was promoted twice and have excellent references. I initiated a customer follow-up program that increased sales by 22 percent within 12 months. I get along well with others, am a good team worker, and am willing to travel or work any hours as needed.

Strengths and skills statement

Good worker traits and skills statement

I am hard working, self-motivated, and willing to accept responsibility. When may I come in for an interview?

Goal statement

If you were an employer who supervised people with skills similar to John's, how might you react to his calling you in this way? If you needed someone like this, would you give John an interview?

Yes _____   Maybe _____   Definitely Not _____

Use the Telephone to Get Interviews

Most people say they *would* or might give an interview if they had an opening. Not everyone, but most. Because of this common response, you can conclude that using a phone script based on your JIST Card is a very effective way to use the telephone for a job search.

You should also notice that the script used above takes most people about 30 seconds to read. The script is carefully designed so that, in just that short time, you present a great deal of information to a prospective employer. Based on many years of experience, the JIST Card/phone script approach has been carefully constructed to reduce the opportunity for an employer to interrupt you (remember, it is only 30 seconds) and it does not allow for a "no" response.

Many job search programs use the JIST Card/phone script approach and the experience of the many thousands of job seekers who have used this approach has been that it takes from 10 to 15 cold-contact phone calls to get one interview. That may sound like a lot of rejection, but most people can easily make 10 to 15 calls in less than an hour. In two hours of making phone calls, most people in these programs get two or more interviews. How many job search methods are you aware of with that kind of a track record?

As I will demonstrate, you can adapt your phone script for use in calling people you know, as well as in making cold contacts to employers. In both situations, the telephone can be used as a time-efficient tool for finding jobs in the networked (or hidden) job market.

Parts of an Effective Phone Script

The phone script I have presented here assumes that you will contact a person who does not know you and who may or may not have a job opening. An example of this situation would be if you were making cold calls to organizations listed in the *Yellow Pages* or online.

As you gain experience making phone calls, you will adapt what you say to specific situations. For learning purposes, I suggest you write and use your phone script in the specific way I outline below. This approach has been carefully crafted based on years of experience, and it is effective.

I have divided the script into five sections. As I review each section, complete the related section in the Phone Script Worksheet found later in this chapter.

1. **The introduction**—This one is easy. Just add your name to the blank space on the Phone Script Worksheet. Write your name as if you were introducing yourself.

2. **The position**—Always begin your statement with "I am interested in a position as..." and write in your job objective.

   It takes you only about 30 seconds to read your phone script, and you don't want to get rejected before you begin. So don't use the word "job" in your first sentence. If you say you are "looking for a job" or anything similar, you will often be interrupted. Then you will be told there are no openings. For example, if you say "Do you have any jobs?" the person you are talking to will often say "No." Once this occurs, your presentation will come to a screeching halt in less than 10 seconds.

   Remember that in the new definition of an interview, you are not looking for a job opening, you simply want to talk to people who have the ability to hire a person with your skills—even if they don't have a job opening at the present moment.

   If the job objective from your JIST Card sounds good spoken out loud, then add it to your worksheet. If it doesn't, change it around a bit until it does. For example, if your JIST Card says you want a "management/ supervisory position in retail sales," your phone script might say "I am interested in a management or supervisory position in retail sales."

3. **The strengths and skills statement**—The skills section of your JIST Card includes length of experience, training, education, special skills related to the job, and accomplishments. Rewriting the content from this part of your JIST Card for use in your phone script may take some time because your script must sound natural when spoken. You may find it helpful to write and edit this section on a separate piece of paper before writing the final version on your script worksheet. After completing this, you should read the final version out loud to hear how it sounds. You should read it to others and continue to make improvements until it sounds right.

4. **The good worker traits and skills statement**—Simply take the last section of your JIST Card, containing your key adaptive skills, and make these key traits into a sentence. For example, "reliable, hard working, and learn quickly" from a JIST Card might be written in a phone script as "I am reliable, hard working, and I learn quickly." These are some of your most important skills to mention to an employer, and putting them last gives them the greatest emphasis and may influence the employer to give you an interview.

5. **The goal statement**—The goal of the phone script is to get an interview. In the example I used earlier in this chapter, the final statement was "When can I come in for an interview?" and that is what I suggest you write on your own script. The reason is that this assertive approach tends to work. If you said, for example, "May I come in for an interview?" (or "Could you please, please, let me come in to talk with you?"), that allows the employer to say "No." And you don't want to make it easy for the employer to say no. They can, of course, do that on their very own, without your assisting them.

Tips for Completing Your Phone Script

Use the Phone Script Worksheet to write out your final draft, but write rough drafts out on separate sheets of paper until you are satisfied with your script.

In writing your phone script, consider the tips that follow.

- ✓ **Do your JIST Card first.** If you have not already completed your own JIST Card, you really ought to do so before you write your phone script. Avoid the temptation (I know that you are resisting this) to "wing it" without a script. It just won't work as well. Trust me.

- ✓ **Write exactly what you will say on the phone.** A written script will help you present yourself effectively and keep you from stumbling while looking for the right words.

- ✓ **Keep your telephone script short.** Present just the information an employer would want to know about you and ask for an interview. A good phone script can be read out loud in about 30 seconds or less. This is about the same time it takes to read a JIST Card. Short is better!

- ✓ **Write your script the way you talk.** Because you have already completed your JIST Card, use it as the basis for your telephone script. But your JIST Card uses short sentences and phrases, and you probably wouldn't talk that way. So add some words to your script to make it sound natural when you say it out loud.

- ✓ **Use the words I use.** As you write your phone script, avoid being too creative. Over the years I refined the words used in the examples. In order to avoid specific problems, I suggest you use them as they are presented.

  For example, do not write or say, "Good morning, my name is _____" because that will build a bad habit, which you will realize all too late on one overcast afternoon. Really, I have learned the best words to use through years of making mistakes, and there is no need for you to make the same ones. Start my way, and you can change it to your way after you have mastered mine.

✓ **Practice saying your script out loud.** I know that your neighbors may think you are nuts, but reading your script out loud and perhaps in front of the mirror etches it into your mind in a way that reading it to yourself cannot do. It has something to do with neural pathways and cognitive retrieval stuff. It also may be something more spiritual, having to do with the way we define ourselves, or a combination of all of these. However, the fact remains that reading an honestly prepared phone script out loud helps you accept that all the good stuff your phone script says about you is true. Having this information etched into your subconscious will also help you in an interview.

Phone Script Worksheet

Complete this worksheet with your final script content. It may take several attempts to get it to "sound right" so use separate sheets of paper for your drafts before completing this form. Once you have it the way you want it, write your final script on this worksheet. Later, you can read this on the phone, just as you have written it here.

1. Introduction

Hello, my name is _____

2. The position _____

I am interested in a position as _____

_____

3. The strengths and skills statement _____

_____

_____

4. The good worker traits and skills statement _____

_____

_____

5. The goal statement _____

_____

When can I come in for an interview? _____

Tips for Making Effective Phone Contacts

Now that you have developed your phone script, you need to know how to use it effectively. The tips that follow have been refined over many years and they work! Here are phone contact guidelines you should follow:

✓ **Get to the hiring authority.** You need to get directly to the person who is most likely to supervise you. Unless you want to work in the HR department, you wouldn't normally ask to talk with someone there.

Depending on the type and size of the organization you're calling, you should have a pretty good idea of the title of the person who would be likely to supervise you. In a small business, you might ask to speak to the manager. In a larger organization, you would ask for the name of the person who is in charge of a particular department.

> *The example here assumes you are contacting employers you don't know. For example, let's say that you are calling employers listed in the* Yellow Pages *under a category of businesses or organizations that need people with your skills. Just call them up and ask for the person in charge. This is a type of cold contact that many people have used to obtain interviews that would have been most difficult to obtain any other way.*
>
> *Another approach is to use the want ads or Internet job listings to identify employers who might hire someone like you. For example, you may find that "Metro Hospital" is hiring maintenance workers. But you want to be an office worker: Could you call them? Yes, you could. You could contact the person hiring maintenance workers via e-mail or phone and ask for the person you should speak with about office jobs.*

✓ **Get the name of a particular person.** If you don't have the name of the person you need to speak to, ask for it. For example, ask for the name of the person in charge of the accounting department if that is where you want to work. Usually, you will be given the supervisor's name, and your call will be transferred to him or her immediately.

When you do get a name, get the correct spelling and write it down right away. Then you can use the name in your conversation and can later send them follow-up mail with their name spelled correctly.

✓ **Get past the receptionist or automated answering system.** Most organizations have someone who answers the phone or an automated system to handle incoming calls. In both cases, the function of these systems is to screen incoming calls and get them to the correct person. But both of these systems can also screen you out, so here are some tips to increase your chances of getting to the person most likely to hire you.

1. **Try to get to a real person first**—You can get through most automated answering systems if you have the name of a specific person. If you don't, most such systems have an option that allows you to "push the zero button" or some other way to get to a real person. Remember, you DO NOT want to talk to someone in the human resources department.

2. **Get the name of the person who is most likely to supervise you**—Once you get through to the operator or receptionist, understand that this person is busy and will try to quickly screen your call. Their task is to either refer you to someone who can help you or to block your call from bothering anyone at all. Be nice to these people, this is their job. If you are calling a small organization, simply ask for the name of the manager—or, in a larger organization, ask for the supervisor of the department you want. In most cases, the receptionist or operator will transfer your call.

3. **If you are being screened out**—If you tell them you are looking for a job, they may transfer you to the human resources department (if they have one) or ask you to send a resume, or to come by and complete an application. This is what they are trained to do, but don't allow this to happen unless nothing else works. If they will not give you the name or transfer you to the person you want, say thanks and end your call. But all is not lost: If you really do want to work in this organization, you could:

   ✓ Try e-mail—See if they have a Web site that lists employee names and responsibilities or send an e-mail to any Web address you can find and ask for the name of the person in charge of the area you want. I've sent questions to Web managers or the general "info" address for the organization and had all sorts of questions answered. Write well and be pleasant and professional, because e-mail is often forwarded to the person you really are trying to reach. If one e-mail does not get you the response you want, try another e-mail to someone else at the organization.

   ✓ Call back later—Call back a day later and say you are getting ready to send some correspondence to the manager of the department that interests you. This is true, because you will be sending the manager something soon. Say you want to use the person's correct name and title. This approach usually results in getting the information you need. Say thank you and call back in a day or so. Then ask for the supervisor or manager by name—you will usually get through to the person. You are also more likely to get right through if you call when that receptionist is out to lunch. Other good times are just before and after normal working hours. Less-experienced staff members are likely to answer the phones and put you through. Plus, the boss might be in early or working late, when the more experienced receptionist is not there to screen you out.

WHAT RECRUITERS DO THAT YOU CAN DO FOR YOURSELF

People who earn their living by finding talented workers for employers do a lot of cold calling and e-mailing. They call lots of employers to find out their needs and then look for people who can fill those needs. They do this by defining a need and creating a sense of urgency to fill it. In a similar way, your task is to create this need for the employer and fill it with you and your skills.

Recruiters know that most employers will almost always consider hiring good people. They know that there may not be a job opening now, but there may be one in the future for a good person. So they find out what is ideally needed, then try to find someone that matches, and they earn a fee.

You can do the same thing by learning as much as you can about an organization, then going after the needs of that organization. If they are growing rapidly and you think you can help them, tell them how you would do this. Get to the people in that targeted organization and present the skills you have that will help them solve specific problems.

When Possible, Be Referred by Someone the Employer Knows

Previous examples in this chapter involved cold contacts to employers, where no one referred you. Learning to make these cold contacts is very important, because they can be VERY effective. Cold calls are also difficult for many people, so learning to make them will prepare you to handle them, and I hope, encourage you to make more of them.

 In spite of this, it is almost always better to be referred by someone the employer knows. Here are some tips for making these sorts of "warm contact" calls:

✓ **Tell them your connection.** If you have been referred by someone, immediately give the name of the person who suggested you call. For example:

"Hello, Ms. Beetle. Joan Bugsby suggested I give you a call."

If the receptionist asks why you are calling, say:

"A friend of Ms. Beetle suggested I give her a call about a personal matter."

When a friend of the employer recommends that you call, you usually get right through. It's that simple.

✓ **Adapt your phone script to the situation.** Sometimes, using your telephone script on your worksheet will not make sense. For example, if you are calling someone you know, you would normally begin with some friendly conversation before getting to the purpose of your call. Once you have chatted informally for a while, you can get to the purpose of your call by saying something like this:

"The reason I called is to let you know I am looking for a job, and I thought you might be able to help. Let me tell you a few things about myself. I am looking for a position as..." (continue with the rest of your phone script).

You will encounter other situations that require that you adjust your script. Use your judgment. With practice, it becomes easier!

Your Goal Is to Get an Interview

Quick Reminder

The primary goal of a phone contact is to get an interview. To succeed, you must be ready to get past the first and even the second rejection. You must practice asking three times for the interview!

Here are some suggestions that will help you to meet your objective.

Ask for the Interview Three Times, If Necessary

To increase your chances of getting an interview, you need to practice **asking** for the interview. This often requires you to overcome initial rejections, but you must learn how to handle this by asking again. Here is an example:

Ask once:

> *You: When may I come in for an interview?*
>
> *Employer: I don't have any positions open now.*

Ask again:

> *You: That's OK, I'd still like to come in to talk to you about the possibility of future openings.*
>
> *Employer: I really don't plan on hiring within the next six months or so.*

Be prepared to ask again:

> **You:** *I appreciate that you are busy, so I'll only ask for half an hour or so of your time. I'd like to come in and learn more about what you do. I'm sure you know a great deal about the industry, and I am looking for ideas on getting into your field and moving up.*

Although this approach does not always work, asking the third time works more often than most people would believe. It is essential that you learn to keep asking after the first time you are told no. Of course, you should be sensitive to the person you are speaking to and not push too hard, but it is more often a question of not being persistent enough than being too aggressive. Employers will often assume that a person who overcomes their objections will show the same persistence on the job.

Arrange for an Interview Time and Date

If the employer agrees to an interview, you should arrange a specific time and date. If you are not sure of the employer's correct name or spelling, call back later and ask the receptionist. Also be sure to get the correct address for the interview.

Sometimes Asking for an Interview Does Not Make Sense

Sometimes you will decide not to ask for an interview during your phone call. The person may not seem helpful or you may have caught him or her at a busy time. If so, there are alternative things you can do:

✓ **Get a referral.** Ask for names of other people who might be able to help you. Find out how to contact them, and then add these new referrals to your job search network. When you call them, remember to tell them who referred you.

✓ **Ask to call back.** If an employer is busy when you call, ask if you can call back. Get a specific time and day to do this, and add the call to your "to-do" list. When you do call back (and you must), the employer is likely to be positively impressed. People respect the professionalism of people who keep their word and may give you an interview for just that reason.

✓ **Ask if you can keep in touch every week or so.** Maybe the employer will hear of an opening or have some other information for you. Many job seekers get their best leads from a person they have checked back with several times.

Follow Up and Send Thank-You Notes

It is very important to follow up with the people you contact in your job search. This effort can make a big difference in causing them to remember and help you. Some research suggests that following up with your contacts is among the most effective things you can do in your job search!

Send thank-you notes! It is good manners to thank people who help you. Mail or e-mail a thank-you note right after a phone call. When someone gives you a referral or suggestion, send another note telling them how things turned out. When you arrange an interview, send a note saying you look forward to your meeting. Because a JIST Card is less formal than a resume, attaching one to your thank-you note is an appropriate thing to do.

Get Past Your Fear of Rejection— So You Can Get to "Yes"

Making phone calls is hard work. It sets you up for some rejection and failure. But, as I suggested earlier, think about it: What is the worst thing that can happen?

One way to look at the job search process is as a series of "no's." You need to get a lot of them before you finally get to "yes":

no no no no no no no no no no no no no no no no no no no no no no no no no no no no no no no no no no no no no no no no no no no no no no no no no no no no no no no no no no no no no no no no no no no no no no no no YES

You could think of your phone contact task as getting quickly through the "no's" to get to the "yes." The important thing is to make the contacts so you can get to "yes" more quickly.

Phone Contacts Will Get You Interviews, but Only If You Use Them

You are more likely to make phone calls and send e-mails if you schedule them every day. It is easiest if you plan to make them during a specific time period each day. For example, make your phone calls from 9:00 a.m. to 10:30 a.m. each morning. You should set a goal to make a specific number of calls each day. Most job seekers can make 10 or more calls per hour and 20 or more calls each morning. And they often get one or more interviews through making that number of calls. Not bad for a morning's work!

Chapter 14

Many people dread making phone contacts. If you count yourself among them, try the following:

✓ Begin by calling people you know. Follow up by calling the people they refer you to. That will improve your confidence and give you practice making effective phone contacts.

✓ Role-play your phone contacts, if at all possible. Have another person be the employer, and see if you can overcome their resistance to see you by asking three times for an interview.

✓ Practice contacting the organizations in the phone book that you rated a "3" (indicating you were not at all interested in working there) as described in Chapter 2. That way you can't mess up your career prospects too badly while you practice to improve your phone skills.

There are many other situations where you will need to adapt your basic phone script. Use your own judgment on this. With practice, it becomes easier. Remember that practice doesn't make it perfect—but it does make it better and easier.

Don't practice too long, though, before making real phone contacts.

≡ *Quick Summary*

✓ The telephone is the most effective job search tool. In fact, many job seekers get more interviews by using the phone than with any other method.

✓ JIST Cards make a very nice basis for phone interview scripts. A script takes 30 seconds or less to read. In two hours of making phone calls (while using this technique), many people get two or more interviews.

✓ The five parts of an effective phone script are: 1) Introduction, 2) The position, 3) The strengths and skills statement, 4) The good worker traits and skills statement, and 5) The goal statement.

✓ The most productive phone calls are ones made to people you know. However, by following tips given in this chapter, you can make effective phone contacts with people you don't know, as well. The results will be more interviews and job offers.

✓ Most employers respond well to a short phone contact. The experience of thousands of job seekers is that very few people will be rude to you when you call.

✓ Many people dread making phone contacts, so tips in this chapter help you to overcome your phone phobia. For example: Begin by calling people you know; then call the people they refer you to. That will improve your confidence and make you more effective and efficient.

✓ Follow up all calls and referrals with a thank-you note or e-mail and include your JIST Card.

✓ To get the best results, use e-mail and regular mail to supplement and follow up on your phone calls in an appropriate way.

Job Application Forms Are Designed to Screen You Out

═══Quick Overview

In this chapter, I review the following:

✔ Why applications are not an effective job search tool for most people

✔ Why you still need to know how to complete applications well

✔ How to reduce your chances of being screened out by your application

✔ How to handle troublesome application questions and issues

Applications are not a job seeker's best friend. In this chapter, I explain to you why this is true. Because you are likely to be required to complete applications during your job search, I also provide you with tips for completing them more effectively.

Hardly anyone I know enjoys rejection. One way job seekers avoid it, at a place of possible employment, is by asking if they can fill out an application. Most employers will say "Yes," because it doesn't cost them much to do so. While asking to complete an application is a nonthreatening approach to the job search, it is not a very effective one in most situations.

Why Applications Are Not an Effective Job Search Tool

While most job seekers assume that filling out applications is an important part of the job search process, you need to know that these documents have considerable limitations as a job search tool. Here are some things to consider about their limited value.

Applications Are Designed to Screen You Out

Think about it. An "Application for Employment" creates a barrier between you and anyone who would actually hire or supervise you. In larger organizations there may be hundreds—sometimes thousands—of applications submitted for each job opening. The chance is slim that yours will jump out and be *THE* one.

Quick Case Study

Let me tell you what the director of a large organization's human resource department recently told me.

"I've worked in human resource departments for over 15 years and am now in charge of the personnel functions of a FORTUNE 500 company. We get many thousands of applications per year. I estimate that most of them get less than 60 seconds of attention before getting filed. And we rarely go back and look through filed applications.

"If someone walks in today who meets the criteria of a job opening, they may be referred for an interview. The ones who came in yesterday probably won't. The truth is most of our new employees are referred by our own employees. Maybe 15 percent or so are hired as the result of filling out an application. We accept applications because we are expected to—not because we need to."

Applications Are Normally Used by Human Resources

The people who work in human resource departments are usually very nice. I even have a few as friends. However, unless you want to work in a human resource department, they can't hire you. They can only screen you in or out—and applications are the primary tool they use to screen applicants out.

About 70 percent of all workers in the private sector are employed by businesses with fewer than 250 employees and the most rapid growth of new jobs has been in businesses with fewer than 50 staff.

The majority of smaller businesses don't have a human resource or personnel department and often don't even have applications. As a result, you will miss out on most of the jobs in our new economy if you think of the job search as a process of dealing with personnel offices and filling out their application forms.

A growing number of larger companies don't even have human resource departments because they have decided that spending money to accept, file, and forget applications isn't worth it. Instead, they refer you to the local, state, or provincial employment office which will do their screening for them. Many large corporations also have smaller branch offices and the hiring is done right there, where they don't have a human resource office.

As you can see, the changes in our economy make the concept of filling out applications even less effective than it was in the past.

Applications Allow for Limited Information

Have you ever seen an application that asks you to list your strengths or why you think you would be a good employee? There are a few that do, but 99 percent do not. The typical application form simply collects factual information and allows few opportunities for you to tell them why they should consider you over someone else.

Applications Encourage You to Reveal Your Flaws

If you have limited work experience, do not have ideal education or training credentials, have gaps in your job history, want to change careers, are unemployed or underemployed, have ever been fired, or have anything other than a near-perfect work history, the application will encourage you to reveal it. It was designed to do just that. The reason is that applications were developed by employers to efficiently collect details they can use to quickly screen out those whose qualifications are not ideal.

Applications Provide a Barrier to Getting an Interview

Many situations do not require you to complete an application before getting an interview. If you see the job search as a process of going to employers and asking to fill out an application or send in a resume, then the application becomes a barrier to getting interviews. This is true because, using the traditional application and resume approach, you must first avoid getting screened out before you can get an interview. At the very same time, some job seekers are getting interviews by simply asking for them, even when there are no job openings. They pass directly to the interview without the possibility of being screened out based on their applications.

More on Career Planning and Job Search

Why You Need to Know How to Complete an Application

In spite of their negatives, it is important for you to know how to complete an application well. Here are some reasons.

Employers May Require Them

Some employers may ask you to complete an application before they interview you so they don't have to waste time asking you about the details of your background. Larger organizations may also require you to complete an application in the human resource department before an interview or hiring. You may also be asked to complete an application after the job offer, but before you begin to work. In all these cases, knowing how to complete an application is important.

They Are More Effective for Young and Entry-Level Workers

Research on how people find jobs indicates that filling out applications is a more effective technique for younger people than for more experienced workers.

The reason is that any of the jobs that young people get are low-paying, entry-level jobs that have relatively high turnover and relatively low skill or training requirements. Employers in these situations use applications as an initial screening process to weed out those who clearly are unsuited for these jobs. The information they collect allows the employer to quickly identify good candidates, eliminate unsuitable ones, and make quick hires.

Applications Force You to Deal with Your Flaws

An application is carefully designed to collect negative information. It requires specific answers about your education and training, previous jobs, pay history, dates employed, reasons for leaving, job title you now seek, criminal history, and other details that it may not be to your advantage to reveal. Learning to complete an application in a way that presents your strengths well and avoids emphasizing your weaknesses will help you to avoid getting screened out. It will also prepare you to better answer tough interview questions and write a more effective resume.

THE BEST WAY TO *USE* AN APPLICATION

Quick Advice ☑ Like a resume, many job seekers assume that the function of an application is to help them get an interview. I hope you now see that an application's primary function is to help an employer quickly screen most people out. This is why job seekers who use either a resume or an application as a primary tool for getting interviews will often find the job search to be a frustrating experience.

A better approach, as I have been encouraging you to consider throughout this book, is to find out about openings through people you know or to make direct contact with those within an organization who are most likely to use someone with your skills. Applications and resumes won't work well in getting you interviews, and their best use is after you have set up an interview. Then you can send a resume or fill out an application to provide the prospective employer with more information.

In fact, when I worked in large organizations, I often hired someone before they ever went to the human resources department. I sent them there to fill out the necessary paperwork, including the application form. From the point of view of the job seeker, that is the best time to complete one—after you get the interview or job offer.

Tips to Complete an Application More Effectively

Because an application form is designed to uncover negatives about you so that the employer can quickly screen you out, your first objective is to learn how to complete an application in a way that does not emphasize your weaknesses. You do have to complete the application honestly, but you don't have to provide negative information if you choose not to.

What follows is a variety of techniques you can use to help you complete an application form in a way that is less likely to get you screened out.

Step 1: Master the Basics

You might be surprised at how many people complete applications incorrectly, leave major sections blank, or fill them out in a sloppy way. Employers WILL notice these things and will often form a negative impression before they read much of the application's content. For this reason, pay attention to the basics I present here.

Chapter 15

1. **Read and follow directions carefully.**

    Too many people jump in and start completing an application without reading the directions. For example, don't write if it says print, and don't put your year of birth where the month should have been. Employers notice this carelessness and assume that you will be similarly careless on the job. Work slowly, read and follow the directions, and do it right.

2. **Use an erasable pen, not a pencil.**

    Carry your own blue or black ink ball-point pen to use in completing an application. This presents a much more professional appearance than the pencils typically provided in human resource departments. Most stationery stores carry erasable pens so you can correct any errors. Carry two in case one stops working.

3. **Be neat.**

    Appearance counts. If your paperwork is messy, the negative impression is likely to help you get screened out. So, print if your writing is hard to read, and make your entries as legible and neat as you can.

4. **Be thorough and correct.**

    Complete all sections of the application form and don't leave blank spaces. If the question does not apply to you, write "N/A," draw a line through it, or make some other response. If a section requires you to provide information likely to eliminate you from consideration, consider writing "will explain in interview" or leave it blank rather than volunteering negative information. Have someone check the sample application you complete later in this chapter for any spelling or grammar errors so you will not make similar errors on real application forms.

5. **Be positive, but honest.**

    Although you always want to present yourself in the most positive light, I recommend honesty throughout your job search and do not advise you to falsify your application or anything other employment document. This is very important. For more details, read the sidebar "Tell the Truth in a Way That Does Not Hurt You" that follows.

6. **Add positive information wherever you can.**

    Because most applications don't ask you for your strengths and accomplishments, you should look for a place to mention them anyway. In the work experience section, mention that you were promoted, trained new staff, or other positives wherever you can fit them in. Mention extracurricular school activities, volunteer work, or other accomplishments or proof that would support your ability to do the job. Quantify your achievements with numbers that support your skills. Even if an application does not provide space for positive information, use any available space on the application to include it.

Step 2: Get Past Troublesome Questions and Issues

In the old days, applications often asked information that had nothing to do with your ability to do the job. Questions such as your age, your parents' occupations, and your marital status were common. With changes in the law, you are much less likely to find these types of questions today.

Generally, issues that don't relate to your ability to perform the job should not be considered in the employment process. Even so, some applications (usually used by smaller employers) still ask "illegal" questions. In addition, the legally allowed questions can still create problems for the unwary.

Here are some of the troublesome questions you might get asked, along with suggestions for handling each.

Position desired

Applications often ask what sort of a job you want, what hours and days you want to work, the salary you expect, and other details. How you handle these questions can be very important. If you know of a specific job opening with this employer, you could use that job title.

A safer approach would be to use the general career area or department that your desired job is in. For example, if you were looking for a position as a warehouse manager, you might write "business or shipping/receiving management or related tasks." That approach would leave your options open to be considered for other jobs that might interest you. Saying "anything," however, indicates you don't know what you want to do and that will not impress an employer.

Whatever job objective you do write down defines what you emphasize on the rest of your application and how you emphasize it. For example, if you want to work in the accounting department of a hospital you would emphasize your accounting-related training and education, experience with accounting software, previous work and military experience that was related to accounting, and anything else that directly supports your stated job objective.

TELL THE TRUTH IN A WAY THAT DOES NOT HURT YOU

It is easy to lie on an application (or on a resume or in an interview, for that matter) but it is not a good idea. Many employers will eventually fire you if they find out you lied about any important item on your application. A better approach is to consider the following options:

Leave a sensitive question blank

If completing any application item truthfully is likely to be interpreted as a negative by an employer, consider leaving that section blank. You can explain that item later in an interview or after being offered a job, if it is important. I cover a variety of answers to problem questions in Chapters 5 and 16, and you may find some of them useful in answering certain questions on an application.

Look for jobs that don't require an application

If it is likely that you would be screened out based on an honest response to an application question, you may want to avoid using applications as a job search tool altogether. For example, if you have been convicted of a felony, most applications will require you to reveal this, and if you do, that will be likely to result in you not being considered. A job search can avoid the application-screening process and often does. So, if you have a serious problem that an application would reveal, you'll be better off looking for interviews in a way that does not first require you to complete an application so that you have the opportunity to make your case in an interview and ask to be considered on your ability to do the job.

For less serious situations, such as being fired, the words you choose to explain what happened are very important. Always look for a way to express yourself that puts you in a positive light.

The fact remains that an application is more likely to do you more harm than good. If you do fill one out, be sure that it is as good as you can make it (while still being truthful) and that it has nothing in it that could eliminate you from consideration.

Health and disabilities

Health-related absences and accidents are expensive to an employer, so you may be screened out if you've had a history of either. The issue here is whether or not your health will keep you from doing a good job and being a dependable worker. Unless you have a problem that will keep you from doing the job, you should say your health is "excellent." Don't mark "fair" or even "good" without a good reason. Such responses will usually get you screened out.

Some applications have a checklist to screen for all sorts of specific medical problems. If the application doesn't ask, you may be asked similar questions in a pre-employment medical screening. If you do have a medical problem that limits your ability to do the job, or if the problem is long-term or can get worse, you have a problem that may be resolved only by changing your job objective.

Some conditions, such as chronic back pain, dizzy spells, seizures, or various physical and emotional disabilities, make it very difficult to find employment. Unfortunately, the very nature of an application makes it even harder to find a job with such conditions.

One solution here is to get good career counseling in the preparation for and selection of a job objective. If the job does not require what you can't do, there is no longer a problem, is there? If your condition does not affect your ability to do the job, you could write "I have no limitations that affect my performance on this job," which would be true.

Workers' compensation is pay you get for a job-related injury or illness that prevents you from working. Some employers assume that those who received this pay in the past are accident-prone or unwilling to work. If you did receive this pay and the application asks this question, consider leaving this section blank and discussing it in an interview if it comes up.

The Americans with Disabilities Act (ADA) is legislation that is designed to protect the rights of workers with disabilities. In a general way, it prohibits employers from considering disabilities in their hiring decisions unless those disabilities prevent the worker from doing the job without reasonable accommodation.

Another law, the Health Insurance Portability & Accountability Act (HIPAA), limits employer access to personal health and/or medical history information and limits their ability to ask health-related questions.

Both of these laws limit an employer from using health- or disability-related issues in the hiring process. If you want additional information on these laws and how they affect your job search, a librarian can help you find related information. Or, check out the Web site www.halftheplanet.com for excellent information related to these matters, as well as links to many other related sites.

Attendance

Most applications will not ask you about your attendance, but some do. If you have a good attendance record, say so, even if the application does not ask this. For example say "only two days absent out of the past year." If you have a good long-term record but were ill recently and have now recovered, you could say something like this:

> *"Over the past five years, I have had an excellent attendance record, missing fewer than three days a year for four of the past five years."*

Education and formal training

Present any education and training that supports your job objective in as positive a way as possible. Because the space for this on an application may be limited, be prepared to use what space there is to your advantage.

Many applications ask for education but not training information. If you received formal training in a setting other than a traditional school (the military is one good example), consider including it in the education section of the application. This would be particularly true if the training you received supports the job you now seek. Before completing the education section, first look over the rest of the application. If there are small or no sections you can use to include the training you received in technical, trade, business, military, or other programs, look for ways to squeeze this information into the education section.

If you attended but did not complete high school, college, or a training program, do not emphasize that fact. Instead, indicate that you "attended" and mention the job-related courses or major you took. If you went to three schools but graduated from only one, emphasize just the school you graduated from, if space is limited.

Of course, if you are recently graduated from school you should mention anything you did while in school that might create a positive impression such as "kept grades in top half of class while working part-time to support myself," or "practiced in school band 10 to 20 hours a week in addition to class work."

Military experience

Military experience is just as important as any civilian job, schooling, or training. The military has the largest training and education program in the world. In addition, the levels of responsibility held by military members are often much higher than anything available to civilians of equal age and training.

If the military section of an application does not let you present your training and experience well, use the education, work experience, and other sections of the application to present this. Present the information in civilian terms and emphasize the things that support your job objective. Include specific numbers to support your skills, such as civilian-equivalent budget, number of people trained or supervised, and so on.

Quick Tip A good resource for military transition is www.careerOINK.com because it provides crosswalks from military jobs to related civilian job descriptions.

Salary and working conditions

Many applications ask you to state your current pay requirements. Many employers will quickly eliminate anyone who wants "too much" or "too little" because they assume those job seekers will be either unhappy with the pay or are not qualified.

Your best approach is to NOT give a specific pay number. Instead, write "open" or "salary negotiable," because you do not yet want to be screened out from consideration based on this factor. If you want to write in a number, write in a very wide salary range, such as "mid-teens to low twenties," "low to mid-thirties," or "$10 to $20 per hour."

Are you willing to work evenings if necessary? Weekends? The best response is to write (if asked) "will consider" or, if you do have a strong preference, write something like "prefer daytime hours, but will consider other shifts." The same approach applies to questions about relocation, travel, and other issues. While you don't have to take a job you don't want, you do not want to be screened out too early in the process, either.

Previous work experience

Employers look at what you have done in previous jobs to support what you want to do now. This is a section of the application that troubles many job seekers. It is unusual for anyone to have an "ideal" work history, yet you must learn to present yourself as a person who has a good chance of succeeding in the job you seek now. Following are some common problems job seekers have related to work experience, and tips to help deal with them on an application.

Gaps in employment

If you have gaps between jobs, the odds are that you did something constructive during that time. If you went to school, had part-time jobs (self-employed), raised children, received career counseling, or did anything else, mention it. It provides a reason for the gap.

If the gap was short, looking for a job is an acceptable reason. You can also avoid using specific employment dates if they display gaps in your history. For example, put "Summer 2002 to Spring 2003" for one job followed by "Spring 2003 to Present." For larger gaps, you can simply use the years, such as "2001 to 2002" or "2000 to Present."

Job titles

If the job title you had does not accurately describe your responsibilities or duties, consider changing it. For example, if you were a "Customer Service Representative" but supervised a department of people, you could use the more generic and descriptive "Department Head, Customer Service and Support." Use judgment on this and select new titles that would be helpful in communicating what you did. However, make sure you do not misrepresent your actual responsibilities. Consider checking first with a previous employer to see if they would object to this.

Job descriptions

Some applications provide a tiny space to describe your job duties. In these cases, select statements indicating your responsibility or achievements like "supervised staff of seven in a three-state area," or "served over 3,000 people a month," or "opened and closed store, deposited $10,000 per week in bank." Use numbers to support your responsibilities if possible, as in the previous examples. You don't have room for many words, so use them well.

Getting fired

Most people get fired over what could be called a "personality conflict." Whatever the reason, *never* write the word "fired" on an application. Is there any way you could express, in a more positive way, your reason for leaving? If, after you left, you went to school or took a job paying more money, mention those things under "reason for leaving past jobs." If you are currently unemployed, think of some way to avoid saying you were fired. If all else fails and you did nothing criminal, what does the truth sound like? For example, "The job I left just did not work out the way I wanted. My boss wanted to do everything herself, and I could not use my own ideas," could be reworded on an application as "looking for a more responsible and demanding position."

Previous supervisors and what they might say about you

If you worry about what your ex-supervisor would say about you, there are two things you should do:

1. **Find out. Call up and/or go see your old boss.** Tell him or her you are looking for a new job and are concerned about what he or she would say to a prospective employer wanting a reference. You can usually negotiate what, exactly, the boss will say. Make sure both you and the boss are clear what will be said to reference inquiries, and say thanks. You could then follow up your visit with an e-mail or letter reviewing what was discussed. Include a draft letter of recommendation that they could modify to their satisfaction, sign, and return to you as a signed original.

2. **Get an alternate source.** If your ex-boss will say harmful things about you, consider giving the name of another responsible person in your old organization who will say good things about your performance.

Too little or "no" experience

If you have had no, or limited, paid work experience, you must fall back on what experience you do have. Look carefully at volunteer, education, training, hobbies, and other experiences. Some of these could qualify as jobs or provide the equivalent experience. Note something positive in the available application space, even if it is not requested. For example, write "I worked in a variety of part-time jobs while going to school full time," or "My studies allowed little free time, and I concentrated my spare time on homework and family responsibilities," or "I am new to the job market but am now ready to put my complete energy into the career I have carefully chosen," or whatever else you might say that is positive.

If you have received job-related training, mention this again. For example, you could say "I have over 18 months of intensive job-related training, including over 150 hours of hands-on experience with equipment similar to yours." Once again, try to use numbers in your statements to support your skills or accomplishments.

Too much experience or education

If you feel you have "too much" work experience or education for the position you seek, perhaps you should be looking for a more responsible job. It would be common sense that employers would prefer people who are "overqualified" for their jobs, but many do not. The issue with too much experience or education is the employer's concern that you will not be satisfied with the job and the pay they offer and you will leave as soon as you can. But if you have good reasons for considering jobs with lower pay or responsibility levels, explain why. You could write, for example, "My children are now grown, and I now want a creative and challenging position that does not require relocation," or "I am very interested in positions paying from the mid-twenties (or whatever) and above."

If you have had many jobs, cluster the older ones under a heading like: "1995 to 1999—A variety of increasingly responsible jobs in the sales and service areas." If you received any promotions on the job, say "Customer Service Supervisor, promoted to Director of Operations" under job title, or wherever this information is appropriate.

Arrest record

Current law does not allow an employer to inquire about your arrest or criminal history unless it is related to your ability to do the job, or if you have been convicted of a felony.

The key word here is "convicted." Employers have a need to know of a convicted embezzler, for example, who is applying for a job as a bank teller. If you were charged but not convicted, our legal system defines you as innocent. Only you, of course, can know the truth about your particular situation, but if you were not convicted you don't have to say you are guilty of anything. The files of juveniles are usually closed and you do not have to reveal any arrest records from that time in your life.

If the application asks if you've ever been arrested, and you have, leave this section blank as you are not required to answer it in most situations. If the arrest was minor, you could write "minor traffic violations," or whatever is appropriate.

If your arrest record is more serious, consider using job search techniques that do not let you get screened out based on an application. You should also consider not looking for certain jobs where your conviction would be a problem for the employer. For example, people who were convicted of theft should not look for jobs handling money. You may want to (and be qualified to) do such work, but it is unwise to seek it.

More and more employers will check your criminal history before you are hired, particularly in government positions, child-related work, or jobs where theft would be a likely problem. If you do have problems in this area, Chapter 16 offers additional advice on how to handle it.

Go out and collect several real applications from employers, then complete them as well as you can. This will give you experience in answering the types of questions you will be asked. Then ask someone you trust to look at your applications and suggest ways you might improve your responses or correct errors you made.

You can also take a completed application with you on your job search and refer to it for details you need to complete others, such as addresses, phone numbers, dates, and other specifics.

Transportation

Some jobs require you to have your own car or have a valid driver's license. If you don't have what is requested, write "I will obtain a car if hired," or another appropriate comment.

Certification, licenses, and other credentials

If you have job-related credentials that are needed for the job you seek, mention them somewhere on the application, even if the information is not requested.

Volunteer activities

If asked, list activities that support your job objective and include specific skills used, as well as responsibilities or achievements that support your job objective. If these activities are an important part of your experience, consider including them in the work experience section of an application.

Hobbies and recreational activities

Some applications ask for this information and if so, list those that support your job objective in some way. If these activities made money or received recognition, mention that. For example, "I designed and developed prototype craft items now sold throughout the state," (which indicates good sales skills and self-motivation) or "I competed and coached an average of 20 hours a week on various gymnastics teams for over six years while maintaining a B average," (indicating you are a hard worker with good time management skills).

Future plans

Emphasize your interest in doing a better job through specific education, training, career advancement, hard work, and superior performance.

References

Some applications may ask you to list people the employer can contact to find out more about you as a worker. The best references to include are those who know your work and will say positive things about you. Consider such people as your coach, teachers, managers from other departments you know from previous jobs, heads of organizations for which you do volunteer work, or professionals with whom you have worked on prior jobs. Friends and relatives won't be objective about you and employers don't usually contact them for that reason. Whomever you select, be sure to ask them if it is okay to list them and find out what they would say about you before listing them as a reference.

Many of your previous employers will not give references over the phone due to company policy or fear of legal action being brought against them. For this reason, it is often helpful to ask previous employers to write you a letter of recommendation in advance. Consider asking them to include specific positives in their letters that would help you in your search for a new job. For example, if you had excellent attendance, got along well with others, or were promoted, ask them to mention these things in their letter. You can then provide these written letters of reference to prospective employers when asked.

≡≡≡≡*Quick Summary*

- ✓ Applications are not a very effective job search tool because they are designed to screen you out.
- ✓ Applications are usually used by human resources. Most small businesses don't have an HR department and often don't even have applications. Therefore, if you think of the job search as a process of dealing with HR offices and their forms, you will miss out on most of the jobs in our new economy. Most HR departments serve as a barrier between you and the prospective hiring manager or employer.
- ✓ Applications allow for only limited, mostly negative information.
- ✓ Applications encourage you to reveal your flaws, not your strengths.
- ✓ Some studies indicate that completing applications is a more effective approach for young people and those seeking entry-level jobs.

Chapter 15

✓ It is still important to know how to fill out an application effectively because:

➤ They are often required.

➤ They force you to confront your flaws and learn how to deal with them effectively.

✓ When completing an application form, be sure to keep the following basics in mind:

1. Read and follow directions carefully.

2. Use an erasable pen, not a pencil.

3. Be neat and thorough.

4. Be positive, but honest.

5. Add positive information, wherever you can and quantify it.

✓ Follow the tips for dealing with difficult application questions and issues presented in this chapter.

✓ Above all, be truthful in filling out the application. Dishonesty will most likely only get you fired eventually. In addition, your integrity is far more important than any job.

CHAPTER 16

More Answers to Specific Problem Interview Questions—

And a List of 94 Frequently Asked Questions

══ Quick Overview

In this chapter, I review the following:

✔ How to answer problematic interview questions

✔ Legal and illegal questions

✔ Answers to many specific problem questions relating to work history and personal situations

✔ 94 interview questions to prepare for (i.e., think about and practice answering) prior to interviewing

This chapter builds on what I covered in Chapters 4 and 5, where I presented the most important points you need to improve your interviewing skills.

This chapter adds three more elements to your interviewing skill set:

1. A quick review of the basic methods I covered in Chapter 4, along with additional details.

2. Brief reviews of a variety of specific interview questions not presented in Chapter 5, along with tips on how to respond to them.

3. A list of 94 frequently asked interview questions.

The odds are very high that you could be eliminated from consideration for jobs based on your answer (or, more likely, your lack of a good answer) to one or more of the issues I bring up in this chapter.

None of us is perfect. We all have specific things about ourselves and our past that could or will be a problem for some employers. You may have "too much" or "too little" education or training, gaps in your work history, you may be "too old" or "too young" or have other characteristics that will concern some employers. Some of these things you really can't change, but it is your responsibility to make these matters less of an issue in a decision to hire you over someone else.

I mentioned earlier in this book that about 80 percent of all people who get interviews do not, according to employer surveys, do a good job in answering one or more interview questions. These problem questions vary for each person and depend on your situation. The job seeker's inability to answer these problem questions is a very big obstacle in the job search and has kept many, many good people from getting jobs they are perfectly capable of handling. They didn't get those jobs because they failed to convince the employer that they had the skills and other characteristics to do the job. In many cases they left the employer with a "sense" there was a problem that was not resolved to their satisfaction. That is to say that the job seekers would have gotten the job offer if they had done better in the interview.

One of the difficulties with problem questions is that they are often not asked by the employer in a clear way, or are not asked at all. For example, if you live a long distance from the employer's job site, the interviewer may be wondering why you would be willing to commute daily to a distant location. His concern may be that you would leave once you found a job closer to home. He may never directly ask the question that really concerns him, so you would not have the opportunity to address his concern, and that job is likely to go to someone else. It is not fair, but it is the way it is.

So the issue here is not your ability to *do* the job, rather the issue is your ability to communicate clearly that you *can and will* do the job well. This chapter will help you quickly identify problem questions an employer may pose about your particular situation, and give you some ways to handle them in a truthful and positive way.

One way to approach this chapter is to skip to the questions that may be a problem for you and your situation. Focus your attention on answering these questions well and you are likely to get more job offers. Due to limited space, most of my tips for answering a given question are quite brief. There are also many other questions you might be asked that I did not cover, although I did cover the ones that are a concern for most people. While many of the problem areas may not directly concern you, reading them all will give you ideas for answering the ones that do directly relate to you more effectively.

A Quick Review of How to Answer Problem Interview Questions

Employers are people, just like you, and they want to make a good decision when hiring someone. Think about it—hiring the wrong person will cause them much extra work and grief. If the new employee does not perform well, they will have to spend extra time supervising that person. If the employee does not stay in the job long, the employer will have to hire and train all over again. If the person they hire does not work out and has to be replaced, this creates a situation that most employers desperately want to avoid—firing someone.

For this and other reasons, employers are highly motivated to hire a "good" person. They want someone who has the skills to do the job and will usually base this decision on the applicant's past work experience and education. These "credentials" are very important in considering one person over another, and if you don't meet the minimum criteria, you aren't likely to be considered.

Assuming that you have completed the activities in the previous chapters of this book, you know your skills and the types of jobs that best suit you. This means that you are seeking jobs for which you do have the necessary skills and, at least, the minimum credentials. This being the case, how well you perform in the interview will often be the key factor in an employer giving you a chance over someone else who has better credentials. You see, it is not always the best person who gets the job, it is often the one who has the best communication skills—the one who does best in the interview.

To be considered, you must meet or exceed an employer's expectations. It is important to understand what an employer will be looking for during an interview. Recall from Chapter 4 the discussion of employer expectations: The three major employer expectations are 1) appearance, 2) dependability, and 3) credentials.

Notice that I put credentials third? This is because I assume that you have the minimal credentials to be considered for the job in question. Appearance is first, because if you create a negative impression (as about 40 percent of all job seekers do) you are unlikely to be considered at all. That leaves Expectation #2 as the one that most employers will focus on during the interview.

The 10 Most Frequently Asked Problem Questions

Way back in Chapter 5, I provided detailed answers to 10 interview questions. I selected those questions carefully because they are representative of the types of questions that most often create problems for people in an interview. Often, the actual question will not be phrased in the same way, but the employer is usually asking one of those questions in some form. That is why I proposed in Chapter 5 that, if you can provide a good and honest response to each of the 10 questions, you will be prepared to answer most other interview questions better.

Because I provided detailed answers in Chapter 5 to each of the questions that follow, I won't repeat them here. The list of questions may help you recollect them, though.

Ten Most Frequently Asked Problem Interview Questions

1. Why don't you tell me about yourself?

2. Why should I hire you?

3. What are your major strengths?

4. What are your major weaknesses?

5. What sort of pay do you expect to receive?

6. How does your previous experience relate to the jobs we have here?

7. What are your plans for the future?

8. What will your former employers (or teachers, if you were recently a student) say about you?

9. Why are you looking for this sort of position and why here?

10. Why don't you tell me about your personal situation?

A Quick Review of the Three-Step Process for Answering Interview Questions

In answering any interview question, it is essential that you understand what the employer really wants to know. In some cases, this will be quite obvious and you can answer directly. Questions regarding credentials and job-related skills often have no hidden agenda and can be answered in a forthright manner.

However, the big problem for most job seekers is the fact that many interview questions are not what they seem to be at all. Some questions, like "Why don't you tell me about yourself?" don't seem to have a direct answer. Others, such as "Do you come from this area?" often have hidden agendas (in this case, the employer is probably trying to find out if you are likely to remain in this area due to family or other ties).

To help you answer these less-than-direct questions, I have developed a simple technique that you can use to answer most interview questions. The technique, called the Three-Step Process for Answering Interview Questions, is covered in detail in Chapter 4. A quick review follows here.

The Three-Step Process for Answering Interview Questions

Step 1: Understand What Is Really Being Asked. This usually relates to Employer's Expectation 2, regarding your adaptive skills and personality: Can we depend on you; are you easy to get along with; and, are you a good worker?

Step 2: Answer the Question Briefly, in a Non-Damaging Way. Acknowledge the facts, but present them as an advantage, not a disadvantage.

Step 3: Answer the Real Question by Presenting Your Related Skills. Once you understand the employer's real concern, you can get around to answering the often hidden question by presenting your skills and experiences related to the job.

To perform Step #3 effectively, recall the Prove It technique from Chapter 5, in which you identify key statements and accomplishments to use. Briefly, the steps of the technique are 1) Present a Concrete Example, 2) Quantify, 3) Emphasize Results, and 4) Link It Up.

Together, the Three-Step Process and Prove It techniques form the basic approach to answering problem questions, and it is most important that you understand and use these techniques to improve your interviewing skills.

Legal and Illegal Questions

Technically, this is a free country, and interviewers can *ask* whatever they wish. Dumb questions, questions in poor taste, and personal questions can all be asked. It's what employers *do* that can get them in trouble with the law. It is illegal to hire or not hire someone based on certain criteria. It is also very difficult to prove that an employer actually does that.

As a job seeker, the more important issue might be whether or not you want the job. If you want to insist that you do not have to answer a certain question, fine. However, realize that the question was probably intended to find out whether you will be a good employee. That *is* a legitimate concern for an employer, and you have the responsibility, if you want the job, of letting them know you will be a good choice.

There are situations (thankfully, very rare) where an interviewer's questions are offensive. They may be offensive in the way they are asked or because of the type of questions asked. If that is the case, you could fairly conclude that you would not consider working for such a person. You just might, in this sort of situation, tell that employer what you think of them. You might also consider reporting them to the authorities. (Yes, this would be a situation where a thank-you note would not be required.)

Some laws that protect you from discrimination

Several major laws present real problems for employers who can be proven to illegally discriminate against protected groups in their hiring:

✓ Title VII of the Civil Rights Act (enacted in 1964 and still very much in effect) makes discrimination on the basis of race, sex, religion, or national origin illegal in hiring discussions.

✓ The Americans with Disabilities Act requires that an employer provide an equal opportunity for an individual with a disability to participate in the job application process and to be considered for a job.

There are situations where a specific job might require an answer to some questions that might appear to be illegal for other jobs. For example, a firefighter would need to be in good physical condition and health-related questions are acceptable. They may be required to climb a ladder carrying 100 or more pounds of weight.

Another example would be a bartender, who would need to be at least 21 years old.

These are examples of legitimate job-related questions that an employer can ask when interviewing for these jobs. In general, an employer is not allowed to ask for or consider information that is not related to a person's doing the job. A bartender, for example, would typically not be required to carry 100 pounds up and down a ladder...

According to the U.S. Equal Employment Opportunity Commission (EEOC) whose Web site is at http://www.eeoc.gov, in a recent year some 270,000 allegations were filed with the commission and its 82 state and local counterparts.

Inc. magazine reports that complainants numbered just over 150,000—some had lodged more than one charge. The number of complaints has been rising sharply, up about 30 percent in just two years and 2,200 percent in the past two decades.

Many people now sue simply for being terminated, even though the employer did nothing wrong. It can cost employers thousands of dollars just to defend themselves through the charge-filing stage, where claims are brought before the

EEOC or a state agency. Defending these suits also costs time and results in substantial loss of revenue even when there is no valid basis for a complaint. As a result, many employers are becoming increasingly careful when they hire, screening people far more thoroughly so that they are less likely to have to terminate someone later. Other employers are simply hiring fewer people.

What to do about "illegal" questions

Just like many other people, some employers are jerks. I know for a fact that some base their hiring decisions on things that should not be an issue at all—things such as age, religious affiliation, weight, family status, physical beauty, race or ethnic background, and other inappropriate criteria. I also know that my suggestions on dealing with this are controversial to some.

This is a free country. People have the freedom to say or believe almost anything. It is their actions and behaviors that most often get them in trouble. What this means is that employers can ask almost anything they want in an interview or on an application. Some people would disagree, saying that an employer does not have this right. Our constitution gives all of us the right of free speech, including the right of an employer to ask inappropriate questions. The problem arises when that information is used to hire one person over another based on certain considerations.

There are a variety of laws that provide punishment for employers who base hiring decisions on certain criteria. Employers do have legitimate concerns about the people they hire and want to be as certain as they can be that the person they hire can and will be productive in the job to be filled.

Turn your negative into a positive

So let's assume that your concern is that you might be unfairly discriminated against because of your status. Let's also assume that you are reasonably well-qualified for the job you seek. Given this, you need to understand that highly qualified people with no apparent "problems" often are unable to obtain jobs after many interviews. The labor market can be very competitive, and others may get the jobs simply because they have better qualifications. I also know that less-qualified people often get offers simply because they do well in the interview. Because you can't easily change your situation, you will need to improve your interview skills to give you an edge.

Begin by considering how an employer might be legitimately concerned about you or your situation. Might they think that you would be less reliable, less productive, or in some other way less capable of doing the job? If so (and the typical answer here is that some might), practice an answer that indicates the problem will not be an issue in your case.

Chapter 16

For example, if you have young children at home (an issue, by the way, that men are rarely asked about), it is to your advantage to mention that you have excellent child care and don't expect any problems. In addition, look for a way to present your "problem" as an advantage. Perhaps you could say that your additional responsibilities make it even more important for you to be well-organized, a skill that you have developed over many years and fully expect to be applied in the new job. In other words, turn your disadvantage into an advantage.

Smart interviewers use open-ended questions to avoid problems and still get the information they want

Employers want to get the information they need to make a safe, profitable hiring decision. You, the candidate, want some privacy and a fair chance to be considered based on your merits. Open-ended interview questions generally achieve both goals.

For instance, instead of an employer asking "Are you living with anyone?" she may phrase the question as "Do you foresee any situations that would prevent you from traveling or relocating?" The employer may want to know if you have any limitations regarding work schedule, or if you have roots in the area that will encourage you to stay. The less direct question allows you to decide what information about your private life applies to the job at hand. Of course, if you are not prepared for such a question, you can provide information that might damage your chances.

So, you see, employers will often want to know details of your personal situation for legitimate reasons. They want to be sure that you can be depended on to stay on the job and work hard. This is Employer Expectation # 2 and is of great concern to most employers. Your task in the interview is to provide information indicating that, yes, you can be counted on to do the job. Often, if you don't get that idea across, you will simply not be considered.

Answers to Specific Problem Interview Questions

The questions that follow fall into two basic types. The first deals with issues most people experience and that are often legitimate issues for an employer to explore. This includes things such as gaps in your employment or being fired from a previous job. Employers are more likely to ask about these matters in a direct way. The second type of question presents issues that many consider inappropriate for an employer to consider when making a decision to hire, such as age, race, and gender. Employers are much more likely to use indirect questions regarding these concerns.

Many of the questions I review here are ones that many workers experience. They are not sins and you will find that if you learn to handle them well, they will not become a major problem in being considered for a job.

Even the suggestion that some of the things in this chapter might be regarded as "problems" by an employer will make some people angry. For example, some would object to any mention that someone over 50 might experience discrimination in the labor market—although anyone over 50 knows that their age makes it harder to get a good job. Others will resent that employers would even consider such things as race, religion, national origin, child care, and other "politically sensitive" matters in evaluating people for employment. The fact remains, some employers do consider these things despite the fact it is unfair or even illegal to do so.

Employers, as I have said before, are simply people. They want to be assured that, yes, you will stay on the job for a reasonable length of time and do well. Sometimes, you just need to get this message across.

You also have to realize that very, very few interviewers have had any formal interview training. They are merely trying to do their best and may, in the process, bumble a bit. They may ask questions that, technically, they should not. Consider forgiving them in advance for this, especially if their intent is simply to find out if you are likely to be reliable. That is a legitimate concern on their part, and you will often have to help them find out that, in your case, their concerns are unwarranted.

In that context, I suggest you consider your situation in advance and be able to present to the employer that, in your case, being "overqualified," or having children, or being over 50, being a new graduate, or whatever your situation, is simply not a problem at all, but an advantage.

So, to help you deal with the reality of the job search (and at the risk of offending someone), I have included questions that are a bit sensitive. However, I think that you, as a job seeker, need to accept what is and look for ways to overcome problems. It can be done. It is true that some employers are unfair. In fact, some employers do consider things in making hiring decisions that should not be a factor. In the interview, learn to be candid and present your problems as potential advantages.

You just can't ever be certain what will concern an employer. Like all people, some will have concerns that just will not make sense to others. Some will even make assumptions that may or may not be true.

For example, I once had a boss who did not believe in hiring managers who had college degrees. His position was that those without degrees were often just as good or better—and would be happy being paid less money. I'm not at all sure that he was right, but I do know that he had this attitude and few managers with college degrees were on his staff. As you might guess, he did not himself have a degree, and I suspect that his real concern was to avoid hiring someone who had better credentials than he did.

Gaps in your work history

Some of the most accomplished people I know have been out of work at one time or another. About one out of five people in the workforce experiences some unemployment each year, a very large number of people. Unemployment is really not a sin, and most bosses have experienced it themselves, as have I.

Quick Advice ☑ The traditional resume technique is to write "20XX to Present" when referring to your most recent job, which makes it look as if you are still employed. If you use this trick, however, realize that it puts you in an uncomfortable position right away. One of the first things you will have to do in the interview is explain that this is not actually the case.

Many people have gaps in their work history. If you have a legitimate reason for major gaps, such as going to school or having a child, tell the interviewer in a matter-of-fact way. By all means, don't apologize or act embarrassed about it. You could, however, add details about a related activity you did during that period that would strengthen your qualifications for the job at hand. This reinforces that you aren't out of touch with what that employer needs; you merely chose not to actively practice it for a while.

Quick Tip During the conversation, it may help to refer to dates in years rather than months. For example, if asked when you worked in the restaurant business, reply, "from 2002 to 2004" rather than "from November 2002 to June 2004." Of course, if pressed, give the exact dates without hesitation.

Being fired!

I remember looking for a new job after having been "fired" from my previous one. Actually, I was "replaced" as a result of internal politics. I hadn't done anything wrong other than to be associated with the wrong boss, one who had lost favor. Still, I feared that the people that remained behind would not give me good references. And it was awkward explaining to potential employers just why I wasn't still working there.

Lots of people get "fired," and it often hurts their chances of getting some jobs. In some cases, employers are afraid that you will be a problem to them as well. Of course, if you were fired for just cause, you need to learn from the experience and:

✓ change your behavior

✓ or consider another career

However, in most cases, we harm our own chances of finding a new job more than being fired requires.

When we don't know how to explain our situation, we don't do a good job in interviews. We too often leave the potential employer wondering just what happened and, not knowing any different, assuming the worst. Leaving an employer with the thought that you are hiding something is a bad way to make a good impression. As a result, you don't get job offers.

Many employers tell me they will not hire someone unless they know why the person left his or her last job. They want to be sure that you are not a potential problem employee. It is clear that you will have to deal with this issue if you want to get hired. The good news here is that many employers have been fired themselves. Normally, people in charge alienate some people or have had interpersonal conflicts or other difficult situations—it goes along with being in charge. If you have a reasonable explanation, many interviewers will understand because they have had similar experiences.

So if you have lost a job, the best policy is usually to tell the truth. Avoid saying negative things about your last employer. Think about how you can put a positive spin on what happened. If you are NOT a big problem to work with, say so—and explain how you are very good at the things that *this* job requires. Tell the truth of what happened in your past job in an objective way and quickly turn to presenting the skills you have to do the job under discussion.

Another very important thing to do if you have been fired is to make sure that you negotiate with your previous employer about what they will say when giving you a reference. Ask for a written letter of reference, too. You can often negotiate this so that you won't be harmed as much as you might fear. All of this can help offset a negative past employer who just may have a simple personality conflict with you. It happens a lot, and it doesn't have to hurt you as much as you may think. Because almost everyone will lose his or her job once, you are in good company.

Get an alternate reference. While you may have had conflict with a previous boss, there are often others at your previous place of employment who thought well of you. If so, it is often wise to get written recommendations from them in advance. You should also contact those people to find out how they might help if asked to provide a reference.

Changing careers or job history unrelated to your current job objective

Chances are this issue isn't as important as you may assume. Sure, the interviewer is curious and wants to get to know you better, but if your past experience were a real barrier, you wouldn't have been invited for an interview in the first place. Stick to a planned schedule of emphasizing your skills and how they relate to the job you are discussing. For instance, a teacher who wants to become a real estate sales agent could point to her hobby of investing in and fixing up old houses. She could cite superior communication skills and an ability to motivate students in the classroom.

Look up the job descriptions of your old jobs and the ones you want now, and find skills that are common to both. Then emphasize those skills in your interviews. The work you did in Chapter 9 will also help you document the skills and other strengths you have to support your current job objective.

"Turtling"—A Basic Technique for Turning a Negative into a Positive

Like a turtle on its back, a problem is a problem only if you leave it that way. By turning it over ("turtling" is what I have come to call this), you can often turn a perceived disadvantage into an advantage. For example:

Too Old: "I am a very stable worker requiring very little training. I have been dependable all my life, and I am at a point in my career where I don't plan on changing jobs. I still have 10 years of working until I plan on retiring. How long has the average young person stayed here?"

Too Young: "I don't have any bad work habits to break, so I can be quickly trained to do things the way you want. I plan on working hard to get established. I'll also work for less money than a more experienced worker."

You can use the turtling technique on most problem questions to turn what some may see as a negative into, in your case, a positive.

Sensitive Questions Having to Do with Your Personal Situation or Status

Most employers are wise enough to avoid making decisions based on things that should not matter. They will hire someone who convinces them that they can do the job well. A good interview allows you to discuss your strengths without lying about them. Your handling of the interview can assure the interviewer that you are not a stereotype—but in order to prevent misconceptions you must know what these stereotypes might be and address them.

For this reason, even if your "problem" does not come up in the interview because the law forbids the question or the interviewer is too uncomfortable to ask, it is likely to be to your advantage to bring it up and deal with it. This is particularly so if you think that an employer might wonder about the issue or that it might hurt you if you don't address it. However you handle the interview, the ultimate question you have to answer is "Why should I hire you?" so provide a good answer, even if the question is not asked quite so directly.

"Too old"

Older workers—particularly those over 50—have a harder time finding new jobs in the labor market. There is research to support that this is so and anyone who is over 50 and has looked for a job, knows that their age can work against them. Among those 50 plus there are a lot of highly qualified managers, technicians, and professionals who have lost jobs due to layoffs. Huge numbers of factory and office workers have lost jobs due to "downsizing" of large companies and other non-performance-related reasons. About a third of these displaced workers end up getting higher paying, better jobs; another third get jobs paying about the same; and the last third end up much worse off. By age, older workers do the worst, with many remaining unemployed, underemployed or dropping out of the labor market.

What is going on? There are some commonsense reasons that few people seem to want to talk about. Many older workers have not kept up with the latest technologies, and their skills are no longer in demand. Younger workers often have better training and technical skills and win jobs over older workers without these. However, I think there are other reasons that have to do with money and employer assumptions about being "overqualified."

People with more experience tend to be paid more. As anyone who has been in the labor market recently knows, the competition for higher-paying jobs is often intense. Unemployment statistics indicate that the more you make, the longer your job search is likely to be. A rule of thumb is that it takes one month per $10,000 in annual pay to find a new job. If you make $50,000 a year, plan on it taking 5 months to find a replacement job at that level of income. Of course, this may fluctuate somewhat depending on unemployment rates and the general health of the economy, but it's a reasonable estimate of the average length of time it takes to find a job at various levels of income (though it could take much less, if you use more effective job search methods).

In making a new hire, most employers will try to avoid hiring someone who was paid more in the previous position. Why? Because they fear that the person earning less than he or she is used to will be unhappy and will leave as soon as a better paying job is available. It is one of the reasons an employer will hire a person with less experience: They figure that such a person will be more satisfied with the pay they get. In addition, many of the new jobs being created in the last decade are in smaller companies that just can't pay as much as many more established firms.

However, in the face of this concern about money, there are some things you can do:

1. First, realize that many of the growing small businesses are run by "older workers" who know what they are doing.

   Experienced older workers have started businesses and consultancies in droves. If you're not ready to start your own business, put your experience to work by approaching larger and smaller businesses and telling how you can help them do even better.

2. Be specific.

   If you know how to develop product, manage, sell, or make any significant contribution, go to the places that need your skills and tell the person in charge what you can do. If you can convince them you can help them make more money than you cost, they may just create a job for you. Make sure that you present your substantial experience and good work history as an advantage. For example, you can probably be immediately productive and are likely to be more reliable than a younger worker.

3. Don't give up.

   Someone out there needs what you can do, but you will have to go out and find them.

According to a survey cosponsored by the Research Committee of the Society for Human Resource Management (SHRM) and the Commerce Clearing House, when employers face an older person across the interviewing desk, they are afraid the person won't be able to adjust to changes in the business environment. Among the specific concerns and comments:

Quick Fact

✓ Older employees have created the greatest challenges for us. Employees hired years ago may not have the education or technical skills to move forward.

✓ Attempts to increase accountability and employ more team-oriented strategies have met with resistance.

✓ Older workers have not adapted to drastic changes in procedures and technology.

A big problem with the "too old" category is figuring out if you truly belong in it. The over-65 growth rate in our country is slowing, and the biggest group taking over the job market is the aging Baby Boomers—those between the ages of 40 and 50. In fact, the Department of Labor tracks the median age of the labor force and reports the following:

Year	Median Age of Labor Force
1978	34.8 years
1988	35.9 years
1998	38.7 years
2008 (projected)	40.7 years

What this means is that about half of all workers are or soon will be over 40 years of age and the numbers of older workers is increasing. So what is "too old?"

Don't let negative preconceptions about age discourage you—there are plenty of ways to combat them effectively during the job interview. For starters, understand that there are fewer younger workers now, so employers will have no option but to compete for the qualified older workers.

To push the interviewer along that path, present your wealth of experience and maturity as an advantage rather than a disadvantage. Older workers often have some things going for them that younger workers do not. Emphasize your loyalty to previous employers, and highlight accomplishments that occurred over a period of time. If you encounter hesitation after the first interview, meet the fear head-on with a question such as "Are you concerned about compensation?" or "If I could reduce your costs significantly, would you be willing to make me a job offer?"

If you have more than 15 years of work experience, draw upon your more recent work for examples of work habits and successes. Select recent activities that best support your ability to do the job you are now seeking and put the emphasis on them. You don't automatically have to provide many details on your work history from earlier times unless it is clearly to your advantage.

Chapter 16

To avoid sounding "too old," mention something "young" like the fact that you own the newest technological gadget, would welcome the refreshing opportunity to operate in a self-directed team situation, or that you have enrolled in a technology course related to the job. Your background research on the organization should reveal a host of ways to plug your up-to-date knowledge and current worthiness.

"Too young"

Younger people need to present their youth as an asset rather than a liability. For example, perhaps you are willing to work for less money, accept less desirable tasks, work longer or less convenient hours, or do other things that a more experienced worker might not want to do. If this is true, you should say so in the interview. Emphasize the time and dedication you put into school projects, and activities you gave up to reach your goals. Above all, conduct yourself with maturity, show some genuine enthusiasm and energy, and you'll leave the interviewer with the impression you need a chance, not a guidance counselor.

If you are turned down in favor of a more experienced worker, don't despair. Keep hammering away at your particular skills, your trainability, and your available years of dedication. Keep doing this and some employer will be happy to hire you.

Overqualified/Too much experience

It doesn't seem to make sense that you could have too much experience, but some employers may think so. They may fear you will not be satisfied with the job that is available and that, after a while, you will leave for a better one. What an employer really needs is some assurance of why this would not be the case for you. If, in fact, you are looking for a job with higher pay, and if you communicate this in some way during the interview, it is quite likely that the employer will not offer you a job for fear that you will soon leave.

This may not be far from the truth. After a period of unemployment, most people become more willing to settle for less than they had hoped for. If you are willing to accept jobs where you may be defined as overqualified, consider not presenting some of your educational or work-related credentials on your resume or at interviews—though I do not necessarily recommend doing this. Be prepared to explain in the interview why you *do* want this particular job and how your wealth of experience is a positive and not a negative.

Employers are afraid, of course, that you will become bored by the job duties and take the next job offer that comes your way. It's a legitimate fear, and one you should resolve in your own mind before you push for the position.

If you do want to continue pursuing the job for whatever reason, go out of your way to assure the interviewer that you aren't a job hopper. Maintain high enthusiasm for the organization's future, and present ways you could grow in this position. Suggest how you could assist other departments, solve long-term problems, build profit, and use your experience to help out in other ways.

Remember that the interviewer is also mentally calculating salary requirements during this time. They don't want to waste their time interviewing someone who will not accept their offer, even though they may have some flexibility to offer more for the right person. Your task is to NOT discuss money until the offer is made. See Chapter 5 for tips on negotiating pay.

New graduate/Not enough experience

Every spring, newspapers across the country blast headlines about how difficult it is for today's graduates to find jobs in their areas of study. Before you start believing the bad press too much, keep in mind that such articles only show one side of the story. Yes, many new grads do find it difficult to find an ideal position with great pay. But this is also true for many more experienced workers.

Remember that small employers are where the action is. The Lindquist-Endicott Report from Northwestern University reports that small- to mid-sized companies tend to be the most active recruiters and large companies do less hiring. Smaller organizations are often more open to letting you take on new projects and directions. This allows many people to take one job and advance more rapidly to better ones.

Many students recognize that they must take control of their careers and make their own decisions. More than 8 out of 10 students surveyed in a Right Associate's Career Expectations and Attitudes Comparison cited their own interests and skills as the major influence on their career choice. Other traditional influences, including family pressure, anticipated salary, and luck or chance, have dropped significantly in importance. When you interview for a position that matches your personality and talents, your natural enthusiasm for that job goes a long way in impressing interviewers.

An advantage that many younger people have is being more comfortable with newer technologies than their elders are. This is an important advantage that helps many younger workers gain an edge over their older, but less technology oriented, competitors. If you fall into the "not enough experience" category, stress any technical expertise you've acquired in school, and emphasize the adaptive skills you identified in Chapter 3 that would tend to overcome a lack of experience.

Again, consider expressing a willingness to accept difficult or less desirable conditions as one way to break into a field and gain experience. For example, indicating that you are willing to work weekends and evenings or are able to travel or relocate may appeal to an employer and open up some possibilities.

Don't overlook acceptable experiences such as volunteer work, family responsibilities, education, training, or anything else that you might present as legitimate activities in support of your ability to do the work you feel you can do.

> Howard W. Scott, Jr., president of Dunhill Personnel System, likes to tell the story of his first job search back in 1959. The broadcast major from Northwestern University ran into walls at almost every turn. Finally, a station manager in Roswell, New Mexico, offered Scott a position at $50 a week. "But I have a degree from Northwestern!" he cried. To which the station manager replied, "I know—otherwise it would have been $40 a week." This is the one thing about interviewing that hasn't changed since our parents' days: The same sacrifices are necessary to break into nearly any field.

Issues related to being a woman

Women have made great progress in many career fields and many more employers, managers, professionals, and other workers in responsible positions are women than ever before. Even so, some employers and some career areas present barriers to women that are different than for men.

Men, for example, are not likely to be asked about their child care issues prior to being hired and are far less likely to experience sexual harassment or gender-related discrimination or prejudice.

Despite the fact that the numbers of women in the workforce have increased rapidly, employers still imagine or experience problems. According to the comments expressed in a survey conducted by the Society of Human Resource Management:

> *"Working women with children have difficulties finding adequate child care in our area. Time off and absenteeism are big issues for our working mothers."*

> *"Gaining coworker acceptance of women in nontraditional roles is a serious problem. Many of our executives are uncertain how to manage women."*

> *"We have more women managers, but few women officers, and none on the board of directors. The glass ceiling is a reality."*

Interestingly enough, women employers are often just as concerned as male employers are about a woman's family status. Employers of both genders assume that a woman will more be more likely to have child-related problems and want to be certain that this will not become a work-related problem.

U.S. Department of Labor statistics indicate that about 90 percent of all working women are in their child-bearing years. Of these women, about 80 percent have or are expected to have one or more children. More than half (54 percent) of all working mothers now care for one or more children under age 5. The stress, not to mention the financial hardships of paying for full-time child care, can create potential disruptions for women in the workplace.

> A Harvard Business Review study documented that "on average, working mothers put in an 84-hour work week between their homes and their jobs; working fathers put in 72 hours, and married people with no children put in 50." Those numbers are staggering: A mother essentially holds down two full-time jobs. In addition, the care of elderly parents generally falls on the shoulders of women in our country. For a woman with or likely to have children or elderly parents, the number one task is to assure the interviewer that they don't intend to abandon their families but do intend to devote the necessary time to the job.

Again, it's simply a matter of turning the situation into a positive. Why not present your resourceful nature by giving an example of how you secured reliable child care? Or, illustrate your management skills by describing how you handled work responsibilities when your child was ill and you needed to be at home. Be prepared to back up your loyalty claims with actual numbers of days missed from previous jobs.

Don't make the mistake of assuming that just because a woman interviews you, it isn't necessary to bring up the child care issue. Even though she may be in the same boat herself, empathy rarely plays a role in landing you a position in a competitive job market. I've personally discussed candidates with women managers who mentioned that child care could pose a huge attendance problem with some of the potential hires. An interviewer's main focus is hiring someone who can do the job—regardless of whether they are a man or a woman.

It seems almost laughable that with the number of women in today's workplace, some interviewers would still be uncertain how to manage women. However, sensational headlines of sexual harassment and discrimination have trickled down to all levels of an organization. According to Carol Price, an educator and lecturer with Career Track who specializes in giving women power presentations, it's best to begin establishing your equal status the second you walk in the room. "Once you do that, I really believe gender issues go away," she says.

Chapter 16

More on Career Planning and Job Search **473**

OK, so how do you "establish equal status" without appearing like a militant on a mission—another image of women that frightens employers? Simply look like you belong at the interview. "That means my head is held up, my shoulders are back, I walk in without hesitation, and I put my hand out," says Price. The handshake in particular is crucial. "A handshake was originally devised to prove we were weaponless. In a job interview, that translates to 'you and I are equal in value' when my hand goes out," Price says.

During the interview itself, do not complain about or even mention the lack of opportunity for women at your current or last job as the reason you are seeking new employment. In fact, don't bring up the fact that there may be questions about your competency at all. Assume you are accepted and you will be, Price advises.

> *"I know there are jerks out there who won't see you as worthwhile if you have ovaries. But the bottom line, at minimum, is that they set up an appointment with you. At worst, they have to see you for quota purposes. At best, they are interested in your skills. So if you go in with the attitude 'He won't think I'm as good as Bill simply because I'm female,' you act that way. You start believing your own press and then you're in serious danger."*

In a book titled *Managing a Diverse Work Force*, author John P. Fernandez asked people to respond to a series of statements regarding women in the workplace. They were asked to either agree or disagree with each of the following statements:

1. The increasing employment of women has led to the breakdown of the American family.

2. Many women obtained their current position only because they are women.

3. Pluralism will force us to lower our hiring and promotion standards.

4. Many women use their gender as an alibi for difficulties they have on the job.

5. Many women are not really serious about professional careers.

6. Many women are too emotional to be competent employees.

The results:

✓ 35 percent of the women surveyed and 27 percent of the men did not agree with any of these statements

✓ 46 percent of the women and 45 percent of the men agreed with one to two statements

✓ 16 percent of the women and 22 percent of the men agreed with three to four of the questions

✓ 3 percent of the women and 7 percent of the men agreed with five to six of the statements

What this means is that about a third of those men and women surveyed do not accept stereotypes about women, but about two-thirds do. It is to those two-thirds that your interview responses must be directed.

Issues related to men

While it is seldom brought up, there are certain biases that tend to be held against men, just because of their gender. Men are expected to have steady employment and not take time off for raising a family or caring for older parents. Those who do not aspire to higher status can be quickly branded "losers." You will also find few males in occupations dominated by women, such as grade school teacher, clerical worker, and nurse. While some would argue that this condition is a result of these jobs paying poorly and having low status, it is clearly not always the case. Just as with women, but in different ways, men are "expected" to behave in certain ways, accept certain responsibilities, and quietly accept the limitations imposed on them.

In the recent past, many men have been frustrated in their inability to move up in pay and stature. A big reason for this is the large number of Baby Boomers who are competing for the limited number of management jobs, and the greater number of educated and qualified women in the workforce who want the same things. There are higher percentages of women graduating from high schools and from colleges now than there are men, and some experts predict that this will result in long-term reductions in earnings of men compared to women. As a result, the competition for jobs has become tough.

Even so, there are few situations where being a man will work against you, particularly if you have a good work history. For example, how many men get questions about their plans to have or care for children, or the possibility that they will make a move from the area because their wife takes a more prestigious job in another city? I know that I've never been asked about this in past employment interviews.

Sexual preference

You may be astounded to find that I am willing to bring this up at all. However, these days unmarried men and women may create suspicion as to their sexual preference in some interviewers' minds.

More on Career Planning and Job Search

The fears are twofold. The first is that that employers to not want their workplace to become a stage for airing social concerns to the detriment of producing products or services. The Society of Human Resource Management reveals that its respondents said, "We have not encountered any pressures from gay/lesbian groups directly. However, employees continue to voice their concerns about having to work with these groups and the potential risk—real or perceived—that they pose," and "In our traditional, conservative culture, managers have deeply ingrained biases and fears of gay and lesbian employees."

Another concern has to do with money. Rapidly increasing health-care costs are a serious problem for most organizations. Some employers are concerned about being forced to insure "domestic partners" because this could substantially increase their health care costs. And, let's face it, some employers don't want to hire someone with a higher potential for HIV-related costs or simply do not want gay people on their staff.

Although I have advocated directly attacking stereotypes in other categories, I advise gay people to adopt the military's "don't ask, don't tell" policy related to this issue. The risks of divulging such personal information are too great to bring up in an interview, and your sexuality is not something you should have to discuss in a job interview, anyway.

Military experience

Employers who have not had military experience themselves often have mistaken stereotypes about those with military experience. The truth is that military people are just like everyone else, except that they are perhaps just a bit more responsible than the average. Some of the stereotypes of military people can work in your favor, some won't.

Here are some common problem areas and suggestions for dealing with these preconceptions in a positive way.

Employers want people who can get along with others: Some people assume military personnel will be overly aggressive. Not true, of course, but a stereotype you can easily handle by being friendly and "normal." If you think this may be an issue, emphasize community service you have done, the importance to you of family and friends, and things you have done in and outside of the military that helped others.

Employers need people who work well in teams and solve problems: Another common misconception is that military personnel are too likely to follow orders rather than being creative. More and more jobs require the ability to work as part of a self-directed team that is expected to solve problems with creative input from each member. The truth is that the military has been training team cooperation and creative problem solving for many years. To overcome any negative stereo-types, you simply need to emphasize your team building and problem solving skills and experiences.

Employers may wonder about why you left or assume that you don't have "civilian" skills: Most people don't realize how large the military is and that each year more than 300,000 people leave the military. Be sure to bring up why you left the military to put the interviewer's mind at rest that it had nothing to do with the concept of being "fired." In most cases, ex-military people have served their country well, have benefited from excellent and expensive training, are more edu-cated and technologically trained than the average person their age, and have had far more management experience or other responsibility than average. The fact is that ex-military are among the most talented and dedicated people avail-able, people who have worked hard and have a proven track record for getting difficult things done. Your responsibility in the interview is to make sure the employer knows these things about you.

Use civilian dress and language: To reinforce your abilities as a civilian worker, avoid wearing military tie pins, rings, or other military jewelry or indicators. Completely avoid using any military jargon and replace it with terms that civil-ians use. Emphasize job-related and other skills you have that are needed in the civilian jobs you seek. The Web site at www.careerOINK.com has crosswalks from military to civilian jobs and the descriptions list the skills needed in these jobs; emphasize these skills and give examples of when you used them and any results you obtained. Do emphasize that your military experience developed skills impor-tant to all employers, including discipline, responsibility, and dependability.

Racial or ethnic minorities

The largest minority groups in this country are African-American and Hispanic, although there are many smaller groups of recent immigrants, Native Americans, and others.

The issue here is discrimination. The good news is that most employers will fairly consider hiring a person based on his or her qualifications. In fact, many employ-ers go out of their way to give minorities fair consideration and actively recruit minorities.

The problem is that some employers are less likely to hire a qualified minority based on negative stereotypes. Unfortunately you are not likely to know which employers are being fair and which are not. Wondering why you are not getting a job offer will drive you nuts, so my best advice is this:

1. Assume that the interviewer is being fair, and will consider hiring you based on your skills and abilities.

2. In the interview, be yourself and focus on the skills you have to do the job. This is the same advice I give to everyone and it is important that follow this procedure.

3. Consider what stereotypes an employer might have and make sure you present details about your situation that would disprove them.

If you have limited English proficiency, this will be a problem for many employers and you will need to bring this up. Suggest that you are a good worker, are learning English rapidly, and consider how your language skills would allow you to help the employer provide better service to those who speak your native language.

Recently moved

Employers are often concerned that someone who has recently moved to an area does not have roots there and may soon leave. If you are new to the area, make sure the employer knows you are there to stay. Provide a simple statement that presents you as a stable member of the community rather than someone with a more transient lifestyle. It may be helpful to mention any family or friends who may live nearby or other reasons you plan to stay in the area.

Have a disability

Biases against those with disabilities are common enough that the government has passed the Americans with Disabilities Act to prevent unfair discrimination. But negative assumptions about people with disabilities are the true barrier you are up against in the interview, no matter how many government agencies exist to back up your eligibility.

According to a Society of Human Resource Management survey, many respondents indicated that accommodating employees with disabilities presents difficulties for their organizations. Among the specific comments: "We are a small organization, and accommodation of physical requirements for disabled workers and time off for illness and medical treatment cause disruption to work and schedules." "Some disabled workers are looked upon with disdain by their managers and peers. We have to overcome these attitudes."

I assume you will not seek a job that you can't or should not do. That, of course, would be foolish. So that means you are seeking a job that you are capable of doing, right? That being the case, you don't have a disability related to doing a particular job at all. The employer will still use his or her judgment in hiring the best person for the job, and that means people with disabilities have to compete for jobs along with everyone else. That is fair, so you need to present to an employer a convincing argument for why they should hire you over someone else.

Most importantly, don't assume that the person chatting with you understands the technical details of your handicap. I see nothing wrong in casually mentioning how you have worked around your disability in other positions. Just remember to remain matter-of-fact in your explanation. If you avoid a defensive tone at all costs, you will not only put the interviewer at ease but also assure him or her that your future colleagues will admire your abilities and attitude, too.

> Technology has provided opportunities to overcome disabilities in the workplace that you should become aware of. For example, speech recognition software allows those who find keyboarding challenging (such as those with arthritis or other conditions that affect hand and wrist activity), and magnification features in operating systems such as Windows that allow those with visual challenges to more easily read text on a computer screen. These are low-cost options that you can use to overcome potential challenges to your disability on the job.

Negative references

Most employers will not contact your previous employers unless you are being seriously considered as a candidate for the job. If you fear that one of your previous employers may not give you a positive reference, here are some things you can do:

- ✓ List someone other than your former supervisor as a reference, someone who knew your work there and who will put in a good word for you.
- ✓ Discuss the issue in advance with your previous employer and negotiate what they will say. Even if not good, at least you know what they are likely to say and can prepare potential employers in advance.
- ✓ Get a written letter of reference. In many cases, employers will not give references over the phone (or negative references at all) for fear of being sued. Presenting a letter in advance assures that you know what is said about your performance.

Criminal record

It should be obvious that a resume or application should not include negative information about yourself. So if you have ever been "in trouble" with the law, you would certainly not mention it in these documents. Newer laws prohibit an employer from including such general questions on an application as "Have you ever been arrested?" and limit formal inquiries to "Have you ever been convicted of a felony?"

In this country, we are technically innocent until proven guilty, and that is why employers are no longer allowed to consider an arrest record in a hiring decision.

Being arrested and being guilty are two different things. Arrests for minor offenses (i.e., misdemeanors) are also not supposed to be considered in a hiring decision. The argument has been that minorities are more likely to have arrest records and consideration of arrest records in a hiring decision is, therefore, discriminatory.

A felony conviction is a different matter. These crimes are more serious and current employment laws do allow an employer to ask for and get this information and to use it in making certain hiring decisions. For example, few employers would hire an accountant who had been convicted of stealing money from a previous employer. Certain types of arrest records, such as those for child molestation, are also allowed to be considered by an employer in making certain hiring decisions. For example, few employers would place a person with this kind of record in charge of a daycare facility.

If you have an arrest or conviction record that an employer has a legal right to inquire about, my advice is to avoid looking for jobs where your record would be a negative. The accountant in the example above should consider changing careers. Even if the applicant did get a job by concealing his or her criminal history, that person could be fired at any time in the future. Instead, I might suggest they consider selling accounting software, starting their own business, or getting into a completely different career unrelated to managing money.

As always, your interview should emphasize what you can do rather than what you can't. If you chose your career direction wisely and present a convincing argument that you can do the job well, many employers will, ultimately, overlook previous mistakes. As you prove yourself and gain good work experience, your distant past becomes less and less important.

Background checks, polygraph, or other test?

Many employers screen applicants before hiring. This is more common for jobs where theft can be a problem, for jobs that involve work with children, and for positions that require driving. Background checks may include drug screening, credit history, criminal history, verification of education and training, checks with past employers, and other inquiries depending on the position. In some cases an employer will not consider hiring someone unless they agree to these background checks.

Some employers are also using computerized or paper and pencil tests to identify people who are likely to be dishonest or have other experience or personality-driven, job-related problems.

While it is unlikely you will be asked to take a polygraph or "lie detector" test, here is some information to consider. The Employee Polygraph Protection Act of 1988 prevents employers from using polygraph tests for pre-employment screening or during the course of employment unless the following situations are involved:

1. An employee is reasonably suspected of involvement in a workplace incident that results in economic loss to the employer, and the employee had access to the property that is the subject of an investigation.

2. A prospective employee of an armored car, security alarm, or security guard firm who protects facilities, materials, or operations affecting health or safety, national security, or currency and other like instruments.

3. A prospective employee of a pharmaceutical or other firm authorized to manufacture, distribute, or dispense controlled substances who will have direct access to such controlled substances.

In general, you need to convince an employer that you can be trusted to do a good job. If you have done a good job in preparing your responses, I suggest that you agree to background checks for jobs that interest you. If you have a serious problem in your background, you need to consider in advance how you will handle employer requests to check your background.

Quick Advice

☑ If you do have a major problem that is likely to screen you out if an employer becomes aware of it, avoid careers and jobs where your past would be a problem. Use job search methods that are less likely to require this information as part of the screening process. You can then explain your situation, and why it will not be a problem now, after you get a job offer.

16 Tricky, But Legal Questions

Most employers avoid asking sensitive questions in a direct way. Instead, they will ask indirect questions during the interview in hopes of finding out what they are not "allowed" to ask more directly.

The questions that follow are all legal, and they give you the opportunity to let an employer know that you and your situation will not be a problem. Think about what might concern an employer regarding your particular situation and plan to cover this during your interview, even if you are not asked in a direct way. Your good answer to one of these questions will give you the opportunity to put an employer's real, but perhaps unstated concern to rest.

What can you tell me about yourself?

I've mentioned this question before, and repeat it now because it is probably the number one question you are likely to be asked, and it almost always kicks off the interview. Again, don't be tempted to go back to childhood and talk about your hardworking parents, your dog, and other trivia. Describe yourself in terms of what the interviewer wants to hear: your work ethic, your skills that apply to this job, your educational background, and other relevant positives.

© JIST Works

Chapter 16

What is your greatest strength?

Overall, this is such a positive question that few people have a problem coming up with an answer. Where they trip up is in not supporting that answer. So if you want to emphasize your people skills, for instance, back it up with a short example of how that translates in the workplace. Then brace yourself for its counter question:

What is your greatest weakness?

I talked about this question back in Chapter 5, and mention it here to remind you to choose something that isn't overly negative. Being a workaholic or a perfectionist or too critical of your own work isn't necessarily a strike against you. Mention something that is a negative, but do this in a way that turns that weakness into a strength.

See Chapter 5 for additional tips on this.

What would you like to accomplish during the next ten (or five) years?

Talk about what you want to do for that employer, not for yourself. "I'd like to cut production costs by at least 5 percent and find ways to streamline the layout procedure so that we can add publications without adding staff," is a much better answer than "I'd like to be making 25 percent more in salary and own my own magazine."

How long have you been looking for another job?

Never give an actual timeframe! Casually reply, "Time isn't a factor because I'm searching for the position that best matches my skills and goals."

What type of person would you hire for this position?

Flashback: You're casting your ballot for class president and mark the box for your opponent out of modesty. In doing so, you lost then and you'll lose now if you don't choose yourself! "I'd hire someone who, beyond a shadow of a doubt, has the skills and people experience to handle this job. I would definitely hire myself."

Are you willing to take a pay cut from your present position?

You aren't willing to discuss salary yet, so politely say so. "Because we are still in the process of getting to know one another, I'd feel more comfortable talking about salary once we agree on employment" (or something to that effect).

Why do you want to work for our organization? Or, Why should we hire you?

These questions are really one and the same and are at the heart of every question in any interview. Appropriate responses are covered in some detail in Chapter 5.

Why do you want to leave your present job?

Do not, under any circumstances, complain about your past jobs or employers. Doing so will make you seem negative and appear to be someone who is likely to have problems in a new job. More appropriate answers include this being a step in your career plans or wanting a better job location. "After introducing a more nutritious menu plan to the day care center and establishing a fun yet informative healthy lifestyle program for the after-school crowd, I've reached the top of the ladder at this smaller firm. I want the opportunity to use my expertise and continue to grow in a larger organization."

Be prepared to answer why you left all of the jobs listed on your resume.

How do you normally handle criticism?

Aah, an easy question if you take it on the chin well. However, most of us aren't that admirable and we have to put a twist on this common question. "Obviously, criticism comes from not doing the job properly, and I'm eager to correct any mistakes or misunderstandings the minute they arise. I'm grateful to the person who cares enough to help me out in that respect."

How do others view your work?

Just who are "others"? Colleagues, supervisors, clients, subordinates? The ability to see yourself from all perspectives is a plus in this situation. "The people I manage know that I will set the example before I ask them to make a sacrifice of time or convenience. My colleagues understand that I am sympathetic to how our departments must work together for the common good. My supervisors are impressed with my dedication and realize that if I promise something, I will deliver it. In addition, clients view the product that my department produces as a symbol of quality."

WHY DID YOU LEAVE?

To help you form an acceptable answer to the "Why did you leave?" question, use the acronym CLAMPS:

C = Challenge.	You weren't able to grow professionally in that position.
L = Location.	The commute was unreasonably long.
A = Advancement.	There was nowhere to go. You had the talent, but there were too many people ahead of you.
M = Money.	You were underpaid for your skills and contribution.
P = Prestige.	You wanted to be with a better organization.
S = Security.	The organization was not financially stable.

Chapter 16

How do you feel about working overtime and on weekends?

Even if this job prospect does not appeal to you, this question can be answered so that your response does not harm you. "I have no problem devoting evening hours and weekends to getting a special project done. I also believe that a balanced life leads to a fresh, energetic employee who is less likely to burn out, so I try to pace myself for a consistent, dependable job performance over the long run, too."

What do you do for fun in your spare time?

This question has a dual motivation. First, the interviewer is confirming your response to the "Will you work overtime?" question. If you replied "yes" to that question, but then outline a lifestyle that involves weekends at a cabin, evenings at the gym, and commitments to various nonprofit and community events, it's unlikely you'll cancel those plans to work overtime.

On the other hand, this is also an opportunity for the interviewer to confirm those things he or she can't legally ask, such as if you have a family, if you attend church, etc. "My in-laws have a cabin by a nearby lake, and the children enjoy going there on weekends. I accompany them when I can, but sometimes work-related projects prevent that. Of course, the grandparents welcome those times so they can spend one-on-one time with the kids."

Describe your typical day.

Naturally, leave out the fact that you aren't a morning person or you start winding down at 4:30 p.m. to hit the parking lot by 5 p.m. This is your opportunity to advertise how well you organize yourself and conceptualize long-term projects. "I keep a calendar on my desk with appointment times recorded on the left side and tasks to accomplish that day on the right. I allot time each day to stay in touch with other departments and to return any missed phone calls or e-mail promptly. Overall, my entire day is focused on providing customers with a top-notch product."

What do you like most about your present boss?

For most candidates, it's not too hard to find something nice to say in response to this question. Focus your answer on the type of supervision your boss provides and not necessarily on a personality type. "I appreciate the regular feedback" is a more useful response than "I enjoy the fact that he/she always has an upbeat attitude," even though both are certainly positive answers.

What do you like least about your present boss?

You knew this was coming based on the previous question. Again, stick to management principles and skip the personality conflicts. Interviewers also like to pose the "What do you like best/least about your present job?" set of questions as well. As I have advised before, continue to look at your current job's opportunities rather than specific unappealing tasks. "I don't like to type my own memos" is honest, but short-sighted.

94 FREQUENTLY ASKED INTERVIEW QUESTIONS

Here is a list of questions most often asked by recruiters who interview new graduates at college campuses. While some of the questions may not apply to your situation, they will give you a good idea of the types of questions a trained interviewer might ask you in an interview. Look over the list and check any that would be hard for you to answer well. Then practice coming up with positive answers for those problem questions!

1. What are your future vocational plans?

2. In what school activities have you participated? Why? Which did you enjoy the most?

3. How do you spend your spare time? What are your hobbies?

4. What type of position most interests you?

5. Why do you think you might like to work for our company?

6. What jobs have you held? How were they obtained?

7. What courses did you like best? Least? Why?

8. Why did you choose your particular field of work?

9. What percentage of your school expenses did you earn? How?

10. How did you spend your vacations while in school?

11. What do you know about our company?

12. Do you feel that you have received a good general training?

13. What qualifications do you have that make you feel that you will be successful in your field?

14. What extracurricular offices have you held?

15. What are your ideas on salary?

16. How do you feel about your family?

17. How interested are you in sports?

18. If you were starting school all over again…?

19. Can you forget your education and start from scratch?

20. Do you prefer any specific geographic location? Why?

(continued)

Chapter 16

(continued)

21. Do you have a girl (boy) friend? Is it serious?

22. How much money do you hope to earn at age _____?

23. Why did you decide to go to the school you attended?

24. How did you rank in your graduating class in high school? Other schools?

25. Do you think that your extracurricular activities were worth the time you devoted to them? Why?

26. What do you think determines a person's progress in a good company?

27. What personal characteristics are necessary for success in your chosen field?

28. Why do you think you would like this particular type of job?

29. What is your father's occupation?

30. Tell me about your home life during the time you were growing up.

31. Are you looking for a permanent or temporary job?

32. Do you prefer working with others or by yourself?

33. What types of people are your best friends?

34. What kind of boss do you prefer?

35. Are you primarily interested in making money?

36. Can you take instructions without feeling upset?

37. Tell me a story!

38. Do you live with your parents? Which of your parents has had the most profound influence on you?

39. How did previous employers treat you?

40. What have you learned from some of the jobs you have held?

41. Can you get recommendations from previous employers?

42. What interests you about our product or service?

43. What was your record in military service?

44. Have you ever changed your major field of interest? Why?

45. When did you choose your major?

46. How did your grades after military service compare with those you previously earned?

47. Do you feel you have done the best work of which you are capable?

48. How did you happen to go to post secondary school?

49. What do you know about opportunities in the field in which you are trained?

50. How long do you expect to work?

51. Have you ever had any difficulty getting along with fellow students and faculty? Fellow workers?

52. Which of your school years was most difficult?

53. What is the source of your spending money?

54. Do you own any life insurance?

55. Have you saved any money?

56. Do you have any debts?

57. How old were you when you became self-supporting?

58. Do you attend church?

59. Did you enjoy school?

60. Do you like routine work?

61. Do you like regular work?

62. What size city do you prefer?

63. When did you first contribute to family income?

64. What is your major weakness?

65. Define cooperation.

66. Will you fight to get ahead?

67. Do you demand attention?

68. Do you have an analytical mind?

69. Are you eager to please?

70. What do you do to keep in good physical condition?

(continued)

Chapter 16

(continued)

71. How do you usually spend Sunday?

72. Have you had any serious illness or injury?

73. Are you willing to go where the company sends you?

74. What job in our company would you choose if you were entirely free to do so?

75. Is it an effort for you to be tolerant of persons with a background and interests different from your own?

76. What types of books have you read?

77. Have you plans for further education?

78. What types of people seem to rub you the wrong way?

79. Do you enjoy sports as a participant? As an observer?

80. Have you ever tutored another student?

81. What jobs have you enjoyed the most? The least? Why?

82. What are your own special abilities?

83. What job in our company do you want to work toward?

84. Would you prefer a large or a small company? Why?

85. What is your idea of how industry operates today?

86. Do you like to travel?

87. How about overtime work?

88. What kind of work interests you?

89. What are the disadvantages of your chosen field?

90. Do you think that grades should be considered by employers? Why or why not?

91. Are you interested in research?

92. If married, how often do you entertain at home?

93. To what extent do you use liquor?

94. What have you done that shows initiative and willingness to work?

Practice, Practice, Practice

It is not enough to read and think about problem questions. As I have said before in this book, interviewing is the art of conversation and interaction. In order to get better at answering problem questions, you do need to think about your responses in advance. This is particularly true for those problem questions that you fear will hurt you if you are asked them in an interview,

You need to practice your interviewing skills *out loud*. If possible, get someone to act as an interviewer and have that person recite problem questions to you. Use the Three-Step Process (presented in Chapters 4 and 5) to answer most questions, and your interviewing skills will surely improve.

⟹ *Quick Summary*

✓ Employers are highly motivated to hire a "good" person. They want someone who has the skills to do the job (usually based on the applicant's past work experience and education).

✓ How well you perform in the interview will often be the key factor in an employer giving you a chance over someone else who has better credentials. It is not always the best person who gets the job; it is often the one who has the best communication skills.

✓ To be considered, you must meet or exceed an employer's expectations.

✓ Together, the Three-Step Process and "Prove It" techniques form the basic approach to answering problem questions, and it is most important that you understand and use these techniques to improve your interviewing skills.

✓ Technically, interviewers can ask whatever they wish. It's what employers do that can get them in trouble with the law. It is illegal to hire or not hire someone based on certain criteria. It is also very difficult to prove that someone actually does that.

✓ Title VII of the Civil Rights Act makes discrimination on the basis of race, sex, religion, or national origin illegal in hiring discussions. The more recent Americans with Disabilities Act requires that an employer provide an equal opportunity for an individual with a disability to participate in the job application process and to be considered for a job. In general, interview questions should focus only on your ability to do the job.

✓ Begin by considering how an employer might be legitimately concerned about you or your situation. Then look for a way to present your "problem" as an advantage ("turtling"). Your task in the interview is to provide information indicating that, yes, you can be counted on to do the job. Often, if you don't get that idea across, you simply will not be considered.

✓ In this chapter, answers to specific problem questions are given. Most of these questions are more likely to be an issue in a traditional interview, and many are a bit sensitive. One good thing about the traditional interview is that you can accurately guess and prepare for the questions most likely to be asked.

✓ Keep in mind that very few interviewers have had any formal interview training.

✓ By preparing and practicing answers to the many questions presented in this chapter, you improve your chances of performing well in an interview considerably, which often leads to getting a job offer.

Tips on Surviving and Coming Back from Unemployment

≡≡≡*Quick Overview*

I briefly touched on the problems involved in being unemployed in Chapter 1, but more suggestions are provided here.

Being out of work is not fun for most people and is devastating to some. It may help you to know that you are not alone in this experience, and I've included some information here on what to expect and some suggestions for getting through it.

Some Problems You May Experience

Here are some feelings and experiences you may have after losing your job.

✔ **Loss of professional identity.** Most of us identify strongly with our careers, and unemployment can often lead to a loss of self-esteem. Being employed brings respect in the community and in the family. When a job is lost, part of your sense of self may be lost as well.

✔ **Loss of a network.** The loss may be worse when your social life has been strongly linked to the job. Many ongoing "work friendships" are suddenly halted. Old friends and colleagues often don't call because they feel awkward or don't know what to say. Many don't want to be reminded of what could happen to them.

✔ **Emotional unpreparedness.** If you have never before been unemployed you may not be emotionally prepared for it and may be devastated when it happens. It is natural and appropriate to feel this way. You might notice that some people you know don't take their job loss as hard as you have taken it. Studies show that those who change jobs frequently, or who are in occupations prone to cyclic unemployment, suffer far less emotional impact after job loss than those who have been steadily employed and who are unprepared for cutbacks.

Emotional Stages to Expect During Your Time Unemployed

Losing your job can be similar in its emotional impact to the loss of a close friend or family member. I can tell you from personal experience that such strong feelings are not easy to avoid or control. There have been many studies done on how to deal with loss, and it may help you to know in advance that your emotional response to job loss is normal.

Psychologists have found that people often have an easier time dealing with loss if they know what feelings they might experience during the grieving process. Grief doesn't usually overwhelm us all at once; it usually is experienced in stages.

Stages of Loss or Grief

Shock: You may not be fully aware of what has happened.

Denial: Denial usually comes next—you cannot believe that the loss is true.

Relief: Then relief enters the picture for some, and you feel a burden has lifted and opportunity awaits.

Anger: Anger often follows—you blame (often without cause) those you think might be responsible, including yourself.

Depression: Depression may set in some time later, when you realize the reality of the loss.

Acceptance: Acceptance is the final stage of the process—you come to terms with the loss and get the energy and desire to move beyond it. The "acceptance" stage is the best place to be when starting a job search, but you might not have the luxury of waiting until this point to begin your search.

Knowing that a normal person will experience some predictable grieving reactions can help you deal with your loss in a constructive way. The faster you can move through the stage of loss and begin an active search for a new job, the better off you will be.

Keep Healthy

Unemployment is a stressful time for most people, and it is important to keep healthy and in shape. Try to do the following on a regular basis:

✓ **Eat properly.** How you look and your sense of self-esteem can be affected by your eating habits. It is very easy to snack on junk food when you're home all day. Take time to plan your meals and snacks so that they are well-balanced and nutritious. Eating properly will help you keep the good attitude you need during your job search.

✓ **Exercise.** Include some form of exercise as part of your daily activities. Regular exercise reduces stress and depression and can help you get through those tough days.

✓ **Allow time for fun.** When you're planning your time, be sure to build fun and relaxation into your plans. You are allowed to enjoy life even if you are unemployed. Keep a list of activities or tasks that you want to accomplish, such as volunteer work, repairs around the house, or hobbies. When free time develops, you can refer to the list and have lots of things to do.

Face Family Issues

Unemployment is a stressful time for the entire family. For them, your unemployment means the loss of income and the fear of an uncertain future, and they are also worried about your happiness. Here are some ways you can interact with your family to get through this tough time.

✓ **Do not attempt to shoulder your problems alone.** Be open with family members even though it is hard. Discussions about your job search and the feelings you have allow your family to work as a group and support one another.

✓ **Talk to your family.** Let them know your plans and activities. Share with them how you will be spending your time. Tell them that your time without a job will end and that you need everyone to help by cutting expenses and being supportive in other ways until you get your next job.

✓ **Listen to your family.** Find out their concerns and their suggestions. Perhaps there are ways they can assist you.

✓ **Build family spirit.** You will need a great deal of support from your family in the months ahead, but they will also need yours.

Chapter 17

✓ **Seek outside help.** Join a family support group. Many community centers, mental health agencies, and colleges have support groups for the unemployed and their families. These groups can provide a place to let off steam and share frustrations. They can also be a place to get ideas on how to survive this difficult period. More information about support groups is presented later in this chapter.

✓ **Participate in an online support or discussion group.** The Internet provides many options for connecting with people who have similar circumstances. Search for groups that deal with these issues, such as www.joblayoffsupport.com. These sites often offer not only an opportunity to post messages on discussion boards or participate in live chat rooms, but also job search advice and links to additional sites or information that may help you cope with unemployment.

Help Your Children Cope

If you have children, realize that they can be deeply affected by a parent's unemployment. It is important for them to know what has happened and how it will affect the family. However, try not to overburden them with the responsibility of too many of the emotional or financial details.

✓ **Keep an open dialogue with your children.** Letting them know what is really going on is vital. Children have a way of imagining the worst, so the facts can actually be far less devastating than what they envision. Let them know that they are safe and protected no matter what and that this is a temporary set-back.

✓ **Make sure your children know it's not anybody's fault.** Children may not understand about job loss and may think that you did something wrong to cause it. Or they may feel that somehow they are responsible or financially burdensome. They need reassurance in these matters, regardless of their age.

✓ **Children need to feel they are helping.** They want to help, and having them do something like taking a cut in allowance, deferring expensive purchases, or getting an after-school job can make them feel as if they are part of the team.

Also, some experts suggest that it can be useful to alert the school counselor to your unemployment so that they can watch the children for problems at school before the problems become serious.

Reduce and Deal with Stress

Here are some coping mechanisms that can help you deal with the stress of being unemployed:

✓ **Write down what seems to be causing the stress.** Identify the "stressors," and then think of possible ways to handle each one. Can some demands be altered, lessened, or postponed? Can you live with any of them just as they are? Are there some that you might be able to deal with more effectively?

✓ **Set priorities.** Deal with the most pressing needs or changes first. You cannot handle everything at once.

✓ **Establish a workable schedule.** When you set a schedule for yourself, make sure it is one which can be achieved. As you perform your tasks, you will feel a sense of control and accomplishment.

✓ **Reduce stress.** Learn relaxation techniques or other stress-reduction techniques. This can be as simple as sitting in a chair, closing your eyes, taking a deep breath and breathing out slowly while imagining all the tension going out of you with each breath. There are a number of other methods, including listening to relaxation tapes, which may help you cope with stress more effectively. Check the additional source material books which offer instruction on these techniques. (Many of these are available at your public library.)

✓ **Avoid isolation.** Keep in touch with your friends, even former coworkers, if you can do that comfortably. Unemployed people often feel a sense of isolation and loneliness. See your friends, talk with them, e-mail them, and socialize with them. You are the same person you were before unemployment. The same goes for the activities that you may have enjoyed in the past. Evaluate them. Which can you afford to continue? If you find that your old hobbies or activities can't be part of your new budget, perhaps you can substitute new activities that are less costly.

✓ **Join a support group.** No matter how understanding or caring your family or friends might be, they may not be able to understand all that you're going through. You might be able to find help and understanding at a job-seeking support group. These support groups consist of people who are going through the same experiences and emotions you are. Many groups also share tips on job opportunities, as well as feedback on ways to deal more effectively in the job search process. *The National Business Employment Weekly,* available at major newsstands, lists support groups throughout the country. Local churches, the YMCA and YWCA, and libraries often list or even facilitate support groups. A list of self-help clearinghouses, some of which cover the unemployed, is available from the National Self-Help Clearinghouse at www.selfhelpweb.org.

Chapter 17

Keep Your Spirits Up

Here are some ways you can build your self-esteem and avoid depression:

- ✓ **List your positives.** Make a list of your positive qualities and your successes. This list is always easier to make when you are feeling good about yourself. Perhaps you can enlist the assistance of a close friend or caring relative, or wait for a sunnier moment.

- ✓ **Replay your positives.** Once you have made this list, replay the positives in mind frequently. Associate the replay with an activity you do often; for example, you might review the list in your mind every time you go to the refrigerator!

- ✓ **Use the list before performing difficult tasks.** Review the list when you are feeling down or to give you energy before you attempt some difficult task. Do what you fear the most first.

- ✓ **Recall successes.** Take time every day to recall a success.

- ✓ **Use realistic standards.** Avoid the trap of evaluating yourself using impossible standards that come from others. You are in a particular phase of your life; don't dwell on what you think society regards as success. Remind yourself that success will again be yours.

- ✓ **Know your strengths and weaknesses.** Know your strengths. What things are you good at? What skills do you have? Do you need to learn new skills? Everyone has limitations. What are yours? Are there certain job duties that are just not right for you and that you might want to avoid? Balance your limitations against your strong skills so that you don't let the negatives eat at your self esteem. Incorporate this knowledge into your planning.

- ✓ **Picture success.** Practice visualizing positive results or outcomes and view them in your mind before the event. Play out the scene in your imagination and picture yourself successful in whatever you're about to attempt.

- ✓ **Build success.** Make a "to do" list. Include small, achievable tasks. Divide the tasks on your list and make a list for every day so you will have some "successes" daily.

- ✓ **Surround yourself with positive people.** Socialize with family and friends who are supportive. You want to be around people who will "pick you up," not "knock you down." You know who your fans are. Try to find time to be around them. It can really make you feel good.

- ✓ **Volunteer.** Give something of yourself to others through volunteer work. It will help you to feel more worthwhile, and may actually help you to develop new skills.

Avoid Depression

Are you very depressed? As hard as it is to be out of work, it also can be a new beginning. A new direction may emerge which will change your life in positive ways. This may be a good time to re-evaluate your attitudes and outlook.

- ✓ **Live in the present.** The past is over and you cannot change it. Learn from your mistakes and use that knowledge to plan for the future—then let the past go. Don't dwell on it or relive it over and over. Don't be overpowered by guilt.

- ✓ **Take responsibility for yourself.** Try not to complain or blame others. Save your energy for activities that result in positive experiences.

- ✓ **Learn to accept what you cannot change.** However, realize that in most situations, you do have some control. Your reactions and your behavior are in your control and will often influence the outcome of events.

- ✓ **Keep the job search under your own command.** This will give you a sense of control and prevent you from giving up and waiting for something to happen. Enlist everyone's aid in your job search, but make sure you do most of the work.

- ✓ **Talk things out with people you trust.** Admit how you feel. For example, if you realize you're angry, find a positive way to vent it, perhaps through exercise.

- ✓ **Face your fears, and try to pinpoint them.** "Naming the enemy" is the best strategy for relieving the vague feeling of anxiety. By facing what you actually fear, you can see how realistic your fears are.

- ✓ **Think creatively, stay flexible, take risks, and don't be afraid of failure.** Try not to take rejection personally. Think of it as information that will help you later in your search. Take criticism as a way to learn more about yourself. Keep plugging away at the job search despite those inevitable setbacks. Most important, forget magic—what lies ahead is hard work!

If your depression won't go away, or leads you to self-destructive behaviors such as abuse of alcohol or drugs, you may wish to consider asking a professional for help. Many people who have never sought professional assistance before find that in a time of crisis it really helps to have someone who can listen and who can give needed aid.

Consult your local mental health clinics, social services agencies, religious organization, or professional counselors for help for yourself and family members who are affected by your unemployment. Some assistance may be covered by your health insurance or, if you do not have insurance, counseling is often available on a sliding scale fee based on income.

Chapter 17

Create a Plan of Action

It is hard being unemployed. Part of the problem is that your routine is no longer structured by work and it is easy to sit around and eventually get depressed, or waste lots of time on unimportant activities.

This is why it is most important for you to create a new schedule for your daily activities. Plan out your week and days in advance and you are much more likely to get the more important things done that it's so tempting to put off. Creating this plan will also help you to avoid feelings of worthlessness. Keep busy, do the difficult job search activities every day (make calls, send e-mails, and go out on interviews), and let each day take care of itself.

Just do your best, that's all anyone can do.

Manage Your Finances While Out of Work

As you already know, being unemployed has financial consequences. While the best solution to this is to get a good job in as short a time as possible, you do need to manage your money differently during the time between jobs. Following are some things to think about.

Apply for benefits without delay

Don't be embarrassed to apply for unemployment benefits as soon as possible, even if you're not sure you are eligible. This program is to help you make a transition between jobs, and you helped pay for it by your previous employment. Depending on how long you have worked, you can collect benefits for up to 26 weeks and sometimes even longer. Contact your state Labor Department or Employment Security Agency for further information. Their addresses and telephone numbers are listed in your phone book.

Prepare now to stretch your money

Being out of work means lower income and the need to control your expenses. Don't avoid doing this, as the more you plan, the better you can control your finances. Consider joining a food co-op where you can volunteer an hour or so month and receive co-op food prices. Do a key word search for "Food Co-op" for your area.

Examine your income and expenses

Create a budget and look for ways to cut expenses. The worksheet that follows can help you isolate income and expense categories, but your own budget may be considerably more detailed. I've included several columns in the expense category of the worksheet that follows. Use the "Normal" column to enter what you have been spending in that category during the time you were employed. Use the

"Could Reduce to" column for an estimate of a number that you will strive for by cutting expenses in that category. The "Comments" column is for your comments on how you might cut expenses.

Monthly Income and Expense Worksheet

INCOME

Unemployment benefits _____

Spouse's income _____

Severance pay _____

Interest/Dividends _____

Other income _____

Total _____

EXPENSES	Normal	Could Reduce to	Comments
Mortgage/Rent	_____	_____	
Home maintenance/ Repairs	_____	_____	
Utilities:			
Electric	_____	_____	
Gas/Oil heat	_____	_____	
Water/Sewer	_____	_____	
Telephone	_____	_____	
Cable	_____	_____	
Food			
Restaurants	_____	_____	
Groceries	_____	_____	
Car payment	_____	_____	
Fuel/Maintenance/ Repairs	_____	_____	
Insurance	_____	_____	

(continued)

Chapter 17

(continued)

EXPENSES	Normal	Could Reduce to	Comments
Other loan payments	_____	_____	
Health insurance	_____	_____	
Other medical/ dental expenses	_____	_____	
Tuition, other school costs	_____	_____	
Clothing	_____	_____	
Entertainment	_____	_____	
Taxes	_____	_____	
Job hunting costs	_____	_____	
Other expenses	_____	_____	
_____	_____	_____	
_____	_____	_____	
_____	_____	_____	
_____	_____	_____	
TOTALS	_____	_____	

Tips to conserve your cash

While unemployed, it is likely that your expenses will exceed your income, and it is essential that you be aggressive in managing your money. Your objective here is very clear: You want to conserve as much cash as possible early on so you can have some for essentials later on. Here are some suggestions for doing this:

✓ **Begin right away to cut all nonessential expenses.** Don't put this off! There is no way to know how long you will be out of work, and the faster you deal with the financial issues, the better.

✓ **Discuss the situation with other family members.** Ask them to get involved by helping you identify expenses they can cut.

✓ **Look for sources of additional income.** Can you paint houses on weekends? Pick up a temporary job or consulting assignment? Deliver newspapers in the early morning? Can a family member get a job to help out? Any new sources of income will help, and the sooner the better.

✓ **Contact your creditors.** Even if you can make full payments for awhile, work out interest-only or reduced-amount payments as soon as possible. When I was unemployed, I went to my creditors right away and asked them to help. They were very cooperative, and most are, if you are reasonable with them.

✓ **Register with your local consumer credit counseling organization.** Many areas have free consumer credit counseling organizations that can help you get a handle on your finances and encourage your creditors to cooperate. You may receive certain benefits by working with them , like lower loan rates at banks or credit unions and a positive statement on your credit report. Look in your local *Yellow Pages* under "Credit and Debt Counseling."

✓ **Review your assets.** Make a list of all your assets and their current value. Money in checking, savings, and other accounts are the most available, but you may have additional assets in pension programs, life insurance, and stocks that could be converted to cash if needed. You may also have an extra car that could be sold, equity in your home that could be borrowed against, and other assets that could be sold or used if needed.

✓ **Reduce credit card purchases.** Try to pay for things in cash to save on interest charges and prevent overspending. Be disciplined; you can always use your credit cards later, when you are getting desperate for food and other basics.

✓ **Consider cashing in some "luxury" assets.** For example, sell a car or boat you rarely use to generate cash and to save on insurance and maintenance costs.

✓ **Shop for bargain essentials.** Try to lower costs for home/auto/life insurance and other monthly or major expenses. Shop for used clothes and other needed items. Shop for food bargains. Whatever you can do to cut costs is a good thing.

✓ **Deduct job hunting expenses from your taxes.** Some job hunting expenses may be tax deductible as a "miscellaneous deduction" on your federal income tax return. Keep receipts for employment agency fees, resume expenses, and transportation expenses. If you locate work in another city and you must relocate, moving expenses may be tax deductible. Contact an accountant or the IRS for more information. Certain education expenses related to updating your skills may also be deductible.

✓ **Delay or eliminate home improvements, vacations, and other non-essential expenses.** Don't make the mistake of starting big or expensive projects while unemployed. Doing so keeps you from the job search and also consumes your limited cash reserves.

✓ **Ask for discounts.** Most of us pay the asking price but discounts can often be obtained for almost anything if you ask for them.

Review Your Health and Other Coverage

You already know that it is dangerous to go without health insurance, so there is no need to lecture you on this, but here are some tips:

✓ You can probably maintain coverage at your own expense, under the COBRA law, if you worked for an employer that provided medical coverage and had 20 or more employees. To continue your health coverage under this law, you must notify your former employer within 60 days of leaving the job.

✓ Contact professional organizations you belong to; they may provide group coverage for their members at low rates.

✓ Speak to an insurance broker, if necessary, to arrange for health coverage on your own or join a local Health Maintenance Organization.

✓ Practice preventive medicine. The best way to save money on medical bills is to stay healthy. Try not to ignore minor ills. If they persist, phone or visit your doctor.

✓ Investigate local clinics. Many local clinics provide services based on a sliding scale. These clinics often provide quality health care at affordable prices.

✓ In an emergency, most hospitals will provide you with services on a sliding scale, and most areas usually have one or more hospitals funded locally to provide services to those who can't afford it.

Search Out and Use Special Programs for the Unemployed

Take advantage of food stamps, free health clinics, unemployment compensation, education grants for tuition, special programs of all kinds for the unemployed and "needy."

I know, you are proud, and it's embarrassing to ask for or accept certain types of help. But consider that many social services and other programs exist for the very purpose of helping people when they need it. If you have or will be working for a big chunk of your life, consider also that your tax and charitable contributions are the source of the funds that support all those programs. You have been or will be paying for these programs for most of your life, yet probably won't use them much, if at all.

This is why you should seek out and use the many free or low-cost services and programs. Here are some specific suggestions:

✓ Contact your area's United Way referral service and ask if they have a print or online directory of community programs for someone in your situation. The local newspaper may also publish a similar resource. Many of the programs mentioned here will be noted in these resources.

✓ Check out any programs available from your local state or provincial employment service. I already suggested you collect any unemployment insurance you qualify for, but see what other programs are offered. The unemployment office sometimes has free career counseling, job search programs, educational funds, or other programs. Many areas have special and free skills training programs or referrals for the unemployed, including funds to go to school.

✓ See if you qualify for food stamps. You can get eligibility rules and local application procedures from the Web site at www.fns.usda.gov/fsp.

✓ If you are pregnant or have babies, you may qualify for special food programs. Check with your local welfare or food stamp office.

✓ Most communities have free or low cost health clinics, mental health services, and many other programs that provide services you are used to paying for that are available for free or low cost for those with limited incomes.

✓ Ask your church what services might be available. Some have confidential food programs, counseling programs, job search assistance, and other programs.

✓ While many people don't know about them, your local township, county, town, parish, or province often has surplus food, emergency housing assistance, and other financial help available.

✓ The federal government makes a long list of food programs available to local schools, government programs, and qualified groups to use or distribute to low income and unemployed. If you qualify, you can get free canned fruits, vegetables, or meats, eggs, beans, infant formula, cheese, pasta, cereal, grains and other foods. Check out the Web site www.fns.usda.gov/fdd for details.

These are just a few of the many examples of the kinds of help you can get if you look for it. Don't hesitate to seek out free or low cost services that are available for those with limited incomes or who are unemployed, if you need them. Assume that you qualify and apply as needed for programs. Later, you will repay the many kindnesses you receive by paying your taxes and helping others in a similar situation in large and small ways.

Quick Summary

✓ Remember that it's normal to experience a sense of loss and depression during unemployment.

✓ Take care of yourself by eating healthy and reducing stress in your life.

✓ Address family issues by helping each other cope with your situation.

✓ Avoid depression and negative thoughts and people.

✓ Create a plan of action, including how you'll manage your finances.

✓ Take advantage of special programs for the unemployed.

Chapter 17

Your Career Management Plan—*How to Keep Your Job Once You Have It*

This chapter was contributed by Karine B. Blackett, MS.

═══Quick Overview

In this chapter, I review the following:

✔ What a career management plan involves

✔ Developing a Career Work Plan

✔ Establishing career goals and continuing to stretch further

✔ Techniques for keeping your job once you have it

✔ Becoming a lifelong learner

✔ Tips for climbing the career ladder within an organization

✔ How to keep your job satisfaction high in the absence of promotion

✔ How to know it's time to start looking for employment elsewhere

✔ How to always be employable

Now that you've read the preceding chapters, it is my hope that you've started to use the techniques outlined. In fact, it would not surprise me if you already have had several job interviews, in addition to job offers. Once you have accepted a job, it is important to develop a plan to manage your career.

Landing a good job when unemployment is high is no easy task. Competition in the job market is always fierce. Add to this the fact that the average person will change careers and jobs at least 7 to 9 times over his or her lifetime, and you can see why job stability and longevity is becoming increasingly important.

In the past, a person could be reasonably assured of working at the same company for 20 or more years. Some people in my father's generation worked for one company from high school graduation until retirement. Unfortunately, in this age of rapid technological changes and corporate mergers and consolidations, the current workforce has no such guarantees of lengthy employment.

In light of the volatile employment times in which we live, it would be significantly advantageous to keep the jobs we have until we can move up the career ladder or move on to more lucrative or satisfying positions. Ideally these moves would be under our control, but often times, these moves are involuntary and sudden. Therefore, to be ready for the unexpected, it is vitally important to have a Career Work Plan in place.

The Career Work Plan

I believe the most important step in creating a Career Work Plan is to formulate goals. The question, "What are your career goals?" must be answered to your satisfaction before you do anything else. In doing this, you are creating a foundation to base educational and employment decisions on. Without career goals to work toward, you will randomly meander through chaotic economic times, never knowing where you really want to go. Many people skip the step of creating goals and, although they end up somewhere, it is rarely where they want to be.

If you are just beginning your career in the traditional college years, a long-term career goal may be more abstract than for a person with 20 years of work experience. For example, if you are just starting out, your goal may be to "work for a company where I can advance in position, responsibility, and salary every few years until the age of 50." I would refer to this sample goal as "stable." Of course, we have learned that employee tenure rarely gives a person the opportunity to work for one employer over the course of 30 years.

With that in mind, the new graduate may formulate more attainable goals such as "work for companies using my talents and gifts accepting new opportunities as they translate up the career ladder until I have enough money to retire or become self-employed." I would refer to this sample goal as "fluid." A fluid career goal is one that is likely to serve you better in the long run.

Because things in your life change, to create a more fluid Career Work Plan, you should create sub-goals. In other words, set goals you can reach within three months, six months, and a year. For example, if you have a goal of getting an office and a five percent raise in a year, that is something you can strive for. Under this goal, start making goals for the types of projects and new opportunities you would like to tackle. You can start looking at your day planner as a daily goal list. Write down the goals for the day so that you do not lose sight of them as you put out the fires that will come your way and eat up your time.

Quick Tip There is a 15/85 rule to follow when you look at your time for the day. Do the 15 percent of the things on your list that will give you 85 percent of the results.

As you gain experience in the job market, your career goals may become more specific. An example of a stable career goal may be "work for Company XYZ until career advancement halts, then cross-train or transfer to competing company until retirement." An example of a fluid career goal may be, "work in the electronics industry until related opportunities arise providing similar or advanced income potential until retirement or ability to become self-employed."

The Career Work Plan is a step-by-step method of reaching your goals. As when formulating your career goals, your Career Work Plan can also be formulated as stable or fluid. Regardless of whether your Career Work Plan is stable or fluid, there are certain things you should consider when writing it.

Steps in the Career Work Plan

1. Develop your career goals.

2. Decide if your goals are stable or fluid. Base your career work goals on those criteria. Then, consider what you like to do, what your talents are, and what qualifications you have. Decide whether you are willing to relocate or prefer to stay in one general area. With this information you should be able to generate a picture of your career goals. Even if your goals are a bit fuzzy, you need to start somewhere. Set a long-term career goal. From that goal, your sub-goals will flow.

3. Identify any problems or blocks to reaching your career goals and develop a plan of action to reconcile them. The most common problems and blocks to a career goal are related to education, experience, and economic health. Other potential problems are personal work habits and how well you handle certain environments, such as dealing with negative people or stress in the workplace. Once identified, you may find that some problems may not be problems at all.

4. List ALL alternatives for reaching your career goals. This list should be as extensive as possible. Some generic guidelines may help categorize your alternatives for reaching your career goals. For example, if you have formulated a "stable" career work plan, you would be likely to consider all governmental, military, and large-industry jobs as methods to reach your goal. If you have formulated a fluid career work plan, you would conversely consider all new-business, technological, and dot.com jobs as methods to reach your goal. Other alternatives may include technical training, vocational schooling, traditional college, and military training.

(continued)

Chapter 18

(continued)

5. Evaluate your alternatives for reaching your career goals. You should list the pros and cons of each alternative separately. Be as objective as you can when making your lists. Carefully weigh any alternative that involves a long-term educational commitment against potential lost income. If you choose a career based on an educational commitment of several years (for example, you want to become a lawyer and are currently in undergraduate school, during which time you would have limited or no income), figure out the number of years it would take to recoup the costs. Keep in mind you will change careers between 7 and 9 times over your lifetime. Your education should pay off, but it is important to see the cost of it in black and white.

6. Choose an alternative for reaching your career goals. This is a difficult step for many people. Some people simply don't like to make decisions. However, I guarantee if you don't make a decision in your Career Work Plan, someone will do it for you and you will probably not like the results. It may also be advantageous to consider the opinion of friends and family when choosing a method for reaching your goals. Remember, your career path is ultimately your choice.

7. Follow up evaluation on progress toward your career goals. Regularly evaluate your progress toward meeting or exceeding your goals. This should be done at least twice a year. Don't give up too early, but don't hold on to a sinking ship either. If you feel you are making progress, press on toward the prize. However, if you feel like you are losing ground, it is important to carefully assess your situation and determine whether or not your lack of progress is within your control. You can use yardsticks that are external, such as your income and number of promotions. You can also use personal yardsticks such as your satisfaction level and whether the position is meeting your creative and intellectual needs.

8. Make changes, if necessary.

Based on your evaluation, you will need to cut your losses or hang in there for the long haul. If you are feeling completely lost at this point in your career work plan, you should begin again to reformulate a career plan goal. If you are currently employed, this is a good time to start a Career Work Plan that will either take you further in the field you are in or help you reformulate your life so that you are heading in the direction you truly wish to go.

Techniques to Keep Your Job and Climb the Career Ladder

Here are some simple strategies you can use to stay in a job you like and move forward in your career.

1) Just Show Up

An employer once told me the funniest excuse for an employee not coming in to work was "I have a problem with my eyes this morning. I just can't see coming in to work today." Funny as that may be, the employee didn't think it was very funny when his job was cut. It may sound absurdly simple, but one of the best ways to keep your job once you have it is to just show up. Employers rarely tolerate absenteeism; chronic lateness; or vague, frequent illnesses. Not showing up for your job disrupts workflow and costs an employer real money. Those who don't show up, usually don't last very long.

Sometimes the person who has been at the job the longest automatically climbs the career ladder when positions become available. Even if you don't have the best education and skills, your loyalty and peseverance often translate into career advances. While this isn't always to an employer's advantage, many companies prefer to promote from within, thereby increasing employment longevity and morale.

2) Cross-Train

The second important technique you can use to keep your job is cross-training. Even during periods of layoffs and downsizing, most companies keep the employees who can do more than one job. If you can demonstrate the ability to do many jobs in an organization, regardless of your length of employment with the company, you are unlikely to receive a first-round pink slip. In this, the old rule "last one hired, first one fired" does not always apply.

Some companies have formal cross-training programs in place while others do not. Regardless, you should always express an interest to your boss that you would like to learn more about other positions within a company. Most supervisors feel employees are more dedicated to their employer when they voice an interest in cross-training. This dedication helps you keep your job. It could also very well land you a promotion, further adding to your job security and tenure.

3) Lifelong Learning—The Value of Continuing Education

There is no such thing as having too much education in my opinion. Knowledge is power, and although it may not always be utilized, it can never be taken away from you. Knowledge makes you valuable to your employer.

Chapter 18

A fundamental concept of successful organizations is that CEOs surround themselves with people more competent than they are. While this is intimidating to some, it works to the benefit and longevity of a company. Therefore, no matter what level of education you currently have, always consider yourself a lifelong learner and strive to become more knowledgable than your coworkers and bosses.

There are numerous ways to advance your current level of education. The huge increase in distance learning and online college courses has opened up post-secondary educational opportunities to nearly everyone. You can be working full-time and still further your education with night courses or distance learning programs. Weekend seminars often provide continuing education credit to participants. Community education programs routinely offer courses on money management, investing, and taxes, among other things.

In addition, many organizations pay for all or part of continuing education after an initial period of work. If your employer supports continuing education, seriously consider taking the company up on it. It's an excellent way to justify your bid for career advancement within a company. Ask your supervisor if this is available to you, or look in your employee handbook.

> Knowledge can also intimidate your employer and coworkers. For this reason, it is advisable to always present your knowledge as "wisdom." Wisdom is defined as a combination of "knowledge" and "love." In other words, don't boast about your grade point average, IQ score, number of degrees, and so on. If you do, you will come across as arrogant, thereby making your employer and coworkers defensive. Rather, subtle references to your education come across as much less threatening to coworkers and bosses.

Maintaining Healthy Job Satisfaction

As you saw in earlier chapters, job satisfaction is often based on more than money. Working conditions, type of work, benefits, and the like are often more important than money when determining job satisfaction. A general rule of thumb to remember about job satisfaction is the fact that NO job is perfect. There will always be things about a job you don't like—even if you work for yourself. The important concept to grasp here is the ratio of things you like to things you don't. It seems to make sense that if you dislike more than 4 of 10 job duties, it's probably time to start looking elsewhere. However, before you turn in your two-weeks notice, it may be advisable to do one or more of the following:

1. Discuss your unmet expectations with your employer. When job dissatisfaction rears its ugly head, it usually involves unmet expectations. For example, if you expect to be treated with courtesy by your employer and

instead you are treated with contempt, your expectation for treatment has failed. Conversely, if your employer expects that you will work until 5 p.m. and you consistently cut out at 4:50 p.m., the employer's expectation has failed. It's critical in maintaining healthy job satisfaction to discuss your expectations with your employer and vice versa. Most dislike doing this because it can involve conflict. However, if you are miserable in your job, what do you have to lose? And what, perhaps, to gain?

2. Ask your supervisor about cross-training opportunities. If you are feeling particularly dissatisfied in your job and that feeling is not directly related to unmet expectations, maybe you should consider asking for a transfer or cross-training opportunities. Many people get bored in their jobs, or they feel underutilized after a period of time. An excellent way to boost your job satisfaction and morale is to ask your supervisor about cross-training opportunities. You can present the idea in terms of adding value to the organization as it is not in their best interest to have only one or two people who know specific duties, processes, or procedures. If cross-training is granted, the bonus is longer employment with one employer, which normally translates into a better-financed and often earlier retirement.

3. Enroll in continuing education courses. As I have explained, continuing your education is advantageous to your career longevity and upward mobility. In addition, continuing education provides you with something to do that is enjoyable and makes you feel purposeful and satisfied. You also add value to the company by the additional skills and knowledge you gain.

4. Change career fields by getting a new degree. Some employees become disenchanted with their choice of career after time. This is often a result of people not having a good idea what they are truly interested in and how their skills match up with their work. One of the best ways to perk up your job satisfaction is to make a decision about changing career fields by getting a new degree. This can be especially true if your employer pays for all or part of higher education expenses. The fact that your employer may be paying you to get a more satisfying job in and of itself can make a crummy job much more satisfying.

Spend time completing the worksheets in Chapters 9 and 10 to explore your interests and define your skills.

During the interim between looking for a better job and finding one, it is advisable to make the best of the bad situation. Some of the career management techniques listed in this chapter can help maintain healthier job satisfaction.

Additionally, it often helps to maintain a proper perspective about your unsatisfying job—"it's just a job." A job that you don't like is simply a means to an end—survival until a better job is found. You have probably heard the phrase, "Don't quit your day job." This applies to this situation as well. Use your day job to survive while you use your other time actively seeking a better position.

The simple fact that you have a Career Work Plan, alternatives to reach your goals, and updated skills/education will often buffer your level of job dissatisfaction. Those with a plan simply go to work expecting to get a more satisfying job soon.

Always Be Employable

People change jobs and careers more often now than ever before. Some changes are voluntary and others are not. Therefore, it is advisable to always be employable. In order to do this, I recommend the following.

1) Join Professional Organizations

Most major industries have representative professional organizations. These professional organizations are an invaluable source of information for the job seeker as well as those who are employed. They often provide insight into the latest trends in the industry via newsletters or professional magazines. This can keep you ahead of the experiential learning curve and help guide you in making decisions related to your Career Work Plan.

The news about the future of a particular industry may be good and lead you to continuing education in your current career area, or it may be bad and lead you to cross-training and/or education outside your current career area.

To find professional associations online simply attach the words "professional organizations" to your field in a search engine and scan the results. Another option is to use the *Yellow Pages* to contact people who are in the field and ask them what organizations they would recommend.

 A final method to find professional organizations is to visit the Web sites listed in Chapter 11.

2) Enroll in Continuing Education Courses

Continuing education classes are often subsidized by employers. There are very good reasons for this. First, employers want their employees to be knowledgable and competent. Second, continuing education often revives employees' interest in their work and directly improves their job satisfaction and productivity. Thirdly, by enrolling in a continuing education course every year or two, you continue to make yourself more employable should you find yourself looking for a new job.

3) Subscribe to Industry Publications

Keep abreast of the latest trends and technologies in your industry by reading professional publications. Anticipate what is coming and be ready to jump on board should your current job become outdated. Most publications also have a classified section in the back of magazines and newsletters informing you of job opportunities in your field. It is easy to find industry publications online utilizing a simple word search. You can also go through your local library. Again, it's a good idea to ask those in the field which publications they recommend.

4) Network

Networking is just as important in getting a job as it is in flourishing in the job once you have it. I don't believe you can ever have too many network contacts. It is important to periodically let them know your employment status, continuing education efforts, and other pertinent information. More often than not, you will not be perceived as a bother to your network contacts. Rather, they are usually quite flattered that you are interested in working for them or someone they know. Furthermore, a very large percentage of jobs are landed by networking—as you should know well by now.

5) Volunteer

People who volunteer are perceived as dedicated and sometimes idealistic or altruistic. These are all great qualities employers often look for, so include volunteer activities on your resume. Volunteering is also a great way to network.

Pick an organization that you would enjoy helping. The options are limitless. Contact local service clubs, hospitals, nursing homes, YMCAs, boys' and girls' clubs, and the like to find out what they may need. In doing this, you may just find yourself a job offer. I know several people who began by volunteering for an organization, only to be offered a paying position later.

6) Develop a Recruiter Relationship

There are numerous local and nationwide employment recruiting agencies. One only needs to go to an Internet search engine and type in the words "employment recruiter" to find a plethora of responses. Some charge for their services. Others bill the employer when an employment offer is made. It is generally more effective to develop a relationship with one particular recruiter within an agency. Calling this person and sending him or her updated resumes every few weeks will keep you in the mind of a recruiter who is actively trolling for employment opportunities.

Chapter 18

7) Maintain an Updated Resume and JIST Card

It may be obvious to say that everything changes, but it does. Your resume and JIST Card should always reflect any expansion of your education, skills, experience, and related activities. This will also give you peace of mind and a jump on the competition if something unexpected happens to your Career Work Plan. I would advise you to review and update these materials at least every 6 months.

Quick Advice

☑ It is also important to remember to update any resume materials you may have online. Personal Web sites, nationwide employment sites, and the like need updating, too.

8) Routinely Peruse Classifieds

Routinely reviewing classifieds in the local newspaper, as well as exploring online sources, is always a good idea. Looking at what is available gives a person the sense of his or her own employability should something unexpectedly happen to a job. Furthermore, it may provide you with ideas for jobs and careers you might not otherwise have considered. Regular searches on major employment Web sites —such as Monster.com, Hotjobs.com, CareerOINK.com, and Careerbuilder.com— often yield expanded employment opportunities in other locations, as you can typically search by city, state, and country.

≡ Quick Summary

- ✓ It is essential to have a Career Work Plan in place to achieve your career goals.
- ✓ The steps in formulating a career work plan are 1) Determine your career goal, 2) List any problems or blocks to that goal, 3) List ALL alternatives for reaching your goal, 4) Evaluate the alternatives for reaching your goal, 5) Choose an alternative for reaching your goal, 6) Perform follow-up evaluation on your progress toward the goal, and 7) Make changes if necessary.
- ✓ Techniques to keep your job and climb the career ladder include 1) Just showing up, 2) Cross-training, and 3) Lifelong learning through continuing education.
- ✓ Maintaining healthy job satisfaction is key to job longevity.
- ✓ Techniques to maintain and improve job satisfaction include 1) Discussing your unmet expectations, 2) Asking about cross-training opportunities, 3) Enrolling in continuing education, and 4) Changing career fields by getting a new degree.
- ✓ You should always be employable. Methods to do so include 1) Joining professional organizations, 2) Enrolling in continuing education courses, 3) Subscribing to industry publications, 4) Networking, 5) Volunteering, 6) Developing a recruiter relationship, 7) Maintaining a current resume and JIST Card, and 8) Perusing classifieds.

APPENDIX

Sources of Additional Information

There are so many books, Web sites, journals, and other career and education information resources available that I would have to write another book to list them. Since I can't do that here, I list those I find most helpful in two groups. The first, "Best Career Information Sources Overall," presents information sources I think are most important or helpful. A second section, "More Sources of Information," adds additional or more-specialized resources not included in the first list.

Both print and Internet sources are mentioned in the lists. A limitation you should consider when using Web sites is that most are commercial ones providing resume listings or are government funded in some way. These sites are very helpful for some uses, but the best information is often not available for free on the Web. The reason is that authors and publishers have not yet volunteered to work for free, and much of the best content requires considerable work and cost to create. For example, the sites that post your resume and allow you to look at job openings are paid for by employers and will often have skimpy information on interviewing, job descriptions, and other information. That is why I include print resources here as well as Internet ones, since print resources will have the best information in some categories until someone figures out how to afford to do otherwise.

There are many worthy resources I do not list here as there just is not space for them all. In an effort at full disclosure, I admit to including more of my own and other JIST titles here. However, I think that it is fair to do so, given the circumstances, and now you know.

Best Career Information Sources Overall

On most major career topics, you can get most or all of what you need from a small number of key resources. I present these resources here.

Information on Industries to Consider

Career Guide to America's Top Industries: This is the most helpful book on this topic. Published by the U.S. Department of Labor as Bulletin 2541, *Career Guide to Industries,* it provides very useful information on more than 40 major industries, including working conditions, education and training needed, advancement, projected growth, earnings, and other details. It is also available online at www.bls.gov in the Publications & Research Papers section.

The North American Industrial Classification System (NAICS): This system organizes all industries into increasingly specific groupings and industries. It was developed by the federal government, and all government systems are now required to use this system. It is useful to identify industries you want to target for your job search or career plans. You can get the entire NAICS listing at the U.S. Bureau of Labor Statistics' Web site at www.bls.gov in the Industries section.

Occupational Information and Job Descriptions

I cover the major resources of occupational information in Chapter 11, but here they are again.

Occupational Outlook Handbook (OOH): Published by the U.S. Department of Labor and updated every two years, it provides excellent descriptions for each of the more than 250 major job titles that cover about 86 percent of the job market. Each job description includes information on the skills required; pay rates; projections for growth, education, and training required; working conditions; advancement opportunities; related jobs; and job-specific sources of additional information, including Web sites. The OOH is available in most schools, libraries, and career counseling centers. *America's Top 300 Jobs* has the same information as the OOH and is more likely to be available for checkout from the library. (JIST)

Enhanced Occupational Outlook Handbook: Includes all the *OOH* text plus brief descriptions for all the related O*NET (Occupational Information Network) jobs and the *Dictionary of Occupational Titles* jobs. —A very useful book. (JIST)

Guide for Occupational Exploration (GOE): The *GOE's* system of organizing jobs based on interests was developed by the U.S. Department of Labor. The system is based on substantial research into how people can use their interests to explore career and learning options, and its structure is used in Chapter 11's interest areas and worksheets. The GOE provides helpful information on all major groups of jobs, including the types of jobs in that group, sources of training or education needed, related school subjects to pursue, related leisure activities and hobbies, and a complete list of job titles within each work group. Descriptions for the more than 1,000 jobs within the various work groups are also included in the GOE, allowing you to identify very specific job opportunities quickly. (JIST)

*O*NET Dictionary of Occupational Titles:* This book is the only printed reference using the new database of information on more than 1,000 jobs tracked by the U.S. Department of Labor. It provides useful descriptions for all the jobs in the O*NET database. (JIST)

Best Jobs for the 21ˢᵗ Century, by Michael Farr with database work by Laurence Shatkin, Ph.D.: This helpful book starts with lots of lists of jobs by earnings, growth rate, and number of openings as well as by level of education and training, interests, personality type, age, and other criteria—plus descriptions for 500 jobs included in the lists. Other books in this series include *300 Best Jobs Without a Four-Year Degree* and *200 Best Jobs for College Graduates.* (JIST)

www.CareerOINK.com: This Web site includes information on more than 14,000 job titles, including much of the information provided in the print resources mentioned above. (JIST)

Government Web sites: You can find the OOH job descriptions under the Publications & Research Papers section of the U.S. Department of Labor's Bureau of Labor Statistics' Web site at www.bls.gov. Another government site at www.onetcenter.org provides access to the O*NET database and related information.

Job Search Information

There are hundreds of books and Web sites on this topic, and *The Very Quick Job Search* has enough information in it to reduce your need for much more, so the only thing I will do here is mention a couple of my books and another JIST book and note that additional resources are included in the "More" section of this list.

The Quick Interview & Salary Negotiation Book: Contains a section of tips likely to make the biggest difference as well as sections with more detailed information on problem questions and other topics. (JIST)

Seven Steps to Getting a Job Fast: A short and inexpensive book that presents the most important points to increase your career planning and job search effectiveness. It might make a good birthday present for an unemployed friend or relative! (JIST)

Cyberspace Job Search Kit, by Mary Nemnich and Fred Jandt: Provides excellent advice for looking for information and jobs on the Web. (JIST)

Information on Resumes and Cover Letters

The Very Quick Job Search also covers this topic pretty well, and here are a couple of books I've written and another JIST book on resumes for additional examples. I also include other resume books in the "More Sources of Career, Education, and Related Information" section.

The Quick Resume & Cover Letter Book: This is one of the top-selling resume books (thank you very much). It is very simple to follow, has good design, and includes lots of good sample resumes written by a variety of professional resume writers. (JIST)

America's Top Resumes for America's Top Jobs includes more sample resumes, organized by job title, than any other resume book ever published. It has a wonderfully diverse collection of resumes from professional resume writers that cover almost all major jobs and life situations, plus brief but helpful resume-writing advice.

Cyberspace Resume Kit, by Mary Nemnich and Fred Jandt: A very thorough book on writing and submitting electronic resumes.

Information on College and Postsecondary Training

An excellent book called *The College Majors Handbook with Real Career Paths and Payoffs,* by Neeta Fogg, Paul Harrington, and Thomas Harrington, provides information on major college courses of study along with data on the actual jobs and earnings of graduates in each and advice in making a good decision on a course of study. (JIST)

Two books by Laurence Shatkin, *Quick Guide to College Majors and Careers* and *Quick Guide to Career Training in Two Years or Less,* provide good reviews of all major postsecondary training options along with the related jobs each will prepare you for. (JIST)

Useful Web sites include

✓ National Association of Colleges and Employers (NACE)—www.naceweb.org—Run by an association of college career counseling centers and interested employers. Lists job openings as well as information for students.

✓ Peterson's Education Center—www.petersons.com—From a major publisher of college and training guides; includes lots of information on colleges, financial aid, internships, career and resume sites, and more.

✓ College Planning Network/Internet College Exchange—www.collegeplan.org—Lots of information for students considering college and adults returning to school, including a list of all major college Web sites; sorts that allow you to identify colleges that meet your criteria, apply to them, and learn about financial aid available; and links for parents and counselors.

Guides to Career Web Sites

CareerXRoads, by Gerry Crispin and Mark Mehler: A very helpful book that reviews more than 2,500 job and resume sites, including many industry and niche sites.

Best Career and Education Web Sites, by Rachel Singer Gordon and Anne Wolfinger: An excellent book that reviews the most useful Web sites (JIST).

The Riley Guide, by Margaret F. Dikel (www.rileyguide.com): This excellent Web site provides information on all major career and job search topics as well as links to other information sites. Topics include preparing for the job search; resumes and cover letters; targeting and researching employers; executing your job search campaign; job listings; networking, interviewing, and negotiating; and salary guides.

Other Important Resources

Libraries: Most libraries have some or all of the books mentioned above, provide free Internet access, and offer many other resources. Their most important resource is the librarian, so don't hesitate to ask for help finding what you need.

People: One of the best sources of information is talking to people who hold jobs that interest you. Ask them what they like and don't like about their work, how they got started, the education or training they needed, and other information. Most people will be pleased to give you advice you can't get any other way.

Career counseling: A good career counselor can help you explore career, training, or education options. Take advantage of these services if they are available to you from a school or other source. Adult education programs and some community colleges provide career-planning courses or programs that you might also consider.

More Sources of Career, Education, and Related Information

Note that these resources are in addition to the ones I recommend in the "Best Career Information Sources Overall" section. You should be able to get most of the books mentioned here at any bookstore (if not in stock, they can special order for you) or at large book-selling Web sites like Amazon.com.

Most Visited Career Web sites

There are systems out there that keep track of how many people visit each Web site, and I've included below the career-related sites that have the most traffic, organized into general groups and listed in order of traffic volume. I'm not suggesting that they are all good, but these are the ones that are used by the most people.

General Sites: Most of these sites will accept your resume for employers to review and list job openings for you to consider as well as provide at least some resume and job search advice.

www.monster.com; www.careerbuilder.com; www.hotjobs.com; www.flipdog.com; America's Job Bank (www.jobsearch.org); www.net-temps.com; www.vault.com; www.4jobs.com; www.job.com; www.employment911.com; www.nationjob.com; www.employmentguide.com; www.careerboard.com; www.topusajobs.com; www.directemployers.com; www.jobwarehouse.com; www.wetfeet.com; www.careersite.com; www.snagajob.com; www.coolworks.com; www.jobbankusa.com; www.sologig.com; www.bestjobsusa.com; www.careermag.com; www.localcareers.com; www.summerjobs.com; www.preferredjobs.com; www.jobfind.com; www.careershop.com; www.employmentspot.com; www.groovejob.com; www.career.com; www.hiregate.com; www.americanjobs.com; www.4work.com; www.worklife.com

College Sites: These sites are mostly for college grads and include lists of openings, advice for recent grads, links to other sites, and a variety of related information.

www.collegegrad.com; National Association of Colleges and Employers (www.nacelink.com); www.collegejournal.com; www.collegerecruiter.com; www.experience.com; www.campuscareercenter.com; www.aftercollege.com; www.collegecentral.com; www.gradunet.co.uk; www.jobpostings.net; www.aboutjobs.com; www.collegejobboard.com; www.careerfair.com; www.entryleveljobs.net

Managers and Executive Sites: These sites are oriented to managers, CEOs, and more highly compensated executive positions.

www.6figurejobs.com; www.careerjournal.com; www.execunet.com; www.chiefmonster.com; www.spencerstuart.com; www.ekornferry.com; www.netshare.com; www.futurestep.com; www.mba-exchange.com; www.mbajungle.com

Niche Industry and Job Types: These sites focus on specific types of jobs or industries.

www.dice.com; www.jobsinthemoney.com; www.computerjobs.com; www.hcareers.com; www.careerbank.com; www.healthcaresource.com; www.leisurejobs.com; www.jobscience.com; www.allretailjobs.com; www.jobsinlogistics.com; www.brokerhunter.com; www.computerwork.com; www.engcen.com; www.healthjobsusa.com; www.allnurses.com; www.medzilla.com; www.nursetown.com; www.salesjobs.com; www.telecomcareers.net; www.techies.com; www.destinygrp.com; www.nursingspectrum.com; www.legalstaff.com; www.nursingcenter.com; www.hirebio.com; www.lawjobs.com; www.engineerjobs.com; www.tvjobs.com; www.jobs4hr.com; www.engineeringjobs.com; www.tech-engine.com; www.taxtalent.com; www.airlinecareer.com; www.bioview.com; www.justtechjobs.com

Diversity Sites: Good sites for minorities and diversity information and links.

www.latpro.com; www.hirediversity.com; www.imdiversity.com

International Sites: These are English-language sites that list jobs available in other countries as well as information on applying and living there.

www.workopolis.com; www.jobstreet.com; Monster Canada (www.monster.ca); www.seek.com.au (Australia); www.monster.co.uk (United Kingdom); www.gojobsite.co.uk; Reed Executive (www.reed.co.uk); www.jobserve.com; www.totaljobs.com; www.careerone.com.au (Australia); www.monsterindia.com; www.planetrecruit.com; www.workthing.com; Monster Ireland (www.monster.ie); www.nixers.com; www.topjobs.co.uk; www.gisajob.com; www.jobshark.ca (Canada); www.stepstone.com; www.jobnet.com.au; www.jobpilot.com; www.doctorjob.com

International Sites (non-English): These sites are for looking for jobs outside the United States, and they are not in English.

www.infojobs.net; www.anpe.fr (France); www.arbeitsamt.de (Germany); www.bumeran.com; www.monster.es (Spain); www.jobpilot.de (Germany); www.monster.fr (France); www.moj-posao.net; www.monster.be (Belgium); www.monsterboard.nl (Netherlands); www.monster.se (Sweden)

More on Job Seeking and Job Success

Here are several JIST resources about job seeking itself:

- ✓ *Career Success Is Color-Blind: Overcoming Prejudice and Eliminating Barriers in the Workplace,* by Ollie Stevenson
- ✓ *Dare to Change Your Job and Your Life,* by Carole Kanchier, Ph.D.
- ✓ *FBI Careers: The Ultimate Guide to Landing a Job as One of America's Finest,* by Thomas H. Ackerman

✓ *How to Be Happy at Work,* by Arlene S. Hirsch
✓ *Inside Secrets to Finding a Career in Travel,* by Karen Rubin
✓ *Inside Secrets of Finding a Teaching Job,* by Jack Warner and Clyde Bryan, with Diane Warner
✓ *Job Offer: A How-To Negotiation Guide,* by Maryanne L. Wegerbauer
✓ *Job Search Handbook for People with Disabilities,* by Daniel J. Ryan, Ph.D.
✓ *Networking for Job Search and Career Success,* by L. Michelle Tullier
✓ *Sales Careers: The Ultimate Guide to Getting a High-Paying Sales Job,* by Edward R. ("Ted") Newill and Louise M. Kursmark
✓ *Ten Steps to a Federal Job: Navigating the Federal Job System,* by Kathryn Kraemer Troutman
✓ *The Unauthorized Teacher's Survival Guide,* by Jack Warner and Clyde Bryan, with Diane Warner

More on Occupational Information

The Dictionary of Occupational Titles (DOT): This is an older book published by the U.S. Department of Labor that provides brief descriptions for more than 12,000 job titles. The government replaced the DOT system with the newer O*NET database, but the DOT's many very specialized job titles are still considered an important career counseling resource for some occupational areas. You can also find these descriptions at www.careerOINK.com

America's Top Jobs Series: Each of the books in this series provide descriptions for the top jobs in each area; career planning and job search tips; and details on growth projections, education required, and other information. (JIST)

✓ *America's Top 101 Computer and Technical Jobs*
✓ *America's Top 101 Jobs for People Without a Four-Year Degree*
✓ *America's Top Medical, Education, & Human Services Jobs*
✓ *America's Top White-Collar Jobs*
✓ *America's Top Military Careers: Official Guide to Occupations in the Armed Forces*

Guide to America's Federal Jobs: This comprehensive book describes where to find job vacancy and application information as well as how to create a federal resume and how to interpret government job classification information.

Health-Care Careers for the 21st Century, by Dr. Saul Wischnitzer and Edith Wischnitzer: This book describes more than 80 allied health careers and provides information about the training and daily work demands.

More on Resumes and Cover Letters

Here are some miscellaneous useful resources for information on job search correspondence and other documents:

✓ *Best Resumes for College Students and New Grads,* by Louise M. Kursmark
✓ *Cover Letter Magic,* by Wendy S. Enelow and Louise M. Kursmark
✓ *Expert Resumes for Health Care Careers,* by Wendy S. Enelow and Louise M. Kursmark
✓ *Expert Resumes for Managers and Executives,* by Wendy S. Enelow and Louise M. Kursmark
✓ *Expert Resumes for Manufacturing Careers,* by Wendy S. Enelow and Louise M. Kursmark
✓ *Expert Resumes for People Returning to Work,* by Wendy S. Enelow and Louise M. Kursmark
✓ *Expert Resumes for Teachers and Educators,* by Wendy S. Enelow and Louise M. Kursmark
✓ *Gallery of Best Cover Letters,* by David F. Noble
✓ *Gallery of Best Resumes for People Without a Four-Year Degree,* by David F. Noble
✓ *Gallery of Best Resumes,* by David F. Noble
✓ *Resume Magic,* by Susan Britton Whitcomb
✓ *Sales and Marketing Resumes for $100,000 Careers,* by Louise M. Kursmark
✓ *Same-Day Resume: Write an Effective Resume in an Hour,* by Michael Farr
✓ *The Edge Resume and Job Search Strategy,* by Bill Corbin and Shelbi Wright
✓ *Federal Resume Guidebook,* by Kathryn Kraemer Troutman

Index

A

D

Index

E

H

I

Index

K–L

M

Index

Index

T